The Simons of Manchester

Manchester University Press

The Simons of Manchester

How one family shaped a city and a nation

Edited by
John Ayshford, Martin Dodge, H. S. Jones,
Diana Leitch and Janet Wolff

Manchester University Press

Copyright © Manchester University Press 2024

While copyright in the volume as a whole is vested in Manchester University Press, copyright in individual chapters belongs to their respective authors, and no chapter may be reproduced wholly or in part without the express permission in writing of both author and publisher.

An electronic version of this book has been made freely available under a Creative Commons (CC BY-NC-ND) licence, thanks to the support of The University of Manchester, which permits non-commercial use, distribution and reproduction provided the author(s) and Manchester University Press are fully cited and no modifications or adaptations are made. Details of the licence can be viewed at https://creativecommons.org/licenses/by-nc-nd/4.0/

Published by Manchester University Press
Oxford Road, Manchester, M13 9PL

www.manchesteruniversitypress.co.uk

British Library Cataloguing-in-Publication Data
A catalogue record for this book is available from the British Library

ISBN 978 1 5261 7638 7 hardback

First published 2024

The publisher has no responsibility for the persistence or accuracy of URLs for any external or third-party internet websites referred to in this book, and does not guarantee that any content on such websites is, or will remain, accurate or appropriate.

Front cover: Ernest and Shena. Photograph of Henry from Modern Flour Milling Machinery (Henry Simon Ltd, 1898), courtesy of Martin Dodge. Photographs of Emily, Shena and Ernest are from Shena Simon papers, Manchester Central Library, courtesy of Manchester Archives+.

Back cover: (L) The Simons' family home of Lawnhurst, Didsbury, as a hospital during the First World War. Courtesy of Martin Dodge. (R) Wythenshawe Hall, c.1950s. Source: Manchester Local Image Collection, courtesy of Manchester Archives+.

Typeset
by Cheshire Typesetting Ltd, Cuddington, Cheshire

Dedication

John Ayshford dedicates this book to his grandparents, Eunice and John Evans, and Derek and Pamela Ayshford

Supported by The Simon Fund, University of Manchester
and by the John Rylands Research Institute

Contents

List of plates	page ix
List of figures	x
List of contributors	xiv
Foreword *Margaret and Matilda Simon*	xvii
Acknowledgements	xix
List of abbreviations	xxi
Family tree	xxii
Introduction *The editors*	1

Part I: Cosmopolitan Manchester and the Simons

1 Context, cosmopolitanism and connectivity: the German diaspora in Manchester   9
Margaret Littler

2 The appeal of a Buddha: Henry Simon, industrialist and philanthropist (1835–99)   33
Janet Wolff

3 'Her compass always pointed to service': the life of Emily Simon (1858–1920)   61
Diana Leitch

4 The shy campaigner: the life of Ernest Simon, politician and social reformer (1879–1960) 89
John Ayshford and Brendon Jones

5 A confirmed outsider: the life of Shena Simon, feminist and education campaigner (1883–1972) 119
John Ayshford and Brendon Jones

Colour plates

Part II: The Simons' contribution to society

6 Busy making good money: the development of the Simon engineering businesses 151
Martin Dodge

7 Shena Simon: feminism, civic patriotism and the strength of local government 194
Charlotte Wildman

8 Building Jerusalem: the Simons' role in housing reform and town planning 218
Stephen V. Ward and Martin Dodge

9 Burghers and citizens: the Simons and the University of Manchester 251
H. S. Jones and Chris Godden

Conclusion 274
The editors

Index 289

Plates

1. Henry Simon Ltd marketing map (1886).
2. Henry Simon Ltd marketing map (1892).
3. Henry Simon Ltd marketing map (1896).
4. Simon Carves advert promoting their work designing and building new colliery plants for the NCB (1950s).
5. Certificate bestowing Ernest Simon the Freedom of the City of Manchester (1959).
6. Map of Manchester in 1935 from *The Rebuilding of Manchester* (1935).
7. Portrait of Henry Simon by Clara von Rappard.
8. Portrait of Ernest Simon by Thomas Cantrell Dugdale (1944/45).
9. Emily Simon.
10. Shena Simon (*c.* 1920).
11. Ernest, Joan, Shena, and Alan and Martin Simon at Broomcroft (1958).
12. The stained-glass window at Lawnhurst with the word 'Maitri'.
13. The plaque at Wythenshawe Hall commemorating Ernest and Shena's purchase and gifting of the Hall and park to Manchester.
14. Card from the Simon Calendar (*c.* 1890).
15. Lawnhurst (2023).

Figures

0.1	The four Simons.	2
0.2	Advertisement for Henry Simon Ltd (1898).	5
1.1	The German Protestant church, Greenheys; now part of the University of Manchester (unknown date).	15
1.2	The Beyer building in 1898 (?).	18
1.3	The British Association for Advancement of Science meeting, Manchester 1887.	22
2.1	Henry Simon (c. 1880s). From *Rathschlaege für meine Kinder* (c. 1899).	32
2.2	Seal of the Deutsche Reichsregentschaft.	35
2.3	The first page of the letter Heinrich sent to Henry on 25 February 1859.	37
2.4	The cover of *Rathschlaege für meine Kinder*. Source: private family papers.	39
2.5	Mary Jane Simon (née Lane).	40
2.6	Henry's former home 'Darwin House', 84 Palatine Road, Didsbury.	41
2.7	First page of the letter Henry sent to Emily on 31 July 1878.	43
2.8	Simon's Bridge.	45
2.9	Manchester Crematorium.	47
2.10	Architect's invoice for Lawnhurst 1892.	48
2.11	Exterior of Lawnhurst (c. 1899–1920).	49
2.12	'Maitri' engraved on the Simon family memorial at Manchester Crematorium.	55
3.1	Emily Simon (date unknown).	60
3.2	Aerial view of the Oaks Estate.	62
3.3	The Larches.	65
3.4	Emily with Eleanor, Victor, Eric, Margaret and Henry.	67

List of figures   xi

3.5	The Simon family (1896) on the cover of *Henry Simon's Occasional Letter to Millers at Home & Abroad*, XXXVII, (January 1897).	72
3.6	Two entries from January 1899 about Emily in the Didsbury National School Log Book (1898–1911).	74
3.7	Emily with Helene, Ernest and Henry, Margaret, Eric and Victor and two unidentified women (*c.* mid-1890s).	77
3.8	Eric, Harry and Victor in uniform during the First World War.	78
3.9	Red Cross nurses at Lawnhurst.	79
3.10	Lawnhurst as a hospital during the First World War.	80
3.11	Emily in Red Cross uniform during the First World War.	82
4.1	Caricature of Ernest Simon from *News Review* (19 June 1947).	88
4.2	Ernest as a young child.	90
4.3	Ernest as a teenager.	91
4.4	Ernest (*c.* 1900s).	92
4.5	The cover of *The Smokeless City* (1922).	95
4.6	Ernest with Roger (1914).	96
4.7	Ernest and Shena campaigning during the 1922 General Election.	99
4.8	Ernest and Shena (seated to his left) during the 1924 General Election.	100
4.9	The map of the reimagined Manchester city centre in *The Rebuilding of Manchester* (1935).	104
4.10	Ernest (*c.* 1930s).	105
4.11	Ernest inspecting American war planes being manufactured (1942).	108
4.12	Ernest with William Haley, Jennie Lee, Aneurin Bevan and Shena (*c.* 1947–51).	109
4.13	Ernest in the Lake District.	113
5.1	Shena Simon (*c.* 1940–50s).	118
5.2	Shena with her mother Jane Boyd Potter (*c.* 1884).	120
5.3	Shena (*c.* 1907–12).	122
5.4	Shena with Roger (1914).	125
5.5	Shena during her tenure as Lady Mayoress.	127
5.6	Shena with Roger, Antonia and Brian (*c.* 1921/1922).	129
5.7	Shena (*c.* 1930s).	131
5.8	'If Lady Simon became Educational Dictator'. From *Teachers' World* (31 October 1934).	133
5.9	Shena with her grandson Alan and her daughter-in-law Joan (1943).	136
5.10	The cover of *Three Schools or One?* (1948).	138
5.11	Shena at the laying of the foundation stone at Wythenshawe civic centre (1969).	141
5.12	Shena (*c.* 1960s).	143

List of figures

6.1	Title page from Henry Simon Ltd promotional catalogue (1898).	153
6.2	The City Corn Mill in Ancoats, operated by Arthur McDougall, where Henry installed his first complete roller milling system in 1878.	155
6.3	The internal layout of the Daverio designed roller milling machine used by Henry Simon in his first installations.	156
6.4	The first marketing map Henry published (1883).	158
6.5	Diagram of a Simon System gradual reduction roller milling installation from the 1880s.	160
6.6	W. Wheldon, 'North Eastern coalfield: colliery pit-head and coking ovens 1' (c. 1845).	162
6.7	Letter from Henry Simon to the editor of the *Manchester Guardian* about the installation of the Simon-Carves Ovens at Pease's West Collieries.	163
6.8	The Mount Street offices.	163
6.9	Cover of a promotional booklet for a new grain elevator designed by Henry Simon Ltd for the Manchester Ship Canal Company (c. 1915).	170
6.10	The Cheadle Heath factory (1927).	172
6.11	Presentation of the birthday portrait to Ernest by J. Mallard, Shop Stewards' Convenor, Henry Simon Ltd (1945).	177
6.12	The span of the SEG companies and departments by the start of the postwar period.	179
6.13	Brand marketing for the SEG in the postwar period.	180
6.14	Ernest in a 1951 Henry Simon Ltd publicity photo.	183
6.15	The expanded SEG site at Cheadle Heath (c. 1954).	185
6.16	The tower containing a working model flour mill at Cheadle Heath topped off by a prominent 'SIMON' sign.	186
6.17	Simon-Carves Ltd advert celebrating their awarding of the Hunterston atomic power station contract.	188
7.1	Shena in 1912.	195
7.2	A news clipping about Shena's protest at the lack of women managers at St Mary's Hospital.	200
7.3	Shena and Ernest visiting a babies' hospital (1922).	201
7.4	Shena's campaign pamphlet for the 1924 local elections.	202
7.5	Shena's campaign leaflet to voters in Wythenshawe (1934).	206
7.6	The cover of Shena's pamphlet, *Local Rates and Post-War Housing*.	209
7.7	Shena receiving the Freedom of the City of Manchester.	213
8.1	Dense Victorian terraced housing in Hulme, an inner neighbourhood of Manchester (1920s).	219
8.2	Sketch plan of the Jersey Street Dwellings.	221

8.3	Report of Emily's speech at the ceremony marking the completion of the Didsbury Garden Suburb.	225
8.4	The practical case for low-density housing to allow daylight made in the influential Tudor Walters report.	226
8.5	Ebenezer Howard commenting on Patrick Abercrombie's report on Wythenshawe.	228
8.6	The announcement of the council's decision to purchase the Wythenshawe estate.	229
8.7	The deed plan for the purchase of Wythenshawe Hall and grounds by the Simons (1926).	230
8.8	Parker's sketch plan of the estate (1931).	232
8.9	Shena Simon captured in a press photo of the ceremonial digging of the first sod on the site of the first privately constructed homes in Wythenshawe.	233
8.10	The cover of *Moscow in the Making* (1937).	236
8.11	Newspaper clipping from the *Daily Times* (Chicago) (30 October 1942).	240
8.12	Letter from the President Franklin D. Roosevelt to Ernest, 22 December 1942.	241
8.13	Zoning plan for Wythenshawe from *Wythenshawe Plan and Reality*.	245
9.1	The foundation stone of the Physics (now Rutherford) Building laid by Henry Simon in 1899.	254
9.2	Shena receiving her honorary degree from the University of Manchester (1966).	258
9.3	A satirical sketch of Ernest as an Athenian statesman.	262
9.4	Ernest having received his honorary degree from the University of Manchester (1944).	269
10.1	The Simon family at Pendyffryn Hall near Conwy (1896).	275
10.2	Ernest, Shena and Brian and Roger at the golden wedding anniversary of Shena's parents, John Wilson Potter and Jane Boyd Potter (1931).	276
10.3	Heinrich Simon (1805–60).	277
10.4	Emily Simon's obituary in the *Manchester Guardian*.	278
10.5	Shena and Ernest on holiday (*c.* late 1920s – early 1930s).	280
10.6	Bust of Henry Simon.	282
10.7	Bust of Ernest Simon.	283
10.8	The signature plaque above Lawnhurst.	284
10.9	Lawnhurst and Broomcroft shown here on the Ordnance Survey 10-foot plan (1893).	284
10.10	The Simon memorial.	285

Contributors

John Ayshford is a doctoral researcher in history at the University of Manchester. Interested in the history of political thought, his doctoral studies focus on radical republican themes in the ideas of John Stuart Mill. He has written articles for the *Journal of Liberal History* and, reflecting his longstanding interest in the Simon family, he co-curated an exhibition in 2022 on Ernest and Shena Simon's role in the creation of Wythenshawe.

Martin Dodge is a Senior Lecturer in the Geography Department at the University of Manchester. He has worked at Cardiff University and University College London. Much of his research is currently focused on the historical geography of Manchester's transport and town planning. In 2018 he co-wrote *Manchester: Mapping the City* (Birlinn, 2018) and in 2022 he co-curated a public exhibition, *Who Built Wythenshawe?*

Chris Godden is a Senior Lecturer in Economic History at the University of Manchester. He has published on the history of economic ideas in the early part of the twentieth century, and the pedagogy of economic history. In 2017, he was the editor of a special issue of the *Bulletin of the John Rylands Library* marking the centenary of the death of the Manchester historian, Mark Hovell.

Brendon Jones works in the Directorate of the Student Experience at the University of Manchester as Residential Life Manager in the Halls of Residence. His PhD, which he completed at the University of Manchester, focused on Manchester Liberalism between 1918–29 with special reference to the career of Ernest Simon. He authored the entries for Ernest and Shena Simon in the *Oxford Dictionary of National Biography* and has written articles relating to Liberal Party history. He is currently working on an article which analyses the views of the Manchester Liberal MPs, including Ernest Simon, on the first Labour government.

Stuart Jones (H. S. Jones) is Professor of Intellectual History at the University of Manchester. He is a specialist in the intellectual history of the nineteenth and twentieth centuries, with a particular focus on Britain and France, and in the history of universities. His books include *Intellect and Character in Victorian England: Mark Pattison and the Invention of the Don* (Cambridge University Press, 2008). He is currently completing an intellectual biography of James Bryce for Princeton University Press, and editing *Manchester Minds: A University History of Ideas* for Manchester University Press.

Diana Leitch MBE is the former Deputy University Librarian of the John Rylands University Library of Manchester and Associate Director of the John Rylands Library. A chemist by academic discipline, she was a member of the JISC Electronic Resources Committee and deeply involved in the transformational digitisation of printed books, periodicals and other works both in the UK and internationally. She is a local and family historian and has written many articles and books on these subjects.

Margaret Littler is Professor Emerita in the School of Arts, Languages and Cultures at the University of Manchester, where she taught primarily in German studies. Her research interests include gender studies, migration studies and the new materialist philosophy of Gilles Deleuze. She is co-author (with Brigid Haines) of *Contemporary Women's Writing in German: Changing the Subject* (Oxford University Press, 2004) and has also published widely on the Turkish German authors Zafer Şenocak, Emine Sevgi Özdamar and Feridun Zaimoglu. Her online exhibition *Germans in Manchester* was initially curated at Manchester Central Library in 2015.

Stephen V. Ward is Professor Emeritus of Planning History at Oxford Brookes University. He has edited the international academic journal, *Planning Perspectives* and is a past president of the International Planning History Society. His books include: *The Garden City* (E. & F. N. Spon, 1992), *Selling Places* (E. & F. N. Spon, 1998), *Planning the Twentieth-Century City* (John Wiley & Sons, 2002), *Planning and Urban Change* (Sage, 2004) and *The Peaceful Path* (University of Hertfordshire Press, 2016). In 2022 he received the International Planning History Society's Sir Peter Hall Award for Lifetime Achievement in Planning History.

Charlotte Wildman is a Senior Lecturer in Modern British History at the University of Manchester. She is an expert in the history of cities, the North, women and local government. Her first book, *Urban Redevelopment* *and Modernity in Liverpool and Manchester*, was published by Bloomsbury Academic in 2016, and she is currently working on a project on crime, and working-class homes and family life.

Janet Wolff is Professor Emerita in the School of Arts, Languages and Cultures at the University of Manchester. She has also taught at the University of Leeds, the University of Rochester (USA) and Columbia University. She is the author of a number of books on aesthetics and the sociology of art. Her most recent books are a memoir/social history, *Austerity Baby* (Manchester University Press, 2017), and (co-edited with Peter Beilharz) *The Photographs of Zygmunt Bauman* (Manchester University Press, 2023).

Foreword

Margaret and Matilda Simon

When we first heard that this book was being planned, we were intrigued. Now that it has been brought to life, it is a real pleasure to read of the achievements of our grandparents and great-grandparents set within their historical and Mancunian contexts, and indeed to discover more about them than we already knew.

Ernest and Shena were part of a family continuum of radicalism and commitment to social progress that can be traced back to Heinrich Simon (Henry's uncle) and his role in the 1848 Frankfurt Parliament and its struggle for German democracy. We learnt as children about this, and about Henry's founding of Simon Engineering and Simon-Carves and his and Emily's philanthropy and social consciences, and we were very aware of Ernest and Shena's public activities. Our own parents had strong socialist and feminist principles, and political debate was ever-present in our family life. This inheritance has undoubtedly influenced our own career choices and political involvements.

Shena and Ernest were also, of course, our Granny and Grampy Simon. We were only seven and five when Ernest died, and he remains as a rather austere and slightly daunting figure in our memory, although visits to their home Broomcroft were exciting, given that its size and lifestyle were so very different from our own. Christmas was enlivened by the Simon Engineering works brass band playing for the family on the Broomcroft verandah, for example.

Our father, Roger, remembered Ernest as a parent who loved the outdoors and introduced his children to the joys of mountain walking, especially in Switzerland and in the Lake District, where Ernest leased a very basic cottage from the National Trust in 1929. He took the family and went there alone too, to work and relax; walking the fells, cooking simple meals on a paraffin stove and sitting by the log fire. There he also composed limericks, showing the lighter side of him, not often apparent to others.

Our memories of Shena are more vivid. She was as cerebral as Ernest, but better with small children. When old enough, we travelled unaccompanied to visit her by train from London, passing the Jodrell Bank telescope and the works tower labelled 'SIMON' in Cheadle Heath, before alighting at Stockport to go to Didsbury. Memorable days out once included a tour of the 'slum clearance' taking place in Hulme and the construction of the new tower blocks with deck access. There was also always a trip to see a Gilbert and Sullivan opera. She was kind, and interested in us, and Margaret was happy to be a student in Manchester in the last year of Shena's life, and able to visit her regularly.

That our grandparents and great grandparents have merited this comprehensive portrait of their lives, many years after their deaths, is a tribute to their very significant contributions to Manchester and to the politics of housing, education and social progress. These issues remain ones of vital importance and frequent debate today, and this book provokes thought about how we might approach them now. We are grateful for this recognition of them, and acknowledge with thanks all the painstaking research that has gone into this project.

Acknowledgements

We would like to acknowledge the following organisations, institutions and people for their role in helping us produce *The Simons of Manchester*. We firstly express our gratefulness to the Simon Fund whose financial sponsorship made it possible for us to produce this book. We are also grateful to the John Rylands Research Institute for supporting our research. Furthermore, we would like to thank the staff at Manchester University Press, especially Emma Brennan and Humairaa Dudhwala, for enabling us to create this volume.

    We are also very appreciative of the help we received from the descendants of the Simons of Manchester – Margaret Simon, Matilda Simon, Helen David and Andrew Simon – when writing this booking. Andrew was a fount of information on the Simon family, and Margaret and Helen kindly provided us with privileged access to private family papers as well as permission to include previously unseen family photos in the book. Margaret was also particularly hospitable in letting us study these items at her home. Much of the project relied on material held by Manchester Central Library and the University of Manchester Library Special Collections. We would therefore like to thank the archivists and curators at Archives+ at the Central Library and those at the John Rylands and the University of Manchester Main Libraries for affording us the vital access to the historic documents we needed. Among the many people who kindly assisted us from these institutions, we would like to highlight the help afforded to us by John Hodgson, Janette Martin, Karen Jacques and the imaging team at the John Rylands. We would also like to thank these bodies for their permission to use images relating to the Simon family held in their respective archive collections.

    A number of other people provided the editorial team with excellent additional assistance. Beyond contributing to our volume, Margaret

Littler, Charlotte Wildman and Brendon Jones generously provided useful feedback on draft chapters and ideas regarding the scope of the book. We also wish to convey our thanks to Sue and Paul Good, and Rosemary Eshel who gave us access to unique historical sources and information. Furthermore, we also are grateful to Christian Klein for his role in allowing us to display his image of the *Deutsche Reichsregentschaft* seal held by the Bundestag in the book. Finally, additional thanks are due to the following people for the extra help we received from them: Neil Humphrey and Gillian Whitworth, Ingrid Holden and Libby Edwards, Imogen Allen and Benjamin Clare, David Leitch, Rachael Evans, Stephen Parker, Matthew Jefferies, Eva-Maria Broomer and Graham Dilliway.

Abbreviations

ESD	Manchester Central Library, Papers of Lord Simon, First Baron of Wythenshawe, Ernest Simon's Diary
ESP	Manchester Central Library, Papers of Lord Simon, First Baron of Wythenshawe
GRO	General Register Office
HSC	Henry Simon Correspondence
JRL	John Rylands Library
MCL	Manchester Central Library
SEGA	Simon Engineering Group Archive
SSP	Manchester Central Library, Papers of Lady Simon of Wythenshawe
UOMVCA	University of Manchester, Vice-Chancellor's Archive

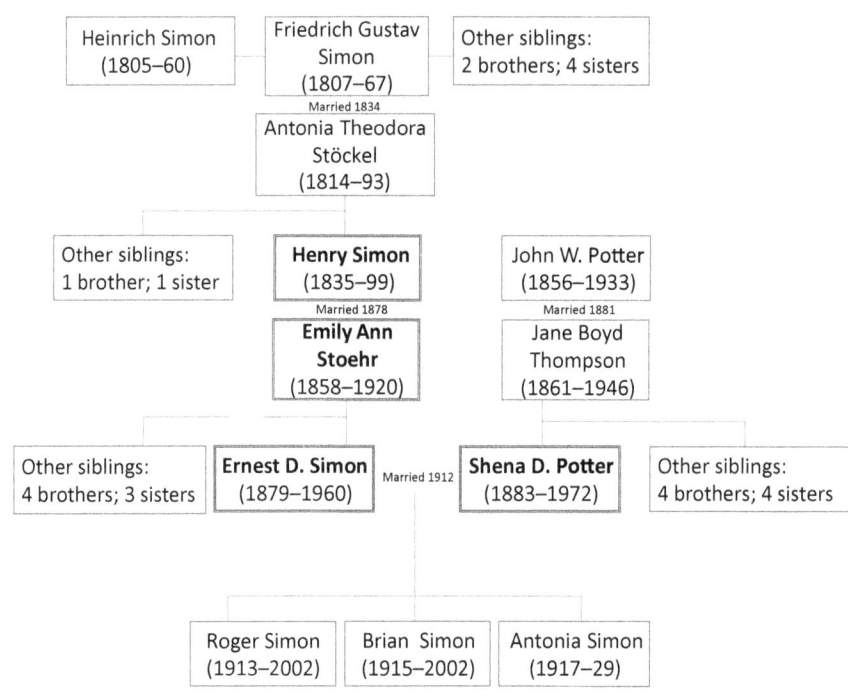

Simplified family tree of the four major protagonists in the Simons of Manchester (highlighted in bold).

Introduction

The editors

This book traces the history of two generations of the Simon family of Manchester: Henry Simon (1835–99), his wife Emily Simon, née Stoehr (1858–1920), their eldest son Ernest (1879–1960) and his wife Shena, née Potter (1883–1972). The Simons may now be little more than a name in the collective memory of Manchester, but in their time they made a formidable impact on the city, its social institutions and its politics. Some sense of their importance is given by an indication of the institutions and buildings that would not have existed, or might not have endured, without the Simon family's contribution: these range from the Manchester Crematorium to Jodrell Bank, from Withington Girls' School to the Hallé Orchestra, from the laboratories where Ernest Rutherford did his path-breaking research to the Wythenshawe Estate, in its time the largest council estate in Europe.

That story certainly tells us what could be done with great personal wealth in the late Victorian period and even in interwar Britain. But while affluence was clearly a necessary condition of the Simons' roles not just as philanthropists but as social reformers, it was equally clearly not a sufficient condition, and this book attempts to explore the sources of this record of innovation. It explores the formation and transmission of a distinctive family ethos shaped by their German ancestors, the experience of being part of a tight-knit German community in Manchester and by the wider Manchester mercantile elite of which Henry Simon became such an influential member. It analyses the ethic that underpinned the success of the two businesses that Henry Simon founded, but it also traces the values that shaped the family's contribution to public life.

The book aims to give due weight to each of the four individuals, so as to ensure that Emily, in particular, emerges from the shadows. But the overall purpose of the book is to study the family collectively. The rationale for that is primarily that there was a powerful family tradition of public

0.1 The four Simons: (in order from top-left to bottom-right) Henry, Emily, Ernest and Shena. Source: *The Simon Engineering Group* (1953) and SSP M14/6/7.

service, deliberately transmitted. That tends to privilege the male line: it was a Simon family tradition, and Emily and Shena married into it. But they also made important contributions to the shaping of the family ethos. The marriages of Henry and Emily and of Ernest and Shena were strong partnerships in which the wife played an important role not just as homemaker but also as philanthropist and public figure. So this is far more than the story of Henry Simon and son.

The structure of the book mirrors these two aims. The first part focuses on the four Simons as individuals, although the four biographical chapters are framed by a study of the Manchester German community as a whole. The second part is thematic, and while the chapters mostly focus on one or two members of the family in particular, the objective is to ensure that a sense of the family as a unit comes through. The central focus is on their work in and for the city of Manchester: its economy, its housing and social infrastructure, its city council, its schools, its university.

Margaret Littler's opening chapter, a study of the German community in Manchester, is intended primarily to explain something of the background to the lives of Henry and Emily Simon. She emphasises wealthy Germans' integration both into the city of Manchester and into mainstream European culture and commerce. Her chapter highlights just how many of Henry Simon's civic, cultural and philanthropic interests, from the Hallé Orchestra to progressive educational methods, were nurtured by the Manchester German community. Janet Wolff's study of Henry Simon reveals him to have been anything but a business-obsessed Gradgrind: a culturally sophisticated man (so much was already known), he is shown to have been endowed with a hitherto undiscovered religious sensibility focused, however, on 'right doings' as the essence of religion. He was curiously drawn to eastern religions, to Buddhism in particular, and the man who placed Darwin at the top of his list of first-rate books also included Schopenhauer in his top ten. Diana Leitch then depicts Henry's second wife, Emily, as a strong-willed woman whose strength of character held the family together. Emily then assumed a much greater public profile during her long widowhood, notably during the First World War, when she allowed her home to be used as a Red Cross hospital under her management.

John Ayshford and Brendon Jones together contribute two co-authored studies of Ernest and Shena Simon. Ernest is painted as someone who self-consciously taught himself to overcome what might have been a debilitating shyness to become not only a successful businessman but also an energetic and creative civic leader and public intellectual both in Manchester and nationally. He would have been the first to admit that his marriage to Shena was the prerequisite for his achievements as a public figure. Theirs was a deeply fulfilled marriage that was at the same time a close working partnership that they modelled more or less explicitly on that of their friends, Sidney and Beatrice Webb. Shena was herself perhaps the most vivid and remarkable of the four characters: she had a personability and ease of manner that Ernest lacked, but she was also a powerful and sometimes overbearing political operator. She was a vocal feminist and a long-term campaigner for educational equality, but, like Ernest, she could lack finesse in handling those for whom she had a low regard. As she said of herself, she could afford to be unpopular.

Having introduced the four protagonists in this way, the book goes on to study their contributions, individual and collective, in several domains: business, local government, housing and higher education. Martin Dodge's chapter on the Simon engineering businesses over a period of ninety years traces the roots of the business success that underpinned the family's public activities. Dodge identifies key drivers of the success of the businesses, both under Henry's and Ernest's leadership: under Henry, engagement with the application of scientific research combined with business acumen, displayed for instance in the shrewd use of patents; under Ernest, confidence in his ability to select key senior managerial staff and a willingness to delegate, combined with a ruthlessness in dealing with those he found to be underperforming. The next chapter, by Charlotte Wildman, then provides a comprehensive assessment of Shena's work in local government. When Shena was elected to Manchester City Council in 1924 there were still very few women on borough councils, especially in the large cities, and the chapter forms an important case study of a woman in municipal politics. It examines Shena's contribution on the key issues of housing, education and women's employment rights, and shows her to have been notably prescient as an advocate of municipal taxation reform as the precondition of the continued vitality of local government. The chapter adds to a small but growing body of recent literature which is challenging the supposed notion of decline in the strength of local government and civic culture in the first part of the twentieth century. The chapter on housing reform and urban planning, by Stephen Ward and Martin Dodge, neatly tells a story in which each of the four made a significant and distinctive contribution. It shows that Ernest's standing as a major civic and national voice on housing policy was prefigured by both Henry's and Emily's involvement in working-class housing schemes. And while it was Ernest who was the housing expert, it was Shena who took the leading role in the development of the Wythenshawe estate. A particularly striking feature of the chapter is that it shows that Ernest's distinctive vision for democratic town planning was shaped by the extensive international visits he made, with Shena, before and during the Second World War. Ernest was notably keen to use these visits to study urban planning in different contexts: European democracies, the Soviet Union and the United States. The Simons of Manchester, and Ernest in particular, were immersed an important set of international debates on postwar reconstruction.

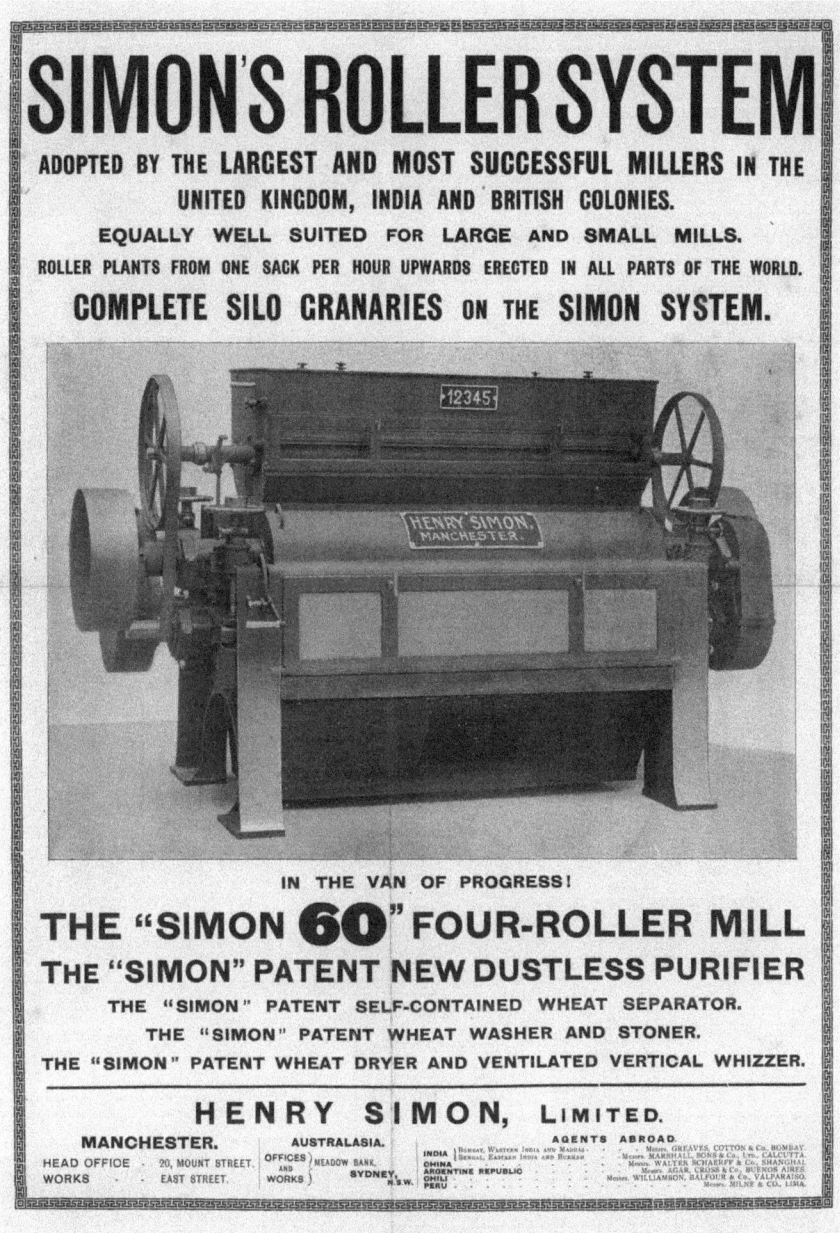

0.2 Advertisement for Henry Simon Ltd (1898). Source: Martin Dodge.

Finally, H. S. Jones and Chris Godden explore the Simon family's long connection with the University of Manchester and its precursors. Ernest and Shena were at the heart of the University community for many decades, and Ernest used his position and experience as a powerful lay officer to give him credibility in the important public debate on the social role of universities from the Second World War to the eve of the appointment of the Robbins Committee. Ernest's substantial personal investment in social science research, notably through the Simon fellowship scheme, was conceived as a contribution to the cause of citizenship education, to which he devoted much of his public work from the 1930s onwards, and the chapter teases out some of the tensions between promoting socially useful research and nurturing educational breadth.

There is, inevitably, much that is not in this book. It does not stretch back to explore Henry Simon's German ancestors, or indeed Emily's ancestors either, in any great depth; and neither does it stretch forward to consider the trajectories of Ernest and Shena's children or indeed their grandchildren. Equally, we do not trace the national political careers of Ernest and Shena, although there is much to be said about the Liberal Summer Schools, the Campaign for Nuclear Disarmament, population control and comprehensive schooling. The Simons offer plenty of opportunities for future researchers. Our central focus here is on the relationship between the family and the city of Manchester and its environs. It is the interaction between the family and the city that gives this story its interest.

PART I

Cosmopolitan Manchester and the Simons

1

Context, cosmopolitanism and connectivity: the German diaspora in Manchester

Margaret Littler

The presence in late Victorian and Edwardian Manchester of a substantial and influential German population has long been acknowledged, as has their contribution to the industrial and commercial growth for which the city is famed. In those days, the Midland Hotel housed a German restaurant, German music and musicians featured prominently in concert programmes, and German businesses were trading in textiles, engineering, chemicals, banking and retail. Names such as S. L. Behrens & Co., Schunck, Souchay & Co., Steinthal & Co., Prieger, Stoehr & Co. and Ermen & Engels must have been familiar among cotton manufacture and trading circles. Terry Wyke describes nineteenth-century Manchester as 'a city whose warp was textiles and whose weft was migrants', and rapidly expanding industry was undoubtedly a major factor drawing German migration.[1] It has been estimated that in 1851 there were around 1,000 German-born residents in Manchester, and that by 1891 Germans were the single largest foreign element in the city.[2] But by the early twentieth century this presence is assumed to have disappeared, and definitively so as the result of two devastating wars. The sinking of the *RMS Lusitania* in May 1915 is often cited as a turning point in the souring of Anglo-German relations, resulting in anti-German riots across Manchester and Salford, targeting businesses with German-sounding names.[3] Unlike Bradford, where the district called Little Germany bears witness to the prominence of Germans in the nineteenth-century wool trade, the cosmopolitanism of 'Cottonopolis' appears to have vanished without trace. This chapter considers both the complex reasons for the Germans' presence in Manchester and the nature of their influence, in terms of the achievements of individual migrants, and also of the networks that they joined, formed and maintained. The actors in this story include civic institutions, science and technology, religious tolerance, political liberalism, educational reforms, music and other 'rational recreation' such as gymnastics and mountaineering. Even if many of those who came settled, naturalised and had British descendants, their presence opened up vectors of connectivity with mainland Europe, so that their migration may be viewed less as a one-off movement than as a traffic of ideas, technologies, commerce and culture that endured. To view their migration in this way reveals an impact that goes far beyond the lifespans of prominent individuals and even the devastation of two world wars.

Prussia

To assess the 'push' factors driving German migration, one must recall that 'Germany' as a unified nation did not exist for much of the nineteenth century, but instead a German Confederation of thirty-nine German states – dominated in the north by Prussia and in the south by the Austro-Hungarian Empire.[4] Emerging from the Congress of Vienna in 1815, this confederation was politically weak, and a disappointment to liberals hoping for a united German nation after liberation from Napoleon.[5] When Frederick William IV acceded to the Prussian throne in 1840, there were hopes of greater political freedoms and German unity. Demands for constitutional rule came from German universities such as Jena, Giessen and Breslau, where student organisations (*Burschenschaften*) had long been the advocates of liberalism and national unity.[6] The end of the Napoleonic Wars had seen a revival of German universities; as centres of a new nationalism, they also enjoyed a renaissance in many disciplines – particularly in science.[7] But the increasing strength of the liberal movement in the 1840s was met with reactionary measures, severe censorship and state control of universities. When revolution broke out in France in 1848, unrest soon spread through the German states, and in May a preliminary assembly was convened in Frankfurt am Main to prepare elections for a new national assembly to replace the German Confederation and its (unrepresentative) Diet. Prominent among those tasked with drawing up a new constitution was the lawyer August Heinrich Simon (henceforth Heinrich Simon) (1805–60), uncle of Henry Simon (1835–99). The proposed constitution included principles such as equality before the law, freedom from arbitrary arrest, freedom of religious observance and freedom of the judiciary from political interference. (Heinrich Simon himself had resigned in 1845 as a judge in the Prussian State Service, in protest against a law regulating the conduct of public servants.)[8] When, in March 1849, the Prussian king refused to reign on the terms of constitutional monarchy presented to him by the Frankfurt Parliament, Heinrich, who already faced a charge of high treason for his outspoken opposition, went into exile in Switzerland. There he gathered some of his family around him, including his nephew, whom he encouraged to study engineering at the Zurich State Polytechnical School, and subsequently to seek employment in Manchester in 1860. There he had the support of other political exiles from 1848, such as the physician and paediatrician Louis Borchardt (1816–83) and the merchant Emil Moritz Stoehr (1827–77), whose daughter Emily became Henry's second wife.[9]

Manchester

The commercial opportunities and relative social and political freedoms in northern English towns meant that German migrants felt at home in Manchester, away from the political repression and conservatism of their homeland, and they were widely accepted there.[10] The city welcomed immigrants who showed a willingness to work hard, bring prosperity and assimilate to local cultural norms. Jonathan Westaway also notes the sympathy of the Manchester liberal and nonconformist middle classes for the political struggles of German liberals, as well as their admiration for German cultural capital.[11] Their own brand of liberalism was focused more on free trade and regional autonomy than the German desire for national unity, but, as Christopher Clark has pointed out, they shared a sense of 'provincial patriotism, defence of "liberty" and resistance to the expansion of state power'.[12] So perhaps it is not surprising that a *Deutscher National Verein* was founded in Manchester in 1848 to support the German liberal cause, that on 30 March that year a public meeting was held at the Manchester Athenaeum with speeches only in German supporting the revolutionaries and that German companies in Manchester raised £500 for families affected by the violence.[13] Such liberal sympathies were further alienated by the increasingly militaristic and autocratic nature of the Second Empire founded in 1871 as a result of war, not popular uprising.

The Manchester to which Germans were drawn was a relatively new city with a rapidly increasing population, an expanding industrial workforce and a growing, prosperous middle class.[14] From a Lancashire town trading in textiles from water-powered mills in the Pennine valleys, Manchester was transformed into a modern industrial urban centre. A population of 95,000 in 1800 grew to 310,000 by 1841, due to the rapid expansion of the textile and related industries.[15] Alan Kidd and Terry Wyke point to the transition from thermal to kinetic energy as the driving force in the city's transformation; the steam engine made it possible to convert heat into controllable work, and this had a dramatic impact on the topography of the city. Industry became concentrated in the centre in the form of huge steam-powered cotton mills and giant warehouses, with canals linking them with markets elsewhere.[16] Industrialisation on this scale made Manchester synonymous with the Industrial Revolution, associated with enormous wealth, unchecked pollution and the appalling living conditions of the workers. When the town of Chemnitz became known as 'the Saxon Manchester', due to its similar industrial pre-eminence in textiles and machine tools production, it was not entirely a compliment.[17] *Manchestertum* became a pejorative term for free-market capitalism in nineteenth-century Prussia.[18]

Much of what we know of the negative impacts of industrialisation in Manchester is from the young Friedrich Engels (1820–95). He originated from the town of Barmen (now part of Wuppertal), a textiles town on a tributary of the Rhine, which in the early nineteenth century 'mushroomed into a "German Manchester" of spinners, weavers, dyers and manufacturers'.[19] Appalled in his youth by the condition of industrial workers in his home town, and radicalised by his reading of G. W. F. Hegel, Ludwig Feuerbach and Moses Hess, he was sent to Manchester in 1842 to work in his father's cotton trading business Ermen and Engels, which also built Victoria Mill at Weaste in Salford. Far from distracting him from radical politics, as his father had intended, Engels' apprenticeship in Manchester informed his critique of the inequalities exacerbated by modern capitalism in *The Condition of the Working Class in England* (published in German 1845). Engels read contemporary studies exposing the impact of industry on public health, attended meetings at the Owenite Hall of Science and befriended leading Chartists, whom he identified as practically representing working-class consciousness.[20] But he also had first-hand access to the impoverished slum dwellings of the workers, due to his personal relationship with the Irish mill worker Mary Burns. As Tristram Hunt writes, 'Mary Burns acted as his underworld Persephone', taking him into the slums of the Irish community and instructing him on the living and working conditions of the most impoverished industrial workers.[21] In addition to the driving force of steam, Engels identified class struggle as a spatial dynamic at work in Manchester. The workers were crammed into overcrowded, polluted slums next to the factories and the wealthy industrialists lived in suburbs on the outskirts, their routes into the city lined with smart shops and warehouses which 'suffice to conceal from the eyes of the wealthy men and women of strong stomachs and weak nerves the misery and grime which form the complement to their wealth'.[22] As Hunt points out, Engels produced a pioneering analysis of class zoning:

> Engels appreciated the city's spatial dynamics – its streets, houses, factories and warehouses – as expressions of social and political power. The struggle between bourgeoisie and proletariat was ... tangible in the street design, transport systems, and planning process ... Class conflict and the social divides wrought by private property were embedded in the very flagstones of the city.[23]

Engels was impressed by the level of education of many mill workers, and was convinced that the destitution in which they lived would ignite revolution from below. However, he also rubbed shoulders with the very bourgeois elites he condemns in *The Condition*, and from whom he had to hide his 'irregular relationship' with Mary Burns. This secrecy, and his legitimate fear of Prussian police spies, account for his use of pseudonyms and frequent changes of address in the city. But he did join the gentlemen's clubs frequented by German merchants, subscribed to their charitable societies and enjoyed riding out with the Cheshire Hunt.[24] Notwithstanding Engels' polarised view of class conflict, many of Manchester's affluent Germans were only too aware of the problems industrialisation had caused, pursuing a path of philanthropy and reform rather than revolution. It was their integration into the life of the city, and simultaneously into mainstream European culture and commerce, that enabled them to become part of the fabric of Manchester itself, its intellectual, educational, civic and cultural life. In addition to the steam engine and the forces of capitalism, migration emerges as another transformative force shaping Manchester's institutions, built environment and middle-class culture.

Jews, Protestants and Unitarians

The German population in industrial northern England was also a largely Jewish population, the more prosperous of them secular Jews who were well-integrated in the city's bourgeois commercial and social life. Many less affluent and more religiously observant Ashkenazi Jews from Eastern Europe worked predominantly in immigrant workshops for the clothing and furniture trade.[25] The Simon family were secular Germans from Breslau in Silesia. Their ancestor 'Hirsch' Simon (1730–92) had been born into a poor Jewish community and accrued his wealth in one of the few occupations open to Jews in eighteenth-century Prussia: the management of currency.[26] But he espoused the German-Jewish Enlightenment with his commitment to a broad education, interest in secular science, liberal politics and progressive values. His descendants converted to Protestantism in 1805, which enabled their upwardly mobile social status and access to professional careers. In Prussia, Jews were excluded from university teaching, and to a large extent from the civil service, whereas in nineteenth-century Britain, Jews had relative freedom and protection (although English universities were largely closed to non-Anglicans until the 1850s). Those Jewish Germans who settled in England were drawn both by commercial interests and relative social freedoms.[27] They tended to identify as Germans rather than Jews, to promote German culture and to establish German organisations, always open to an English membership and audiences. Their acculturation is all the more evident in contrast with the more religiously observant East European Jews who settled in the later nineteenth century, and whose close-knit community has been called 'a voluntary ghetto'.[28] In contrast, the Reform movement led by figures such as Tobias Theodores strove to modernise Judaism and integrate into secular bourgeois society, and was arguably a more dynamic force for change precisely due to their level of social, commercial and civic integration in the city. Edward Behrens (1837–1905), a wealthy shipping merchant and managing director of his father's cotton manufacture and export business S. L. Behrens & Co., was a member of the Reform Synagogue, and his wife, Abigail Behrens, was a founding member of the philanthropic Jewish Ladies' Visiting Society, set up in 1884 to promote healthy food and housing for impoverished Jewish families.[29]

Many of the manufacturing, mercantile and professional families in Manchester were nonconformists, and among these, the Unitarians were both disproportionately influential and particularly welcoming to foreigners and dissenters of all kinds. Due to its non-Trinitarian, undoctrinaire theology, it was also acceptable to secular Jews or Jewish converts:

> Socially and culturally dominant, Unitarian Chapels offered immigrants direct access to a small but influential mercantile and manufacturing élite prominent in the government and public life of Manchester. As German immigration increased after 1850, a German-Unitarian nexus was to be crucial in the educational, intellectual and cultural life of the city.[30]

The Doctrine of the Trinity Act made it legal to be Unitarian in England from 1813, and Unitarianism claims the first trained female minister in any denomination, who happened also to be German: Gertrud von Petzold (1876–1953). Cross Street Unitarian Chapel was both a cultural and religious hub, hosting meetings of the Literary and Philosophical Society (founded 1781) until 1799. William Gaskell was Unitarian minister at the chapel along with Samuel Alfred Steinthal (1871–93), the brother of the wealthy cotton merchant Henry Michael Steinthal (1821–1905), who was also a member of the congregation. The Jewish calico printer Salis Schwabe (born Salomon ben Elias; 1800–53) converted to Anglicanism in 1831 and joined the Unitarian Church around 1842. Like many other middle-class Germans who gravitated to Unitarianism, Salis and Julia Schwabe frequented the house of Elizabeth and William Gaskell in Plymouth Grove.

The German Protestant church on Wright Street (now the Stephen Joseph Studio in Lime Grove) opened in 1855, holding services in German. Greenheys, as the area was then known, was populated by many wealthy German immigrants, and the church was active in collecting for charity, notably for the infirmary, but increasingly for German-based charities. Celebrations of the Kaiser's birthday indicate a more unquestioningly patriotic sentiment than was common among the more liberal Germans, but Su Coates remarks that its solemn Protestantism made it 'not truly foreign or potentially heretical', and therefore acceptable to Manchester's middle classes.[31] However, the church was closed during both world wars, and was sold in 1948, the congregation moving to a new location in Stretford.[32] This church is not to be confused with the German Mission Church and school in Cheetham, near Ducie Bridge, presided over by the Reverend Joseph Steinthal from 1853 until his death in 1877.[33] Both church and school aimed to help poor and itinerant Germans, and were dependent on donations from the wealthier German community. Coates presents Joseph Steinthal as a charismatic individual, outspoken in his criticism of the lack of support for his church from his wealthy countrymen, many of whom he called 'modern cosmopolitans – viz. Jews – who have thrown off the mosaic Gospel' and made life easy for themselves, or indeed had embraced 'that comfortable religion Unitarianism'.[34] This must surely have been directed at his namesake (and relative by marriage) the Rev. Samuel Alfred Steinthal of Cross Street Chapel, and the other Germans drawn to the Unitarian faith.

One endeavour that seems to have overcome many confessional and political divisions among the German population was philanthropy, and a charity to which principally Germans subscribed was the Society for the Relief of Really Deserving Distressed Foreigners, founded in 1847 (as was the Jewish Board of Relief).[35] It supported impoverished foreigners of any origin (though clearly not the feckless or professional beggars), often paying for their passage home. Thus, as Su Coates suggests, the presence in the city of destitute foreigners was probably an embarrassment to wealthy foreign merchants, and as it happens the majority of recipients *were* German. The shipping merchant Martin Schunck (father of chemist

1.1 The German Protestant church, Greenheys; now part of the University of Manchester (unknown date). Source: MCL ref. M63706.

Henry Edward Schunck) was its chairman from 1847 to 1873, and its subscribers over the years included members of the Behrens, Schuster and Schwabe families, the cotton merchants Charles Souchay and Henry Michael Steinthal, the Reverend Joseph Steinthal, Frederick Zimmern (managing director of Steinthal & Co.), alderman Philip Goldschmidt (the first foreign-born mayor of Manchester), the cotton and silk merchant Henry Gaddum, Friedrich Engels and Ernest Delius.[36]

Commerce and industry

The Napoleonic Wars had already driven many wealthy German merchant families to settle in Manchester in the early nineteenth century, when Napoleon's Continental Blockade of 1806 imposed a trade embargo on English goods. These included the manufacturer and exporter of cotton textiles Soloman Levi Behrens (arrived 1814), the calico printer Salis Schwabe (Glasgow 1818, Rhodes in Middleton from 1832), the textile and shipping merchant Johann-Carl Schunck (1808), grandfather of Henry Edward Schunck, and members of the banking and cotton trading Schuster family (1808). In Prussia, the Continental System damaged the fortunes of the Simon family, though it failed in its aim to isolate Britain. Herman Simon (1781–1851), father of Heinrich, lost much of his family's wealth due to the blockade on trade with Britain, but it also brought many successful German businesses to England, long before the political exiles of 1848.

Manchester was not the only destination for German textiles companies, as demonstrated by the Behrens family. Nathan Behrens (cousin of Soloman Levi Behrens), based in Bad Pyrmont (now Lower Saxony), imported cotton and woollen goods from England to the German market. His son Jacob Behrens (1806–89) settled in Bradford in 1838, established the company Jacob Behrens & Co., exporting woollen products to Germany and France, and became a government advisor on international trade.[37] Louis Behrens, Jacob's brother, established a branch of Jacob Behrens & Co. in Tib Street, Manchester, which was later run by Jacob's son, the engineer Gustav Nathan Behrens (1846–1936).[38] Thus, two branches of the same family were active in Manchester at the same time (the shipping merchant Edward Behrens managed S. L. Behrens & Co.). As we will see, Gustav Behrens was to play a role in the musical life of the city and was a close friend of Henry Simon. Gustav's son Leonard Behrens was Hallé Concert chairman in 1958, continuing the family's support for the orchestra.

German industrial and textile-producing areas were the source of many of these migrants: Silesia (home of the Simons), Westphalia (Schwabe, Engels) and Saxony (Beyer). The early industrialisation of cotton production in England threw handloom weaving in Silesia into crisis after 1815, when Prussia's free-trade policy led to the flooding of the market with

English cotton products. Then mechanisation of Silesian linen weaving further threatened the livelihoods of handloom weavers, resulting in a famous uprising in 1844 in which damage to factory owners' property and machinery was brutally punished by military force.[39] Competition with British weaving technology also lay behind the migration of Charles Frederick Beyer (born Carl Friedrich Beyer, 1813–76), the son of poor handloom weavers in Plauen, Saxony.[40] His talent in drawing earned him a state scholarship to study draughtsmanship at Dresden Polytechnic, after which he was sent to Manchester in 1834 to report on weaving machine technology. He then declined offers of work in Saxony and returned to Manchester, where he was employed as mechanical draughtsman by Sharp, Roberts & Co., manufacturers of a self–activating mule for spinning machines, the very machinery that put an end to handloom weaving.[41] Beyer so impressed his employers that they put him in charge of the other branch of the business: locomotive design. He regarded aspects of British locomotive design as unmechanical, and introduced many technical innovations that took account of the dynamics of engine design. In 1853, he entered into partnership with Richard Peacock (a Unitarian, son of a Yorkshire lead miner), with whom he designed the Gorton Foundry for locomotive manufacture, delivering the first engine in 1855. The company expanded rapidly, and Beyer employed an assistant from Plauen, Hermann L. Lange in 1861, knowing that he would have the same training and theoretical knowledge as himself (technical school in Karlsruhe and engineering experience in Berlin).

Beyer was convinced that industry should be closely informed by science, and that university education could make this link. The model of the German technical university was far removed from the British university tradition, and it served industry much better. He was also a philanthropist, building churches and schools for his employees in Gorton, and rebuilding the church on his country estate in Llantysilio, North Wales (where he is buried). In his lifetime he campaigned and raised funds for the chair of engineering at Owens College (1868), founding the first applied science department in the North of England, on the model of the European polytechnic schools. He entirely funded the building of the Beyer Building to house the departments of biology and geology, and helped to raise funds for the move of the college to its current site on Oxford Road and for the construction of the John Owens Building. Dying without heirs, he was the single largest donor to Owens College, leaving a bequest of around £104,000 in 1876. He had made it clear to the then principal of Owens College, Prof. Greenwood, that he favoured a broad-based university education: 'Professor Greenwood has stated that, from personal intercourse, he knew Mr Beyer shared the opinion that the prosperity of such institutions was best secured when all the various branches of liberal and scientific knowledge were pursued in common.'[42]

1.2 The Beyer building in 1898 (?). Source: University of Manchester Library. Reference: UPC/2/234. Copyright the University of Manchester (CC BY-NC-SA 4.0).

There are clear parallels with Henry Simon, whose career in Manchester also began with work on European railways, who knew the superiority of German (and Swiss) technical training and whose major technological innovations drew inspiration from his travels abroad.[43] In Simon's case it was the Austrian roller milling technology he used to revolutionise flour milling and the coke oven design using waste products that he observed in France.[44] In his *Rathschlaege für meine Kinder* [*Advice for my Children*] he wrote:

> *Keep your eyes open* when travelling. I picked up the coke-oven business by looking about me, when on an excursion in France … A couple of hundred English Engineers had the same facilities to SEE the importance of this system, being with me at the same time, but they did *not*.[45]

Similarly, Simon was convinced of the importance of scientific training for engineers, donating funds to Owens College for the construction of a new physics laboratory designed by his friend the physicist Arthur Schuster. Similarly to Beyer, he also promoted a broad-based university education that included languages, and he endowed the Henry Simon Chair of German Literature in 1895. German was on the curriculum from the inception of Owens College in 1851, taught by Tobias Theodores, who was also tutor to the children of William and Elizabeth Gaskell, and a pioneer of Reform Judaism.

Chemistry and physics

Akin to the fragmented nature of the German states, German universities were dispersed centres of learning, but the universities of Giessen, Heidelberg and Berlin were pre-eminent in the teaching of experimental science.[46] Justus von Liebig (1803–73), widely regarded as the originator of organic chemistry, had a teaching laboratory at the university of Giessen that drew chemists from all over Europe. Liebig famously disparaged English science when addressing a meeting of the British Association in Liverpool in 1837: 'England is not the land of science. There is only widespread dilettantism, their chemists are ashamed to be known by that name because it has been assumed by the apothecaries, who are despised.'[47] On a further British lecture tour in the early 1840s, he convinced Prime Minister Sir Robert Peel and Prince Albert, among others, that there should be Royal College of Chemistry in London. When it opened in 1845, its first director was a Giessen-trained chemist, August Wilhelm von Hofmann, whose interest in aniline derived from coal tar inspired his student William Perkin, who produced the first useable synthetic colour, mauve, in 1856. Simon Garfield points out that other scientists before Perkin had produced synthetic dyes, but without a sense of their usefulness in industrial processes. For a scientist like Perkin to seek commercial application of his discovery also seemed a betrayal of pure science, even to Hofmann. But 1851 seems to have been a tipping point in the changing relationship between industry and science. Garfield points to the Great Exhibition of 1851 and its exposure of a lack of technical education in Britain, and to the founding of Owens College that year, at which chemistry professor Edward Frankland (who had studied with Robert Bunsen in Marburg) warned that Britain's textiles industry lacked a sufficient basis in science.[48]

Liebig's research laboratory in Giessen and Gustav Kirchhoff and Robert Bunsen's work in spectroscopy in Heidelberg were nodes connecting the trajectories of many Manchester scientists whether they worked in industry, as independent 'devotee scientists', at the Mechanics' Institution or at Owens College, where the connection between science and industry was being forged. James Sumner has noted the growing professionalisation of science in mid-nineteenth-century Manchester, where devotee scientists with private means still conducted research, often alongside business ventures. Without the institutional framework of a university appointment, they relied on institutions such as the Literary and Philosophical Society, the Natural History Society, the Mechanics' Institution, the Hall of Science and the Royal Manchester Institution to communicate and support their research.[49] One such scientist was Henry Edward Schunck (1820–1903), born in Manchester to Martin Schunck, an export shipping merchant, whose own father, Carl Schunck, had settled in Manchester in 1808, having fought on the side of Britain in the American War of Independence. Carl Schunck founded a textile shipping company Schunck and Mylius, later Schunck, Souchay & Co.[50] The company expanded into manufacturing and Henry Edward worked for a while at its calico printing works in Rochdale, before devoting himself entirely to research. He studied for his PhD with Liebig in Giessen, and did important work on indigo and madder dyes, becoming very eminent in the field of industrial chemistry, while conducting his research from a private laboratory at his home in Kersal. He was a leading member of the Literary and Philosophical Society, a governor of Owens College (though never employed there), and in 1895 made a large donation to the college for the endowment of chemical research. On his death he bequeathed his laboratory to the university, where the entire building was rebuilt on Burlington Street in 1904.[51] Liebig's work was also influential in informing early studies of the effects of industry on public health. It had become evident that the slum dwellings, air pollution from factory chimneys and the toxic effluent from dyeworks in the already polluted rivers were all serious risks to health. Liebig's adaptation of 'miasma theory' proposed that diseases such as cholera were caused by the decay of animal and vegetable matter, and formed the basis for demands for improved sanitation in towns. Lyon Playfair (1818–98), later a Liberal MP and government minister under Gladstone, was manager of a calico printing works at Clitheroe, appointed Professor of Chemistry at the Royal Manchester Institution and served on the 1843 Royal Commission to examine public health in large industrial towns. He had trained with Liebig in Giessen and supported the agenda to improve water supplies and sewage disposal in industrial towns. Robert Angus Smith (1817–84) came to Manchester as Playfair's assistant, but was also Giessen-trained, and went on to form an inspectorate for the control of air pollution (he was the first to coin the term 'acid rain').[52] Both Playfair and Smith were well networked with industrialists in the Manchester Lit and Phil, which both informed their work and enabled them to encourage compliance with regulatory controls. As James Sumner points out, this civil engineering response to public health was 'a palatable basis for reform: poor sanitation, not the system that produced poverty, could be blamed for the worst of the city's ills'.[53] Of course Engels had little faith in the benevolent concern of rich industrialists, writing in the Preface to *The Condition of the Working Class in England*: 'Have they done more than paying the expenses of half-a-dozen commissions of inquiry, whose voluminous reports are damned to everlasting slumber among heaps of waste paper on the shelves of the Home Office?'[54]

The network emanating from Liebig's laboratory in Giessen and Bunsen's department in Heidelberg did, however, have a direct impact on the founding of science departments at Owens College, which became the Victoria University of Manchester in 1903. The Unitarian Henry Enfield Roscoe (1833–1915) was an important link in this network, having studied chemistry in Heidelberg with Gustav Kirchhoff and Robert Bunsen, and continued his collaboration with Bunsen after return to Britain in 1857, where he was appointed to a chair of chemistry at Owens College. They did pioneering work in photochemistry, and carried out the first flashlight photography using magnesium as a light source.[55] Roscoe was instrumental in bringing German scientists to work with him in Manchester, such as Carl Schorlemmer and Arthur Schuster.[56]

Carl Schorlemmer (1834–92) studied chemistry in Heidelberg (with Robert Bunsen) and Giessen (with Liebig). In 1859, he became personal assistant to Henry Roscoe at Owens College, and remained in Manchester for the rest of his life. He was elected as Fellow of the Royal Society in 1871, and in 1874 he was appointed to the first chair of organic chemistry in Britain, at Owens College. Three years later the first volume of what would be his and Roscoe's unfinished great *Systematic Treatise on Chemistry* was published. He is known for his research on paraffin hydrocarbons, and as a theorist, historian of science and co-founder (with Liebig) of the new discipline of organic chemistry.[57] As Roscoe recalled after his friend's death, Schorlemmer's research into the structure of hydrocarbons made possible the enormous growth of the chemical industries that had generated such wealth and employment.[58] He himself lived modestly, and was known as the 'red chemist' for his life-long commitment to communism. He remained a paid-up member of the German Social Democrat Party, and when Bismarck's first Anti-Socialist Law was passed in 1878, Schorlemmer naturalised as a British citizen to protect himself from persecution. He frequented the Thatched House Tavern, off Market Street, where German scientists from Manchester's chemical industry gathered to talk science, business and German politics. This may have been where he met Engels, and they soon became close friends.[59] Schorlemmer often visited Marx and Engels in London after Engels moved there from Manchester in 1870. At Schorlemmer's burial at the Southern Cemetery in Manchester officiated over by the Unitarian Rev. Samuel Alfred Steinthal, Engels laid a wreath from the German Social Democrat party on his grave. His affectionate obituary for Schorlemmer fondly recalled the facial injuries sustained by his friend in the course of his experiments with unstable substances. He also paid tribute to his unusually Hegelian insight into the dynamic nature of reality:

> He was probably the only important natural scientist of his age who did not spurn what was to be learned from the then much maligned, Hegel, whom he held in high regard. And rightly so. Anyone who wants to achieve something in the field of theoretical, synthetic natural science must view the phenomena of nature not as discrete unchanging units, as is mostly the case, but as dynamic and subject to change. And this can today still be most easily learned from Hegel.[60]

If Marx and Engels taught Schorlemmer the economic foundations of his instinctive communist convictions, Schorlemmer was among those who influenced Engels's scientific materialism and Marx's interest in agricultural chemistry.[61] In his memory, at the instigation of Roscoe and the industrial chemist Ludwig Mond, the Schorlemmer Organic Laboratory was built at Owens College, designed by Alfred Waterhouse and fitted out according to Roscoe's direction, dedicated to the teaching of organic chemistry. In his address on the opening of the laboratory in 1895, Roscoe expressed the hope:

> that the time would soon come when the leaders in chemical industry would appreciate the necessity of a thorough scientific training, as had long been the case in Germany; and that as Giessen was, under Liebig, the means of raising the standard of chemical education throughout the Fatherland, so the chemical department of Owens College might, under the direction of Prof. Dixon and Prof. Perkin, the director of the new laboratory, be pointed out as the institution in England which had done the same for this great empire.[62]

Shortly after the Schorlemmer laboratory was opened, another German scientist was planning a state-of-the-art physics laboratory at Owens College.

1.3 The British Association for Advancement of Science meeting, Manchester (1887). Carl Schorlemmer (seated far right), Henry Roscoe (perched on chair) and Edward Schunck (standing, top right) with other notable scientists. Roscoe is lighting a cigar for Dimitri Mendeleev. Source: University of Manchester Library. Reference: DCH/1/6/6/1. Copyright the University of Manchester (CC BY-NC-SA 4.0).

Arthur Schuster (1851–1934) came to Manchester in 1870, where some of his cotton-trading family had settled in 1808 to avoid the Continental Blockade. He began working in the family firm Schuster Brothers & Co., while also attending Roscoe's evening lectures in chemistry at Owens College. After a degree in maths and physics at Owens College 1871–72, he took his doctorate in Heidelberg 1872–73, working on spectrum analysis with Gustav Kirchhoff. Schuster returned to teach at Manchester and was appointed to a chair of mathematics 1881–88, then a chair of physics 1888–1906. Sumner notes how his career exemplified the professionalisation of university science: 'Schuster [...] unusually combined the patronage opportunities and commercial connections of a wealthy nineteenth-century devotee with the institution-building agenda of a twentieth-century university leader.'[63] Schuster's parents had converted from Judaism to Christianity in the 1850s, around the time when he and his brother Felix Otto (the future banker and free-trade campaigner) were born. This branch of the family moved to England in 1869 after the Prussian annexation of Hesse, and both sons had distinguished careers, exemplifying a new international bourgeoisie.[64] Arthur became known internationally for his scholarship on earthquakes, magnetism, atmospheric electricity and solar eclipses (which took him all over the world). He played a leading role in the formation of the Victoria University of Manchester and its Faculty of Technology, and served on the Education Committee of the Manchester City Council. He designed and raised the funds to build a brand-new physics laboratory in 1898, the fourth largest physical laboratory in the world, and built to serve both teaching and research. Without this world-class facility Rutherford, who succeeded him as Langworthy Professor of Physics in 1907, would not have been able to conduct his world-famous research. Henry Simon laid the foundation stone in October 1898, acknowledging in his speech his lengthy association with the college, his longstanding friendships with both Roscoe and Schorlemmer and his optimistic vision of scientifically informed industry.[65]

German clubs: the Albert Club and the Schiller Anstalt

Germans in Manchester joined the existing clubs frequented by middle-class businessmen, such as the Brazenose, the Bridgewater and the Reform Club.[66] But they also formed their own clubs based on the German concept of the '*Verein*' as a voluntary association promoting 'polite conviviality', self-improvement and 'rational recreation'. The Albert Club and the Schiller Anstalt were two such gentlemen's clubs, founded by Germans but open to their English peers, and which, as Westaway puts it:

> fostered the creation of a bourgeois and cosmopolitan culture, in which and through which German immigrants could become Anglicised and celebrate

their German-ness, while Manchester's middle classes could be exposed to German ideas and German cultural capital.[67]

The name of the Albert Club (1842–88), a tribute to Prince Albert, was a reflection of the dual identity of its founding members.[68] It contained a library, newsroom, billiards room, dining room, smoking room, card and committee rooms. Originally it was formed by a group of young Germans, but by 1869 half of its 120 members were English. Martin Schunck was one of the first trustees. Other members included Samuel Moore (a close friend of Engels) and Godfrey Ermen (Engels senior's business partner), architect Edward Salomons (1828–1906), Dr Louis Borchardt (a friend of Heinrich Simon), Dr Eduard Gumpert (a friend of Marx and Engels) and Charles Souchay (a leading calico printer and cotton merchant). Engels was on the committee in the 1860s and kept up his membership after moving to London in 1870. According to Coates it was a very 'harmonious' club, but closed in 1888, possibly eclipsed by the success of the Schiller Anstalt.

In the autumn of 1859, German-speaking Europe celebrated the centenary of the birth of German poet and dramatist Friedrich Schiller (1759–1805). Long before there was a unified German nation, Schiller was its 'intellectual founding figure' for the values championed in his works: freedom of the individual, universal human rights and protection against tyranny.[69] The same centenary was celebrated on 11 November 1859 at the newly opened Free Trade Hall in Manchester, followed in 1860 by the founding of the Schiller Anstalt (1860–1911/12), a social and cultural club for the Germans in Manchester, which became famous for the quality of its chamber concerts.[70] This coincidence illustrates the convergence in Manchester of the capitalist ideology of free trade and the humanist ideals embodied by Schiller's work. The physician (and refugee from 1848) Dr Louis Borchardt was its first chairman, Charles Hallé one of the founding vice-chairmen and Philip Goldschmidt was a founding member. Members included Adolf Schwabe (brother-in-law of Salis Schwabe, who took over the Middleton calico printing business on the death of Salis in 1853), silk merchant Henry Edwin Gaddum, Louis Behrens (of Jacob Behrens & Co.) and his cousin S. L. Behrens. Engels joined in May 1861 and was its chairman 1864–68, although he claimed that his friend the physician Eduard Gumpert had persuaded him to join, and he complained that it reminded him of the Fatherland in the way it was run like a police state.[71] Around Engels there formed a radical group in the institute, including Gumpert, Carl Schorlemmer, Wilhelm Wolff and occasionally Marx. Wolff (1809–64), like Henry Simon, came from Silesia and studied in Breslau, but his origins were much humbler and his politics more radical. Having worked with Marx and Engels rallying communist solidarity in Europe in the 1840s, he fled first to Switzerland then to England in 1851. Louis Borchardt knew him from Breslau and urged him to come to Manchester in 1854. There he made a living teaching languages and remained a close friend of Marx and Engels, but renounced radical politics.[72] His was an overlapping but different trajectory from that of Henry Simon, who became president of the Schiller Anstalt as a wealthy industrialist in 1898, but resigned in January 1899 in protest at the institute's plans to celebrate the Kaiser's birthday. If the united Germany that had formed in his absence could not be reconciled with Simon's liberal and reformist ideals, perhaps the celebration of German culture became all the more important.

Music

One of the lasting traces of the Schiller Anstalt remains its concert programmes, printed in German and featuring German music played by prominent German musicians of the time. These are documentary evidence of the cosmopolitan cultural capital that Germans brought to Manchester in the form of music performances. It is well known that the pianist and conductor Charles Hallé (born Karl Halle, 1819–95) founded the Hallé Orchestra after moving to Manchester in 1853, having fled the unrest of 1848 in Paris, but it is less evident how much he owed to German musicians and music-lovers for the success of his ventures. The engineer and businessman Gustav Behrens (son of Jacob Behrens in Bradford) was a close friend and supporter of the Manchester Gentlemen's Concerts that Hallé attempted to revive before founding his own orchestra in 1858. Behrens was also on the committee that Hallé assembled to establish a music school in Manchester, the Royal Manchester School of Music (founded 1893).[73] And after Hallé's death in 1895, when the orchestra was in financial difficulty, Henry Simon, Gustav Behrens and James Forsyth secured the future of the orchestra by setting up the Hallé Concerts Society, formally incorporated in 1899. Three of the orchestra's first four principal conductors were German: Charles Hallé himself (1858–95), Hans Richter (1899–1911) and Michael Balling (1912–14). The prominent Manchester cellist Carl Fuchs (1865–1951) had studied in Frankfurt am Main and St Petersburg before settling in Manchester in 1888. Here he was principal cellist for the Hallé Orchestra, a founding member of teaching staff at the Royal Manchester College of Music (RMCM), and from 1895 to 1914 he was the cellist in Adolph Brodsky's quartet. On the outbreak of war in 1914, Fuchs (by then a British citizen) was interned in Ruhleben camp in Berlin as an enemy alien, returning to Manchester in 1919 to continue his teaching and performing career.[74]

Given Hallé's fame, it can be important to recall that there was already a lively public music culture in the city before he arrived, but that this was also indebted to German educational ideas. Rachel Johnson's study of the music programmes of the Royal Manchester Institution, the Manchester

Mechanics' Institution and the Athenaeum demonstrates the importance of music in these institutions dedicated to 'education, rational recreation and moral improvement'.[75] She points out that despite the paternalistic social engineering aspect of using music to refine the tastes, enlighten the views and improve the morals of the working classes, the provision of reasonably priced concerts and lectures on music did much to diversify audiences, to cross social and professional boundaries and to encourage serious engagement with music as an art form. The admission of women to concerts and lectures on music, for example, paved the way for admission of women to other courses at these institutions.[76] Johnson also points to the overlap in leadership between the three institutions, and the prominence of the Unitarians Benjamin Heywood (1793–1865), George William Wood (1781–1843) and *Manchester Guardian* founder John Edward Taylor (1791–1844) as supporters of their use of music for social improvement. Heywood was both founder and first president of the Mechanics' Institution (1825–40), inspired by the French, Swiss and German models of vocational and technical education, and an advocate of progressive educational ideas such as balancing bodily health and mental vigour. He provided a gymnasium for the institute in 1830–31, soon converted into a reading room by the disapproving directors.[77] Heywood was also convinced of the beneficial effects of music education, and thought it should be available, as in Germany, to rich and poor alike as a subject in schools rather than a luxury reserved for the wealthy.[78]

Educational reform and 'rational recreation'

Heywood's progressive educational ideas were ahead of his time, but by the 1850s they chimed with those of many other Unitarians and German immigrants influenced by Swiss and German educationalists, such as Johann Heinrich Pestalozzi and Philip Emmanuel von Fellenberg. Friedrich Fröbel (1782–1852) who studied with Pestalozzi, was particularly influential in England, with his education theory based on nurturing the unique needs and potential of the individual from an early age, with an emphasis on play, being outdoors and physical activity. He coined the term *Kindergarten*, and the *Kindergarten* movement spread to Britain in the 1850s.[79] The Unitarian minister W. H. Herford had visited a Fröbel school in Switzerland in 1847, and he founded one in Lancaster in 1850. He later founded the Manchester *Kindergarten* Association in 1872, and in 1873 opened a co-educational school with Louisa Cabutt that later moved to Lady Barn House in Withington. Exploratory play, fresh air, rambling and physical activity were important features of the curriculum, and for the first ten years of its existence, almost half of the pupils at Lady Barn House had German names.[80] Henry Simon's children all attended the school, and as Brian Simon recalls, 'As headmaster Herford emphasised discovery, activity, curiosity, in place of traditional didacticism, with the aim of teaching children "to *think*", that is "to observe, compare and judge facts and ideas for themselves" rather than depend on verbal memory in learning.'[81]

Closely linked to these progressive educational ideas, the influence of German gymnastics had a lasting impact on the outdoor movement, rock climbing and mountaineering in England. Starting in a grass-roots nationalist gymnastics movement (*Turnerschaft*) founded in Prussia by Friedrich Ludwig ('*Turnvater*') Jahn in 1811, by the 1860s in Britain German gymnastics promoted the same kind of balance between physical health and intellectual activity as was found in Fröbel's pedagogy.[82] A *Turnverein* was founded in Manchester in 1860 to promote German gymnastics and enhance social life with excursions and gatherings, combining educational, social, cultural and sporting activities. Lacking its own premises, it seems to have been based at the Mechanics' Institution. Unlike the single-pursuit sports clubs common in Britain, the *Verein* embodied a more holistic German model of physical culture based on harmonious mind–body balance. This was also alien to the 'athletic fetishism, anti-intellectualism and a boorish gospel of team sports' promoted in British public schools.[83] Gymnastics was not only an indoor pursuit, it included rambling, cultural excursions and recreation combined with instruction. Jonathan Westaway points to its influence on the British outdoor movement from the 1860s, and on the transformation of approaches to rock climbing and mountaineering in Britain. Bouldering, the application of gymnastics to the climbing of short, technically demanding rocks, without ropes, was pioneered by the son of a German exile from 1848 in London, Oscar Eckenstein, and is the antithesis of Alpine mountaineering with its collaborative endeavour and competitive conquest of summits. Climbing in the local Pennine hills or the Lake District was accessible to all, whereas Alpine mountaineering was governed by upper-middle-class 'unspoken gentlemanly codes'.[84] The son of W. H. Herford and his German wife Marie Catherine Betge (also a teacher with progressive educational views) became a leading rock climber of the prewar years, his name Siegfried Wedgwood Herford signalling his dual heritage and encapsulating the cosmopolitanism of Manchester bourgeois culture. As Westaway remarks, this points to an understanding of 'bourgeois' that is less tied to origins than to a specific way of being in the world: 'In Manchester it was possible to be both German and British and to exhibit a "specific cultural praxis" somewhere in between, though it became more difficult after the Boer War and impossible after 1914.'[85] The First World War undoubtedly changed British attitudes to the Germans in their midst, moving some to change their names (Steinthal to Stonedale, Salomons to Sanville) and others to assimilate more completely. But the legacy of Manchester's connections to European science, commerce, education and culture endures in its universities, its music, its schools and outdoor recreation. Its cosmopolitanism as well as its strong regional identity are rooted in its nineteenth-century industrial prime.

Notes

1 Terry Wyke, 'Rise and Decline of Cottonopolis', in Alan Kidd and Terry Wyke (eds), *Manchester: Making the Modern City* (Liverpool: Liverpool University Press, 2016), p. 71.
2 See: Jonathan Westaway, 'The German Community in Manchester, Middle Class Culture and the Development of Mountaineering in Britain, c. 1850–1914', *English Historical Review*, 124:508 (2009), 571–604; Mervyn Busteed, 'A Cosmopolitan City', in Kidd and Wyke (eds), *Manchester: Making the Modern City*, p. 227.
3 Tom McGrath points out that those targeted included Russians and other Eastern Europeans, and families whose sons were fighting for Britain in the War, 'Hidden Histories, Stephen Joseph Studio, University of Manchester', https://ifthosewallscouldtalk.wordpress.com/2019/08/20/hidden-histories-stephen-joseph-studio-university-of-manchester/ (accessed 31 July 2023). Nicoletta Gullace also observes that the riots which followed the sinking of the *Lusitania* had a 'random xenophobic quality to them' with Britons with foreign sounding-names along with Belgians and Russians attacked. See: Nicoletta F. Gullace, 'Friends, Aliens, and Enemies: Fictive Communities and the Lusitania Riots of 1915', *Journal of Social History*, 39:2 (2005), 352. It can be no coincidence that German families changed their names in 1915, among them the family of Edgar and Caroline Steinthal, who became Stonedale, and the family of architect Edward Salomons, who became Sanville in 1906.
4 By 1866 some of these states had merged, but thirty-four still remained.
5 See: Fanny Lewald, *A Year of Revolutions*, translated, ed. and annotated by Hanna Ballin Lewis (Oxford: Berghahn, 1997), p. 11.
6 It should be noted that German liberals espoused a secular nationalism, not a chauvinistic one, and were in favour of a unified nation-state governed by constitutional rule, so liberalism and nationalism were not as antithetical as they may now appear.
7 Brian Simon, *The Monument at Murg* (Leicester: The Pendene Press 1998), pp. 62–3.
8 Simon, *The Monument at Murg*, pp. 64–74 (pp. 66–7). As Simon points out, Karl Marx's *Rheinische Zeitung* was targeted by Prussian censorship in 1843, and Marx himself fled to Paris (p. 66).
9 Brian Simon, *In Search of a Grandfather: Henry Simon of Manchester* (Leicester: The Pendene Press: 1997), pp. 23–4, 42–4.
10 Busteed, 'A Cosmopolitan City', p. 229.
11 Westaway, 'The German Community in Manchester', 571.
12 Christopher Clark, *Iron Kingdom: The Rise and Downfall of Prussia 1600–1947* (London: Allen Lane, 2006), p. 56, cited by Westaway, 'The German Community in Manchester', 578.
13 Busteed, 'A Cosmopolitan City', p. 229.
14 Parliamentary representation was only granted to Manchester after the 1832 Reform Act, and it was granted city status in 1847, by which time it was already a centre of industry and international trade. See: Alan Kidd and Terry Wyke, 'Making the Modern City', in Kidd and Wyke (eds), *Manchester: Making the Modern City*, pp. 1–27.
15 See Tristram Hunt's 'Introduction' to Friedrich Engels, *The Condition of the Working Class in England*, trans. by Florence Wischnewetzky, ed. Victor Kiernan (London: Penguin, 2009), p. 7. Engels' book was the result of his first two years in Manchester, and was published in German in 1845. An English translation was published in the US in 1885, and not until 1892 in the UK.
16 Kidd and Wyke, 'Making the Modern City', pp. 2–4.
17 A longstanding friendship agreement between Manchester and Chemnitz lapsed during the forty years of East German Communism (during which it was named Karl Marx Stadt), but was revived after unification in 1990.
18 To this day a '*Manchesterhose*' is the German term for corduroy trousers.

19 Hunt, 'Introduction' to Engels, *The Condition of the Working Class in England*, p. 2.
20 Hunt, 'Introduction', to Engels, *The Condition of the Working Class in England*, p. 11. In his biography of Engels, Hunt notes that on his return to Manchester in the 1850s he became disillusioned by the 'embourgeoisification' of the city's working class and even the Chartists, who were too willing to compromise with middle-class reformers. Tristram Hunt, *The Frock-Coated Communist: The Life and Times of the Original Champagne Socialist* (London: Penguin, 2010), p. 190.
21 Hunt, *The Frock-Coated Communist*, p. 100.
22 Engels, *The Condition of the Working Class in England*, p. 86.
23 Hunt, 'Introduction', to Engels, *The Condition of the Working Class in England*, p. 21.
24 Roy Whitfield, *Frederick Engels in Manchester* (Salford: Working Class Movement Library, 1988), pp. 30, 97. According to Whitfield, even Jenny Marx disapproved of the liaison with Mary Burns (p. 23).
25 Bill Williams, *Jewish Manchester: An Illustrated History* (Derby: DB Publishing, 2008), pp. 28–36.
26 This was true also of the Lewald family, the relations of Henry's grandmother Wilhelmine Lewald. In the absence of a central mint in Prussia, the Lewalds administered the mint in Königsberg, while the Simons worked at the mint in Breslau. Simon, *The Monument at Murg*, p. 37.
27 See: Lucia Morawska, 'Outlandish Names on the Provincial Doors: German Jews in Victorian Bradford and their Expression of Identities', *Identity Papers: A Journal of British and Irish Studies*, 2:1 (2017), 33–4. Notably Jacob Behrens, who exported woollen goods to the German market, also set up business in Manchester, so the influence of some of these families was widespread.
28 Williams, *Jewish Manchester*, p. 32.
29 Williams, *Jewish Manchester*, pp. 68–72.
30 Westaway, 'The German Community in Manchester', 574.
31 Su Coates, 'Manchester's German Gentlemen: Immigrant Institutions in a Provincial City 1840–1920', *Manchester Region History Review*, 5:2 (1991–92), 24.
32 McGrath, 'Hidden Histories'.
33 See: Busteed, 'A Cosmopolitan City', pp. 228–9. Coates claims that Steinthal worked there for thirty-five years until 1888, but he died in 1877.
34 Coates, 'Manchester's German Gentlemen', 25.
35 Bill Williams has the society recorded as The Society for the Relief of Really Destitute and Deserving Foreigners, but appears to mean the same organisation. Williams, *Jewish Manchester*, p. 30.
36 Coates, 'Manchester's German Gentlemen', 26–7.
37 See: Morawska, 'Outlandish Names on the Provincial Doors', 29–58.
38 The company still trades as Behrens Textiles: www.behrens.co.uk (accessed 18 August 2023).
39 This rebellion is immortalised in Heinrich Heine's poem *The Silesian Weavers* (1844) and in Gerhard Hauptmann's 1892 naturalist drama *The Weavers*. It was a rallying cry to many German liberals and socialists in advance of 1848. Engels translated Heine's poem into English, seeing the Silesian weavers' revolt as a precursor of communist revolution. Hunt, *The Frock-Coated Communist*, p. 125.
40 Manchester Science and Industry Museum archive, MS0001/ 134, Ernest F. Lang, 'The Early History of our Firm', *Beyer & Peacock Quarterly Review*, 1:2 (April 1927), 13–24.
41 Richard Roberts invented the self-acting 'mule' in 1824 and patented an improved version of the machine in 1830. According to Roy Whitfield, Mary Burns was employed as an operative of this machinery for Ermen and Engels. Whitfield, *Frederick Engels in Manchester*, pp. 19, 21.
42 Lang, 'The Early History of our Firm', 21.

43 Henry Simon had contracts with Beyer, Peacock & Co. when working on European railways in the 1860s–1870s. See: Simon, *In Search of a Grandfather*, p. 40.
44 Simon, *In Search of a Grandfather*, pp. 105–17.
45 Private family papers, Henry Simon, *Rathschlaege für meine Kinder* (Manchester: c. 1899). Emphasis in the original.
46 Oxford and Cambridge had chairs of physics and chemistry, but taught mainly the history of science.
47 Simon Garfield, *Mauve: How One Man Invented a Colour that Changed the World* (London: Faber and Faber, 2000), p. 20.
48 Garfield, *Mauve*, p. 46.
49 James Sumner, 'Science, Technology and Medicine', in Kidd and Wyke (eds), *Manchester: Making the Modern City*, pp. 128–30.
50 As so often happens, the company names reveal family connections: Martin Schunck married the daughter of Johann Jacob Mylius of Frankfurt am Main, and Charles Isaac Souchay (1799–1872) was a merchant who settled in Manchester and married Helene Elisabeth Schunck. He had studied in Giessen with Liebig.
51 Other influential German industrial chemists who were linked to the Mechanics' Institution but not employed by a university included the inorganic chemist Ludwig Mond, who studied with Bunsen in Heidelberg and founded Brunner, Mond & Co. at Winnington, Northwhich, and Mond Nickel in Canada, which produced soda. Two of Mond's companies were among the four that became Imperial Chemical Industries (ICI). With Roscoe, Mond founded the British Chemical Society and was its first president in 1888. Ivan Levinstein attended the precursor of Berlin's Technical University and founded an aniline dye works at Blackley, which later became part of ICI. He was president of the Manchester Chamber of Commerce. Charles Dreyfus studied chemistry in Strasbourg, then founded the Clayton Aniline Company, and became president of the Manchester Zionist Society.
52 Sumner, 'Science, Technology and Medicine', pp. 131–32.
53 Sumner, 'Science, Technology and Medicine', pp. 130–31.
54 Engels, *The Condition of the Working Class in England*, p. 33.
55 Robert H. Kargon, 'Roscoe, Sir Henry Enfield', in *Oxford Dictionary of National Biography*; 'Sir Henry Enfield Roscoe', *Manchester Guardian* (20 December 1905), p. 4.
56 Peter J. Davies, 'Sir Arthur Schuster 1851–1934' (Unpublished PhD dissertation, University of Manchester, 1983), pp. 6, 12–16, 18.
57 P. J. Hartog, revised by Anthony S. Travis, 'Carl Schorlemmer', in *Oxford Dictionary of National Biography*.
58 'The Owens College: Opening of the Schorlemmer Laboratory', *Manchester Guardian* (4 May 1895), p. 9.
59 It is also possible that they met at the Schiller Anstalt, of which both were members.
60 Friedrich Engels' obituary, published in *Vorwärts* 153, 3 July 1892. Also at: www.mlwerke.de/me/me22/me22_313.htm (accessed 18 August 2023). My translation.
61 Ian Angus, 'Marx and Engels and the Red Chemist: The Forgotten Legacy of Carl Schorlemmer', *Climate and Capitalism: An Ecosocialist Journal* (21 March 2017). See: https://climateandcapitalism.com/2017/03/21/marx-and-engels-and-the-red-chemist/ (accessed 18 August 2023). Sumner mentions also the influence of John Watts' lectures at the Hall of Science on Engels' scientific materialism. Sumner, 'Science, Technology and Medicine', p. 130.
62 Schorlemmer was indeed followed as chair of organic chemistry at Owens College by William Perkin Jr (1860–1929), son of the creator of mauve aniline dye; 'The Schorlemmer Memorial Laboratory', *Nature*, 52: 1333 (16 May 1895), 63–4. See: www.nature.com/articles/052063a0 (accessed 18 August 2023).
63 Sumner, 'Science, Technology and Medicine', pp. 119–69. For biographical details, also see: Davies, 'Sir Arthur Schuster'.

64 Westaway, 'The German Community in Manchester', 585.
65 The speech is reproduced as an appendix in Simon, *In Search of a Grandfather*, pp. 139–51.
66 The Reform Club on King Street was designed by architect Edward Salomons and J. Philpot-Jones (1869), and the Schiller Anstalt's premises at 66 Nelson Street were renovated by Salomons and Steinthal in 1885. Rhona Beenstock, 'Edward Salomons: A Sociable Architect', *Manchester Region History Review*, 10 (1996), 91–2.
67 Westaway, 'The German Community in Manchester', 582.
68 The Albert Club was originally in Clifford Street, off Upper Brook Street. From 1859, it was housed in Dover House, on the corner of Dover Street and Oxford Road. Some remains of the Albert Club were found when excavating the site for the National Graphene Institute which is now located on Clifford Street. 'X Marx the Spot!', *Mail Online* (1 March 2013) www.dailymail.co.uk/news/article-2286608/X-Marx-spot-Workers-remains-Victorian-club-frequented-Friedrich-Engels-prepared-write-Communist-Manifesto.html (accessed 20 August 2023).
69 Stefan Berger, *Germany: Inventing the Nation* (London: Hodder Arnold, 2004), p. 47.
70 The Schiller Anstalt was located first in Cooper Street, then at 250 Oxford Road, and finally at 66 Nelson Street.
71 Coates, 'Manchester's German Gentlemen', 23.
72 Whitfield, *Frederick Engels in Manchester*, pp. 49–51.
73 The Royal Manchester College of Music was amalgamated with the Northern School of Music in the 1970s to form the current Royal Northern College of Music. See: Geoff Thomason, 'Hallé's Other Project: the RNCM', *Manchester Memoirs*, 149 (2012), 104–23.
74 The Carl Fuchs archive is held at RNCM Archives, reference CF. See: www.mdmarchive.co.uk/connecting-manchesters-music-archives (accessed 20 August 2023).
75 Rachel Johnson, 'The Agency of Music in Industrial Society: A Comparative Study of the Royal Manchester Institution, Manchester Athenaeum and Manchester Mechanics' Institution, 1834–1860', *Journal of Victorian Culture*, 27:1 (2022), 97.
76 Johnson, 'The Agency of Music', 115–16.
77 Westaway, 'The German Community in Manchester', 588.
78 Johnson, 'The Agency of Music', 106.
79 Advocates of the *Kindergarten* movement in Manchester included Julia Schwabe, wife of Salis Schwabe.
80 Westaway, 'The German Community in Manchester', 598.
81 Simon, *In Search of a Grandfather*, p. 59. (Simon quotes from Herford).
82 On Jahn see: Berger, *Germany: Inventing the Nation*, p. 13.
83 Westaway, 'The German Community in Manchester', 591.
84 Westaway, 'The German Community in Manchester', 595. Westaway also notes that mountaineering was 'part of the international bourgeois cultural capital' of the Schuster Brothers Arthur and Felix Otto (585).
85 Westaway, 'The German Community in Manchester', 600–1. He notes that Siegfried Wedgwood Herford was killed in the First World War, fighting for Britain. Three of Henry Simon's sons were also killed while serving in the British Army. See Chapter 3 in this volume by Diana Leitch.

2.1 Henry Simon (*c.* 1880s). From *Rathschlaege für meine Kinder* (*c.* 1899). Source: private family papers.

2

The appeal of a Buddha: Henry Simon, industrialist and philanthropist (1835–99)

Janet Wolff

In a letter dated 19 February 1889, Henry Simon wrote to his brother-in-law Oscar Stoehr in Bombay.[1] He says he has taken the liberty of sending him the *Pall Mall Budget* (a weekly digest of the *Pall Mall Gazette*, published from 1868 to 1920) to the end of the current year, as he had mentioned he had little to read. Henry says it contains 'a very good collection of weekly news and literary notices', and that he hopes that when reading it Oscar will think of him. A bit of news next:

> I yesterday lunched at the club with young Lathbury who has been ordered out to India, and is leaving next week. We played a game of billiards together and he beat me.[2]

Then, after some family gossip about Oscar's brother Emil, a somewhat surprising request:

> If ever you come across a nice bronze representation of Buddha – not too colossal, say not over 2 ft. high, I should very much like to acquire it, even at some serious expense. Should you not find this perhaps you could find a smaller one – anything from 6 inches upwards. I do not mind spending a good many pounds on a larger one if really fairly executed, and you could simply pack it up and send it to me when you find such, and I will remit, or pay to your account in such a way as you may desire.[3]

It is surprising given Henry's expressed hostility to religion. In his biography of his grandfather, Brian Simon tells a story of Henry's reaction to a request to contribute to a Manchester Jewish cause in the 1890s:

> Henry pointed out the danger of creating a misunderstanding. His mother had been Christian, his father's family Jewish a hundred years earlier and there could only be gratitude for the connection with Jewish intelligence and 'family-kindness'. But 'an abyss of quite infinite dimensions' separated him

from the Jewish faith, as also any other 'religious faith'; agnosticism, pure and simple, was the only moral position for a 'man of science'.[4]

His passion for science is manifest in letters, advice to his sons, an important address he gave on the occasion of the laying the foundation stone of the new physics laboratory at Owens College in Manchester in 1898, and in maxims and aphorisms he printed in calendars he produced and circulated over a number of years.[5] An exchange with his son's, Ernest's, housemaster at Rugby school in January 1897, insisting Ernest be allowed to focus on science rather than classics, might also suggest rather a Gradgrind philosophy of life and education.[6]

And yet this is very far from the case with Henry Simon. He was a highly cultured man, fluent in several languages, extremely well read in literature, deeply involved in music and the arts. Perhaps his view on religion is well expressed in a quotation from one of his calendars: 'Religion consists less in solemn phrases than in right doings.'[7] And another, clearly open to the best of religion: 'The acts and practice of religion, to wit, sympathy, charity, truthfulness, purity, gentleness, kindness.'[8] One can see that Buddha might fit well with such a notion of faith and morality.[9]

* * *

Henry Simon arrived in Manchester in 1860 at the age of twenty-five, with a degree in engineering from the newly established Zurich State Polytechnical School. He was born in Brieg, Silesia, on 7 June 1835, and named Gustav Heinrich Victor Amandus Simon.[10] His father, Friedrich Gustav Simon (known as Gustav), was a civil servant and a director of one of the first German railways. His mother, Antonie Theodora Stöckel, published three novels in later life. Gustav died relatively young, in 1867, but Antonie lived another twenty-six years, and Henry visited her frequently in Brieg until her death in 1893. He attended the local *Gymnasium* (grammar school). But when his uncle Heinrich, brother of Gustav, left for Switzerland after the 1848 revolution, Henry and his parents decided to join him in Zurich. There Henry studied at the Zurich School of Industry, as Brian Simon records:

> Here was a new-type school, in parallel to the gymnasia, which recruited pupils at 13 for a modern education geared towards science and technology, preparing for such careers and higher education. Henry's interest in this field had already been stimulated as a child by familiarity with the workshops of the Silesian railway in which his father held a responsible position, so that he apparently had free access.[11]

In 1853, at the age of eighteen, Henry returned to Prussia to study science and mathematics at the University of Breslau. Two years later he embarked on his studies at the Zurich Polytechnic, acquiring advanced knowledge in theory of machines, mechanical drawing, machine construction and building construction. The course also involved excursions to sites of industrial development in Germany and Switzerland. As Brian Simon points out, Henry was already making contacts that would prove valuable later in his professional life.

Heinrich had been actively involved in the all-German assembly in Frankfurt 1848, leader of a group of about fifty of the 'moderate left' and then elected to the Constitutional Committee. With the failure of the Parliament in Frankfurt, Heinrich was among the small, increasingly radicalised group, that transferred to Stuttgart – known as the *Rumpfparlament* – and was elected to the Reich Regency of five. Confronted by military force, this too failed; and Heinrich, charged with high treason, fled to Switzerland, taking with him the seal of the Reich Regency. At some point this came into the possession of his nephew Henry, who brought it to Manchester.[12] After over a century it was formally returned to the German Government by the Simon family in 1990.[13] It is now on display in the Bundestag in Berlin.

In the last year of his life Henry proudly claimed the radical tradition of his family, and in particular of his uncle Heinrich, a very great influence on him as a young man. He explained his resignation as President of the Schiller Anstalt as a protest against that body's celebration of the

2.2 Seal of the Deutsche Reichsregentschaft. Source: C. Klein, German Bundestag, Exhibition on Parliamentary History, 2023.

Kaiser's birthday. Concerned that they were ignoring reactionary trends in Germany, he wrote on the 31 January 1899:

> I do not fit in with the new German political spirit. I am the oldest descendant of a family which was heavily involved in the 1848 uprising, and I cannot renounce the idealistic aspirations of those times.[14]

In fact, his arrival in Manchester had everything to do with 1848 and with Heinrich's own connections with friends and colleagues in the German community there. Dr Louis Borchardt and Henry M. Steinthal were partners in Heinrich's copper mine business in Murg, Switzerland; Borchardt had, like Heinrich Simon, been a fugitive from the failed 1848 Revolutions in Germany. Borchardt, also like Heinrich Simon, was from Breslau, Silesia (now Wrocław in Poland). Heinrich wrote to Henry (at the time completing military service in Berlin) on 25 February 1859 to say that he has written to Emil Stoehr in Manchester (another 1848-er, from Baden) asking him to arrange a job for Henry for the middle of the following year. He enclosed Stoehr's reply and encouraged Henry to get in touch with him.[15] After military service, Henry worked for a time in a machinery construction company, Roehrig & Koenig near Magdeburg, and at Heinrich's suggestion then returned to Zurich to prepare for his emigration to Manchester. Over the coming four decades he established himself as a highly successful engineer and later a great philanthropist and civic activist. He married twice and had eight children; the youngest was only five years old when he died at the age of sixty-four in July 1899.

* * *

In his first years in Manchester, Henry worked as a consulting engineer, travelling a great deal during that time. He was appointed superintendent and resident engineer for railway contracts in Russia by Messrs Jametel of Manchester. During 1861 and 1862, he was based between Warsaw and Vilna, supervising work on the railways there. Over the next two years he travelled in Italy and France for business on his own account; much of 1867 was spent in Paris in connection with the English section of the International Exhibition there. In Manchester he opened an office at 20 Deansgate, and in 1868 moved to 7 St Peter's Square. From 1884, the company offices were based in a five-storey building at 20 Mount Street in central Manchester, near the old Central Station (now the Manchester Central Convention Centre). According to Brian Simon, in 1868 Henry appears in a local trade directory as 'Civil and Consulting Engineer, Contractor, Exporter of Machinery and Agent for Foreign Patents'.[16] For the next few years he worked hard establishing commercial and business links with British firms and also companies in Europe. His real breakthrough came in 1878, with his adoption of a radically new method of flour milling – the use of roller mills to replace the mill stones that had been used to grind

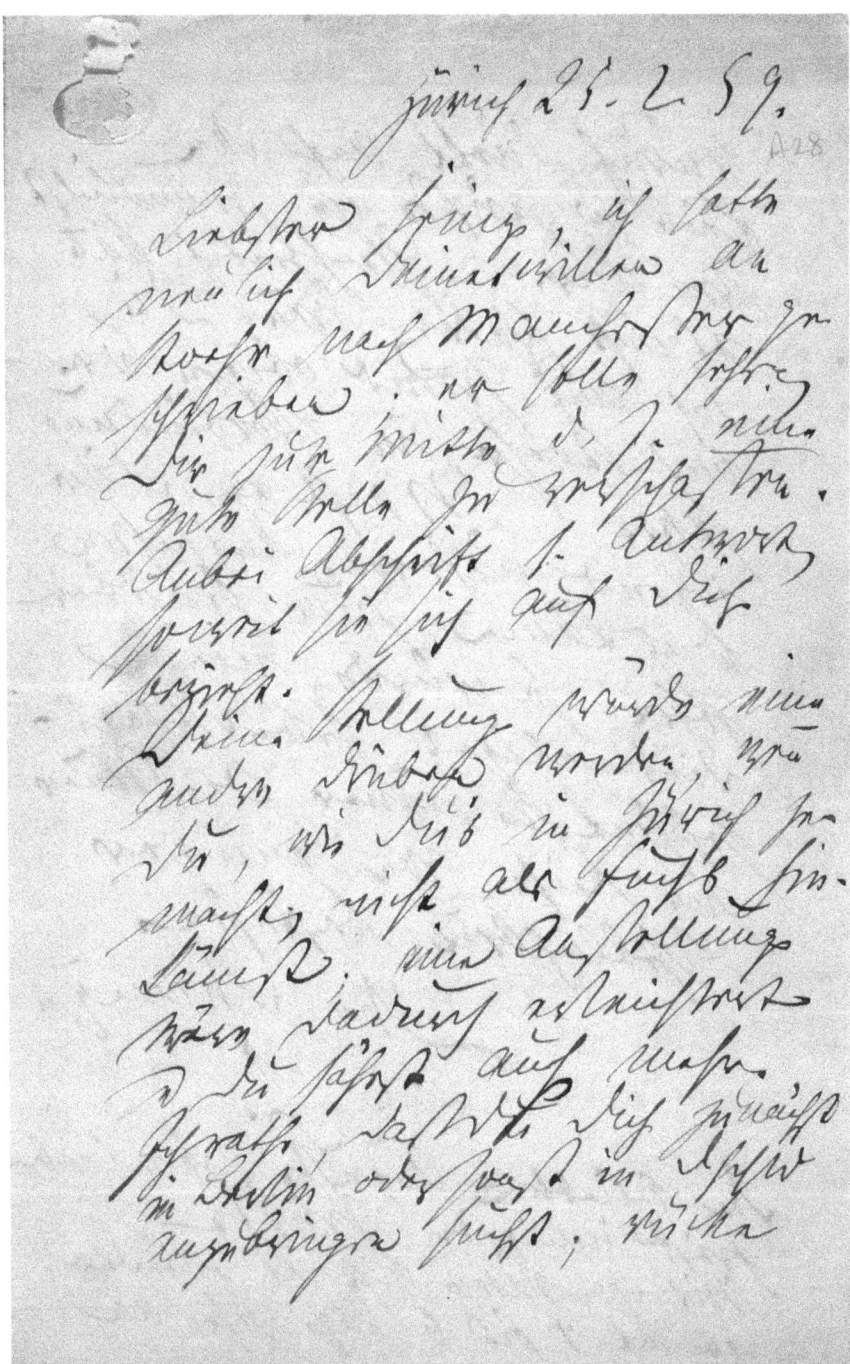

2.3 The first page of the letter Heinrich sent to Henry on 25 February 1859.
Source: University of Birmingham, the Simon papers HS/A/91. Copyright the University of Manchester (CC BY-NC-SA 4.0).

wheat. In 1881, he designed the first completely automatic roller flour mill for F. A. Frost & Sons at Chester; within another decade or so he had over 400 mills around the world using the Simon System. His milling business became a limited company, Henry Simon Ltd, in 1897. In addition, his success was compounded in 1881 with a second invention, a new industrial process for by-product coking, formed in partnership with François Carves. Simon-Carves became a limited liability company in 1896. From the late 1870s he was therefore well established and able – in due course – to support a large family comfortably, build a beautiful new house and become active in civic and philanthropic enterprises.

Throughout his years in Manchester, Henry had strong ties with families in the German community – Stoehr, Steinthal, Behrens, Eckhard and others. The executors of his will were Gustav Behrens and Gustav Eckhard (his second wife's brother-in-law). His second wife, Emily, was the daughter of Emil Stoehr, who nearly twenty years earlier had facilitated his entry into Manchester society. The Unitarian minister Rev. Samuel Alfred Steinthal officiated at his first wedding and at his funeral; his nephew, Edwin Alfred Steinthal, was architect with his partner Edward Salomons (son of a German Jewish cotton merchant) of Henry's Didsbury villa, Lawnhurst.[17] Henry was a member of the German Liedertafel music association (founded 1841) and the Schiller Anstalt (founded 1860).[18] Apparently in 1898, though by then in extremely poor health, he seriously considered accepting the post of German consul in Manchester.[19] And throughout his life, for work, family and health reasons, he visited Germany very frequently.

* * *

In a diary entry in 1912, Ernest Simon recalls his mother reading him a diary his father, Henry, had kept between 1864 and 1867, when he was between the ages of twenty-eight and thirty-two and still establishing himself in work and life in Manchester.

> The most striking point is his desire for friendship and family life, the latter he got at Stoehr and Steinthal. 'Mein Königreich für einen Freund'.[20] He clearly found it as difficult as I do to make real friends. He was pessimistic and generally unhappy as to his chance of making money and being able to marry, which he passionately wanted, seeing in himself the possibilities of a happy family life. He demanded of a wife 'Schönheit, Güte, Verstand and Geist' [beauty, goodness, understanding and spirit] and says it can't be found in Manchester. Suggests a German educated in Paris.[21]

In a letter to his son Harry (27 January 1899), Henry tells him he suffered real loneliness before he was married. Earlier, in a series of reflections and pieces of advice he composed for his children in Venice in 1888 – *Rathschlaege für meine Kinder* – he recalls advice from his uncle Heinrich on the topic of marriage. The collection is written in a mixture of English and German. This one, in German, relates that when Henry, as a young

2.4 The cover of *Rathschlaege für meine Kinder*. Source: private family papers.

2.5 Mary Jane Simon (née Lane). Source: *Henry Simon of Manchester* (1997).

man, had been enamoured of a young woman, Heinrich counselled prudence, telling him that if you buy a new horse and it proves to be a mistake that is not too great a tragedy. On the other hand, it is a more serious mistake to choose the wrong wife, the misfortune being irreparable.²²

In fact, the woman Henry married was not German and not (as far as I know) educated in Paris. She was Mary Jane Lane, of Higher Broughton, aged twenty-three (to Henry's thirty-five) on the date of their marriage, 25 January 1871.²³

At the time of the wedding, Henry was living in Clifton Avenue, Fallowfield; during their short marriage they moved into Darwin House in Didsbury (named by Henry – like his son Ernest Darwin Simon – in honour of one of his heroes in science). They had one child – Ingo, born on the 7 May 1875. Mary Jane died of laryngeal croup on 17 April 1877, before Ingo's second birthday. It seems Henry had help with the child from a children's nurse, Annie Jackson; there are short letters from her to him when he was travelling, reporting on Ingo's activities. (One, dated only 'Friday morning', says that Ingo 'sings all day long'; and a letter of 3 October 1878 from Henry to Emily Stoehr, who would soon become his second wife, says 'Ingo is singing loudly in his bed'. I suppose there is nothing unusual about a child doing this, but it seems worth remarking given Ingo's later training and career as a professional singer.)²⁴

2.6 Henry's former home 'Darwin House', 84 Palatine Road, Didsbury. Photo courtesy of David Leitch.

Many letters from Henry to Emily are preserved in documents kept by the family – much of this archive is now in the John Rylands Library in Manchester. It is interesting to learn, from a letter dated 19 June 1878, that three-year-old Ingo apparently went to stay with Emily and her family during one of Henry's absences (the letter is headed Union

Carlsbad). He says he is 'longing badly for my boy', and that he is happy to know that he is exceedingly well taken care of – 'better than at his own home under present circumstances'. This was before he and Emily were married, and even before they became engaged. It is clear that after their marriage (30 November 1878) Emily cared for Ingo as her own son, and he felt her to be his mother. (Ingo writes in one of Henry's letters to 'Dear Mama Em', and signs 'your loving son Ingo'.) It seems that Henry proposed to Emily on the 30 July 1878, which I deduce from a lovely and touching letter he wrote to her the next day (handwritten, but with his work address – 7 St Peter's Square – at the top). It is eight pages long, and it is tempting, but for lack of space, to reproduce the whole of it here. He opens with this:

> Dear Emily
>
> I understand it so thoroughly that you were startled yesterday. I also quite feel that you should have time to try and know your own heart.
> I would <u>not for the world</u> have you give a promise that you might at any time feel hard to keep.
> I should consider it the greatest possible blessing for me and Ingo if you could after mature reflection really make up your mind to become my wife.

He says he has always found it difficult to speak about his own good qualities, but that he has known her since childhood (she, the child of his friend and sponsor Emil Stoehr, was two years old when Henry arrived in Manchester), and that she should not consider herself unworthy to fill Mary Jane's place.

> Soon after the death of good Mary Jane – in dire need of sympathy – I mentally looked around for someone to fill that awfull [sic] void.
> My mind rested on you from the beginning.
> Your kind disposition of character, your conscientiousness, your whole manner and ways were <u>always</u> highly sympathetic to me. So they were to Mary Jane. She often expressed this to me and others. And it is a pleasant feeling to me that you did know and like her. I know your character is certainly noble enough to feel no jealousy of my memory of her.

He adds that it is right that Emily should consider his age (at the time she was twenty and he forty-three) – that he realises she might have envisaged a different life than the one with him. That he is aware he would be taking her away from her 'exceptionally beautiful home' (in Alderley Edge) to a much simpler house, and that she should consider that 'I am by no means a rich man, and that I have to work hard'.

> Lastly you may know that I am of a somewhat serious and taciturn disposition, but my appearance is worse than the reality ... I mean well – I have a heart capable of loving deeply and longing – longing for love and affection – and I have a deep veneration for all that is pure, good and noble and really high.

> 7 St Peters Sqr. 31. July 78
>
> Dear Emily
> I understand it so thoroughly that you were startled yesterday. I also quite feel that you should have time to try and know your own heart. I would not for the world have you give a promise that you might at any time feel hard to keep. I should consider it the greatest possible blessing for me and Ingo if you could after mature reflection really

2.7 The first page of the letter Henry sent to Emily on 31 July 1878. Source: JRL HSC, Box 1. Copyright the University of Manchester (CC BY-NC-SA 4.0).

He tells her again that she should take her time deciding, and to telegraph him when she is ready to see him.[25]

It is not known when the official engagement was, but the wedding took place in November that year.[26]

* * *

Henry was right to tell Emily that he had to work hard. The year of the marriage was the year of his first important roller mill installation, and one assumes only the start of accelerating success (and increasing wealth). Their first child (of seven) was Ernest, born in October 1879, followed by Harry a year later, Eleanor (Nell) the next year, Margaret in 1883, and Victor, Eric and Dorothea in 1886, 1887 and 1893.[27] One measure of growing success is the fact that the 1881 census already records, alongside the family, a governess, a cook and two other servants. By 1891 there was a governess, a cook and three housemaids. (A newspaper report on Henry's funeral lists, among the eight carriages of family mourners, two carriages of servants.)[28] Throughout, he worked hard, travelled frequently and often dealt with the stresses of his occupation and businesses. There were a couple of cases of patent litigation in the 1890s. Anthony Simon writes that even towards the end of his life Henry could not relax.

> [H]is heart was no longer strong, and as age advanced upon him he worried more and more about his business; he slept badly, with a notebook and pencil at his bedside, and few nights passed in which he did not once or more turn on the light to make a note of some point that had struck him.[29]

Despite this, it was the period of his many civic and philanthropic endeavours, especially during the 1890s. He was the first chair of the Manchester Labourers' Dwellings Company, and one of the initiators and first directors of the Manchester Pure Milk Supply Company. With C. P. Scott he founded Withington Girls School, intent, as Brian Simon writes, 'on providing a sound education for daughters'.[30] He established a chair of German literature at Owens College (from 1903 the University of Manchester), and was a leading benefactor of the new physics laboratory at the College, giving a speech on 4 October 1898 on the laying of the foundation stone of the laboratory.[31] He also sponsored the explorer Fridtjof Nansen for his expedition to the North Pole.[32] As already mentioned, he served as president of the Schiller Anstalt from 1898 (until his resignation on political grounds in January 1899). And at the very end of his life, he provided funds for the construction of a footbridge over the Mersey river, linking Didsbury and Northenden to facilitate access for Didsbury's poor to allotments on the other side of the river. The bridge was built in 1901, two years after Henry's death.[33]

One of his most notable acts was the establishment of the Manchester Crematorium in 1892. This was something he had taken a strong interest

2.8 Simon's Bridge. Photo by Janet Wolff.

in, travelling abroad to Paris, Milan and Zurich and elsewhere to acquire knowledge about the technology involved. The practice was very new in England, the only existing crematorium at the time being in Woking, where the first cremation took place in 1885.[34] The debates at the time, on topics of health, sanitation, aesthetics and overcrowding of cemeteries, are quite fascinating. One rather interesting discussion concerned whether, when the time came, God would be able to raise a body at the resurrection – would this be impossible from ashes? As Bishop Fraser opined, in his sermon in Bolton in 1874:

> The omnipotence of God is not limited, and He would raise the dead whether He had to raise our bodies out of churchyards, or whether He had to call our remains ... out of an urn in which they were deposited 2,000 years ago.[35]

Problems of foul play and exhumation are discussed in debates at the time, and the risk of what is politely (though still terrifyingly) referred to as 'premature burial'. One text reads: 'Are our readers aware that many cases have happened wherein a person has been buried whilst alive? Think of the eternity of horror on the two or three minutes awakening, and the hopeless struggle to free oneself.'[36] In this context, a consensus was emerging on the great advantages of cremation instead of burial.

In Manchester, discussions on the subject had begun in the late 1880s, and a Cremation Society for Manchester and District was formed, deciding at a meeting in 1890 on the erection of a crematorium. A limited company was set up, with Henry Simon as chairman. The Duke of Westminster served as president. The project gained 275 subscribers, a significant number of them (forty-five) with German names.[37] The architects appointed were Salomons and Steinthal, who also designed Lawnhurst. Henry himself designed the furnaces for the crematorium. On his death (and of course he himself was cremated), Emily Simon offered to provide an organ for the crematorium in his memory.[38] Outside the crematorium building is a large memorial to the Simon family.

* * *

The Simon family had moved into Lawnhurst by 1893. There had been an earlier house, also called Lawnhurst, belonging to a Samuel Taylor and his wife, Mary. This house was demolished, and Henry Simon bought the land and commissioned a new building from architects Salomons and Steinthal. The date carved above the front door is 1891, though a list of accepted estimates from the architects (to a total of £12,498, including architects' charges) is dated 4 April 1892.

It seems likely the building (or extension) work carried on after they moved in. In a letter to Harry of 22 October 1897, Henry writes 'The smoking room will now be ready in a day or two, all except furnishings, curtains &c.'[39] The large garden required the employment of a head gardener and three assistants, the former earning 30 shillings a week (as well as having a house in the grounds to live in).[40] Mary Stocks, Ernest Simon's biographer, describes life for the young children growing up in Lawnhurst:

> The size of this house, and the extent of its grounds, bear witness to the degree of prosperity which the Simon business concerns had achieved by that date. At Lawnhurst the young Simons led country lives, kept animals, made hay, and played games. It was a happy home, with money to spare for education, travel, hospitality, and philanthropy. It was an intellectually alert home, in

2.9 Manchester Crematorium. Source: *Cremation in Great Britain* (London: The Cremation Society of England, 1909), p. 29.

which books were read and discussed, and in which the humanist agnosticism of Henry Simon was, during his life, and remained after his death, the dominant Simon philosophy.[41]

As she says, at the time, Didsbury – now part of the city of Manchester and only five miles from the centre – was a separate village. Indeed, in a letter to Emily from Darwin House (also in Didsbury – now West Didsbury),

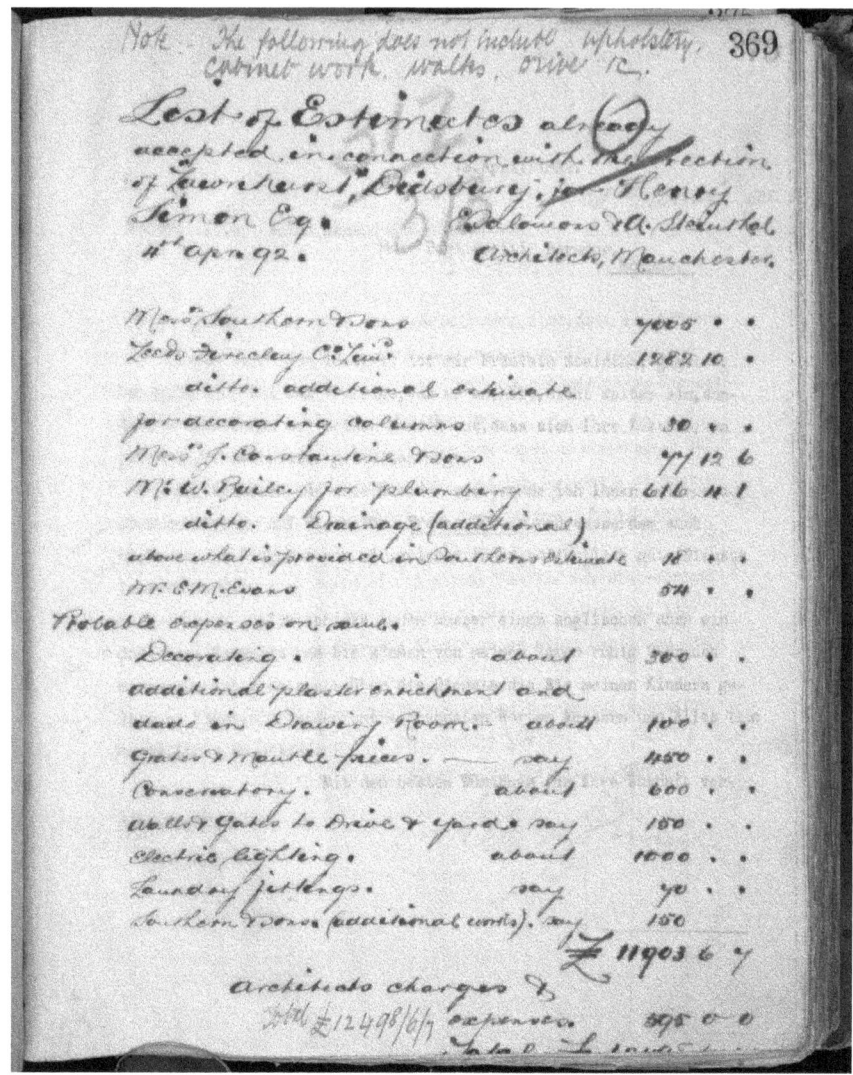

2.10 Architect's invoice for Lawnhurst 1892. Source: JRL SEGA, 56, 'Father's Letters 1887/1902'. Copyright the University of Manchester (CC BY-NC-SA 4.0).

undated but filed with letters from late 1878, Henry writes teasingly: 'You are quite wrong in your geography if you think that Didsbury has anything whatever to do with Manchester, except that it is near by [sic].'[42] As for Stocks' comment on size, and the measure of prosperity, this is perhaps attested to in the next census – 1901, two years after Henry's death. It records as resident Emily, Ernest, Harry, Eleanor and Dorothea; three students, aged nineteen, twenty and twenty-one; a cook, kitchen maid, nurse, three housemaids and a waitress. The gardener Joseph Towe and his wife

2.11 Exterior of Lawnhurst (c. 1899–1920). Source: SSP M14/4/24.

Fanny lived in the gardener's cottage, and the coachman Richard M. Loud in the coachman's cottage.

Towards the end of the substantial archive of letters from Henry to his son Harry, now on Lawnhurst headed notepaper, Emily and Harry's sister Eleanor (Nell) take over from Henry, as he becomes more and more ill. The letters make for sad reading. On 6 May 1899, Emily writes (to 'My dear boy') first with news about lovely weather, tennis, Victor's school match, but then reports that Henry is a little unwell:

> Father drove to Pendleton this afternoon to call on Mr. Darbishire and is afraid he caught cold. Which I trust he did not as he was really just recovered from this last weakness and feeling better.

On 10 June, she says 'Father's state continues most unsatisfactory … he had a very uncomfortable night and has not been up at all today … Today for the first time he has felt too weary to read as usual.' Two days later she reports that another doctor, Dr Steele, has attended, and says he may have a morphine injection if he cannot rest without. On 18 June, she says he is so ill and has difficulty breathing, requiring night nursing. Still optimistic, she writes on 20 June that he is sitting up in bed, but 'recovery will be slow'. After that the letters are from Nell, alternating 'better news' with worse news through the rest of June. Finally, Emily writes again on 13 July:

> My dear boy. I cannot spare you the blow it hurts so to give. Father will not be with us much longer; he is growing weaker. You will wish to be with us all and be with the dear Father whenever you can. I will expect you tomorrow ... We must help each other by love to bear the sorrow we share. Your very loving Mother.

Henry died on 22 July.[43]

* * *

Two weeks after Henry Simon's death, on 9 August 1899, Gustav Behrens received a vitriolic anonymous letter, written on Manchester Reform Club notepaper. Behrens had been working with Henry Simon and James Forsyth to appoint a new conductor for the Hallé Orchestra after the unexpected death in 1895 of Charles Hallé, and to secure the continued existence of the orchestra itself.

> Dear Behrens.
>
> Your friend Simon is dead. Of course his shameful treatment of Cowen caused his brain to go wrong. I have been waiting to see if the same would happen to you. I can assure you there are thousands that would rejoice to hear of the death of that Richter. You must feel uncomfortable in your mind when you think of your abominable conduct to Cowen. Yours – One that knows you well.[44]

Richter was Hans Richter, perhaps then the most famous conductor in the world and at the time the principal conductor of the Vienna Opera. He was offered the conductorship of the Hallé Concerts on 3 November 1895, in a combined approach with the Liverpool Philharmonic Society, though in the end he was not able to take up the position for another four years. Cowen was Frederic Cowen (born Cohen), pianist, composer and conductor, who had conducted the Philharmonic Society in London as well as orchestral and choral concerts in Melbourne. With strong support from Liverpool, he was appointed to conduct the Hallé for the 1896–97 season, and then again the following year. By that time, Richter wrote to say that he was at last able to be free of his Vienna contract and to come to Manchester for October 1899. In the months leading up to Richter's arrival in Manchester, Cowen had managed to orchestrate a campaign in favour of his own retention on a permanent basis, the anonymous letter being from one who took his side in the case.[45]

The initiative for the rescue of the Hallé had come from Gustav Behrens, who then involved James Forsyth, Charles Hallé's business manager and founder of the Manchester music shop (still existing today). They asked Henry Simon to join them to act together as guarantors for the next three seasons of concerts. The task of finding a new conductor was their most urgent one, but they also needed to establish the future of the concerts. Before the 1898–99 season – the last of the three guaranteed seasons – they formed the Hallé Concerts Society, incorporated in June

1899 under the Companies Act with, initially, fifty members. In all this, even as his health was failing, Henry was actively involved, including a visit to Vienna in 1896 to meet with Richter.[46] Early in this four-year saga, he was defending Cowen against an apparently critical report in the *Manchester Guardian*. On 13 February 1896, he wrote to the critic (Henry Hiles) to object to his negative views on Cowen.

> Dear Sir,
>
> As one of the guarantors of the Halle concerts, I take the liberty, which I hope you will excuse, of writing to you with a desire to express my thanks for the letter which you have written to the 'Guardian' with regard to our appointment of Mr. Cowen.
>
> The leaderette in the Guardian with regard to this subject was really written in such an uncalled for style, that I was very much astonished indeed. It was throwing cold water over the best appointment which we could make under the circumstances, and was certainly not affording a hospitable welcome to Manchester, or in any way encouraging Mr. Cowen.[47]

The next day he wrote to C. P. Scott, editor of the newspaper, explaining the history of his involvement in this enterprise.

> Mr. Behrens was consulted, as an old friend of Sir Charles, by the family and trustees, and after conversation with me, it was settled between the trustees and three guarantors, viz., Forsyth, Behrens and myself, to continue the concerts for the present season, and to guarantee a possible loss in equal shares between us three guarantors.

He says this will be for no personal profit to the guarantors, except to Forsyths 'a reasonable remuneration for their professional work, similar to that, in principle, which they received from Sir Charles Halle before'. He predicts possible future disagreements with Liverpool, and says 'Mr. Cowen, Mr. Brodsky and Mr. Forsyth will meet at my house on Tuesday week for a general conversation, and a settling, as it were, of the politics and budget for the next season.'[48] He continues:

> You ought also to know – but this must not be made public in any way – that the arrangement with Cowen is only made for the coming season, so we are quite at liberty to look about during that time for anybody better, should he not fill his place.

He ends by noting that he is pleased that Mr Hiles has withdrawn his critical remarks the day before, in a letter in the *Guardian* 'which seemed dictated by a desire to counteract as much as possible the evil effect of that leaderette'.

Two years later, the pages of the *Guardian* were mobilised by both sides of the Cowen/Richter debacle. On 4 October 1898, the paper published a long leader reviewing the situation, proclaiming itself pro-Richter. Meanwhile, Richter himself appears to have received anonymous letters (presumably from the pro-Cowen supporters), and wrote at length to

Behrens to declare 'I am incapable of tackling any work if I am to be followed and interrupted by malicious and intriguing people – for I have no weapons against infamy.' Gustav Behrens and Henry Simon telegraphed in reply: 'Please do not allow yourself to be misled by malicious individuals. You quite mistake position of affairs here. You are expected with open arms.'[49] This was Henry's final important civic project. He sometimes had to miss meetings because of ill health, but the commitment and the passion for the right outcome were there to the last.

* * *

In his (post) proposal letter to Emily, Henry admits to a 'somewhat serious and taciturn disposition'. Anthony Simon writes of him that 'he did not readily admit familiarity' and, commenting on Henry's tendency to privacy, attributes this to 'his naturally retiring nature' (as well as, in later years, to his failing health).[50] In some of his letters he gives the impression of strictness, moral rectitude and lack of humour, and in business affairs he was clearly able to be very firm when required. In one letter (1 December 1887) he gives notice to 'Miss Emile', governess to the children.

> I maintain that you have disappointed us with regard to your musical knowledge, for although you said you did not play much yourself you gave us to understand that you were capable of directing the musical practicing of our children. We told you at the time that that was a most important thing ... In our estimation your musical knowledge is absolutely insufficient to usefully direct the practicing of young children.[51]

On another occasion he writes to a J. T. Cammell giving him a month's notice, finding that 'your general accomplishments are not those which I require', noting particularly 'the want of theoretical education as an Engineer'.[52] His many letters to Harry (and in one or two cases to Ernest) often contain advice and instruction (to follow freehand drawing, to go in for pure sciences); on one occasion he returns Harry's letter because it is too untidy.[53] His correspondence with his sons' teachers (Mr Yeo at Fettes College for Ingo, then Dr James at Rugby for Ernest and Harry) is quite forthright and insistent on his ideas for their education.[54] And one can easily get the impression, from Henry's inclination to cite (and, in the case of the calendars, circulate) moral reflections and even certainties, of a humourless and self-important man. And yet this picture quite overlooks the other side of his nature – warmth, affection, a deeply embedded capacity for love. As his early letter to Emily says, he does have a heart capable of loving, and that letter and others at the time make very clear his devotion to the very young Ingo. The letters to Harry are affectionate, often light and jokey (of course Harry was between the ages of eleven and eighteen in those years, some to him still at home when Henry was travelling abroad, the majority during his time as a pupil at Rugby). He has a range of warm greetings and signatures ('Enrico caro', carissime Henrice', 'Henricissime', 'Harryboy', and 'fatherly father', 'paternally eternally', 'Papa H', 'lovingly'). And, after all, the calendar mottos include many positive and congenial quotations. For instance, 'The greatest pleasure of life is love'.[55]

As noted earlier, in relation to the Schiller Anstalt incident in 1899, Henry's commitment to a liberal politics never wavered. Among some late letters are several examples of this. On 20 March 1889, he wrote to the editor of the *Manchester Guardian*, taking issue with their Berlin correspondent's criticisms of the *Volks Zeitung*, which he insists 'is a respectable radical paper of I believe about 40 years standing'. Apparently, the correspondent 'stigmatises that paper as having used "scurrilous and mendacious terms" in speaking of the Emperor William I', who had died the previous year – Henry asks for a justification of this claim by providing an abstract of these terms. On 7 February 1896, writing (in German) to a Herr Bamberger in Berlin, he sends him a copy of the *Manchester Guardian*, which – unlike *The Times* – represents liberal England and not the interests of the aristocracy. A few days later he is writing (in German) to Dr Albert Wolffson in Hamburg, again saying that only the *Guardian* reports sensibly on international, and especially German, politics. However, he takes a more conservative position on trade union issues in a letter to Mr Volkhofsky (19 October 1897), writing firmly in defence of the employer in the face of what he fears will be excessive union power.

> I have been a radical and a sincere well-wisher of the working-classes all my life, and nothing would grieve me more than that anyone – and especially someone like you – should think of me as one of the many people who being themselves fairly well off lose their heart for those who are not, and become selfish; but I would have to console myself, in that case with Schopenhauer who so clearly says in his writings that, as long as you have a good conscience, and know yourself, what you are, you need not mind what others think.

But he continues:

> The present pernicious war between Capital and Labour finds me – I say so with great regret – distinctly on the side of what I prefer to call the Captains of Industry and not to revile by the evil-smelling name of Capitalists …
>
> Any good workman can find work by changing his place if the conditions do not suit him.
>
> The capitalist can not [sic] do that. He has what has been accumulated by him, and possibly by his father, in bricks, mortar and machinery, and he is tied to the spot, and it is he who is the slave of these circumstances, and of Trade Unionism.[56]

One wonders whether he ever exchanged thoughts and views with Friedrich Engels, himself a former chairman of the Schiller Anstalt. If the liberalism never faltered, socialism was always a step too far.[57]

* * *

To the side of the rather grand staircase at Lawnhurst are five beautiful and impressive stained-glass windows, about four metres high. At the top of each is a motto – very much in keeping with Henry's calendars and with his *Rathschlaege* for his children. Two are in French: *Repos ailleurs* (rest elsewhere – this apparently from the Afrikaner writer Jacob Daniel du Toit), and *Fais ce que doit, advienne que pourra* (do your duty, come what may). Another is German: *Erst wägen, dann wagen* (translating more or less as 'look before you leap'). In Latin: *Spernere mundum, spernere nullum* (despise the world, despise nothing). This last is also one of the recommendations in the *Rathschlaege* where Henry explains that by despising the world he means despising outward appearance and superficiality. In a mixture of English and German he elaborates – the worthless, 'carriages, horses, servants with cocards, powdered hair and shoulder knots, luxurious fare and life'. By 'despise nothing' he means that everything has its function in the world and is worth understanding and studying.[58]

There is one final motto, a single word: *Maitri* (Plate 12). This, it transpires, is Sanskrit and means benevolence, loving-kindness, friendliness. The concept is central to Buddhism. So Henry's letter to Oscar Stoehr in India, asking him to look for a statue of Buddha, is perhaps not so out of character. Not only that – in the detail of Henry's will we find this item bequeathed to his trustees:

> The Watch by Frodsham with the Sanscrit [sic] word 'Maitri' on the back and with the words 'Heinrich Simon 7*th* June 1873' inside being the date on which I received it from my said late wife as a present.

The late wife was Mary Jane (as Emily outlived him), and we can only wonder what the word might have meant to them – whether, indeed, the young wife introduced it into their marriage. In any case, it reappears twenty years later in Lawnhurst. After Henry's death, it appears once more – engraved on one of the pillars of the family memorial at the crematorium.

It can also be found on the gravestone in Millencourt Cemetery on the Somme for Henry and Emily's youngest son Eric, killed in action in France in 1915, below the Star of David acknowledging his conversion to Judaism on his marriage.

* * *

Henry's letter about trade unions cites Schopenhauer (perhaps somewhat strangely, in that context). I have wondered before about Henry's great attachment to this philosopher. In Ernest's 1912 diary, when he quotes his father's own diary, he adds a note about Henry's views on writers – 'hates Hegel and Kant, likes Schopenhauer'. The *Rathschlaege* begins with a list of 'First Rate Books', 'which I remember having *much* enjoyed'. Darwin tops the list. Schopenhauer's *Lichtstrahlen* (rays of light) is among

2.12 'Maitri' engraved on the Simon family memorial at Manchester Crematorium. Photo by John Ayshford.

the other nine.[59] Without knowing very much about Schopenhauer (other than the generally held view that he is 'the philosopher of pessimism'), I have for some time been perplexed to have learned that, supporting (and funding) Nansen for his Arctic exploration, Henry sent him a copy of the same volume by Schopenhauer to take on his travels. He had met him at an Owens College dinner in 1892 and visited him in Norway later that year, taking Ingo with him. In February 1897, after the successful expedition, Nansen was a guest at Lawnhurst, a visit recorded by Henry in a special issue of his *Occasional Letter* in April of that year which also reproduced a speech he gave at a reception for the explorer.[60]

Even the editor of a collection of Schopenhauer's works begins his introduction to the book with these words. 'Schopenhauer has become synonymous with a thoroughly pessimistic worldview. In defiance of tradition ... he proclaimed we live "in the worst of all possible worlds".'[61] And yet Henry wrote to Nansen, when sending the book, that it was to him 'what to a fervent Christian ... the Bible is said to be'.[62] There is never even a hint of a pessimistic outlook in anything written about – or by – Henry Simon. But of course, his reading of the philosopher is more careful and more subtle. One could perhaps say that the real message is that one must make the best of any bad or difficult situation – a philosophy of acceptance and resignation and an escape, however fleeting, from suffering, primarily through the routes of asceticism, compassion and aesthetic experience. These ideas were strongly influenced by Indian philosophies, to which

Schopenhauer was introduced in Weimar by the orientalist Friedrich Majer in the winter of 1813–14.[63] References to Hindu texts, the *Bhagavad Gita* and the *Upanishads*, recur in his writings.

> From 1845 onwards, Schopenhauer referred to himself several times to friends and acquaintances ... written and oral as a 'Buddhaist', and in 1856 he even bought a Buddha statue and had it gilded.[64]

This may be as near as we can get to an answer to the question of why Henry Simon was interested in acquiring a little Buddha statue from India. And the sad coda to the story is that, as related in the following chapter, Oscar Stoehr, to whom he wrote in February 1889, died about three months later at the age of twenty-three in a tragic accident in India.[65] It is unlikely that the Buddha ever made it to Didsbury.

Notes

1. Oscar Stoehr, born in 1866, was a Lieutenant, serving in the Bengal Sappers and Miners section of the Royal Engineers. See Chapter 3 in this volume, by Diana Leitch.
2. Diana Leitch believes this Lathbury was Stanley Chandos Lathbury, son of Henry Lathbury, a China and India merchant. Whether or not he went to India, he was in Fulham ten years later. By 1895, he had become involved in theatre, and he went on to some fame as a Shakespearean actor. The club was very likely the Clarendon, of which Henry was a member (see: Brian Simon, *In Search of a Grandfather: Henry Simon of Manchester 1835–1899* (Leicester: The Pendene Press, 1997), p. 41). Some of his letters use Clarendon Club notepaper. The Club opened in Mosley Street, Manchester, in 1869, and had a billiard room on the upper floor. See: *Manchester Guardian* (12 April 1869), p. 4; 'The Clarendon Club, Mosley Street and St, Peter's Square', *Architects of Greater Manchester* 1800–1940, https://manchestervictorianarchitects.org.uk/buildings/the-clarendon-club-mosley-street-and-st-peters-square (accessed 18 August 2023).
3. JRL SEGA, 56, 'Father's Letters 1887/1902', 19 February 1889.
4. The family had converted to Christianity in the early nineteenth century. Simon, *In Search of a Grandfather*, p. 22. In an interesting family development, Henry's youngest son Eric converted to Judaism to marry a Jewish woman, Winifred Levy Simon. See Brian Simon, *Henry Simon's Children* (Leicester: The Pendene Press, 1999), p. 91.
5. For example: 'The scientific spirit is of more value than its products, and irrationally held truths maybe more harmful than reasoned errors. T. Huxley', *Fragments of Thought Gathered by Henry Simon* (Edinburgh: printed by R & R Clark Limited, 1900), no. 34. The calendars were inspired by one made by Emily as a gift for Henry – beautifully handmade, wrapped in silk-stitched covers, and contained in a carved wooden box. (For images of the box and calendar, see: HSC Temp/1 at https://luna.manchester.ac.uk/luna/servlet/.) In a letter to Sir Henry Thompson (8 May 1894), Henry writes: 'Your letter about my Calendar arrived at breakfast this morning, and gave us a great deal of pleasure. Yes, the literary part, in fact everything about the Calendar is by myself ... As you speak so kindly of the Calendar I think I may tell you that originally Mrs Simon made for me, on one of my birthdays, a hand-written calendar containing quotations for each day of the year – an immense piece of labour. The quotations were taken from the English, French and German, and it was of course rather easier to select 365 good mottos from three languages than from one as I now do.' See: 'Father's Letters 1887/1902'.

6   'Father's Letters 1887/1902', Henry Simon to Robert Whitelaw, 7 January 1897.
7   No. 196, Bishop Fraser in *Fragments of Thought*.
8   No. 194, Old Inscription in *Fragments of Thought*.
9   Andrew Simon, great-grandson of Henry Simon, recalls a letter from Henry to his son Harry, probably written from the Bay of Naples around 1890, in which he says he has found an interesting little idol (perhaps ancient Roman) which they should place in their 'gods corner' when he returns home. Private correspondence (6 October 2023).
10 At the time, Brieg was in the Prussian Empire. It is about thirty miles south-east of Breslau. Now it is Brzeg, in south-west Poland. The primary source of information on the life and work of Henry Simon has been the biography written by his grandson Brian Simon. See: Simon, *In Search of a Grandfather*.
11 Simon, *In Search of a Grandfather*, p. 28.
12 Heinrich died only a few months after Henry left for Manchester, drowned in an accident in the Wallensee at Murg in Switzerland. One must assume that all his papers and possessions were brought to Manchester by Henry sometime after that. Brian Simon, *The Monument at Murg* (Leicester: The Pendene Press, 1998), pp. 11–12.
13 Simon, *The Monument at Murg*, pp. 69–70, 85–91.
14 Simon, *In Search of a Grandfather*, p. 161. The Schiller Anstalt, founded in 1860, was a social and cultural club for Germans in Manchester.
15 University of Birmingham, The Simon Papers HS/A/91, Heinrich Simon to Henry Simon, 25 February 1859. www.digitalcollections.manchester.ac.uk/view/EX-CADBURY-SIMON-HS-A/91 (accessed 8 August 2023).
16 Simon, *In Search of a Grandfather*, p. 40.
17 His marriage to Emily was in a Church of England church in Alderley Edge. Also see: Rhona Beenstock, 'Edward Salomons – A Sociable Architect', *Manchester Region History Review*, 10 (1996), 90–5. Web.archive.org/web/20070221173757/http://www.mcrh.mmu.ac.uk/pubs/pdf/mrhr_10_beenstock.pdf (accessed 23 October 2023).
18 On the Liedertafel and other German organisations, see Mervyn Busteed, 'A Cosmopolitan City' in Alan Kidd and Terry Wyke (eds), *Manchester: Making the Modern City* (Liverpool: Liverpool University Press, 2016), especially the section on Germans in Manchester pp. 227–30.
19 Simon, *In Search of a Grandfather*, p. 130.
20 'My kingdom for a friend.' It's not clear whether Ernest is actually quoting Henry's diary here, but it seems so.
21 ESD, 25 June 1912.
22 Private family papers, Henry Simon, *Rathschlaege für meine Kinder* (Manchester: c. 1899), p. 13. According to Brian Simon, these writings were printed and bound together as a book by Emily after Henry's death. Simon, *In Search of a Grandfather*, p. 37. Although the opening page has 1888 as the date, p. 16 has 15.vii.91, which suggests the compilation began in Venice in 1888 and was added to later.
23 Brian Simon has a couple of things wrong about Mary Jane. He has the year of marriage as 1874, and – for some reason – Mary Jane as an Australian woman. See: Simon, *In Search of a Grandfather*, p. 42. The marriage register has a date of 25 January 1871, and gives her address as Kensal Craig, Higher Broughton. Her father, William Lane, was born in Manchester in 1809 and her mother, Matilda Gibson, in 1811 in Rochdale. Mary Jane was born in Manchester on 14 May 1847.
24 For these letters, see: JRL HSC, Box 1.
25 JRL HSC, Box 1, Henry Simon to Emily Stoehr, 31 July 1878. Underlining in the original.
26 Simon, *In Search of a Grandfather*, p. 42.

27 Simon, *In Search of a Grandfather*, p. 43.
28 'Funeral of the late Mr. Henry Simon', *Manchester Courier* (26 July 1899), p. 7.
29 Anthony Simon, *The Simon Engineering Group* (Cheadle Heath: privately printed, 1953), p. 5.
30 Simon, *In Search of a Grandfather*, p. 60.
31 The speech is reproduced as an appendix in Simon, *In Search of a Grandfather*, pp. 139–51. Extracts are included in Simon, *The Simon Engineering Group*, pp. 6–10.
32 Simon, *In Search of a Grandfather*, pp. 102–4.
33 Simon, *In Search of a Grandfather*, pp. 124–5.
34 *Cremation in Great Britain* (London: The Cremation Society of England, 1909), p. 21.
35 *Cremation in Great Britain*, p. 13. See also J. Harvey Simpson, *Cremation in Manchester and Elsewhere* (Manchester: James Collins & Kingston Limited: 1902), pp. 20–7.
36 Simpson, *Cremation in Manchester*, p. 70.
37 Simon, *In Search of a Grandfather*, pp. 119–20. A different source gives the numbers as 65 out of a total of 288, in 1892: 'A Brief History of Cremation: The Manchester Experience', *Manchester Genealogist*, 37:2 (2001).
38 'Joint Stock Company: The Manchester Crematorium', *Manchester Guardian* (14 December 1899), p. 5.
39 JRL HSC, Box 3, Henry Simon to Harry Simon, 22 October 1897.
40 Simon, *In Search of a Grandfather*, p. 75.
41 Mary Stocks, *Ernest Simon of Manchester* (Manchester: Manchester University Press, 1963), pp. 6–7.
42 JRL HSC, Box 1, Henry Simon to Emily Simon (late 1878?).
43 For these letters, see: JRL HSC, Box 3.
44 Michael Kennedy, *The Hallé Tradition. A Century of Music* (Manchester: Manchester University Press, 1960), p. 126. Kennedy goes on to say that the writer was discovered to be a churchwarden.
45 The whole drama is related in detail by Kennedy, *The Hallé Tradition*, pp. 115–26.
46 Simon, *In Search of a Grandfather*, p. 101.
47 'Father's Letters 1887/1902', Henry Simon to Henry Hiles, 13 February 1896.
48 'Father's Letters 1887/1902', Henry Simon to C. P. Scott, 14 February 1896. Mr Brodsky is Adolph Brodsky, violinist, whom Hallé brought to Manchester in 1895 to be leader of the orchestra and teach at the music college with Hallé had founded in 1893. Hallé died within a few weeks of his arrival. In 1896, Brodsky became Principal of the Royal Manchester College of Music.
49 Kennedy, *The Hallé Tradition*, pp. 120, 124–5.
50 Simon, *The Simon Engineering Group*, pp. 4–5.
51 'Father's Letters 1887/1902', Henry Simon to Miss Emile, 1 December 1887.
52 'Father's Letters 1887/1902', Henry Simon to J. T. Cammell, 2 November (no year given).
53 JRL HSC, Box 3.
54 'Father's Letters 1887/1902', John S. Yeo, 31 December 1890, 7 January 1891; Henry Simon to Herbert Armitage James, 7 January 1897, 20 February 1897.
55 Attributed to Sir William Temple. *Fragments*, no. 323.
56 'Father's Letters 1887/1902', Henry Simon to C. P. Scott, 20 March 1896; Henry Simon to Herr Bamberger, 7 February 1896; Henry Simon to Albert Wolffson, 10 February 1896; Henry Simon to Mr Volkhofsky, 19 October 1897.
57 Henry Simon and Engels had a mutual friend, Carl Schorlemmer, himself a communist. Henry acknowledges him in his speech on laying the stone for the physics laboratory at Owens College on 4 October 1898 (Simon, *In Search of a Grandfather*, p. 139). On Engels' chairmanship of the Schiller Anstalt, see Tristram Hunt, *The Frock-Coated Communist: The Life and Times of the Original Champagne Socialist* (London: Penguin, 2010), p. 211.

58 Simon, *Rathschlaege für meine Kinder*, p. 9.
59 Simon, *Rathschlaege für meine Kinder*, p. 5.
60 Simon, *In Search of a Grandfather*, pp. 102–4. Nansen admired Lawnhurst so much that he asked to borrow the plans, and had his own house, Polhøgda near Lysaker, built on their design. See Janet Wolff, *Austerity Baby* (Manchester: Manchester University Press, 2017), pp. 152–4. Henry's 1897 speech is reproduced in Simon, *In Search of a Grandfather*, pp. 153–7.
61 Wolfgang Schirmacher, 'Living Disaster: Schopenhauer for the Twenty-first Century', in Wolfgang Schirmacher (ed.) *The Essential Schopenhauer* (London: Harper Perennial, 2010), p. vii.
62 Roland Huntford, *Nansen: The Explorer as Hero* (London: Abacus/Little, Brown and Company, 2001 [1997]), p. 204.
63 Arthur Hübscher, 'Arthur Schopenhauer', www.britannica.com/biography/Arthur-Schopenhauer (accessed 20 August 2023); https://plato.stanford.edu/entries/schopenhauer/ (accessed 20 August 2023).
64 Urs App, 'Schopenhauers Begegnung mit dem Buddhismus', *Jahrbuch der Schopenhauer-Gesellschaft*, 79 (1998), 53–4. For a considered discussion of the parallels and differences between Buddhism and Schopenhauer's philosophy, see: Peter Abelson, 'Schopenhauer and Buddhism', *Philosophy East and West*, 43:2 (1993), 255–78.
65 See Chapter 3 in this volume by Diana Leitch.

3.1 Emily Simon (date unknown). Source: *Henry Simon of Manchester* (1997).

3

'Her compass always pointed to service': the life of Emily Simon (1858–1920)

Diana Leitch

When Emily Simon died in 1920, the *Manchester Guardian* reported her death as that of 'Mrs Henry Simon' with no mention of her first name in the article.[1] Of the quartet studied in this book, Emily is the one who is lost to history. To a degree that is inevitable, for the archival record is sparse. Closely inspecting the materials which do exist, however, does enable a reconstruction of her ancestral Germanic mercantile background and her extended family. In unearthing her familial history, we not only learn of the rich set of social networks which linked the business communities of Manchester and Bradford together, but we also gain a much fuller sense of her philanthropy, political activism and work in the community as well as the many tragedies in her life and that of the wider Simon family.

Stoehr connections

She was born Emily Anne Stoehr on 27 April 1858 at the family home, 20 Cecil Street, in the All Saints district of Manchester where her parents, Emil and Helene Stoehr, had lived since 1856.[2] Many immigrants from continental Europe already lived in this semi-rural area on the southern edge of the city. The 1861 census recorded that nearby at 14 Ducie Street four German men were lodging with a retired grocer called Benjamin Bishop. One of them, a civil engineer, aged twenty-five, was called Heinrich (sic) (later Henry) Simon who would later become Emily's husband.[3] From Cecil Street the family – Emily, her parents, Emil and Helene Stoehr, and her older brother, Charles, and younger sister, Matilde – moved in 1860 to Oakfield, a house on the 'Oaks' Estate in Rusholme, south Manchester, adjacent to The Firs on Ladybarn Lane. In 1845, plots were offered for the creation of 'respectable residences' and over the next ten to fifteen years several notable families, including the Stoehrs, moved in. Oakfield was one of the grand mansions on a horseshoe-shaped road called Oak Drive off Didsbury/Wilmslow Road in Rusholme. Some of their neighbours in 1861 were famous in the history of Manchester. The innovative mechanical engineer Joseph Whitworth (1803–87) lived at The Firs. Alfred Waterhouse (1830–1905), the architect of Manchester Town Hall, lived at Barcombe Cottage. On Oak Drive was Mary Louisa Orrell (1829–96), widow of the mill-owner and former mayor of Stockport Alfred Orrell (1815–49). In 1871, she was to become Joseph Whitworth's second wife. Families of German origin included Henry Michael Steinthal (1821–1905) and his wife Wilhelmine Pauline Steinthal (1827–83), who lived with their seven children at a house called Hollywood (probably the house later known as the Hollies). The merchant Edward Behrens (1837–1905) moved in later that decade to a large house called The Oaks on the corner of Old Hall Lane.[4] The area was known to Rusholme locals as the home of the cotton magnates. A photograph of the Stoehrs' house, Oakfield, was taken by a German-born photographer, Helmut Carl Friedrich Martin Petschler (1832–70), who lived nearby in Egerton Road, Fallowfield. He specialised in snow scenes and Carte Visage photographs.[5]

3.2 Aerial view of the Oaks Estate. Source: Martin Dodge.

After the Stoehrs moved on from Rusholme, Oakfield was later occupied by the journalist and leader writer on the *Manchester Guardian*, Charles Edward Montague (1867–1928) and his family in close proximity to his father-in-law, Charles Prestwich (C. P.) Scott (1846–1932), editor of the *Manchester Guardian*, who was by then living at The Firs.[6] Emily's parents, Emil Moritz Stoehr (1827–77) and Helene Margarethe Stoehr, née Worms (1831–1908), were of German birth and already had one child, Charles William Stoehr (1856–1926), born in 1856 at 20 Cecil Street. Emily was the second child, and after her seven more siblings were to follow: Matilde, Marie-Louise Christine, Emil Moritz, Oscar Henry, Clara Helene, Susanne and Friederich (Fritz) Otto.[7]

Little is known about Emil Moritz Stoehr's origins in Germany except that he came from Sachsen Altenburg and was born on 23 February 1827. His marriage certificate suggests that his father was Wilhelm Stoehr, a postmaster.[8] Emil seems to have fled from the German state of Baden in 1848 after the suppression of the March revolution of that year, and he arrived in Manchester via Hamburg. Simon family legend had it that Emily had inherited a torn newspaper cutting from 1848 offering a reward for Emil 'alive or dead'. His arrival from Hamburg as an alien was recorded by the captain of the ship *Trident* at the Port of London on 1 June 1849.[9] Stoehr declared himself a merchant from Hamburg and received a Certificate of Alien Arrival No. 2009 from the Port authorities. He met up in Manchester with physician Dr Louis Borchardt (1816–83), who was also an exile from the 1848 revolution and came from Breslau. Both of them, together with merchant Henry Michael Steinthal (1821–1905), who had been born in Eccles, had business connections with Heinrich Simon (1805–60) and his mining activities at Murg on Wallensee in Switzerland. It was through Heinrich that they first encountered his nephew, Henry Simon.[10] Emil was a textile merchant; the *London Gazette* of 25 June 1858 recorded that on 3 June a patent for the invention of 'certain improvements in looms for weaving' was granted to Emil Moritz Stoehr of Manchester.[11] He went into partnership with Friederich Carl Prieger, forming the firm Prieger, Stohr (sic) and Company.[12] The Prieger–Stoehr partnership was dissolved in 1867, and from then on Emil had his own company of E. M. Stoehr & Co.[13]

Emil's textile business involved trade with merchants in Bradford, the international capital of the wool industry. It was a town occupied by many merchants of German origin including Jacob Behrens (1806–89), founder of the great firm of Sir Jacob Behrens & Sons Limited which is still operating today in Manchester.[14] Many members of the Steinthal family were merchants there too. The area occupied by the merchants' wool and yarn warehouses was known as 'Little Germany'.[15] It was in Bradford that Emil most likely met Helene Margarethe Worms, who had been born in Hamburg in 1831 and was the daughter of German wool merchant, Charles Worms, and his wife, Emily. Charles Worms arrived from Hamburg at the port of London on 8 January 1837.[16] He worked in Bradford for the Hamburg-based thread manufacturers, Emmanuel & Co. Before 1842, he had been in partnership with Moritz Steinthal (1795–1848) and Hermann Schlesinger (1791–1847) as merchants and yarn dealers in Bradford, but the partnership with Schlesinger was dissolved on 13 December 1841.[17] Charles Worms went on to be a successful and wealthy woollen merchant operating in the 'Little Germany' part of Bradford's merchant quarter. The family lived first at 10 Eldon Place on Manningham Lane and then moved to a much larger mansion, 8 Mount Royd. Helene had two other siblings, Alfred Worms (b. 1831) who died unmarried in Bradford in 1893 and Anna Maria Worms (b. 1834) who married Francis Anton (Frank Anthony) Steinthal (b. 1824), eldest son of Moritz Steinthal, at St Peter's Church, Bradford on 18 September 1858 just a few months after her niece, Emily Stoehr, was born in Manchester.[18] The extended family of the Steinthals, in both Bradford and Manchester, feature recurrently in Emily's life. The daughter of Moritz Steinthal (1795–1848) and Friedericke Emmanuel (1802–66), Wilhelmine, married another Steinthal, Henry Michael, the former business partner of Heinrich Simon and the older brother of Samuel Alfred Steinthal, who would baptise Emily in 1861.[19] The interaction and intermarriage between these Germanic merchant families was extensive both in Bradford and Manchester and between the two cities.

In 1856, Emil Stoehr married Helene Worms at the English Presbyterian Chapel on Chapel Lane in Bradford. After their marriage, Emil and Helene moved to Manchester to live in Cecil Street.[20] Their first child, Charles William, was baptised at Manchester Cathedral, but that is unlikely to indicate an attachment to the Established Church: they had, after all, been married at an 'English Presbyterian' or Unitarian chapel in Bradford.[21] The next two children, Emily and Matilde, were baptised at Platt Chapel, a Unitarian chapel in Rusholme, both on 4 May 1861. The family's attachment to Unitarianism was clear enough. The baptisms at Platt Chapel were conducted by the Reverend (Samuel) Alfred Steinthal (1826–1910), a notable figure in Manchester Unitarianism. On the same day, two of the younger sons, Edwin Alfred and Walter Oliver of Henry Michael Steinthal of Hollywood (sic), Fallowfield, were also baptised by Alfred Steinthal who was their uncle.[22] Henry Michael and Samuel Alfred were both sons of Ludwig Steinthal (1784–1861).

Alfred Steinthal appears at many critical stages in Emily's life. At the time of her baptism in 1861, he was serving as a Unitarian minister in Liverpool working with poor immigrants, but in 1864 he was appointed to Platt Chapel, from where he moved in 1870 to the celebrated Cross Street Chapel, where he was for many years a colleague of William Gaskell. He was a teetotaller, an advocate of women's suffrage and more generally of equality of the sexes and championed many advanced causes.[23] He was a notably vociferous supporter of the abolitionist cause in the United States alongside Massachusetts Unitarian minister Samuel May Jr (1810–99).[24]

In 1866 the family moved from Oakfield to one of the large impressive villas that had been built on the leafy heights of Woodbrook Road and Macclesfield Road on the west slope of Alderley Edge. A residential colony for affluent Mancunian merchants had been established there, made possible by the building of the London and North Western Railway from Manchester in 1843. The villas were Italianate, Tudor, Gothic castellated and Swiss in yellow or red brick, white render or local stone and each stood in a two-acre plot on the former de Trafford estate. The Stoehrs home, The Larches, was the third villa designed by Manchester architect Joseph Stretch Crowther (1820–93) and he himself lived at one of the other villas, Redclyffe Grange, in this early housing development which was complete by 1870. The Larches was near the top of the Edge and had a famous garden.[25]

If the Stoehrs moved in Unitarian circles, that might help account for Helene's early attachment to the cause of women's suffrage, given the link between Unitarianism and early feminism in the nineteenth century.[26] Hers was one of over 1,500 signatures on the Suffrage Petition presented to the House of Commons by John Stuart Mill, Liberal MP for the City of Westminster, on 7 June 1866. The signatures had been collected astonishingly quickly over the course of May 1866 from women of all classes, occupations and marital status across the whole of the UK, and it helped secure the first parliamentary debate on women's suffrage the following year. Mill's attempt to amend the Second Reform Bill to replace the word

3.3 The Larches. Courtesy of Graham Dilliway.

'man' with 'person' was defeated but marked the start of the campaign for the enfranchisement of women.[27] A fellow signatory, Ursula Bright, wife of Mill's ally Jacob Bright MP, lived in Alderley Edge near the Stoehrs and may well have collected Helene's signature for the petition.

Marriage

Emily's father died shortly before his fiftieth birthday in 1877. His death certificate, signed by Dr Louis Borchardt, recorded that he had had a brain tumour and paralysis for several years so Emily and her family would have endured his lingering illness for some time before he died.[28] Helene Stoehr was now a widow, aged forty-five, with nine children to bring up ranging in age from Fritz aged five to Charles William aged twenty. She never remarried and was a widow for thirty-one years until her death in 1908.

At the time of her father's death, Emily was nearly nineteen, and the following year she became engaged to widower, Henry Simon, who was twenty-three years older. It is clear that Henry had known Emily and her family for many years since their days as neighbours in All Saints and that her father was one of his long-term friends. It was indeed Emil Stoehr to whom Heinrich Simon had written to from Switzerland asking if he could find a job for his nephew, Henry, in Manchester.[29] Presumably Emily met Henry's requirements for a wife which he noted in a diary he wrote between 1864–67: 'Schönheit, Güte, Verstand und Geist' [beauty, goodness, understanding and spirit], which he doubted he would find in Manchester![30] The photograph of her taken around the time of her wedding (Figure 3.1) does show her as an attractive young woman. In one of Henry's letters to Emily at the time of their engagement he writes of 'taking you away from your beautiful – exceptionally beautiful – home and bringing you to a much simpler house', and indeed his home at 84 Palatine Road was simple in comparison with The Larches. He obviously also valued the bustling and cheerful family life of Emily's home in comparison to his quiet house where he only had his little son Ingo, aged two, and servants.[31] The couple were married on 30 November 1878 at St Philip's Anglican Church in Chorley (Alderley Edge) near Emily's home at The Larches. The report of their wedding noted that:

> St Philip's Church, Chorley was well filled on Saturday morning on the occasion of the marriage of Miss Emily Stoehr, eldest daughter of Mrs Stoehr of the Larches, Alderley Edge, to Mr Henry Seaman (sic) of Didsbury. The service was conducted by the Rev Mr Consterdine of Chorley, and the party left the church amid a peal of music from the organ. The path from the church was covered with scarlet felt carpet. The bride was simply but appropriately dressed in a plain white silk Princess dress. The bridesmaids were attired in pale blue silk dresses, trimmed with swan's down. The happy party were

conveyed from the church in six carriages. The proceedings throughout were of a very quiet and simple character, owing, we understand to a recent family bereavement. The number of people congregated at the church testified in a very strong manner to the high esteem and respect in which the bride and her family are held everywhere they are known.

The report spelt Henry's surname as Seaman, which is how it was pronounced until the family anglicised the pronunciation in 1915.[32]

Emily, the young bride, left her family home in Alderley Edge for ever and went to live with Henry and son Ingo at Henry's home, 'Darwin House'. Emily and Henry's first son Ernest Emil Darwin Simon was born on 9 October 1879, and was followed in quick succession over the next seven years by Heinrich Helmuth (Harry) (October 1880), Eleanor Christadora (Nell) (January 1882), Margaret Antonia (January 1883) and after a short gap Victor Herman (October 1886) and Eric Conrad (September 1887). All were born at Darwin House. Six years later, Antonia Dorothea (Tony) was born in September 1893 at their new home, Lawnhurst.[33]

As Emily's new Simon family in Didsbury grew, her old Stoehr family in Alderley Edge started to break up. Emily's younger sister, Marie-Louise, married the German immigrant merchant Gustav Eckhard (1851–1929) in 1883.[34] Gustav had started working as a clerk in a 'stuff' and yarn house in Bradford, possibly in a firm owned by another branch of the Eckhard family, and was naturalised just before his wedding.[35] The couple settled initially in Fallowfield before later moving to Didsbury. They and their children were to feature greatly in Emily's later life.

3.4 Emily with Eleanor, Victor, Eric, Margaret and Henry. Source: JRL HSC.

The next of Emily's siblings to leave home was her older brother, Charles William Stoehr (1856–1926), in 1885. He made a typical Alderley Edge marriage when he married Mary Georgina Verena Tonge (1861–1952), known as Verena. She was the eldest daughter of East India merchant, Yorkshireman Richard Tonge, who lived at the biggest mansion on the Edge called Croston Towers, directly opposite The Larches. His business career did not flourish, however. Several business ventures failed. The marriage to Verena produced two sons, Charles Felix Stoehr born 13 January 1886 and Oscar Humphrey Stoehr born 12 April 1889, but in other respects was no more successful than Charles's business career. Verena was very supportive of her mother-in-law, Helene, for many years but eventually moved to live in Llanhyddland Valley, Anglesey, in North Wales where she died in 1952, aged ninety. Charles migrated to South Africa, where he died in Durban in June 1926.[36]

While Verena's life was marked by its longevity, the lives of Emily's siblings, Matilde and Oscar, were cut short. Their deaths represented the first of many losses in Emily's life. In December 1886, Emily's younger sister, Matilde, died at The Larches. She was only twenty-seven and died of ulcerative endocarditis which she had suffered from for six months. Her youngest brother, Fritz Otto, aged fifteen, registered her death.[37] Three years later Oscar was to die aged twenty-three. Oscar had pursued a military career, studying at the Royal Military Academy at Woolwich and proceeding from there to join the Royal Engineers. He was posted to India as a member of the Bengal Sappers and Miners. His group were hewing out a home for the Gurkhas who were with them on the side of the Himalayas. However, he was bored by the remoteness of the place and came down to the plains below the Himalayas for a break, bringing his two greyhounds with him. While there he was accidentally fatally shot when his greyhound playfully jumped on him when he was leaning on his loaded gun against his chest.[38]

There were also problems in this period with another of her brothers, Emil Moritz Stoehr, which no doubt upset Emily. Her husband, Henry, alluded to it in a letter to Oscar in February 1889:

> You will possibly have heard from your mother that Emil has again lost patience with his present occupation and has now made up his mind, against everyone else's advice in the family to go to America and try cattle ranching. He has not at all behaved nicely, in fact is not on good terms with any of his family, even his sisters. It is a great pity and a gross trial for your mother. We all feel very sorry for her. Do not in your letters to your mother mention anything about this unless she has written to you about it, but I thought it scarcely right to write to you about other subjects without mentioning this matter.[39]

Whether or not he tried cattle ranching, he certainly travelled in the Americas and, as this letter indicates, was inclined to drift from occupation to occupation. Born in 1864, he had been educated at Rugby School,

Owens College and then Balliol College, Oxford, where he matriculated in 1887 at the age of twenty-three.[40] He died of bronchial consumption in Bournemouth in 1904, which he had suffered from for two years.[41]

Emily's younger sister, Susannah, married a barrister, Walter John Napier (1857–1945) in Singapore on 23 November 1889.[42] Napier was from an Alderley Edge family. He had been called to the bar in 1881 and worked for a firm of solicitors in Manchester from 1882 to 1888. In 1889, he joined a firm of advocates and solicitors in Singapore. He became a member of the Straits Settlements Legislative Council and was appointed its attorney general in 1907.[43] Walter retired in 1909 and was knighted. Susannah thus became Lady Napier and the couple moved back to Surrey in England. There Lady Napier was a leading light in the Women's Institute and the Surrey County Nursing Association. The *West Sussex Gazette* reported that Walter died at the age of eighty-seven on 22 February 1945.[44] The following year, Susie died at the age of seventy-seven after being struck by a motor vehicle.

At the time of the 1891 census, Emily's mother, Helene Stoehr, aged fifty-nine, was living at a house called Harkness on Barlow Moor Road in Didsbury. Her two youngest children and Emily's siblings, Clara Helene Stoehr, aged twenty-four, and Fritz (Friedrich) Otto Stoehr, aged nineteen, both students, were living with her.[45] They had trajectories that were interestingly different from Emily.

Having been educated at Alderley Edge High School and in Frankfurt, Clara sat the Cambridge Higher Local Examinations in the summer of 1890 and went on to Newnham College, Cambridge.[46] Clara was deeply involved on her return to Manchester from Cambridge in the establishment of the University of Manchester Settlement in Ancoats in 1895 and served as the first head of the Women's House, living at the Ancoats Art Museum while organising the work of the settlement. She stepped down from that role on health grounds in 1898, and later settled in Hindhead in Surrey. There she was an active suffragist: she regularly spoke at meetings, organising rallies and campaigns with other well-known suffragists. Clara followed her mother on the suffrage question; but, as we shall see, her elder sister, Emily, took a very different position. At the beginning of the First World War, Clara was the organising secretary for a hostel for Belgian Refugees in Kensington, London. She possibly influenced Emily who later took in Belgian refugees at Lawnhurst in the early part of the First World War. In 1924, Clara migrated to South Africa and died there twenty years later. She never married.[47]

Emily's youngest sibling, Friedrich (Fritz) Otto Stoehr, was educated at Clifton College in Bristol. Like Rugby, Clifton was one of the public schools favoured by Manchester Unitarians and businessmen of German-Jewish heritage: there are a number of Steinthals and Kyllmanns in the school register, sons of Henry Michael Steinthal and Edward Kyllmann.[48] From

Clifton, Fritz went to Trinity College at Oxford and took a Second in Greats (Classics) in 1894, before going on to study medicine, graduating MBChB in 1899. He served with the Royal Army Medical Corps (RAMC) until 1902 in the Anglo–Boer War. In 1903, he joined, as the medical officer, an expedition which was carrying out a geodetic survey of southern Africa. Between 1903 and June 1906, they were working in what is now Zambia and Mozambique. During this period, he collected plants and birds for the South African Museum and this became his major interest. He also carried out some work for the Belgian Government in the Congo and published a work in French on sleeping sickness, *La Maladie du Sommeil au Katanga*, which was caused by a protozoon carried by the tsetse fly. In 1913, he took an Oxford MD and became a psychiatrist. That year he also married Elsie Maude Stanley Hall, a famous and gifted Australian classical pianist, who had been a child prodigy. His life continued in Africa at his farm in Zambia, practising in Johannesburg and living in Cape Town where he died in 1946.[49] Fritz kept close to his family, writing letters to his mother, Helene, and his two sisters, Emily Simon and Marie-Louise Eckhard, until his death.[50]

Public life

While all the changes in the lives of her siblings and her mother were taking place in the wider world, Emily was firmly based in Didsbury, raising her growing family and supporting her husband in his business interests. Emily's life was not restricted to the private sphere, however. She was actively involved in social, philanthropic and political causes in the community. Her public activity began in 1889 with Emily helping to expand the education of girls in Manchester. She was an advocate of women's education and the development of the ways in which girls were taught. All of Emily's children attended Lady Barn House School in Withington, one of the first co-educational day schools in the country, having been created by the Unitarian Minister, William Henry Herford, and Louisa Cabutt in 1873. While the Simon boys left at eleven to attend public boarding schools, there was limited schooling provision for the Simon daughters at that age. Faced with this paucity, Emily and Henry became the driving forces behind a new local school for girls which taught along modern lines. At a meeting on 16 October 1889, in the drawing room of Miss Caroline Herford at Lady Barn House School where she was now the headmistress, Emily and Henry joined a group which included C. P. Scott and his wife, Rachel, Marie-Louise Eckhard, Mrs Lejeune, Mrs Renold and Professor Core to discuss the creation of a 'higher girls school for Withington and District'. Dr Adolphus Ward, Professor of History at Owens College, was in the chair, and a management committee was formed. A statement from the committee about the educational principles of the school said:

The importance of the natural sciences as a training in accuracy of observation and reasoning was noted and more prominence was to be given to manual training and outdoor games than is usual in girls schools.[51]

Withington Girls' School (WGS) subsequently opened in a house on Mauldeth Road in Withington in April 1890.[52] A year later, C. P. Scott became chairman of the council of the School on 1 April 1891 and his daughter, Madeline, was one of the first four pupils of the school. Henry Simon became the treasurer of council from the beginning and his role was taken over and continued by Emily after his death. All three of their daughters, Eleanor, Margaret and Dorothea, attended WGS.[53]

Emily continued to support the school for over twenty years until she died. In 1897, she gave two seats and a selection of trees for the school playing fields. In 1903, she enabled the school to move from 16 Mauldeth Road to Wellington Road. In 1905 she donated a sanatorium (cottage) in the school grounds and in 1914 she undertook an extension of the building with two new classrooms and the refitting of the laboratory. Finally, in 1920, she endowed the school, in perpetuity, with extensive fields and grounds which are still used for sporting activities behind the main buildings off Wellington Road in Withington. She founded the Emily Simon Scholarship for former pupils of WGS at the University of Manchester, and this is still awarded today.[54] After Emily's death, Shena Simon, who spent her career in education in Manchester, became a member of the management committee in 1925 and thereby maintained the family's connection with the school.[55] The school's four houses are named after the most important founders: Scott, Simon, Herford and Lejeune. Emily's portrait hangs in the WGS entrance hall along with that of the other key founders. She is long remembered there and is named publicly at every annual school founders' day.

Among Henry's papers at the John Rylands Library is a calendar which Emily made by hand for Henry in 1890 which started a great Simon tradition. There is a card for each day of the year with a motto in one of three languages – English, French and German – and the cards for each month are wrapped in a hand-sewn envelope and wrapped with a red silk ribbon and tied with a button (Plate 14). They are all stored in a hand-carved wooden box with the initials 'H. S.' on the lid. Emily chose all the mottos. The whole is delightful still, but very fragile. The tradition of making a calendar with a motto for clients of the Simon companies was established in 1892, and Emily continued to be involved in the choice of mottos for many years.[56] Occasional Letters were also created for clients. The Occasional Letter for 1897 has a picture of the whole family on the front, which was taken while they were on holiday at Pendyffryn Hall near Conwy in Wales in 1896.[57]

At the beginning of the 1890s, the family moved from Darwin House on Palatine Road to their new home, Lawnhurst, on Wilmslow Road in

3.5 The Simon family (1896) on the cover of *Henry Simon's Occasional Letter to Millers at Home & Abroad*, XXXVII, (January 1897). Source: JRL SEGA, 17.

Didsbury village opposite the famous Methodist Training College. Family life continued for Emily revolving round the children and supporting Henry, whose health was not good, as well as her WGS involvement.

In 1899, Henry's health was rapidly deteriorating as a result of heart problems. In his last weeks of life, Emily had little rest or sleep and was getting very tired and overwhelmed despite having a nurse living in. She was ordered by the doctor to rest, to go out every day and to take a sleeping draught at night. Her commitment and devotion to Henry continued to the end. In July 1899, Henry died at Lawnhurst, leaving Emily a widow with responsibility for eight children ranging in age from Ingo, who was now twenty-four, to Dorothea, who was just five years old.[58] One of Emily's first tasks in the early autumn of 1899 was to take Eric, aged twelve, to his new boarding school, Bedales, at Petersfield in Hampshire. Bedales, founded in 1893 and co-educational since 1898, represented a new departure for the family, since Eric's older brothers had gone to Rugby.[59] The progressive ethos of the new school no doubt appealed to those families involved with Lady Barn House School, and the Simons were probably attracted by the school's non-denominational approach to religion, and indeed a degree of secularism implied by the absence of a chapel. The school's founder and first headmaster, John Haden Badley, recalled that 'in these early days many of the children came from thinking manufacturing families of Unitarian connection in the North and Midlands'.[60] Eric met his future wife, Winifred Levy, who was Jewish, at Bedales.[61]

Emily was only forty-one at the time of Henry's death, and thereafter she started to take a more active role in the local community and also to make decisions and undertake roles that she had not done before. Indeed, she also began to be publicly associated with social, philanthropic and political causes. One of Emily's first decisions, with other members of the family, was to pay for an organ in the chapel at the crematorium in Henry's memory. A memorial plaque was installed on the wall in 1900, just below the organ gallery.[62]

In autumn 1899, she also returned to a project she had started on 1 April 1898 before Henry became gravely ill, and that was being a member of a Ladies Committee formed to provide support to Didsbury National School on Grange Lane. The Girls' School log book for the period 1898 to 1911, maintained by the headmistress, records regular visits throughout this period by Mrs Simon, often accompanied by Mrs Mark Ashton, to see the girls' needlework and most importantly to take books for them to read.[63] These are typical entries at the beginning of 1899:

> Jan 13th Began school on Monday after Christmas holidays. Today, Friday, Mrs Simon began a library in this room providing both cupboards and books. Mrs Simon and a friend gave out the books to the girls and told them to bring them next Friday to have them changed.

> Feb 3rd Mrs Simon visited today and gave out the library books. Standard III and IV have used these books for their lesson in silent reading, excepting those who are not fluent readers – they were taken specially by their teacher.

The first entry after Henry died read:

> Oct 13th 1899 Mrs Simon and Mrs Mark Ashton visited this week. They spoke about prizes for needlework and attendance, also said they were bringing some more books for the library – seemed anxious for good results from reading.

Mrs Mark Ashton was the young widow of textile merchant William Mark Ashton, who had died in 1895, and lived at Heyscroft, on Palatine Road between Didsbury and Northenden. She was of German origin like Emily, having been before her marriage Letitia Mary Kessler. Margaret Ashton, the famous Manchester local politician, was her sister-in-law.[64] Emily supported the school in many other ways, including giving them her children's rocking horse for the nursery. In memory of Emily one of the school (now Didsbury C of E Primary School) houses is Simon, alongside Gaddum, Pankhurst and Fletcher Moss.

Emily was admired in Didsbury for her other philanthropic activities and the support that she provided especially to the poor.[65] She was described as a pioneer in the field of social welfare in Didsbury. She founded and built Didsbury Lads Club on Elm Grove and even taught there once a week in 1911. Didsbury's first library was created in that

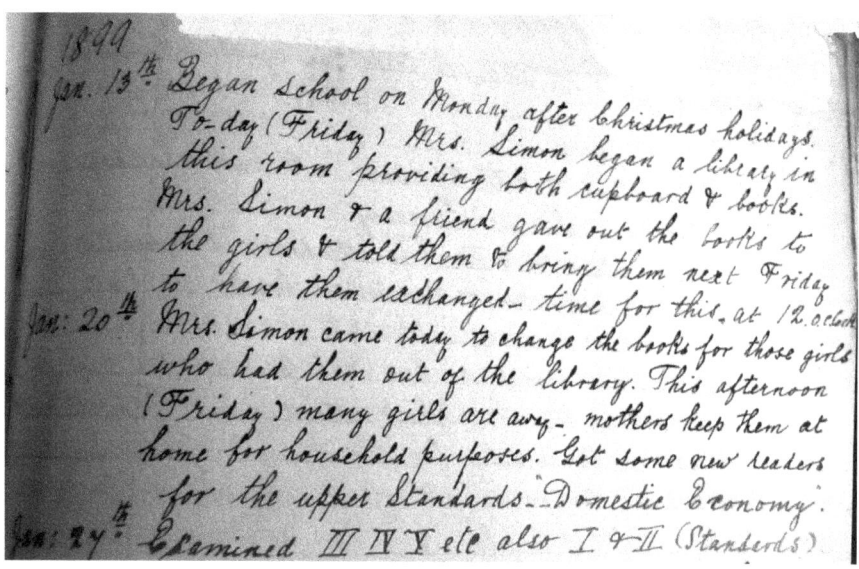

3.6 Two entries from January 1899 about Emily in the Didsbury National School Log Book. Photo by John Ayshford. Access to the log book was kindly provided by Paul and Sue Good.

building and was known in 1908 as Didsbury Institute and Library. She also bought three existing houses in Elm Grove specifically to help women. One (no. 21) was used as a day nursery/creche for babies and young children whose mothers went out to work. A second was used to provide dinners for schoolchildren for the same reason.[66] As a service for women at the other end of life she bought a third house called 'Kirklees' at the end of Elm Grove (no. 16) from William Grunewald, where eight older women, who were poor and friendless, could live with a caretaker. Some had previously been involved with the Simon family. The 1939 census named it as a Home for Old Ladies with the residents being Fanny Brindle, Margaret Treweek, Eliza Holbrow, Nellie Scott, Edith Irving, who was the resident housekeeper, and Regine Sara Stiglitz.[67] The latter resident was a refugee, an enemy alien exemption from internment. This home continued for many years into the 1960s, and a couple of the female members of the family maintained the Simon connections with it. The Help the Aged Housing Association eventually agreed to accommodate the remaining residents and in return accepted the freehold of the house and were able to realise its value. The house was incorporated into Heald's Dairies before it was demolished and replaced by new housing. The Boy Scouts were lent the stables at the back of this house.[68]

One of Emily's other public roles was in the anti-suffrage movement, and it created some friction within the family and its social networks. In August 1909, she held a garden party at Lawnhurst, addressed by the leading anti-suffragist Edith Somervell (wife of the composer Arthur Somervell).[69] In October the same year, the Free Trade Hall hosted a high-profile debate on women's suffrage, pitting the suffragists Margaret Ashton and Helena Swanwick against Mary Ward (the novelist Mrs Humphry Ward) and Edith Somervell again. The two anti-suffragists were invited to stay at Lawnhurst. Ernest, who was pro-suffrage, and whose diary is our source for this, was not impressed: 'they did not speak well, Miss Ashton and Mrs Swanwick were better, & won easily. But ... none of them would convince an inquirer.'[70]

Emily was at that time honorary secretary of the Didsbury sub-branch of the Women's Anti-Suffrage League, and soon took on the same role for the Manchester branch and continued in that position when the league merged with the Men's League in 1910 to form the National League for Opposing Woman Suffrage.[71] Emily wrote letters to the *Manchester Guardian* in August 1911 on the subject. In one of these letters, co-authored with Cordelia Moir on behalf of the National League, Emily took issue with Helena Swanwick, arguing that once the sex disqualification was abolished, adult suffrage would imply that women voters would outnumber men, and that would amount to 'a political and social revolution': as such, 'it ought to be deliberately discussed and decided upon by the electorate of the country before being adopted'.[72]

The issue of women's suffrage could reveal some disagreements within families. Something of the tensions produced within the Simons' social circle by the suffrage controversy emerges from the pages of *The Common Cause*, the suffrage journal largely financed by Margaret Ashton and edited by Helena Swanwick. It reported in October 1909 that Mrs Marie-Louise Eckhard, Emily's sister, had held a meeting to set up a Didsbury branch of the National Union of Women's Suffrage Societies. The report continued:

> Didsbury has been a happy hunting-ground for the anti-suffragists. Out of 10,000 inhabitants 1,000, they say, signed their petition; but an idea of their methods may be gathered from the fact that one of the ladies who joined our committee had herself signed the petition, being told by its bearer, to whom it was explained that she was in favour of Women's Suffrage, that it was 'only against the militants'. Similar stories met us on every hand in the village, and we shall have the strong support of many of the 'petitioners', all the stronger because they feel that they have been cheated.[73]

This drew a riposte from Emily's daughter, Margaret Simon, protesting against 'the tone adopted towards anti-suffragists in the report from Didsbury':

> It can scarcely be unknown to its author that I personally organised nearly all the canvassing for signatures to the Anti-Suffrage petition for Mrs Henry Simon, who is hon. Secretary of the Didsbury sub-branch of the W.N.A.L.. It goes without saying that I gave my canvassers very careful explanations that the petition is against votes for women, and not exclusively against the militant section, and if any statement made by one of them misled the lady referred to in your correspondent's report I very much regret it. But it does not impress one much with the reliability of the lady who takes sufficient interest in the question of votes for women to join the newly formed Didsbury branch of the N.E.S.W.S. [sic] that she was unable, or did not trouble, to read the object of the petition clearly printed at the top of each petition form before appending her signature.[74]

Whatever tensions may have emerged it is clear that these intra-familial divisions were not fatal to family unity and Emily continued to have a close connection with her sister.[75]

In addition to her philanthropy and anti-suffrage campaigning, in the 1910s Emily had started to take holidays in Germany and Switzerland to relax and visit her and Henry's relatives, taking her daughters and nieces with her. In 1910, she visited the Rappards, whose friendship with the Simons stemmed all the way from 1850 when Heinrich Simon fled with Conrad von Rappard to Switzerland.[76] Her mother, Helene Stoehr, who had lived with her at Lawnhurst on occasions, had died in 1908 of cancer and bronchitis at her house, Elm Bank in Alderley Edge, with Emily most likely at her side.[77] Helene was buried with her husband, Emil, and two children, Matilde and Emil Moritz, at St Bartholomew's Church in Wilmslow.[78]

3.7 Emily with Helene (to her right), Ernest and Henry (above her), Margaret, Eric and Victor (sat below) and two unidentified women (*c.* mid-1890s). Source: JRL HSC.

Later years

Emily embarked on another project after her mother's death. From 1909, she compiled a family chronicle which was circulated quarterly to relatives everywhere. It documented weddings, births and social activities.[79] The births of Lindisfarne Hamilton and Patrick Hamilton in 1907 and 1908 to her daughter Eleanor and her husband George Hamilton, of Oliver and John Simon to her son Eric in 1912 and 1914, and of Diana Meek in 1913 to her daughter Dorothea, and also of Harry's four children, Anthony, Monica, Michael and Christopher Simon, would all have been recorded.[80] The effects, however, of the forthcoming war and the continuing tragedies in Emily's life could not have been imagined. In July 1914, most family members, including Emily, attended a very happy occasion, the society wedding of her nephew, Charles Felix Stoehr, Charles William Stoehr's older son, at Holy Trinity Church in Stratford-upon-Avon, to Kathleen Hudson. The couple left for Aden where he was serving with the Royal

Engineers. Kathleen Stoehr, Emily's niece-in-law, returned to England in autumn 1915, but on her way back to join her husband in Aden her ship, *SS Persia*, was blown up in the Mediterranean off the coast of Crete by a German U-Boat, *U-38*. She died, aged twenty-one, with most of the other passengers on 30 December 1915.[81] This was also the year that Emily's youngest son, Captain Eric Conrad Simon, serving with the 2/5th Lancashire Fusiliers, was killed in August 1915. He was buried at Millencourt Communal Cemetery.[82] The word MAITRI and the Star of David are on his gravestone. In November 1915, his older brother, Victor, was awarded the Military Cross.[83] Despite the service of Emily's sons in the army, in the midst of widespread Germanophobia, the Simon family changed the pronunciation of their name from the Germanic 'Seaman' to the anglicised 'Simon' during the war.[84]

More family tragedy was to follow for Emily in 1917 with the deaths of her sons, Victor and Harry, and of her nephew, Oscar Humphrey Stoehr, in the space of three months. Major Victor Simon MC of the Royal Engineers died in France on 5 June 1917 and is buried at Villers-Faucon Communal Cemetery.[85] Oscar died at Scapa Flow, when his ship, *HMS Vanguard*, on which he was a torpedo officer, blew up on 9 July 1917, just a few days before the ship's crew, including Oscar, had taken part in a theatrical party.[86] Major Henry (Harry) Simon of the Royal Field Artillery died on 8 September 1917 following shrapnel wounds from a shell.[87] He left a widow, Edith (née Horsfall) and four small children. There were a few moments of light for Emily that year, however, as two more grandchildren were born: Antonia, the third child of Ernest and Shena, and Tufton Beamish, Margaret's second child.[88] All three Simon

3.8 Eric, Harry and Victor in uniform during the First World War. Source: private family papers.

sons are listed on Didsbury War Memorial. Only one other family in Didsbury lost three sons and that was the Scott family whose names are on the same war memorial.

Emily carried on resolutely through all of this sadness, initially opening up Lawnhurst in 1914 as a place of refuge for Belgian refugees, then running it as a home where wounded soldiers could recuperate. In May 1916, she donated Lawnhurst as an official Red Cross Hospital for the remainder of the war. An additional building was erected to house more patients.[89] Her Red Cross VAD card records her involvement. It says she was engaged from 7 December 1914 and her duties were as housekeeper. She was recorded as giving 'three weeks' half-day duty out of each month since Dec. 1914' and that she had 'also lent her house for a Hospital since May 1916'. She was also vice-president and honorary commandant of the Red Cross Society, Didsbury Branch.[90] Emily lived in two small rooms in her house, and while she ran the hospital, she was not in charge of its medical and nursing services.[91] Volunteer nurses and other staff were recruited locally and one such volunteer was Luly Hassan, a former pupil of WGS, who lived at 198 Wilmslow Road, Withington.[92] WGS gave money to support a bed at Lawnhurst each month throughout the war.[93] It is recorded that the matron at Lawnhurst was Miss Constance Mackay Selbie (1878–1963) of 139 Withington Road, Whalley Range. Mrs Hilda King of Beechwood, Didsbury, was the quartermaster from 1916 and Mrs Beatrice Curzon of Elm Road was the assistant quartermaster.[94]

3.9 Red Cross nurses at Lawnhurst. Luly Hassan is seated, second from right. Photo courtesy of Rosemary Eshel.

On 2 February 1918, the *Manchester Guardian* published the names of ladies whose work had been brought to the attention of the Secretary of State for War for their valuable services rendered in connection with the establishment, maintenance and administration of hospitals in Lancashire and Cheshire. Emily Simon's name was there alongside those of the Marchioness of Cholmondley, Lady Donner (Fallowfield) and many other distinguished women.[95]

National recognition came for Emily's efforts when it was announced in the *Supplement to the London Gazette* on 30 March 1920 that she had been awarded an OBE. The citation read:

> Emily Anne, Mrs. Simon
>
> Vice-President, Didsbury Division, British Red Cross Society; Commandant and Donor, Lawnhurst Hospital, Didsbury.[96]

Strangely, the only other reference to this award was in a now very rare journal, *Milling*, in May 1920. It refers to her being Henry Simon's wife and a cutting from the journal is in a press cuttings book formerly belonging to Ernest and Shena Simon in Manchester Central Library.[97]

Inevitably the stresses and strains of the war and familial tragedies she had suffered throughout her life since she was eighteen, including the death of her father and her beloved husband, and particularly those in the last six years, took their toll. She went with her daughter-in-law, Edith Simon, Harry's widow, and her grandson, Anthony Simon, to visit Harry's grave in autumn 1920, but while in Belgium, she had an accident and

3.10 Lawnhurst as a hospital during the First World War. Source: Martin Dodge.

subsequent poor medical treatment led to a serious illness.[98] Emily died in Didsbury on 7 November 1920 shortly after reaching home. She was sixty-two. Ernest registered her death the next day. The doctor who signed the death certificate was Dr Thomas Ashton Goodfellow MD who gave two causes of death – chronic myocardial degeneration over seven years and cardiac failure. Dr Goodfellow would have known her well as he was the medical officer for Lawnhurst Military Hospital during the war and also the chairman of the Manchester War Committee.[99] Her cremation took place at Manchester Crematorium on 10 November and the service was conducted by the Rev. F. C. L. Hamilton, rector of Northenden. The brief report of the funeral in the *Manchester Guardian* said that as well as family members being present, there were representatives from various local organisations she had supported: the Didsbury Helpers, the Didsbury Lads Club, the Didsbury Liberal Association, the Didsbury Day Nursery and the Withington and Didsbury Branch of the British Red Cross Association.[100] An unnamed person who had served with Emily for five years as a fellow commandant at Lawnhurst wrote in the article in the *Manchester Guardian* how:

> Mrs Simon did noble work ... The men who were so skilfully nursed back to health have full reason to look back on Lawnhurst and bless her memory. We who knew her intimately, loved her ... and we feel that Manchester should be proud of this unostentatious but truly great heart, now passed to a fuller life.[101]

Another former colleague called her 'a Mother of Mothers, whose compass always pointed to "Service"'. We know nothing of the author of this description, except that it was someone writing in a Didsbury Parish Church Review in 1958, having served as a kitchen orderly with Emily, forty years before, over the new year period. Emily had returned from attending the watch night service at (St James) Church and talked to all the patients and staff and was praised for her gracious and kindly personality and care for all the staff.[102]

A memorial service was held at Manchester Crematorium for Emily in December 1920 at which her eldest granddaughter, Lindisfarne Hamilton, aged thirteen, read out a poem she had written entitled:

> 'Grannie'
> The mirth of sunshine and the rain-swept sky
> The smell of earth newly baptised with rain
> The pleasant melancholy of the grey
> Wet mists that robe the wide, wise-hearted moor
> The song of birds in the grey April dawn
> The lore and laughter of her human kind
> She knows no more; for she has passed beyond
> Our human joys and with her lost beloved
> Is happy in a land where the dawn sings
> And music blossoms ... Tears will cease

And we shall joy again in joys of earth
But still enshrined within a thousand hearts,
Her spirit lives, a sacred memory.[103]

Emily's will and its codicil appointed Ernest and Eleanor as her executors and trustees. There were one or two interesting features of this will, dated 1 March 1918. She bequeathed the sum of £500 to her friend Henrietta Hayne Smith, a legacy of £500 to her sister-in-law Verena Stoehr, and to her godson Lennox Napier £100. Each grandchild was to get £100 to enable them to travel. Not surprisingly she left donations to Didsbury Institute and Lads Club but also to another cause she supported – the Benevolent Fund of the Manchester Governesses' Home. The houses and land she had bought in Elm Grove in 1911 were left to Ernest and Eleanor. In the codicil dated 30 July 1920, she voluntarily granted land in Withington off Wellington Road to the Trustees of Withington Girls' School which was to be used as a recreation ground and playing fields for the school.[104]

3.11 Emily in Red Cross uniform during the First World War. Source: *The Simon Engineering Group* (1953).

Miss Grant, the headmistress, writing in the WGS newsletter for October 1920–November 1921 records the 'deep sorrow of the school over Mrs Henry Simon's death and the grateful realisation of all she has done for the school'. She also noted the benefit of Mrs Simon's gift of the playing fields to the school, the donation by Mrs Hamilton and Mrs Ernest Simon of all Emily's books to the school library plus busts and a globe and the fact that pupil Margaret McDougall was awarded the Emily Simon Scholarship to study at the University of Manchester.[105]

In an additional WGS Newsletter written shortly after Emily's death on 7 November 1920, Miss Grant wrote 'she carried on a multitude of quiet deeds of help and courtesy ... neither personal sorrow or fatigue nor the pressure of much business, were allowed to interfere. Her outlook and her faith are fittingly expressed in the words of her calendar for 7 November – "only be strong and very courageous" (Joshua I.7)'.[106] The impact of Emily's philanthropy and support for the local community was long felt after her death and is still recognised today.

Notes

1. 'Mrs Henry Simon', *Manchester Guardian* (9 November 1920), p. 8.
2. Birth Certificate of Emily Anne Stoehr 27 April 1858 in Chorlton upon Medlock, GRO 1858 Vol. 8C, entry 133, p. 467.
3. 1861 England Census, Township of Chorlton upon Medlock, Household Schedule no. 234, p. 58.
4. 'Chancellor's Hotel' www.manchester.ac.uk/discover/history-heritage/history/buildings/chancellors/ (accessed 1 September 2023); Thomas Seccombe, revised by R. Angus Buchanan, Whitworth, Sir Joseph, Baronet, in *Oxford Dictionary of National Biography*; W. C. Williamson, *Sketches of Fallowfield and the Surrounding Manors, Past and Present* (Manchester: John Heywood, 1888), p. 108.
5. https://rusholmearchive.org/fallowfield-brow-and-oak-drive (accessed 10 September 2023).
6. Trevor Wilson, 'Scott, Charles Prestwich', in *Oxford Dictionary of National Biography*.
7. Birth certificate of Charles William Stoehr 2 October 1856 in Chorlton upon Medlock, GRO 1856 Vol. 8C, entry 371, p. 464. Information from the Public Family Tree of the Donaldson Family on Ancestry.com which is maintained by Dr Hugo Donaldson. Material for this tree was researched in 2000 by John Stirland, Donaldson's uncle, who is descended from Marie-Louise Eckhard (née Stoehr), Emily's sister.
8. Information from the Public Family Tree of the Donaldson Family.
9. Port of London Certificate of Arrival, No. 1009 (1849).
10. Brian Simon, *In Search of a Grandfather* (Leicester: the Pendene Press: 1997), p. 34.
11. *London Gazette* (25 June 1858), p. 3066.
12. 'To the Directors of the Manchester Chamber of Commerce', *Manchester Courier and Lancashire Advertiser* (19 May 1860), p. 1.
13. 'Bankrupts, &c', *Daily Post* (Liverpool) (3 January 1867), p. 8; *Slater's Royal National Commercial Directory of Manchester and Salford with their Vicinities 1876* (Manchester: Slater, 1876), p. 492.
14. D. T. Jenkins, 'Behrens, Sir Jacob', in *Oxford Dictionary of National Biography*. Also see: Lucia Morawska, 'Outlandish Names on the Provincial Doors: German Jews

in Victorian Bradford and their Expression of Identity', *Identity Papers: A Journal of British and Irish Studies*, 2:1 (2017), 35–43. For Behrens Textiles, see: www.behrens.co.uk (accessed 31 August 2023).
15 For a study of Bradford's German mercantile community, see: Susan Duxbury-Neumann, *Little Germany: A History of Bradford's Germans* (Stroud: Amberley Publishing, 2015).
16 Port of London Certificate of Arrival (1837) No. 83.
17 *Perry's Bankruptcy Gazette* (1 January 1842), p. 8.
18 1871 England Census, Municipal Borough of Bradford, Township of Manningham, Household Schedule no. 108, p. 28; *Bradford Observer*, 5 March 1868. 'Worms-Steinthal Marriage', *Greenock Advertiser* (24 September 1858), p. 3.
19 Simon, *In Search of a Grandfather*, p. 44.
20 *The York Herald* (12 January 1856), p. 5.
21 Select Births and Baptisms, Manchester Cathedral (19 September 1857). Accessed via www.ancestry.co.uk (accessed 31 August 2023).
22 MCL M59, Platt Unitarian Chapel Baptism Register 1861–1912, p. 4. Emily's younger siblings, Marie-Louise Christine and Emil Moritz, were also baptised at Platt Chapel on 27 February 1864.
23 'The Rev. S.A. Steinthal. Congratulations on his Eightieth Birthday', *Manchester Guardian* (16 November 1906), p. 12.
24 S. Alfred Steinthal, 'On Slavery', *The Times* (30 March 1853), p. 7; 'Manchester Anti-Slavery Conference', *The Anti-Slavery Reporter*, 2:9 (September 1854), pp. 201–16.
25 See: Matthew Hyde, *The Villas of Alderley Edge* (Altrincham: The Silk Press, 1999).
26 For the connection between Unitarianism and feminism in the nineteenth century, see: Kathryn Gleadle, *The Early Feminists: Radical Unitarians and the Emergence of the Women's Rights Movement, 1831–1851* (Basingstoke: Macmillan, 1995).
27 'Parliamentary Intelligence', *The Times* (8 June 1866), p. 5; John Stuart Mill, 'The Admission of Women to the Electoral Franchise' (20 May 1867), in *The Collected Works of John Stuart Mill*, John M. Robson (ed.), 33 vols (London: Routledge and Kegan Paul, 1963–1991), XXVIII, pp. 161–2. 1866 Suffrage Petition Names, p. 30 www.parliament.uk/globalassets/documents/parliamentary-archives/1866suffragepetitionnameswebfeb18.pdf (accessed 2 September 2023).
28 GRO Altrincham, Death Certificate of Emil Moritz Stoehr, March 1874, Vol. 8A (1874), p. 125.
29 Simon, *In Search of a Grandfather*, p. 34.
30 Henry's desired qualities in a wife and his lack of belief that he would find such a woman in Manchester are recorded in Ernest Simon's diary. Emily read extracts of Henry's diary to him in 1912. see: ESD, 25 June 1912.
31 JRL HSC, Box 1, Henry Simon to Emily Stoehr, 31 July 1878. Also see Chapter 2 in this volume by Janet Wolff.
32 *The Advertiser* (Wilmslow and Alderley Edge), 7 December 1878.
33 Simon, *In Search of a Grandfather*, pp. 42–3, 75–6.
34 'Births, Deaths and Marriages', *Manchester Weekly Times*, 21 April 1883, p. 8.
35 The firm of J. C. Eckhard is recorded in *White's Directory of Bradford* in 1861; Certificate of Naturalisation to an alien. Gustav Jacob Conrad Eckhard 14 March (1883) no. 3882.
36 Information provided to author by local historian of Alderley Edge, Graham Dillaway, in 2023; Register of Burials in the Parish of Llanhyddland in the Count of Anglesey, p. 79.
37 GRO Altrincham, Death Certificate of Matilda [sic] Stoehr, 16 December 1886, Vol. 08A (1886), p. 127.
38 'Death of Oscar Stoehr on 29th May', *The Alderley and Wilmslow Advertiser* (7 June 1889), p. 1.

39 JRL SEGA, 56, 'Father's Letters 1887/1902', Henry Simon to Oscar Stoehr, 19 February 1889.
40 A. T. Michell, *Rugby School Register. Vol. 3, from May 1874 to May 1904* (Rugby: A. J. Lawrence, 1904), p. 66.
41 GRO Christchurch, Death Certificate of Emil Moritz Stoehr 26 January 1904, Vol. 2B (1904), p. 484.
42 'Births Marriages and Deaths', *St James' Gazette* (28 November 1889), p. 12.
43 *London and China Express* (19 April 1907), p. 5.
44 *The West Sussex and Farnham Advertiser* (22 February 1945), p. 2.
45 1891 England Census for Civil Parish of Didsbury.
46 ACAD (A Cambridge Alumni Database). https://venn.lib.cam.ac.uk/cgi-bin/search-2018.pl?sur=stoehr&suro=w&fir=&firo=c&cit=&cito=c&c=all&z=all&tex=&sye=&eye=&col=all&maxcount=50 (accessed 10 September 2023).
47 www.exploringsurreyspast.org.uk/themes/subjects/womens-suffrage/suffrage-biographies/clara-helene-stoehr-1867-1944/ (accessed 5 September 2023).
48 E. M. Oakeley, *Clifton College Annals and Register 1860–1897* (Bristol: Arrowsmith, 1897), pp. 169, 310.
49 'Stohr, Dr Frederick Otto', in *S2A3 Biographical Database of Southern African Science*. www.s2a3.org.za/bio/Biograph_final.php?serial=2735 (accessed 1 September 2023).
50 University of Cape Town Libraries Special Collections (Manuscripts and Archives) Elsie Hall Papers ZA UCT BC 10 F3–F5.
51 Withington Girls' School Archive, 'Foundation Document' (1899), www.wgs.org/archive/foundation/foundation-document/ (accessed 11 September 2023).
52 'Withington Girls' School', *Manchester Guardian* (22 April 1890), p. 12.
53 Simon, *In Search of a Grandfather*, pp. 61–3.
54 Withington Girls' School Archive, Withington Girls' School Annual Newsletter October 1920–November 1921; Withington Girls' School Archive, Supplementary Withington Girls' School Newsletter November 1920; 'The Founders of Withington Girls' School', www.wgs.org/about-wgs/history-and-founders/founders-withington-girls-school/ (accessed 11 September 2023).
55 Withington Girls' School Archive, Withington Girls' School Annual Newsletter November 1924–November 1925.
56 JRL HSC Temp/1. See also: HSC Temp/1 at https://luna.manchester.ac.uk/luna/servlet/ (accessed 1 September 2023).
57 JRL SEGA, 17, *Henry Simon's Occasional Letter to Miller's at Home & Abroad*, XXXVII (January 1897).
58 Brian Simon, *Henry Simon's Children* (Leicester: The Pendene Press, 1999), pp. 82–3.
59 Simon, *In Search of a Grandfather*, p. 72.
60 J. H. Badley, *Bedales: A Pioneer School* (London: Methuen, 1923), p. 71.
61 Simon, *Henry Simon's Children*, pp. 90–1.
62 'Joint Stock Company: The Manchester Crematorium', *Manchester Guardian* (14 December 1899), p. 5.
63 The logbook is held by Sue Good who kindly allowed us to study and photograph it.
64 E. France and T. F. Woodall, *A New History of Didsbury* (Didsbury: E.J. Morten Publishers, 1976), pp. 193–7.
65 Ernest recalled in the year Emily died how 'Mother was a wonderful example of unselfishness – her whole pleasure lay in helping others. Everybody in the village who was in need of help automatically went to her – and never in vain.' Private family papers, Ernest Simon, 'Mother', January 1920. Also see: 'Mrs. Henry Simon'.
66 France and Woodall, *A New History of Didsbury*, p. 186.
67 1939 Census County Borough of Manchester Registration District 464-1 Schedule No. 92. Elm Grove Kirklees Home for Old Ladies.

68 Information about Kirklees courtesy of Andrew Simon. Private Correspondence (1 August 2023).
69 'Our branch news-letter', *Anti-Suffrage Review* (August 1909), p. 5.
70 ESD, 26 October 1909.
71 *Anti-Suffrage Review* (September 1909), p. 6; 'Women's Anti-Suffrage League. The Manchester Branch', *Manchester Guardian* (26 May 1909), p. 5.
72 'The Women's Suffrage Issue', *Manchester Guardian* (1 August 1911), p. 10. In calling for a referendum, Emily and Moir echoed the jurist and prominent anti-suffragist A. V. Dicey, who in a series of works made the case for a confirmatory referendum as the condition of the approval of fundamental constitutional changes such as women's suffrage. See: Mads Qvortrup, 'A.V. Dicey: The Referendum as the People's Veto', *History of Political Thought*, 20 (1999), 531–46.
73 'Reports of Societies within the National Union', *Common Cause* (14 October 1909), p. 10.
74 Margaret Simon, 'The Anti-Suffrage Petition', *Common Cause* (28 October 1909), p. 11. Margaret had been appointed 'petition secretary' for the Manchester branch earlier in the year: 'A Report from Manchester', *The Anti-Suffrage Review* (May 1909), p. 8.
75 For instance, in 1912 Emily spent Christmas at the Eckhards'. See: Simon, *Henry Simon's Children*, p. 88.
76 Simon, *Henry Simon's Children*, p. 89.
77 GRO Macclesfield, Death Certificate of Helen Margaretta [sic] Stoehr 19 June 1908. Vol. 08 (1908), p. 98.
78 St Bartholomew's Church, Wilmslow. Records of gravestones and their inscriptions in the churchyard. Grave no. B.b.28.
79 Simon, *Henry Simon's Children*, pp. 84–5.
80 Simon, *Henry Simon's Children*, pp. 112–13.
81 *Stratford-upon-Avon Herald*, 7 January 1916, p. 8.
82 www.cwgc.org/find-records/find-war-dead/casualty-details/44030/eric-conrad-simon/ (accessed 13 September 2023).
83 *Supplement to The Edinburgh Gazette* (6 November 1915), p. 1680.
84 Mary Stocks, *Ernest Simon of Manchester* (Manchester: Manchester University Press, 1963), p. 49. For Germanophobia in Britain during the First World War, see: Panikos Panayi, 'The Destruction of the German Communities in Britain during the First World War', in Panikos Panayi (ed.), *Germans in Britain Since 1500* (London: Bloomsbury, 1997), pp. 113–30.
85 www.cwgc.org/find-records/find-war-dead/casualty-details/235872/victor-herman-simon/ (accessed 4 September 2023).
86 'A Melancholy Coincidence – HMS Vanguard's Theatrical Party', *Sunday Pictorial* (15 July 1917) p. 1.
87 ESD, 8 September 1917.
88 Simon, *Henry Simon's Children*, p. 107.
89 Simon, *Henry Simon's Children*, p. 102.
90 https://vad.redcross.org.uk/record?rowKey=189676 (accessed 14 September 2023).
91 Anthony Simon, *The Simon Engineering Group* (Cheadle Heath: privately printed, 1953), p. 2.
92 https://vad.redcross.org.uk/record?rowKey=99585 (accessed 14 September 2023). We would like to thank Rosemary Eshel for providing the editors with information on Luly Hassan.
93 Withington Girls' School Archive, www.wgs.org/archive/withington-ww1/ (accessed 14 September 2023).
94 'Honours for Nurses', *Guardian* (Runcorn) (15 August 1919), p. 5.
95 'Ladies' Hospital Services', *Manchester Guardian*, p. 7.
96 *Supplement to the London Gazette* (30 March 1920), p. 3804.

97 SSP M14/6/3, 'Civilian War Honours', *Milling* (20 May 1920).
98 Simon, 'Mother'; Simon, *Henry Simon's Children*, pp. 108–9.
99 Death Certificate of Emily Anne Simon 7 November 1920. Deaths in the Sub District of Didsbury in the County of Manchester (1920). Registration District Chorlton. Entry no. 117.
100 'Mrs. Henry Simon'; 'Emily Simon', *Manchester Guardian* (11 November 1920), p. 16.
101 'Emily Simon', *Manchester Guardian*, 11 November 1920, p. 16.
102 Private family papers, *Didsbury Parish Church Review* (June 1958).
103 'New Poets in the Nursery', *Manchester Guardian* (2 August 1923), p. 14; 'Miss Lindisfarne Hamilton's Poem', *Manchester Guardian* (8 August 2023), p. 9.
104 For Emily's will, see: https://probatesearch.service.gov.uk/ (accessed 20 September 2023).
105 Withington Girls' School Annual Newsletter October 1920–November 1921.
106 Supplementary Withington Girls' School Newsletter November 1920.

4.1 Caricature of Ernest Simon from News Review (19 June 1947). Source: private family papers.

4

The shy campaigner: the life of Ernest Simon, politician and social reformer (1879–1960)

John Ayshford and Brendon Jones

Terrified of being judged, nervously quiet and deeply introspective, as a young person Ernest Simon did not seemingly have the hallmarks to become historically important. Yet, over the course of five decades between 1910–60, he would become a notable local and national politician and reformer who left an indelible mark on Manchester and British society. Ernest shaped a whole range of issues as diverse as air pollution, university education and nuclear disarmament, and subsequently various aspects of his work have been studied by academics.[1] Despite scholarly interest, Ernest, however, remains a relatively unknown figure. *Ernest Simon of Manchester*, written in 1963 by his friend and fellow reformer Mary Stocks, remains the only major biographical account.[2] While Stocks' work remains an illuminating and essential source for those interested in Ernest's life, this chapter seeks to build upon her book to provide a revised account of Ernest. Through examination of the plethora of books and articles he authored, alongside his and his wife's extensive papers, this chapter critically examines Ernest's life and considers how his work speaks to today's society.

Childhood and education

Ernest Emil Darwin Simon was born on 9 October 1879. The son of Henry Simon and Emily Simon and the eldest of their seven children, Ernest grew up in a large house in Didsbury in Manchester named after Henry's hero Charles Darwin. The wealthy family lived there until 1892, when they moved into a grand mansion, Lawnhurst. At an early age Ernest and his siblings attended Lady Barn House School. Founded by W. H. Herford, the school taught children along progressive *Fröbelian* lines and appealed to Manchester's numerous liberal-minded German immigrants and civic

4.2 Ernest as a young child. Source: SSP M14/4/24.

elites, such as the owners of the *Manchester Guardian*, the Scott family, who sent their children there including Ernest's lifelong friend John Scott.[3]

After Lady Barn House, Ernest with John Scott attended Rugby School. According to Ernest's reflections recorded in his diary over a decade after he left Rugby, his time there was marked by bullying and loneliness stemming from his chronic shyness:

> at school I was hopelessly ragged, because I never dared to answer. I used to put my waistcoat on before my tie; because ties being I suppose new to me, I was afraid of tying mine in the wrong way. When shaving began, I went up at secret times so as not to be seen … [I] never learnt to talk & tell a story. I never had the courage to laugh till I was 28!![4]

Ernest placed the cause of his shyness on a paucity of mutual understanding with his parents, which led to his inability to learn how to properly converse with them and therefore others. He was unable to speak to his mother about 'difficult matters', and his father's 'reticence' and 'very reserved nature', in conjunction to the age gap between them, hampered their 'companionship'.[5] This lack of understanding, however, was not for

4.3 Ernest as a teenager. Source: SSP M14/4/24.

want of affection between Ernest and his parents. In a 1920 letter to his own children, Ernest described his relationship with Emily as 'about the ideal of relations of mother and son'.[6] Moreover, letters sent from Henry to Ernest and his brother Harry at Rugby show his father as jovial and caring.[7]

At Rugby Ernest specialised in science, something only enabled by the efforts of Henry and Emily in overcoming the opposition of Ernest's housemaster Robert Whitelaw. Achieving highly, he won a place at Pembroke College Cambridge to study engineering.[8] Ernest's years at Cambridge between 1898–1901 were ones he later regretted, for instead of applying himself in studies he wasted his time indulging in hedonistic pursuits. Despite achieving a first-class degree Ernest did little study, having already 'done nearly all the work beforehand at Rugby', and instead sought to find camaraderie with those who enjoyed a high life of opulent pleasure, having 'a sneaking admiration for the bad bold man of wine[,] women & gambling'. Passing his time visiting Newmarket races and playing 'bridge and poker', Ernest failed to make friends, continuing to find interaction with others difficult owing to his shyness.[9]

A guiding faith

After Cambridge, Ernest joined the family businesses. His father having died in 1899, Ernest rose through the ranks of his late father's companies to assume control of them in 1910.[10] Working for the firms afforded Ernest self-belief. He gained a sense of self-exceptionalism arising from a perception of 'intellectual superiority' which cast off much of his nervousness.[11] Ernest realised,

> more & more how often I was right, & how much better an instrument my brain was than the vast majority of brains with which it came into contact. And at about the same time I began to use my brains effectively in life in general, & began to get on with people, & to have real views of my own.[12]

From the late 1900s, Ernest was to undergo an even more significant transformation. Sheepish about asserting his own opinions, Ernest's shyness rendered him open to different ideas, and having resumed his childhood love of books, he came across the writings of leading intellectuals.[13] Ernest was captivated by prominent socialist and science fiction writer

4.4 Ernest (*c.* 1900s). Source: private family papers.

H. G. Wells and was enthralled by his work *First and Last Things* (1908). It stirred within Ernest a strong yearning to work for the common good which he conceived as his own 'religion'.[14] In addition to Wells, Ernest studied Beatrice and Sidney Webb's *Industrial Democracy* (1897) and *The Break up of the Poor Law* (1909). Ernest was in awe of their intellectual prowess, shown in their argument for replacing the antiquated nineteenth-century Poor Law, notorious for introducing workhouses, with a modern, progressive and far-reaching welfare system.[15] Combining both the ideas of Wells and the Webbs, Ernest came to believe that 'one's whole duty' was to work for the happiness of the community, holding the Webbian goal of providing 'equality of opportunity for all' to realise their true potential as the 'good in itself'.[16]

Ernest's sense of public duty was further awakened in the late 1900s and early 1910s by two other main sources. As Ernest recorded in his diary, his understanding of 'religion' took much from John Stuart Mill's essay *The Utility of Religion* (1874). Such was the influence of the Victorian philosopher over Ernest that there is a clear echo of Mill's 'intensely interesting' (as Ernest described it) *Autobiography* (1873) in the 'little autobiography' Ernest wrote for his children which, too, traced his own mental development.[17] The example of his parents also began to mould Ernest's public-spiritedness. Ernest read his father's book of moralistic advice inspired by the teachings of his great uncle Heinrich Simon and wished that Henry had been alive when he had 'began to think for himself' as he would 'have benefitted immensely' from his 'experiences and outlook'.[18] Several years later he depicted his parents in rather glowing terms for his children, describing them as dutiful and selfless citizens to emulate.[19]

Galvanised by his 'religion', Ernest threw himself into political campaigning. Converted as an ardent supporter of the Webbs' Minority Report campaign for the introduction of their own version of welfare provision, Ernest invited them to Lawnhurst in December 1909 before a campaign rally at the Free Trade Hall in Manchester. The visit affirmed Ernest's admiration for the Webbs and soon afterwards he became a director and important financier of their nascent political journal the *New Statesman* founded in 1913.[20] His support of the Webbs reintroduced Ernest to his old Rugby housemate R. H. Tawney, whose role in the Workers' Educational Association (WEA) convinced Ernest to sponsor its work enthusiastically as well.[21] Ernest, however, desired to be more than a financial backer to the causes he supported, but to be actively involved in them. He took elocution lessons so he could gain the confidence to make speeches, and made his first real foray into social reform tackling air pollution in Manchester.[22]

Smoke had blighted Cottonopolis since the Industrial Revolution, with soot caking Manchester's buildings and being breathed in daily by its inhabitants, with the consequence of hundreds of deaths each year.[23]

Having attended a meeting of Manchester City Council's Sanitary Committee in 1910, Ernest learnt of smoke abatement and sought to apply himself towards furthering it and in 1911 became the honorary secretary of the newly founded Smoke Abatement League of Great Britain.[24] The following year he played an instrumental role in the creation of its Manchester branch, the headquarters of which were located at 20 Mount Street, the home of the Simon businesses. With Ernest as its chairman the branch monitored polluting factories and lobbied the council to take the issue of air pollution seriously. In 1913, the council got behind Ernest and tasked him with experimenting in designing better domestic heating methods than coal fires.[25] Ernest's expertise in fighting air pollution saw him appointed by the Ministry of Health to a committee on air pollution, and in 1922 he authored his first book *The Smokeless City* with Manchester social investigator Marion Fitzgerald.[26] Ernest's work made a lasting impact in Manchester. Ardwick-born Labour minister Ellen Wilkinson, speaking about her native Lancashire on BBC radio in 1945, remembered how Ernest's 'overpowering energy and personality' helped to clean 'the skies of our northern cities'.[27] In 1946, the government charged Ernest with leading another committee on Domestic Fuel Policy. Its report, calling for smokeless zones in residential areas, the adoption of cleaner fuels and advanced domestic appliances to reduce the use of coal, was directly echoed by the 1954 Committee on Air Pollution led by Sir Hugh Beaver which paved the way for the momentous Clean Air Act 1956.[28] While the act came in the wake of the 1952 great London smog, 'the spade work' for the act was, according to Beaver, accomplished by Ernest and his fellow 'crusaders' for clean air.[29]

A Beatrice for his Sidney

Upon realising his 'religion', Ernest hoped to find a wife he could work with in the cause of social reform. Impressed by the dynamism of the Webbs and their achievements, Ernest 'wanted a wife who could play Beatrice to his Sidney'.[30] As it happened, in February 1912 Ernest met Shena Potter at a party in Didsbury, introduced by their mutual friend Eva Hubback.[31] Shena, a like-minded Cambridge-educated economist and active feminist campaigner from a wealthy shipping family, made a more than suitable match. Having gone to the London School of Economics in 1907 on the advice of its co-founder Beatrice Webb, she became side-tracked from her studies and had begun her career as a social reformer. When she met Ernest, she was in the midst of campaigning to ensure that the interests of women, particularly those of poorer insecure workers as well as married women, were covered by the provisions of new National Insurance legislation.[32] Ernest corresponded with her over the course of the first part of 1912, and they were to meet another six times before Ernest proposed to her in July. Shena was certainly attractive, but Ernest believed that

4.5 The cover of *The Smokeless City* (1922). Source: SSP M14/6/7.

'character & intellect' and a mutual interest in addressing 'social problems' in a partner outweighed physical beauty.[33] Having just recovered from an operation, he wrote the following in his diary after his proposal:

> So I have lost an appendix & found a wife! ... I always imagined that 'love at first sight' could mean nothing but physical love – which is the very last it meant in this sense. It was purely mental attraction, a feeling that here at last was the woman with whom I could live & be in real sympathy & comradeship.[34]

4.6 Ernest with Roger (1914). Source: SSP M14/4/24.

Marrying in November, they spent their honeymoon travelling around Europe before settling in Didsbury. Married life was, as Ernest recorded in his diary the following year, 'an enormous & increasing success', and in spite of his earlier apprehensions about physical attraction, it was clear that he had fallen deeply in love with Shena.[35]

Two months before their marriage, Ernest had been elected unopposed as a Liberal councillor for Didsbury.[36] Having stood on a platform to combat high rates of infant mortality, Ernest worked to establish council maternity centres to assist new mothers in raising newborns between 1914 and 1915. In his work he campaigned with the recently formed Manchester and Salford Women Citizens' Association, in which Shena was a central figure.³⁷ During the 1910s, Ernest and Shena were to enjoy having their own newborns with the arrival of Roger in 1913, Brian in 1915 and Antonia (Tony) in 1917.³⁸

During the First World War, Ernest lost all three of his younger brothers, Eric in 1915, and Victor and Harry in 1917. Ernest saw the war as a futile, horrendous slaughter which was brought 'home very closely' by the death of Eric. The youngest of Ernest's brothers, he 'could not bear the thought of killing' as a soldier and had resolved to 'kill only vermin'. Having nearly, on Ernest's advice, avoided frontline action, he was killed within three months of going to France.³⁹ Ernest's pain was compounded by his fears of being attacked for his German ancestry due to the prevalence of Germanophobia in Britain during the war. Government propaganda coupled with rumours of German atrocities and fears of enemy agents hiding in plain sight whipped up anti-German hatred. Following the German sinking of the *Lusitania* in May 1915, the feeling reached a climax with nationwide anti-German riots consuming the country. Many Germans and their property were afflicted, including the large community which lived in Manchester. The violence led the government to detain and repatriate unnaturalised Germans.⁴⁰ Against the background of xenophobia and his witnessing of the hatred directed towards prominent local politician Margaret Ashton for her pacifism, Ernest felt compelled to 'lie low and be very careful', 'owing to' his 'German blood'. He even attested for service in 1916 to appear 'patriotic', so his reputation and therefore his means to work for social reform would not be sullied.⁴¹ At the war's close, Ernest had emerged unscathed from any hatred with ambitions to head to Parliament.

Ernest had long harboured ambitions to enter national politics and at the First World War's end he was unexpectedly drawn into the fray of Westminster.⁴² Five days after the armistice, Ernest was on a train to London on his way to see Tawney when he encountered C. P. Scott and a deputation from the Manchester Liberal Federation. Scott and the Liberals were travelling to London in an attempt to secure a reconciliation between the leaders of British Liberalism, David Lloyd George and Herbert Asquith, and invited Ernest to join them. Lloyd George's displacement of Asquith as prime minister in 1916 had divided the Liberal Party and the delegation sought to fix this rupture in light of the impending general election. Both Lloyd George and Asquith, however, proved intransigent to the peace-making efforts of Ernest and his fellow Mancunians, and a few days later Lloyd George and the Conservative leader Bonar Law endorsed their 'couponed' candidates to fight against Asquith's independent Liberals.⁴³ The rupture left many Liberals in the invidious position of having to choose between the alternative leaders, and it proved 'a great mental struggle' for Ernest. After consulting the Webbs, who opposed cooperation with Lloyd George, he decided to back Asquith. While campaigning in Withington for the Asquithian candidate was exciting for Ernest, he despaired at the anti-German demagoguery of Lloyd George and came away from the election fearing for democracy itself.[44]

Ernest's dejection was short lived, however. Returning unopposed as a councillor for Didsbury in 1919, Ernest's re-election coincided with an electoral earthquake in Manchester. Thirty years of Conservative domination was broken by a progressive majority of Liberal and Labour councillors and opened up a major opportunity for him to shape policy. Lloyd George's electoral pledge of 'Homes fit for Heroes' had led to the 1919 Addison Act which enabled local authorities to embark on major schemes of housebuilding, and Ernest as the chairman of the council's housing committee sought to capitalise on this. Exhilarated by the opportunity, he aspired 'to make Manchester's housing scheme the best in the country' to show 'that a municipality can build houses'. Red tape and postwar scarcity of labour and materials, however, proved to be the undoing of Ernest's hopes, with the council only building a fraction of the houses they set out to construct.[45] Ernest's vision for housing in Manchester also saw the committee set in train the preliminaries for the creation of a garden city in Wythenshawe to relieve Manchester's terrible overcrowding.[46]

The whirlwind of Withington

One of the political implications of the post-1914 world was to shake the foundations of British Liberalism. A number of developments since the war, including economic turmoil and the heightening of the class tensions, had left Liberalism 'unequipped' to address major societal problems.[47] For Ernest this was starkly revealed at the 1918 general election. He confided to his diary there was an:

> utter lack on the part of the Liberal Party and the candidates in particular of any knowledge or interest in industrial problems, and the great question of equality.[48]

In the context of postwar industrial strife and mass unemployment, Ernest considered it imperative to address 'working-class discontent with the present economic system'. Consequently, during the winter of 1918–19, Ernest brought together a group of Manchester businessmen who shared his view that the party needed to formulate a new industrial policy. The group invited Ramsay Muir, Professor of History at the University of Manchester, to the meetings of the group and he summarised their discussions in a book, *Liberalism and Industry* (1920). The book proved to be influential, leading the national party to adopt a stance on industrial issues in early 1921. Buoyed by their accomplishment, the Mancunian coterie resolved to invite 'about one hundred younger Liberals to meet in Grasmere' later the same year. Proving to be a success, it set the template for the creation of the Liberal Summer School movement which began the next year. Meeting annually, the Summer Schools acted as forums for influential intellectuals such as John Maynard Keynes and William Beveridge to float their ideas about contemporary economic and social questions. Embraced by the party leadership, the schools increasingly shaped Liberal Party policy as the 1920s progressed.[49]

In November 1921, Ernest became Lord Mayor of Manchester. Ernest's mayoralty was abruptly interrupted when he contracted septic pneumonia in February 1922. With Ernest confined to bed for three months, Shena as Lady Mayoress took on all engagements having already used her position to be proactive and outspoken in civic affairs. Pneumonia being a serious illness before the advent of antibiotics, Ernest feared he could die, but was 'kept alive by brandy & morphia and hourly doses of oxygen!'[50]

The fall of the Lloyd George coalition in October 1922 resulted in a general election, called for 15 November. Ernest's term of office as Lord Mayor came to an end on 9 November and he only had days to campaign as Withington's Liberal candidate before polling day. Dubbed by the *Manchester Evening News* as 'Withington's Whirlwind Candidate', Ernest campaigned on housing and tackling unemployment, but was defeated by 670 votes,

4.7 Ernest and Shena campaigning during the 1922 General Election. Source: SSP M14/4/24.

having been subjected to slander which alleged he was German and therefore anti-British.[51] A second opportunity to contest the seat emerged in 1923 when Prime Minister Stanley Baldwin decided the reintroduction of tariffs required another general election. With the Liberal Party reunited under the old Shibboleth of free trade, Ernest was elected with a majority of 3,918.[52]

Ernest's maiden speech in Parliament focused on housing and his experience of it in Manchester. With a hung Parliament, he believed that cooperation between Labour and the Liberals could be fruitful especially for housebuilding, as had been the case in Manchester.[53] Using his Manchester-honed expertise, he closely scrutinised the legislation which became the Wheatley Act and got his own private member's bill passed: the Prevention of Eviction Act 1924.[54] A radical and pragmatic piece of legislation, it curtailed landlords' ability to arbitrarily evict tenants. Ernest hoped it would 'put an immediate end to the misery, the hardship and the sense of insecurity from which so many tenants are suffering all over the country'.[55] The fall of the first Labour government in October 1924 produced yet another general election and Ernest was defeated in the wake of conservative reaction to the red scares of the Campbell case and the Zinoviev letter.[56]

4.8 Ernest and Shena (seated to his left) during the 1924 General Election. Source: SSP M14/6/9.

Britain's industrial future

The derisory performance of the Liberal Party in the 1924 general election made Ernest review his political allegiances. He had previously wrestled with his party affiliation in 1920, having seriously considered joining Labour largely owing to his admiration of the ideas of Tawney and the Webbs.[57] The seemingly poor prospects for the Liberal Party put stress on Ernest's commitment to Liberalism yet again. Decidedly to the left of the party, he had even found himself agreeing 'with my extreme Labour audience' while standing in a by-election in Dundee in 1924, despite his public 'anti-socialist' platform. Moved by the poverty he had witnessed there, he considered his central 'political aim' was 'to give the best chance to every child, and to remove the excessive inequalities of today', which was for Ernest 'practically the aim of Labour'.[58] Ernest's position was exemplative of the egalitarianism of left-liberalism and its fluid boundary with socialism in the 1920s, but he did not jump ship.[59] Labour's commitment to mass nationalisation struck Ernest as impractical. Moreover, he disliked the party's close relationship with the trade unions; a dislike accentuated by his fear of class conflict engendered by the 1926 General Strike.[60] Ernest thus decided to remain with the Liberals, a decision bolstered by Lloyd George's support for bold new policies.

In 1926, Lloyd George got behind the Summer School movement Ernest had founded and gave it £10,000 from his infamous political fund to finance an inquiry into industrial policy. Ernest played a central role in the inquiry, which culminated in the production of *Britain's Industrial Future* (1928).[61] Amongst a litany of proposals, it advocated a major public works programme to tackle unemployment as well as profit-sharing schemes and worker consultation to abate class tensions. 'The product of a remarkable collaboration between politicians and economists' such as Lloyd George and Keynes, it represented a third way between 'harsh individualism and the employer-autocracy' and statist socialism and laid the foundations to the Liberals' 1929 election manifesto *We Can Conquer Unemployment*.[62]

Back in Manchester, Ernest had stepped down as a councillor in 1925, but he was about to make one of his and Shena's biggest contributions to the city.[63] Manchester's plans to build a garden city looked doomed because of expense. Frustrated by inaction, Ernest and Shena purchased Wythenshawe Hall and 250 acres of surrounding land and presented it unconditionally to the City Council in 1926. Their donation proved decisive, enabling the council to purchase the rest of Wythenshawe and transform it into a garden city.[64] Home life in Manchester for Ernest and Shena was hit by tragedy, however, when Tony was diagnosed with a malignant tumour of the eye which led to her death three years later. Tony's protracted illness and passing was devastating for both Ernest and Shena.

Tony's stoicism moved Ernest to tears, and her resilience in her dying days proved to be an inspiration, allowing him to find serenity in the face of bereavement.[65]

The Liberal Party entered the 1929 general election with a reinvigorated policy agenda. Ernest won his old seat and joined the other fifty-eight Liberal MPs propping up the minority Labour government. Ernest was favourable to the new government, supporting its decisions to continue housing subsidies and to raise the school leaving age, as well as its foreign policy. As the Liberals' spokesman on housing, Ernest worked with Eleanor Rathbone to ensure that the 1930 Greenwood Housing Act would enable municipalities to charge lower rents for poorer families in council houses.[66] However, he soon became disillusioned with Parliament. Ernest's perception of Lloyd George's ineptitude combined with 'the whole atmosphere of personal ambition' left him frustrated, considering Parliament an 'insufferable waste of time'.[67]

In summer 1931, a financial crisis led the leadership of the Labour government to consider cuts to unemployment benefit. It caused a major split in the party and the collapse of the government. With the ensuing formation of the National Government, Ernest was asked to take ministerial office as parliamentary secretary at the Ministry of Health. He accepted on the condition that housing subsidies would not be cut. Frustrated by civil servants' 'lack of enthusiasm and vision' regarding housing, Ernest's ministerial career lasted two weeks before a general election in October.[68] Having become disillusioned with Parliament before his appointment, he had decided not to contest Withington and had to stand in Cornwall. Despite a personal endorsement from Ramsay MacDonald, he was defeated by a Conservative, and thus Ernest's parliamentary career ended for the time being.[69]

How to abolish the slums

Having left Parliament, Ernest was appointed by MacDonald to the government's Economic Advisory Council in 1931.[70] The following year he was knighted. Thinking little of honours, he and Shena had joked about looking forward to the day when he could reject a knighthood. In accepting the title, however, he believed that it would bring influence and thereby enable him to forward the cause of reform, chiefly in housing.[71]

Ever since his appointment as chairman of the Housing Committee on Manchester City Council in 1919, the housing problem in Britain had become a significant concern of Ernest's. After having established himself as a national leading authority on housing in Parliament, he directed his energies towards writing three books: *How to Abolish the Slums* (1929), *The Anti-Slum Campaign* (1933) and *The Rebuilding of Manchester* (1935) to raise awareness of the crisis and promulgate his solutions to it. Drawing on a mass of nationwide statistical evidence and his direct experience of Manchester, Ernest traced the history of housing reform from the Victorian era, highlighting the current terrible conditions of many dwellings and the successes and failures of postwar housing policy.

While the period after the First World War saw unprecedented levels of housebuilding by both the private sector and local councils, this boom in construction benefited the middle classes and did little for the needs of millions of working-class people. 'The very people who were most in need of improved living standards', as Keith Laybourn writes, 'were not ... the chief beneficiaries' of housing expansion.[72] Instead, as Ernest observed, huge numbers of people, including two million children according to his own estimates, were living in vastly overcrowded, damp, flea-ridden houses which were rapidly deteriorating.[73] For Ernest, working-class people had been failed as new housing was simply too expensive and overcrowding was growing worse. The private sector had built houses for sale which were beyond the means of the poor, and new council houses were being leased at rents only affordable for the aristocracy of the working classes.[74]

To solve the crisis Ernest argued that alongside relief for larger families and rent restrictions, subsidies towards municipal house building had to be substantially increased so that newly constructed houses could be affordable for the poor.[75] The history of housebuilding since the nineteenth century had, according to Ernest, shown that as the public regulation of housing increased, so did its quality, and he concluded that the private sector could not build houses as cheaply and to as good a standard as those built by municipalities.[76] Additionally, to ease overcrowding, Ernest believed that slum clearance had to be put on hold until there was a surplus of new dwellings.[77] The eventual abolition of the slums would offer a fantastic opportunity to redesign the city centre. In *The Rebuilding of Manchester*, Ernest with J. Inman and Max Tetlow drew up plans to drastically reshape the city centre. Alongside the construction of 40,000 municipal flats, schools, shops and other amenities, Ernest envisaged the creation of huge parks in the city centre coupled with a grand new exhibition hall and cathedral. To be completed in 1985, it would replace the antiquated ring of Victorian housing surrounding the city centre clustered amongst factory works totally lacking in green spaces.[78]

Underscoring Ernest's arguments was his opposition to Sir Hilton Young, who had been appointed the Minister of Health in November 1931. Young had frustrated Ernest by cancelling subsidies for municipal housing, allowing only the private sector to build new homes. Furthermore, he criticised Young for pressing ahead with slum clearances without, in Ernest's eyes, building enough alternative affordable accommodation to replace demolished housing.[79] Lambasting Young's policy in the *New Statesman* and engaging him head-on in an animated debate on BBC radio, Ernest attacked Young's strategy as catastrophic for the poor.[80]

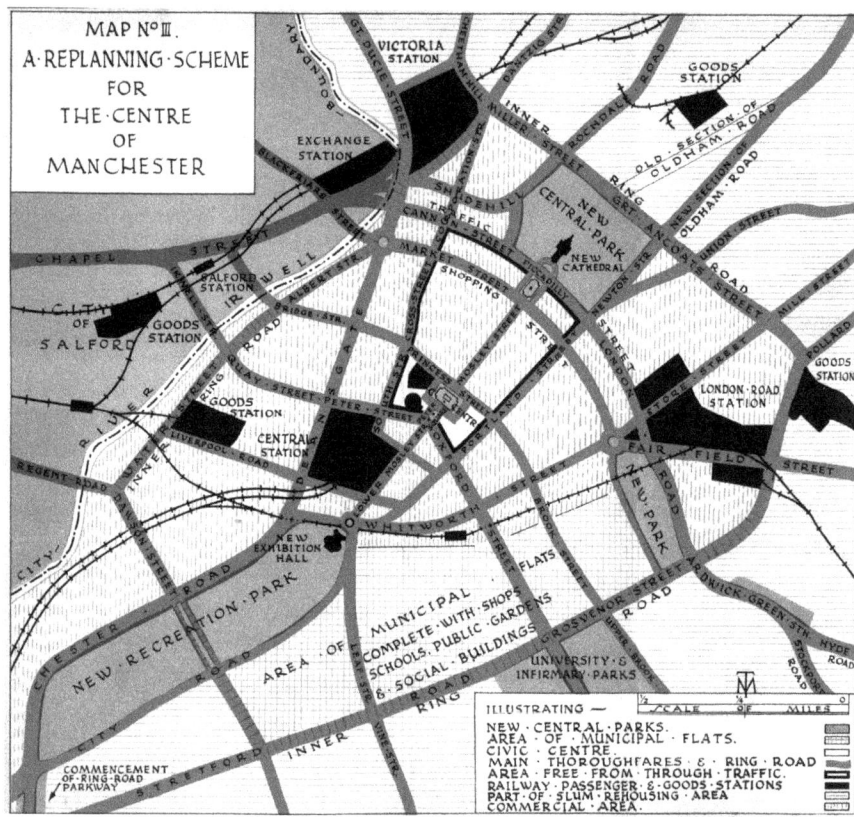

4.9 The map of the reimagined Manchester city centre in *The Rebuilding of Manchester* (1935). From E. D. Simon and J. Inman, *The Rebuilding of Manchester* (London: Longmans, Green and Co., 1935).

Education, democracy and totalitarianism

Like housing, Britain's economic woes were at the forefront of Ernest's mind and were to sow the seeds of his other main campaign in the 1930s: citizenship education. With politicians unable to solve the economic crisis, Ernest believed the public was left 'disillusioned, unhappy and uncertain'. This alienation, coupled with the rise of Nazism in Germany in 1933, led Ernest to fear that citizens could easily be seduced by fascism as the public seemingly had little understanding or interest in democratic government or in the value of freedom.[81] The future of democracy was thus at a crossroads; the great question for Ernest was whether people were 'to live as free citizens of democracies', or become 'the docile followers of a despot'?[82] Ernest believed the answer to safeguarding democracy lay in education and he founded the Association for Education in Citizenship with Eva Hubback in 1934. Attracting a host of leading educationists, intellectuals and politicians, the association aimed to reform education so that school-age pupils could be taught to appreciate liberal and democratic values and to take an active interest in public affairs. Leaving school as informed and engaged citizens, they would not fall victim to the fascist demagogue, but would be able to elect able representatives who could address the complex economic problems facing society.[83]

To work towards protecting popular rule in Britain, Ernest was keen to investigate how democracy functioned elsewhere. In 1938, he toured Switzerland as well as the Nordic nations. Publishing his findings the following year in *The Smaller Democracies* (1939), Ernest was impressed by the active engagement of citizens in civic affairs, their education and their freedom-loving nature. Fascism had been arrested in these countries, as their citizens elected competent democrats who were able to overcome the challenging economic crisis. The Scandinavian countries, in particular, showed to Ernest that healthy democracies with educated citizens could 'overcome the complexities of the machine age' and flourish instead of sinking into economic despair and fascism.[84]

Permeating Ernest's ideas about democracy was a tension between technocracy and active citizenship. On the one hand he felt that expert

4.10 Ernest (*c.* 1930s). Source: SSP M14/4/24.

elite representatives should hold the reins of government. 'Leadership', Ernest argued, was 'just as important in democracies as in dictatorships', and as much as citizens had to become informed about public issues, they had to leave solutions to experts.[85] Citizens had 'to realise their own ignorance and select the right people for Parliament'.[86] Yet, on the other hand, Ernest proclaimed that his 'faith' as a democrat was underpinned by citizen 'self-government in a great variety of small affairs', and in Switzerland he was in awe of the inculcation of democratic virtues through citizen participation in decision-making.[87] Ernest's reconciliation between these polar positions would help shape his most ambitious plan for reform, the rebuilding of Britain after the Second World War.

An equally important factor in shaping Ernest's future postwar plans was a trip to the Soviet Union. In 1936, Ernest and Shena with the academics William Robson and John Jewkes set off to study various aspects of Soviet Moscow, collating their findings in their book *Moscow in the Making* (1937). At the time of their visit, the USSR was a subject of great interest in intellectual circles. In the context of frustration at the economic slump and inequality in capitalist Britain, figures from across the political spectrum were intrigued by the Soviet Union's planned economy and rapid industrialisation. Some, such as Ernest's old friends the Webbs, saw the USSR as a new socialist civilisation, and their own extensive and popular study of the communist nation inspired Ernest and Shena's visit to Moscow.[88]

Hoping to garner lessons from the Soviet experiment, Ernest studied town planning, local government and housing in the capital. He was impressed by the public-spirited enthusiasm and efficiency of the one-party Communist government, as well the collective ownership of land which enabled effective planning. Nonetheless, unlike the Webbs, Ernest was no apologist for the regime and recorded very high levels of overcrowding, vastly beyond anything he had seen in Manchester. Moreover, with their visit coinciding with the beginning of Stalin's great purge, Ernest was critical of the government's repression of any form of dissent. Ernest's experience of the USSR left him to wonder whether the success of planning and the resolve of its government could be replicated in Britain while 'maintaining the freedom of minorities and the kindly tolerance of England?'[89] It was a question which was to remain with him as the catastrophe of the Second World War unfolded.

The Second World War

Upon the outbreak of the Second World War, Ernest volunteered to work for the Ministry of Information. His tenure there, however, was short and mired in bureaucratic mismanagement on the part of the ministry. Shortly afterwards, Ernest's expertise as a leading industrialist was called upon when he was appointed in spring 1940 as the area officer for the Ministry of Aircraft Production in the North-Western Region, and then as regional advisor to the ministry a year later. In 1941 he was also made deputy chairman of the Building and Trade Council at the Ministry of Works. During his tenure, Ernest led two reports: *Training for the Building Industry* (1942) and *The Placing and Management of Contracts* (1944).[90] The reports formed the basis of Ernest's book *Rebuilding Britain – A Twenty Year Plan* (1945). It represented the sum of Ernest's years of experience as an authority on housing and town planning.

To avoid the failures of the interwar period, Ernest argued that the government had to carefully plan postwar reconstruction. For Ernest, not enough affordable homes for the working class had been built during the interwar period as the building industry had been unplanned and therefore prone to booms and busts because of oscillating demand in housebuilding. During boom periods, materials and labour became scarce and therefore expensive, costs which were passed on to the price of erecting homes, which in turn meant they were let at rents which were unaffordable for many working-class people. Ernest had witnessed this first-hand in Manchester following the First World War. Even though he was instructed by the Minister of Health to use ruthless means, as chairman of the Housing Committee he had struggled to find supplies and labour and as a result the council built nowhere near enough houses. During periods of slump, hundreds of workers were left unemployed despite the desperate need for housing, a problem which was worsened by the fact that private builders were inclined not to go to the expense of recruiting additional workers for fear that a slackening in demand would worsen unemployment. To avoid the mistakes of the past, Ernest argued that the government had to control the volume of houses being built through a scheme of mass municipal housebuilding. It would thereby control the rate of construction and help to expand the workforce by guaranteeing employment for builders in line with the 1944 White Paper on Employment Policy which committed postwar governments to ensuring a high and stable level of employment.[91]

Much of *Rebuilding Britain* was inspired by his experience abroad, particularly by a visit to the USA between September and December 1942. Ernest and Shena travelled across America, Shena lecturing on local government and education and Ernest on postwar reconstruction. During his time there, Ernest studied great planning projects in America and, much to President Roosevelt's pleasure, greatly admired the Tennessee Valley Authority.[92] Ernest's prior visit to the Soviet Union underscored much of the book too. Inspired by the example of Moscow, he proposed in *Rebuilding Britain* that 'all land' had to be 'made available' for development, with municipalities able to cheaply and efficiently purchase land to facilitate planning. In addition, he believed that a reconstruction project in Britain had to emulate the determination the Muscovite government had shown in undertaking its own planning scheme. In contrast to the zeal cultivated

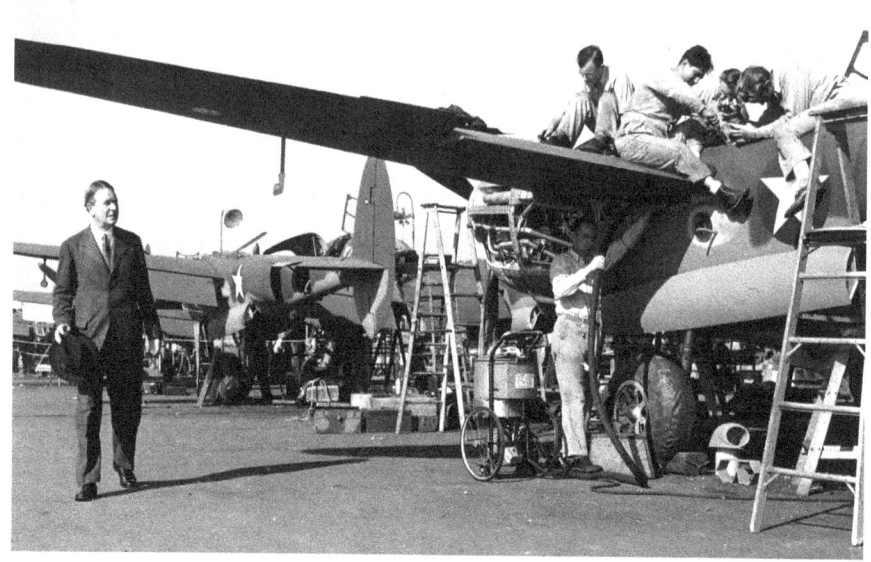

4.11 Ernest inspecting American war planes being manufactured (1942). Source: SSP M14/4/24.

by one-party rule and repression, postwar planning would be realised by the democratic 'drive' of citizens. Here, Ernest resolved his inner tension between technocracy and active citizenship. While the government and expert planners would undertake a long-term programme of housebuilding, the democratic pressure educated citizens would place on the government would ensure it carried out the scheme in full, in a manner which was subject to their criticism and their freely determined wishes.[93] Ernest's proposals in *Rebuilding Britain* were to anticipate the Attlee government's major housing and planning reforms. Aneurin Bevan embarked on a mass municipal housebuilding programme, with the Town and Country Planning Act 1947 nationalising development rights and making it easier for local authorities to purchase land for development.[94]

Comrade Lord Simon

In 1946, Ernest re-entered politics, contesting the Combined English Universities by-election which had been called following the death of Eleanor Rathbone. Ernest had great respect for Rathbone and like her decided to stand as an independent. Emphasising his three decades' experience on the Council of the University of Manchester, Ernest called for the expansion of university education, housing and, like Rathbone, family allowances.[95] Ernest lost to a Conservative with another ally of Rathbone, Mary Stocks, splitting the progressive vote.[96] Following this defeat, and after much deliberation, Ernest resolved to join the Labour Party. Impressed by its leadership and now less concerned about nationalisation, Ernest wrote to Shena, a party member since 1935, of his decision, signing off his missive 'With all my love, darling wife – and soon to be "comrade"'. Having followed Shena in boarding Labour's ship, he soon found himself back in Parliament after Clement Attlee offered him a peerage. Ennobled as Baron Simon of Wythenshawe in 1947, his title reflected his and Shena's pride in Manchester's garden city.[97]

Later that year, Ernest was asked by the government to become the chairman of the BBC. Ernest was largely silent in the Lords during his quinquennium as chairman to maintain the political neutrality of the role. One occasion, however, did require him to speak, when in 1950 Ernest inadvertently found himself at the centre of political controversy that caused a scandal. As chairman, he had decided to ban further broadcasts of a play by Val Gielgud called *Party Manners*. Ernest feared that the comedy, which portrayed a Labour government as corrupt, would undermine people's faith in democracy.[98] The decision, much to Ernest's surprise, dragged him into controversy, with the right-wing press making the accusation that, with the support of the government, he had censored a play that attacked his own party. The Lords debated the controversy, affording Ernest the opportunity to account for his mistakes but also to stress the impartiality of the corporation.[99]

4.12 Ernest with (right to left) William Haley, Jennie Lee, Aneurin Bevan and Shena (c. 1947–51). Courtesy of Helen David.

Ever the investigator, Ernest examined foreign broadcasting as chairman. He was particularly impressed by the decentralised Swiss system and believed that Britain could well benefit from such a system for its nations and regions. As part of his fact-finding, Ernest visited the United States in 1948. Disapproving of what he saw as sensationalist commercial television which did nothing to render Americans 'wiser or better citizens', he came away convinced of the need to retain the BBC's monopoly over broadcasting. This ambition of Ernest's was cemented in his mind by the Churchill government's decision to introduce commercial television.[100] Collaborating closely with Mary Stocks, Ernest joined the National Television Council and campaigned in the Lords to oppose the change.[101] Ernest's efforts were in vain, but his work as the chairman of the BBC had been stimulating for him, and he concluded his tenure there with his analysis of the corporation, *The BBC from Within* (1952).

Ernest's last campaigns

Now in his seventies and with his BBC chairmanship at an end, Ernest did not retire from public life but continued campaigning. In the 1950s, Ernest became convinced that the future of humanity was imperilled by two threats. The first was overpopulation. The fall in the death rate had led to unprecedented population growth over the past two centuries, and Ernest feared its unchecked increase would outstrip the supply of food, condemning millions to poverty. After initially approaching Max Nicholson, head of the Political and Economic Planning thinktank, to investigate the issue further, Ernest ended up as a chairman of the organisation's research group into population.[102] Informed in part by a study Ernest undertook into the 'Population and Resources of Barbados' in 1954, the group published its report entitled *World Population and Resources* the following year. It called for more research into, and action regarding, 'human fertility and methods of regulating it'. In addition to advocating the careful monitoring of population and resources as well as the ecological and social impacts of resource overexploitation, the report also suggested that developing countries receive technological assistance to prevent overpopulation.[103]

Ernest's fears about the danger of overpopulation led to his support of the International Planned Parenthood Federation and the British Family Planning Association and then his establishment of the Simon Population Trust in 1957. To address global poverty and malnutrition, the trust's key objectives were to improve

> understanding of the problems of world population and resources; and to encourage research and education to contribute to the adjustment of population to resources.

Ernest bequeathed £15,000 to the trust with a further £179,000 given after Shena died. The trust promoted male sterilisation and sponsored projects in contraception as well as postgraduate scholarships and educational material on population and reproductive choice. It also contributed to the 1984 UN Conference on Population before closing in 2001.[104]

In addition to overpopulation, the other threat to humanity Ernest feared was nuclear war. The Cold War had sparked a nuclear arms race and in Britain the movement against nuclear weapons became a groundswell in 1958 with the founding of the Campaign for Nuclear Disarmament (CND), the executive of which Ernest joined.[105] Ironically, the origins of the nuclear bomb can be traced back to Rutherford's discovery of the structure of the atom in the physics laboratory at the University of Manchester originally financed by Ernest's father, Henry.[106]

While he was not completely certain about unilateralism, and disapproving of the civil disobedience employed by other CND members, the danger nuclear weapons posed trumped Ernest's qualms. Ernest believed there were three key objectives to secure: an end to British nuclear tests, a government announcement that it would never pre-emptively strike, and the formation of a non-nuclear club of countries.[107] In 1959, Ernest used his position in the Lords to secure a debate on this third goal. Opening the debate, he outlined this nonproliferation proposal which had been originally formulated by his CND ally Bertrand Russell. As the only other nation to have nuclear armaments besides the USA and the Soviet Union, the UK could, Ernest believed, use its influence to get non-nuclear nations to renounce nuclear weapons in return for Britain's own disarmament. Furthermore, he believed that Britain should endeavour 'to persuade the United States and the U.S.S.R. jointly to sponsor a world-wide system of inspection under the auspices of U.N.'. Despite support from Russell and the bishops, the motion was opposed by the Conservative government and the Labour opposition. Nevertheless, as one peer commented, Ernest 'had a field day' in pressing for disarmament.[108]

For Ernest, the only way to successfully achieve nuclear disarmament was for the populace to understand 'the true horrors of the H-bomb'.[109] As the president of Manchester CND, he launched a campaign in 1958 to inform the city's inhabitants about the calamity of nuclear war. The campaign culminated in a packed-out meeting at the Free Trade Hall in Manchester during which an appeal for funds saw donations fall 'like confetti' onto the speakers' stage. The rally allowed Ernest to make clear the devastation of nuclear weapons by presenting how Manchester and its surrounding area would be devasted by a single bomb. In addition to his local educational campaign, Ernest financed the journalist Wayland Young, the son of his former nemesis on housing, Hilton Young, to write a book on disarmament.[110]

Having been on the University of Manchester's council since 1915 and an officer since 1932, Ernest had considerable knowledge of, and interest in, higher education, and his postwar campaigning was to shape its future significantly. With the question of university administration left unaddressed despite years of expansion, and with a lack of investment in higher education putting Britain at risk of falling behind technologically, Ernest believed that the whole university system had to be overhauled.[111] Eager to address these issues, Ernest, in his final appearance in the Lords in May 1960, called on the government to 'inquire and report on the extent and nature of full-time education for all those over the age of 18'.[112] His motion was met with indecision from the government which disappointed him. Ernest's campaigning was not in vain, however, as in December 1960 the government established a committee under the chairmanship of Lord Robbins, granting all that he had requested.[113] The 1963 Robbins Report laid the foundations for the rapid expansion of higher education, and while the increase in the number of female and working-class students fell short of report's expectations, it helped to boost equality of educational opportunity.[114]

Conclusion

In 1959, Ernest was awarded the Freedom of Manchester. A proud Mancunian, he used his speech to reflect upon the achievements of the city and, echoing modern calls for civic devolution, Ernest expounded his belief that Manchester could thrive if it was more independent of central government.[115] It was to be an evening honour for Ernest, however. Eleven months later he collapsed following a stroke during a trip to the Lake District. Shena moved him back to a nursing home in Manchester where she remained by his side until he died on 3 October 1960.[116]

Ernest Simon's life was as intriguing as it was influential. From a chronically shy child, he went on to help improve the housing conditions of millions and enable the opening of higher education to the masses. Spurred by his 'religion', he had a strong work ethic, but his achievements were greatly facilitated by his wealth, his contacts, his assistants and by Shena, who subordinated her political ambitions in order for him to realise his own.[117] Influenced by the Webbs, his own sense of self-exceptionalism, and by his career as a self-described 'autocratic employer', Ernest endorsed top-down planning and placed his faith in experts to solve societal issues.[118] For all his technocratic tendencies, however, he worked for a more egalitarian society which was composed of educated citizens actively engaged in self-government.

Tracing Ernest's work helps to shed light on key historical moments of the twentieth century, from the proliferation of council housing, to British reactions to totalitarianism and postwar reconstruction. Moreover, his historical activism also speaks to contemporary issues afflicting society today. Indeed, many problems which Ernest sought to address sadly remain. Air pollution is responsible for thousands of deaths and respiratory illnesses,

4.13 Ernest in the Lake District. Source: private family papers.

and there is an entrenched crisis of unaffordable housing. Ernest's ideas about civic education, too, seem tragically more apt than ever in light of the international upsurge of right-wing authoritarianism. And, while many would not endorse Ernest's neo-Malthusian outlook, sustainable development, particularly for emerging nations, will be a major challenge this century. Finally, the tumult which the climate emergency and the rise of artificial intelligence will cause to the economy will require something akin to the bold new industrial policy Ernest helped to formulate a century ago. For all these reasons, a study of his life furnishes us with resources for thinking about the challenges of the future.

Notes

1 Ernest's role in shaping interwar Liberalism is discussed in Michael Freeden, *Liberalism Divided: A Study in British Political Thought 1914–1939* (Oxford: Oxford University Press, 1986), pp. 78–126, 252–7. Ernest's campaigning to promote education in citizenship has been examined by several scholars: Guy Whitmarsh, 'The Politics of Political Education: An Episode', *Journal of Curriculum Studies*, 6:2 (1974), 133–42. Rob Freathy, 'The Triumph of Religious Education for Citizenship in English Schools, 1935–1949', *History of Education*, 37:2 (2008), 295–316; Susannah Wright, *Morality and Citizenship in English Schools: Secular Approaches, 1897–1944* (London: Palgrave Macmillan, 2017), pp. 177–99; Hsiao-Yuh Ku, *Education for Democracy in England in World War II* (London: Routledge, 2020), pp. 154–70.

2   Mary Stocks, *Ernest Simon of Manchester* (Manchester: Manchester University Press, 1963). For a recent biography which focuses on his role in the Liberal Party, see: David Dutton, 'E.D. Simon: Intellectual in Politics', *Journal of Liberal History*, 104:4 (2019), 16–27.
3   Brian Simon, *In Search of a Grandfather: Henry Simon of Manchester* (Leicester: The Pendene Press, 1997), pp. 42–3, 59–60, 75–6.
4   ESD, 22 March 1911, 3 February 1920.
5   ESD, 3/4 April 1909, 14 February 1913, 3 February 1920.
6   Private family papers, Ernest Simon, 'Mother', January 1920.
7   Private family papers, Henry Simon to Harry and Ernest Simon, 5 October 1894; Henry Simon to Harry Simon, 20 May 1896. These are copies of the originals which are part of the HSC archive at JRL.
8   Simon, *In Search of a Grandfather*, pp. 67–73.
9   ESD, 3 February 1920.
10 Anthony Simon, *The Simon Engineering Group* (Cheadle Heath: privately printed, 1953), p. xi.
11 ESD, 10 April 1910.
12 ESD, 3 February 1920.
13 ESD, 16 July 1914, 22 March 1911.
14 ESD, 27 December 1908, 11 May 1909.
15 ESD, 19(?) October 1909.
16 ESD, 5 December 1911, 10 July 1912.
17 ESD, 29 August 1911, 3 February 1920.
18 ESD 3/4 April 1909. The book referred to is Henry Simon, *Rathschaelage für Meine Kinder* (Manchester: c. 1899). See: Chapter 2 in this volume by Janet Wolff and Simon, *In Search of a Grandfather*, p. 37.
19 Simon, 'Mother'.
20 ESD, 20 November 1909, 24 November 1909, 11 December 1909; Stocks, *Ernest Simon of Manchester*, p. 29.
21 ESD, 1 December 1909, 19 February 1910.
22 ESD, 11 December 1909.
23 E. D. Simon and Marion Fitzgerald, *The Smokeless City* (London: Longmans, Green and Co., 1922), p. 14.
24 ESD, 16 March 1911.
25 'Smoke Abatement: A Manchester Branch of the League', *Manchester Guardian* (25 April 1912); SSP M14/6/3, 'The British Association', *Engineering* (15 October 1915).
26 *Interim Report of the Committee on Smoke and Noxious Vapours Abatement* (London: HMSO, 1920).
27 Ellen Wilkinson, 'Born and Bred in Lancashire', *The Listener* (29 November 1945), p. 617.
28 *Domestic Fuel Policy: Report by the Fuel and Power Advisory Council* (London: HMSO, 1946), pp. 28–31; *Committee on Air Pollution: Report* (London: HMSO, 1954), pp. 59–60, 67–74.
29 Hugh Beaver, 'The Ministry of Works 1941–1947', in *80th Birthday Book for Ernest Darwin Simon, Lord Simon of Wythenshawe, b. 9th October 1879* (Cheadle Heath: The Cloister Press, 1959), p. 46
30 Brian Harrison, *Prudent Revolutionaries: Portraits of British Feminists between the Wars* (Oxford: Clarendon Press, 1987), p. 285.
31 Stocks, *Ernest Simon of Manchester*, pp. 33–4; ESD, 20 July 1912.
32 Janet Beveridge, *An Epic of Clare Market: Birth and Early Days of the London School of Economics* (London: G. Bell & Sons, 1960), p. 75; Joan Simon, *Shena Simon Feminist and Educationist* (privately printed, 1986), Chapter I, pp. 3–4.
33 Before he met Shena, Ernest had struggled to talk to women due to his shyness and social awkwardness: ESD, 11 May 1909. Mary Stocks writes how 'his diaries

are barren of sex adventure, but in other respects so uninhibited that one may conclude that if such adventure had been present it would have been duly recorded'. Stocks, *Ernest Simon of Manchester*, p. 33.
34 ESD, 3 April 1909, 20 July 1912.
35 ESD, 26 December 1912, 20 May 1913.
36 'Didsbury Ward Election', *Manchester Guardian* (10 September 1912), p. 3.
37 SSP M14/6/3, Ernest D. Simon, 'Bye-Election September 1912. To the Electors of the Didsbury Ward'; ESD, 5 June 1916; Shena Simon 'Women Citizens Associations.–II.', *Common Cause* (14 July 1916), p. 175.
38 'Births', *The Times* (20 October 1913), p. 1; ESD, 26 March 1915, 21 August 1917.
39 ESD, 20 August 1915, 10 June 1917, 8 September 1917.
40 Panikos Panayi, 'The Destruction of the German Communities in Britain during the First World War', in Panikos Panayi (ed.), *Germans in Britain Since 1500* (London: Bloomsbury, 1997), pp. 115, 120–2, 127–8.
41 ESD, 5 December 1915, 11 December 1915, 4 January 1916, 24 January 1916.
42 ESD, 27 September 1910.
43 ESD, 16 November 1918; Trevor Wilson, 'The Coupon and the British General Election of 1918', *Journal of Modern British History*, 36:1 (1964), 28–42.
44 ESD, 26 November 1918, 15 December 1918.
45 E. D. Simon, *A City Council from Within* (London: Longmans Green & Co., 1926), pp. 32–57; ESD, 6 November 1919.
46 Sir Ernest and Lady Simon, 'Wythenshawe', in E. D. Simon and J. Inman, *The Rebuilding of Manchester* (London: Longmans Green & Co, 1935), pp. 37–8.
47 Freeden, *Liberalism Divided*, pp. 8–11; David Dutton, *A History of the Liberal Party Since 1900* (Basingstoke: Palgrave Macmillan, 2013), pp. 77–8.
48 ESD, 26 November 1918.
49 For the poor economic background, see: Keith Laybourn, *Britain on the Breadline: A Social and Political History of Britain 1918–1939* (Stroud: Sutton, 1998), pp. 8–9, 109–10, 126; Michael Freeden, *Liberalism Divided*, pp. 80–1; Ernest Simon, 'The Liberal Summer School', *The Contemporary Review* (September 1929), pp. 274–5.
50 Stocks, *Ernest Simon of Manchester*, pp. 66–7; ESD, 14 April 1922.
51 SSP M14/6/8.
52 'Thursday Night's Declarations', *Manchester Guardian* (8 December 1923), p. III.
53 Hansard (Commons), 18 January 1924, vol. 169, cols 433–8.
54 Stocks, Ernest Simon of Manchester, pp.72–3; SSP M14/6/4, 'Housing (Financial Provisions) Bill. Speech by Mr. E. D. Simon, MP', 17 July 1924.
55 SSP M14/6/4, 'Prevention of Evictions. Speech by Mr. E. D. Simon, MP', 26 March 1924.
56 'Tory Triumphs', *Manchester Guardian* (30 October 1924), p. 9.
57 ESD, 7 February 1920.
58 ESD, 27 February 1925; 'Dundee's Alternative', *Manchester Guardian* (20 December 1924), p. 10; E. D Simon, *How to Abolish the Slums* (London: Longmans Green and Co., 1929), p. vii.
59 See: Freeden, *Liberalism Divided*, pp. 246–57, 294–328.
60 ESD, 27 February 1925; 'Liberals and Labour Party', *Manchester Guardian* (17 November 1926), p. 12.
61 Freeden, *Liberalism Divided* pp. 102–3,105–6.
62 *Britain's Industrial Future: Being the Report of the Liberal Industrial Inquiry* (London: Ernest Benn, 1928), pp. 187–9, 205, 227, 231–8, 267–338; Robert Skidelsky, *Politicians and the Slump: The Labour Government of 1929–1931* (London: Macmillan, 1994), pp. 51–2.
63 Stocks, *Ernest Simon of Manchester*, p. 77.
64 'Correspondence: A Garden Suburb for Manchester', *Manchester Guardian* (1 January 1926), p. 16; 'The Wythenshawe Estate. Buy and Incorporate',

Manchester Guardian (3 May 1926), p. 13; 'The Wythenshawe Estate. Manchester Takes Possession', *Manchester Guardian* (30 September 1926), p. 11.

65 Stocks, *Ernest Simon of Manchester*, pp. 81–2; ESD, 27 May 1927, 'My first fifty years' October 1929.
66 ESD (Parliamentary Diary), 27 July 1929; E. D. Simon, *The Anti-Slum Campaign* (London: Longmans, Green and Co., 1933), p. 40.
67 ESD (Parliamentary Diary), January 1930, 3 July 1931.
68 ESD, 21 September 1931, 22 September 1931, 2 April 1932.
69 SSP M14/6/9, '1931 General Election'.
70 Ernest served on the council's Committee on Economic Information from 1932 which effectively replaced the council. In 1936, he had to resign after he transgressed the committee's 'rule on secrecy' because he mentioned 'an opinion of the Committee when on a deputation to a minister from an organisation he represented'. See: Susan Howson and Donald Winch, *The Economic Advisory Council 1930–1939: A Study in Economic Advice and Recovery* (Cambridge: Cambridge University Press, 2008 [1977]), p. 107.
71 ESD, 2 April 1932.
72 Laybourn, *Britain on the Breadline*, pp. 78–80.
73 Simon, *How to Abolish the Slums*, p. 44; Simon, *The Anti-Slum Campaign*, p. 3; E. D. Simon and J. Inman, *The Rebuilding of Manchester* (London: Longmans, Green and Co., 1935), p. 61.
74 Simon, *How to Abolish the Slums*, pp. 54, 90; Simon, *The Anti-Slum Campaign*, pp. 121–2, 143–4.
75 Simon, *How to Abolish the Slums*, pp. 69–70, 92–5; Simon, *The Anti-Slum Campaign*, pp. 136–41, 147.
76 Simon and Inman, *The Rebuilding of Manchester*, pp. 73–7; Simon, *The Anti-Slum Campaign*, pp. 145–6.
77 Simon, *How to Abolish the Slums*, p. 58–9; Simon, *The Anti-Slum Campaign*, p. 130
78 Simon and Inman, *The Rebuilding of Manchester*, pp. 124–44.
79 Simon, *The Anti-Slum Campaign*, pp. 51–6, 144–6.
80 'The Urgency of Slum Clearance', *The Listener* (9 November 1933), pp. 685–7, 723.
81 Sir Ernest Simon, 'Education for Democracy', *New Statesman* (14 July 1934), pp. 71–2; ESP M11/11/15, E. D. Simon, 'The Need for Training in Citizenship', in E. D. Simon and Eva M. Hubback, *Education for Citizenship* (Ashton-under-Lyne: J. Andrew & Co.,1934), p. 6.
82 Sir E. D. Simon, *The Smaller Democracies* (London: Victor Gollancz, 1939), p. 11.
83 Stocks, *Ernest Simon of Manchester*, p.104; Sir Ernest Simon, 'The Aims of Education for Citizenship', in Sir Ernest Simon and others, *Education for Citizenship in Secondary Schools* (London: Humphrey Milford, 1936), pp. 1–10; Sir Ernest Simon, 'Preface', in Sir Ernest Simon and others, *Constructive Democracy* (London: George Allen and Unwin, 1938), pp. 7, 10.
84 Simon, *The Smaller Democracies*, pp. 174–91.
85 Simon, *The Smaller Democracies*, p. 185; 'Sir E. Simon Examines Democracy', *Manchester Guardian* (5 October 1935), p. 17.
86 'Making Democracy a Success', *Manchester Guardian* (14 December 1932), p. 11.
87 ESP M11/11/15, Sir Ernest Simon, 'The Faith of a Democrat', p. 3; Simon, *The Smaller Democracies*, pp. 25–8, 36–7, 47–50.
88 Sir E. D. Simon, 'Preface', in Sir E. D. Simon, Lady Simon, W. A. Robson and J. Jewkes, *Moscow in the Making* (London: Longmans Green and Co., 1937), pp. v–vi; Richard Overy, *The Morbid Age: Britain and the Crisis of Civilization, 1919–1939* (London: Penguin Books, 2010), pp. 283–96.
89 Sir E. D. Simon, 'Housing', 'The Mossoviet: Its advantages for town planning', 'The Mossoviet is it democratic?', in *Moscow in the Making*, pp. 154–5, 211–15, 219–220, 226–7.

90 Stocks, *Ernest Simon of Manchester*, pp. 112–17.
91 E. D. Simon, *Rebuilding Britain – A Twenty Year Plan* (London: Victor Gollancz, 1945), pp. 15–33.
92 Simon, *Rebuilding Britain*, pp. 133–57; private family papers, Ernest Simon 'My American Visit', 26 December 1942; private family papers, Franklin Roosevelt to Ernest Simon, 22 December 1942.
93 Simon, *Rebuilding Britain*, pp. 127–32, 224, 232–3.
94 Michael Foot, *Aneurin Bevan*, 2 vols (London: Granada, 1982), II: 1945–1960, pp. 68–85; Stephen V. Ward, *Planning and Urban Change*, 2nd edn (London: Sage Publications, 2004), p. 116.
95 ESP M11/16/9, 'Candidature of Sir Ernest Simon. Combined English Universities Parliamentary By-Election 1946'.
96 'Conservatives Win a Seat', *Manchester Guardian* (21 March 1946), p. 6.
97 Stocks, *Ernest Simon of Manchester*, pp. 124–6.
98 ESP M11/6/8, 'Party Manners' Note by S. of W; ESP M11/6/8, 'Party Manners' Personal Statement by Lord Simon of Wythenshawe, 11 October 1950.
99 *Hansard* (Lords), 7 November 1950, vol. 169, cols 192–4.
100 Lord Simon of Wythenshawe, 'Broadcasting in other Countries', *Political Quarterly* 24:3 (1953), 356–86.
101 Hansard (Lords) 25 November 1953, vol. 184, cols 536–45; ESP M11/6/3.
102 Stocks, *Ernest Simon of Manchester*, pp. 141–3.
103 ESP M11/11/15, Lord Simon of Wythenshawe, *Population and Resources of Barbados* (Manchester: privately printed, 1954); *World Population and Resources. A Report by P E P* (London: Political and Economic Planning, 1955), pp. 324–8.
104 Penny Kane, 'The Simon Population Trust: A Brief History', *Journal of Family Planning and Reproductive Health Care*, 28:2 (2002), SPT1–SPT12; ESP M14/6/13, 'The Simon Population Trust', December 1965, p. 3.
105 Richard Taylor and Colin Pritchard, *The Protest Makers: The British Nuclear Disarmament Movement of 1958–1965, Twenty Years On* (Oxford: Pergamon Press, 1980), pp. 3–6.
106 Simon, *In Search of a Grandfather*, p. 127.
107 Stocks, *Ernest Simon of Manchester*, p. 147.
108 For the full debate, see: Hansard (Lords) 11 February 1959 vol. 214, cols 71–178.
109 SSP M14/6/13, 'Speech on the Effects of a Hydrogen Bomb by Lord Simon at the Free Trade Hall, Manchester, May 1958'.
110 Stocks, *Ernest Simon of Manchester*, pp. 149–50; 'Second Stage of Ban the Bomb Rally', *Manchester Guardian* (22 May 1958), p. 16.
111 ESP M11/11/15, Lord Simon of Wythenshawe, *Future Numbers of University Students: The Desperate Need for Technologists* (London: Turnstile Press, 1956); ESP M11/11/15, Lord Simon of Wythenshawe, 'A Royal Commission on the Universities' (Reprinted from *Universities Quarterly*, 1958).
112 For the full debate, see: Hansard (Lords), 11 May 1960, vol. 223, cols 615–732.
113 Stocks, *Ernest Simon of Manchester*, p. 173.
114 Claire Callender, 'Student Numbers and Funding: Does Robbins Add up?', *Higher Education Quarterly*, 68:2 (2014), 175–8.
115 'Address by Lord Simon of Wythenshawe on the Occasion of the Presentation of the Freedom of the City of Manchester 25th November 1959 in the form of a farewell speech to the City Council', *Manchester Review*, 9 (1960), pp. 1–11.
116 Stocks, *Ernest Simon of Manchester*, p. 174.
117 SSP M14/7/13, Mabel Tylecote, *The Work of Lady Simon of Wythenshawe for Education in Manchester*, 28 November 1974, p. 2.
118 ESD, 7 February 1920.

5.1 Shena Simon (*c.* 1940–50s). Source: private family papers.

5

A confirmed outsider: the life of Shena Simon, feminist and education campaigner (1883–1972)

John Ayshford and Brendon Jones

In June 1938, Shena Simon wrote to her friend Virginia Woolf congratulating her on her latest work *Three Guineas* (1938).[1] Shena remarked to Woolf that she was 'personally grateful' for the role her writings had in bolstering her own desire to campaign for reform, in spite of the obstacles she faced from a patriarchal society. Tracing her own career so far as a campaigner, Shena first outlined how her role in 'the suffragette agitation' had made her rebellious, unconcerned about 'other people's opinions of me and my actions'. Later, as Lady Mayoress in Manchester, she explained how she had caused a 'storm' of criticism following a simple protest at there being no women managers at a women's hospital. More recently, on government committees, she had chosen to dissent from her 'men colleagues', opting to write minority reports of her own, and now she was making 'a great nuisance' of herself in her role advising the Board of Education. Shena confessed she 'sometimes wondered whether I ought to adopt a different attitude' but, as she informed Woolf, she resolved that:

> as I am completely independent, in the sense that I don't want 'honours' or appointments or anything from the powers that be, I have decided that, unlike many other women, I can afford to be unpopular. Now, after Three Guineas, I am more confirmed in my belief, and shall probably become more and more of an 'outsider'.[2]

In retrospect, Shena's letter to Woolf encapsulates her character as an independent-minded and strong-willed feminist reformer. Shena's career, which saw her contribute to significant improvements in health, housing and education nationally and in her adopted city of Manchester, was defined by a radical and autonomous streak. Combined with this streak was a privileged financial independence which meant that deference to custom, public opinion and powerful institutions did not moderate Shena's work and ideals. She could quite literally 'afford to be unpopular'. As one friend was to remark on her death, 'the pursuit of truth was more important than popularity' for Shena.[3] Shena's work as a free-thinking reformer touched the lives of many Britons during her lifetime and has done so ever since. Yet for all this she remains relatively unknown, despite her national prominence in her lifetime. This chapter therefore aims to shed light on Shena's historical significance and the influences which buttressed her career as a public servant and reformer.

The chapter follows the writings of historians of education Jane Martin and Hsiao-Yuh Ku who have highlighted Shena's contribution to reforming education and the intellectual underpinnings of her work. Martin, examining her work on Manchester City Council and as an educationist, argues that Shena followed in the tradition of public duty and active citizenship of nineteenth-century middle-class radicals, centred on the positivist idea of the religion of humanity.[4] Ku, in her recent volume on the vanguard of

5.2   Shena with her mother Jane Boyd Potter (c. 1884). Source: SSP M14/4/3.

British progressives who sought to democratise education in the first half of the twentieth century, has illustrated how the social democratic tenet of 'equality of educational opportunity' was the 'foundation' upon which Shena's work rested.[5]

In portraying Shena's life, this chapter builds upon research by Marian Horrocks as well as the educational historian Joan Simon's privately printed biography of her mother-in-law and her articles on Shena's work on the Spens Committee.[6] It also draws upon her and her husband's vast array of papers held by Manchester Central Library and the numerous reports, pamphlets and books she wrote. In doing so, the chapter aims to paint a picture of a forgotten reformer who 'never hesitated to stand up for her convictions'.[7]

Shena Potter

Shena Simon was born in Croydon in 1883. Named Dorothy Shena Potter, she was the second of the nine children of John Wilson Potter (1856–1933) and Jane Boyd Potter née Thompson (1860/61–1946). Both of Shena's parents came from wealthy shipping families. Her mother was the granddaughter of George Thompson, a radical MP and founder of the Aberdeen line, while her father was a lead partner in a firm involved in shipping to Australia. Their union marked an end to a rivalry as John Wilson Potter had worked on the loading of the ship the *Cutty Sark*, the nemesis of George Thompson's ship the *Thermopylae*.[8] Shena, as Joan Simon writes, 'was devoted' to her parents and was close to her elder sister Millicent. Shena was home educated and spent three years between the ages of eighteen and twenty-one working to apply to Newnham College Cambridge. Shena's ambition to study at Newnham, something she had resolved to do 'at a very early age', was initially contrary to the expectations of her parents, who, having sent her brothers to school, believed that she would live a life of domesticity. Shena's ambition was most likely bolstered by her governess Theodora Clark. Clark, a Quaker and a supporter of female suffrage and university education, guided Shena through her studies and undoubtedly sowed the seeds of Shena's free-thinking and feminist outlook.[9]

Shena originally planned to study history at Newnham. It was something she had always been 'passionately fond of' and had excelled in. In the end she opted for economics, a subject she developed an interest in towards the end of her schooling as a result of her encounter with John Stuart Mill's great tome *Principles of Political Economy* (1848) which she read 'with avidity'. Enrolling at Newnham in 1904, Shena began studying for the economics tripos and was taught by Britain's foremost economist, Alfred Marshall. At Cambridge she was to forge lifelong friendships, two notable ones being with Dorothy Osmaston and Eva Spielman (later

Layton and Hubback).[10] While Cambridge was, according to Shena's own recollections, 'heavily chaperoned', university life would have no doubt been liberating. Whereas conformity, paucity of autonomy and social interaction would have governed her and her friends' home lives, university offered new freedoms.[11] As Osmaston recalled:

> for the first time ever we regularly met a circle of men as equals discussing with them: everything from religious beliefs and social evils to sex in a way that would have been impossible in the more conventional relationships of our homes.

Such freedoms allowed Shena's friends to join men in political societies at the university, with Spielman and Amber Reeves (later Amber Blanco White) becoming actively involved in the university's Fabian Society.[12] While Shena was not to follow in their footsteps, she struck up correspondence with principal Fabian Beatrice Webb in 1905 and on her advice Shena decided to study at the London School of Economics after Cambridge.[13]

5.3 Shena (c. 1907–12). Source: private family papers.

At the LSE, Shena undertook research into 'the underlying assumptions of the emergent Labour Party' under Graham Wallas and L. T. Hobhouse. Shena loved being a student at the School from 1907–12. It was 'a most stimulating place' where students and teachers of different sexes, races and ages mixed.[14] It was here that she got to know Beatrice Webb and her husband, Sidney, further. In 1964, she recalled how they were both 'so human and so ready to help any student however insignificant', but Shena's rapport with them was nevertheless hurt, albeit temporarily, by their defamation of her Newnham friend Amber Blanco White following Amber's affair with H. G. Wells.[15]

Shena's time at the LSE proved to be formative as she embarked on a lifelong career as a social investigator. As she recollected, her times there 'were some of the most fruitful of my life'.[16] She took an interest in industrial relations which distracted her from her research. Collaborating with Manchester-born labour activist, James J. Mallon, Shena investigated 'sweated industries' and worked on the 'preliminaries for the setting up of wages boards', the bodies which would set a minimum wage for those in low-paid and insecure industries. To complement her work, she travelled to Australia and New Zealand to study the machinery there for settling industrial disputes.[17]

In travelling to the antipodes, Shena was following in the footsteps of Margaret MacDonald, a prominent figure in the National Union of Women Workers (NUWW). Joining the union and working under Macdonald, Shena came to greatly admire her. In the NUWW, Shena campaigned during and after the passing of the National Insurance Act 1911 to ensure women's interests were covered by the legislation. Motivating Shena's campaign was the fear that wives, domestic servants and low-paid women would have little to no protection against illness and unemployment under the act.[18] The challenges she faced while doing so convinced her that without the vote to directly influence politicians, it would be very difficult to improve the status of women.[19] It led her to deeply sympathise with the suffragette movement formed in Manchester by the Pankhurst family. Having to live with her parents in Westminster upon whom she was financially dependent meant she could not join in suffragette militancy, as they were opposed to it. Shena came to an agreement with her parents: they let her engage in marches and make speeches, as long as she did not do 'anything actively militant'.[20] This constraint on her freedom no doubt frustrated Shena and played a part in underscoring her love of Virginia Woolf's *A Room of One's Own* (1929), a core message of which was that, as Shena wrote,

> until women are economically independent they cannot ... be free to speak or write what they really think. Their opinions – even those expressed in the privacy of the home – must be those which will win favour with the father or husband who holds the purse strings.[21]

Shena's desire for women's enfranchisement was strongly held. Her involvement with the suffragettes went against her prior 'instincts' to be rule-abiding and considerate. As she told Woolf in 1938, 'as a girl' she 'was too much too concerned with other people's opinions' and was afraid 'of hurting their feelings'. Likewise, writing to her husband, Ernest Simon, in 1916, she explained how at Newnham she was 'always most scrupulous about keeping to all the rules – ridiculous as some of them seemed – because I knew I should feel uncomfortable if I broke them, even if I knew no bad results would follow'. Being involved in the movement, however, as she wrote to Woolf, 'turned' her 'into a rebel' and marked the beginning of a career as an increasingly outspoken and free-thinking reformer.[22]

North and south

In February 1912, Shena was invited by her Newnham friend Eva Hubback to a party in Didsbury where she met Ernest Simon. Eva lived in Didsbury in south Manchester and had made the acquaintance of Ernest Simon, a wealthy Mancunian businessman with aspirations to be a social reformer, and thought he would make the ideal match for Shena.[23] While Shena did not suffer from a want of admirers, she had been uncertain about marriage, for although, as she told Eva, she desired a partner, she feared a conventional marriage would confine her to domesticity and the loss of her ability to be a campaigner.[24] It was for this reason that a partnership with Ernest seemed so appealing, as together they could pursue their many shared political causes. Five months later, Ernest proposed to Shena in Oxford. The proposal itself was a success, but not without a hitch, since they both fell out of the canoe on which the proposal took place. It was not 'an ideal place' as Ernest wrote in his diary.[25] They married in November and spent their honeymoon in France, Italy and Monaco, the third destination involving a costly visit to Monte Carlo Casino, before moving to Didsbury.[26] While their bond at first rested in large part on shared ideals, Shena and Ernest soon developed a close romantic partnership.[27] Together they had three children. Their sons Roger and Brian Simon were born in 1913 and 1915 respectively, and in 1917 Shena's hopes of having a daughter were realised when Antonia (Tony) Simon was born.[28]

Moving to Manchester meant that Shena never completed her research, but she still remained active in the NUWW and under its auspices she helped to found the Manchester and Salford Women Citizens' Association. While women could not yet vote in general elections, women ratepayers could vote locally, and so she set up the association to enable women to ensure their interests were represented. By establishing a branch of the association in each ward of Manchester and Salford, the association aimed to organise and educate women so they could 'realise the power they possess as voters' and bring their experience to bear upon local government.

5.4 Shena with Roger (1914). Source: SSP M14/4/24.

The association, which inspired similar organisations in other major cities, gathered much support and helped to increase the number of women on the council. A notable victory for Shena and the Women Citizens came when they successfully lobbied the council, with the help of Ernest on its Sanitary Committee, to introduce maternity centres to provide support for new mothers and arrest infant deaths in 1915.[29]

Civic politician

During the course of the First World War, Shena continued to work for the NUWW, and collaborated with C. P. Scott, editor of the *Manchester Guardian* and a friend of the Simon family, to set up scholarships for women at the University of Manchester.[30] Illness in 1919, however, forced Shena into temporary retirement from public work. During her recuperation, she weighed the conflicting demands of being a good mother and pursuing a career in public service. Given their public work, Shena and Ernest were far from being hands-on parents, with governesses doing much of the raising of their children. Their bond with their children was slightly distant and formal. Shena, according to Joan Simon, struggled to form the closest of attachments with them, especially with her sons. Despite looking after three children under six during her recuperation, Shena doubted her ability as a mother and decided that compromising her public ambitions to be always with her children was not necessarily the best for them, given that 'the nursery governess had much more to offer than she had'.[31]

Any doubts Shena harboured about a career as a social reformer had dissipated by November 1921, when she became Lady Mayoress of Manchester for a year. From the outset, Shena was anything but a passive adjunct of her husband. She used her status to advance the position of women in the city within the first days of her term when she publicly refused to deliver Christmas presents at a women's hospital in protest at the fact it had no female senior staff. After her refusal caused a stir in the press, in March the hospital submitted to Shena's protest and appointed two women to its managerial board.[32] In addition to calling upon women to take up public service to practise 'the religion of humanity', Shena also used her platform to proclaim her radical beliefs. On one occasion she lamented that the majority of women were enslaved by the tyrannical demands of housework, and on another she asserted that boys should be free to play with dolls to foster paternal instincts, for raising children was not the sole responsibility of women.[33] Shena's work as Lady Mayoress intensified in February when Ernest developed pneumonia, and she stood in his stead at official engagements until he recovered.[34] In 1921–22, Shena developed what would become her lifelong interest in education and Manchester's schoolchildren, visiting over fifty schools in the space of a year. As she explained, as Lady Mayoress 'you can ask to see anything you want. I wanted to see schools so … I spent a whole year going round looking and asking questions.'[35]

After her term as Lady Mayoress, Shena stood for election to the council as a Liberal in the Chorlton-cum-Hardy ward in 1923. A cornerstone of her campaign was the representation of women's interests. She stressed that far more women were needed on the council. While it dealt with many matters which affected women, from washhouses to nurseries, only three of the 140 councillors were female. Furthermore, she felt that the votes of women were vital in ensuring the welfare of the city's children. 'The maternal instinct had to be harnessed for the good of the community, and electing a married woman with children' would help to realise this.[36] Though her preliminary bid to be elected failed in Chorlton, the following year she was victorious, having stood on a platform again highlighting the lack of women on the council and calling for the building of more schools in Manchester.[37]

In line with her interests in health and education, Shena sat on the council's sanitary and education committees. As one of the small minority of women councillors, Shena was subject to condescending treatment

5.5 Shena during her tenure as Lady Mayoress. Source: SSP M14/4/3.

from older male colleagues. One peculiar anecdote records that during a meeting of the sanitary committee, she had to assess the quality of oats for horses used in waste collection. After she protested that she did not see the point in this,

> the chairman, a silver-haired alderman, ... left his chair and standing behind her said: 'I understand my dear. No doubt you've not had much to do with horses. A lady too. Allow me to show you how to test the oats with you finger and thumb – thus. Now, I'm sure you see, don't you?'[38]

On the council, Shena began her career in education, attempting unsuccessfully at first to reverse cuts to the council's education budget in 1925.[39] In 1928, however, a victory was won when she campaigned with other councillors from across the political divide to abolish the council's ban on married women teachers; a 'simply ridiculous' ordinance which interfered in the personal lives of women and their partners, as Shena complained.[40] While on the Education Committee, Shena established a strong rapport with Manchester's Director of Education, Spurley Hey, with whom she worked to enhance the provision of education in Manchester in the face of major financial constraints during the 1920s.[41] Hey had great respect for Shena's dedication to work in education in Manchester and correctly predicted that she would become the first chairwoman of the Education Committee. Given their closeness and Shena's commitment to education in Manchester, Hey confided to her that she was one of the 'few members who take a keen and intelligent interest in the work of the committee'. He told her he gave her 'more information [about education in Manchester] than all the other members put together'.[42]

Shena's career on the council coincided with a personal ordeal which left deep emotional wounds. Two years into Shena's term, in 1926, her daughter Tony was diagnosed with a rare form of eye cancer. In 1927, an operation was carried out to remove the eye, but it only provided a period of remission. A further operation was performed, and Tony was given radium and lead treatment, but the cancer kept reappearing. It became increasingly clear that the disease was terminal and Tony died in September 1929, just after her twelfth birthday.[43] The loss of Tony left Shena traumatised. Shena had had such high hopes for her daughter that her loss 'seemed to remove all meaning from life'.[44] The pain of Tony's death affected Shena for decades; its enduring nature is revealed in a memoir written by Shena's friend, the sculptor Mitzi Cunliffe. When Mitzi was pregnant in the early 1950s, Shena sent her some infant sweaters she had knitted herself. Her husband Marcus wrote to thank Shena, informing her that their daughter was to be called Antonia. Shena replied remarking,

> how extraordinary that you should have chosen my favourite name for a girl. I had a daughter named Antonia who was everything a feminist could have wished a daughter to be, with beauty and brains. She died horribly at 12 years of age.

When Antonia Cunliffe was born, Mitzi recalled how Shena

> visited me at home as soon as the hospital released us. When she looked at Antonia in her cot, she was moved to tears and embraced me, weeping. Years later I was told by amazed relatives that she had never mentioned her dead daughter, who had slowly died of cancer, to anyone. It was tabu [sic] to refer to her even within the family circle, so shattering was the tragedy.[45]

Following Tony's death, Shena buried herself in work to distract herself from the pain of her bereavement, but would still wake from sleep many years later 'with ghastly realisation'.[46]

Manchester's garden city

In the same year of Tony's diagnosis, Shena and Ernest purchased Wythenshawe Hall and 250 acres of its enveloping parkland and gave it unconditionally to the council to help spur the development of a garden city for Manchester. Much of the housing in Manchester was overcrowded,

5.6 Shena with Roger, Antonia and Brian (c. 1921/1922).

dilapidated and unsanitary and thus Wythenshawe had been selected as a site to rehouse thousands into modern dwellings amidst green surroundings. In the immediate postwar years, Ernest as a councillor had helped lay the initial plans for the building of a garden city south of the Mersey, and now, in 1926, Shena had been appointed to the council's Wythenshawe Estate Special Committee to oversee its development. The council employed Barry Parker, a leading garden city town planner.[47] Shena developed a close working relationship with Parker, as she had with Hey, and indeed, in 1932, Shena would deliver the casting vote on the committee which ensured that Parker's services were retained by the council so Wythenshawe's design would still retain its garden city ethos.[48] A year earlier, in 1931, Shena had ascended to the chair of the committee and aimed to provide good educational provision in Wythenshawe and amenities for social activities.[49] She also helped to cultivate a sense of community amongst Wythenshawe's first pioneer residents. In 1933, she opened the inaugural meeting of the Wythenshawe Residents' Association and the following year presented prizes at the garden city's first flower show.[50] Such was Shena's concern with the new estate, she even took an interest in the minutest of details from the colour of bricks to grass verges. Her work on Wythenshawe, however, led to the loss of her seat.[51] It had become consuming and, having been promoted to the chair of the Education Committee in 1932, Shena felt she had been voted off the council as she could not pay sufficient attention to her own ward in Chorlton.[52] Furthermore, the development of Wythenshawe was met with accusations of economic extravagance on her part.[53]

Alongside her work on the council, Shena sat on the Royal Commission on Licensing in 1929–31. Unwilling to conform to the less radical suggestions of her colleagues, she wrote a minority report of her own which called for the public ownership of pubs to reduce alcohol consumption.[54] From 1926, Shena also engaged in campaigning to reform municipal finance.[55] She campaigned for central government to contribute a significant percentage of local authority funding, rather than just giving a block grant, in order to give councils the confidence to expand the provision of important social services.[56] Her work in municipal finance led to her being appointed in 1938 to a departmental committee to ensure the uniform implementation of the rates across Britain would not 'cause undue hardship'. Dissenting once again from the majority on the committee, she believed that their measures of relief from hardship were insufficient and that the rates would ultimately put a demanding burden on the poor.[57] Radical overhaul was needed, and she argued a municipal income tax should replace the rating system.[58]

In 1934, Shena tried to return to the council, standing as an independent candidate in Wythenshawe. During the campaign she was struck by illness and, despite Ernest campaigning in her stead, she narrowly lost.[59] In 1935, Shena joined the Labour Party, angered by the government's delay in raising the school leaving age; and the following year she was selected to stand in Moston.[60] Moston was not a safe harbour for a Labour candidate, and she was defeated. Although Shena's career as an elected councillor was over, she was shortly afterwards co-opted as a Labour nominee back onto the Education Committee; a position she would hold until 1970.[61]

Making a great nuisance

With her career set firmly on the path of working in education in Manchester, Shena was simultaneously shaping the future of national secondary education in the 1930s. In 1931, she had joined the Consultative Committee of the Board of Education, replacing her friend and WEA colleague, R. H. Tawney, who had recommended her as his successor. As a self-professed 'disciple' of Tawney, Shena received his valuable advice during her tenure. While the committee was not, as Shena wrote, Tawney's 'best milieu', it was Shena's natural habitat and so, armed with her experience of work on Manchester City Council, she began her work

5.7 Shena (c. 1930s). Source: SSP M14/4/3.

on the Consultative Committee which would pave the way for universal secondary education.[62]

At the time of Shena's appointment, education was highly segregated. After the age of eleven, children were taught at senior elementary, technical or grammar schools. These schools were under different codes of regulations which favoured grammars. While children at grammar schools could stay until they were eighteen, most children at senior elementary schools left at fourteen. Under these various codes, grammar school pupils benefited from smaller classes, better-paid teachers and superior amenities. Furthermore, the majority of grammar school places were fee-paying, with a fraction of places available for free.[63] For Shena, this system of education ultimately meant that access to grammar school education was inaccessible for many working-class children whose parents could not afford fees. Even when working-class children won scholarships, insufficient economic means often forced parents to send their children to work rather than to grammar schools. With most children having to leave education at fourteen, Shena was also critical of the loss of regular health checks and exercise for children and 'the sympathetic help of teachers with many problems connected with their physical and emotional development'.

She lamented how upon leaving school most children ended up in 'a factory, workshop or blind alley occupation, often working long hours in bad atmospheres; and into a world where, instead of consideration for the individual being of prime importance, the financial success of the firm has to be the criterion'.[64] To equalise educational provision, 'a common code of regulations for all post-primary schools' was needed; it was, as Joan Simon writes, 'the key to realising secondary school for all'.[65]

In 1933, the Board of Education tasked the Consultative Committee to investigate 'the framework and content' of education for children over eleven, and Shena saw this as an opportunity to push for an equal code for all schools and universal secondary education.[66] However, she had to overcome the ambivalence of the chairman of the Consultative Committee, William Spens, master of Christi Corpus College, Cambridge, towards a single code. Given his astute chairmanship of past committees, combined with his conservative leanings and connections with elite education, Shena feared that the board had placed him as chairman to check any progressive proposals suggested by the committee. Shena even initially fretted that he might try to water down the goal of the committee's 1926 report calling for the raising of the statutory leaving age to fifteen.[67]

Spens' hesitancy became evident in 1935. Despite the committee having decided it was necessary to consider raising the leaving age and creating parity between the different types of schools for children over eleven, Spens backtracked from this position, arguing that the board should decide whether it was in the committee's remit to do so. This caused uproar among his fellow committee members, and the issue was shelved until 1936, when Spens arranged a meeting with the permanent secretary to the Board of Education to discuss to what extent the committee could make proposals regarding a unified post-primary code. Leaping upon this opportunity, Shena swooped in with her allies, Sir Percy Jackson and E. G. Rowlinson, to secure the formation of a sub-committee to consider the question of a single code. With Shena as its chair, the sub-committee assembled the evidence which lay behind the Consultative Committee's final report in 1938 recommending a single code for an equalised provision of secondary education, organised into grammar, secondary modern and technical high schools, all with a leaving age of sixteen.[68] With similar tact, Shena, without the support of allies, singlehandedly wore down Spens's opposition to abolishing fees for grammar schools, too.[69] Through her influence, the final report resultingly called for places in grammar schools to be free or at a reduced fee according to parents' means (with the ultimate aim of making all places available without charge).[70] As she wrote to Virginia Woolf in June 1938, she had made 'a great nuisance' of herself 'on the consultative committee' and won.[71] While the 1938 report of the Consultative Committee was not immediately endorsed by the government, it directly informed

R. A. Butler's momentous 1944 Education Act which introduced universal secondary education and a higher leaving age.[72]

Alongside her work on the Consultative Committee in the 1930s, Shena found the time to combine her love of the past and her attachment to civic government in writing a major book on local government in Manchester since 1838, published in 1938.[73] Outside the committee, Shena established herself as a well-known voice on education in the pages of national newspapers and educational periodicals, calling for greater equality of educational opportunity. In one article, discussing what she would do if made 'educational dictator', she told readers she would not only make all secondary and university education free, but would even 'abolish all

5.8 'If Lady Simon became Educational Dictator'. From *Teachers' World* (31 October 1934). Source: SSP M14/2/3/2.

private schools except those that are carrying out genuine educational experiments'.[74]

Shena's campaigning for greater equality in education was bolstered by a 1936 trip to study education in Moscow. Her investigations revealed to her that the Soviet Union had realised 'complete equality of opportunity'. Unlike in Britain, where many children began work at fourteen, she observed how in the Soviet Union there was free education from eight to university age, with adolescents only allowed to work limited hours from sixteen. Despite the great strides it had made, however, Shena was critical of the Soviet educational system. For while there was equal educational opportunity, the object of education in the USSR was at odds with individual freedom. Shena asserted that while in Britain the aim of education was to develop children's potential as individuals, in the Soviet Union the tight control of the curriculum and information alongside ubiquitous propaganda moulded children into the 'instruments' of 'the rulers of the U.S.S.R.'.[75]

The Children in War-Time

In 1938, with a war with Nazi Germany looking increasingly likely, Shena began training as an air raid warden. Angered at appeasement and Nazi oppression of women, Shena wrote that if 'standing up to Hitler risked war … it was only logical for me to be ready to take my part in it'. Her training, however, instilled a fear of what air attacks could unleash:

> I must admit that during those days before Munich when I was feverishly fitting gas masks on children I found myself wondering whether it would not be better to let Hitler take Czechoslovakia than have children all over Europe gassed.[76]

Written in 1940, Shena's admission was in a letter to her friend Virginia Woolf. Shena's and Woolf's relationship had begun when Woolf refused an honorary degree from the University of Manchester in 1933, something Shena, as an admirer of her work and member of the university's council, was keen for her to have. Nevertheless, in her letter of refusal an invitation was extended by Woolf to Shena to visit her in London, which was accepted. For Shena the invitation represented, as she wrote in her reply to Woolf, 'a reward' for the 'severe self-restraint which prevented my writing to you like any enthusiastic school girl, when "A Room of One's Own" appeared'.[77] Meeting about twice a year after their first encounter, they became close friends. In addition to corresponding regularly with each other, Shena would travel to Virginia's home in Bloomsbury where they exchanged ideas and sought to learn from the other's experiences. 'Every time I saw her,' Shena wrote, 'I came away feeling stimulated and exhilarated. She made me look at problems from a new angle – even those pertaining to the relations of men and women which I thought I had studied thoroughly.'[78] Likewise, Woolf 'had a particular affection for' Shena and sought to absorb Shena's knowledge and 'imbed' her ideas in what she wrote.[79]

Woolf's writings were a fount of inspiration for Shena; she even carried a copy of *A Room's One's Own* with her everywhere she went. Woolf's work bolstered her determination to campaign for reform and unashamedly advocate her own beliefs.[80] Years later, it is fascinating to deduce from research by Peter H. King that, unbeknownst to either Shena or Woolf, they were relatives. Both were descended from a Scottish smuggler, James Stephen, born in 1670, the 3× great-grandfather of Woolf's father, Sir Leslie Stephen.[81] Their friendship was thus complemented by distant cousinhood. Woolf's suicide in 1941 was saddening for Shena. 'Knowing Virginia,' she wrote to Woolf's widower, Leonard, was 'one of the best things that has ever happened to me.' 'Her death,' Shena added, was 'the worst fatality of the war.'[82] She wrote a eulogy of her and her work, concluding her piece with Woolf's belief that war and exploitation could only be brought to an end by the inculcation of feminine virtues in men.[83]

With the onset of the Second World War, the fears Shena had conveyed to Woolf about the danger air raids posed to children were at the forefront of her mind. At the beginning of the conflict, compulsory education was suspended, with hundreds of schools closed in areas susceptible to bombing. While numerous children had been evacuated, many had never left or were returning from evacuation, with the result that nearly a million children remained in Britain's cities. For Shena, the situation was intolerable. Touring Manchester to survey the state of education, she summed up the problem in a letter to the *Manchester Guardian*:

> Compulsory education has vanished ... Clearly this cannot be allowed to go on. Children are losing precious months of an already far too short educational career, and they are drifting back to a city which is not yet adequately provided against air raids.[84]

Notwithstanding the peril of air raids, Shena was also concerned that without compulsory education, children's welfare was being jeopardised. In a pamphlet published by the WEA entitled *The Children in War-Time* (1939), Shena outlined how, without education, many children were 'running wild' and others as young as twelve were in work. They were missing out on the provision of milk and on medical inspections which were vital to ensuring the health of many children. Furthermore, Shena complained that the Board of Education were hastily reopening some schools without sufficient protection against bombing raids. To redress these issues, Shena outlined in the pamphlet how the educational system could be rebuilt. In addition to calling on the Board to survey and requisition more buildings to allow more children to be evacuated, she argued for the urgent reintroduction of compulsory education, along with the raising of the leaving age to fifteen, which had been agreed but deferred, and the setting of a firm date for further evacuation.⁸⁵ Shena's pamphlet proved an influential intervention, and the board announced soon afterwards the partial reintroduction of compulsory education for April 1940 and greater air-raid protection for schools.⁸⁶

Three Schools or One?

During the war years, Shena worked as a housing officer for the Ministry of Aircraft Production in the North West, organising the billeting of workers who were manufacturing warplanes.⁸⁷ In late 1942, Shena took a break from this work when she and Ernest travelled to America on the invitation of the Ministry of Information to undertake a lecturing tour there to improve ties with Britain's ally. Speaking on British local government and education, Shena took the opportunity to study the school system in the US.⁸⁸ In America, she examined the system of comprehensive education in which all secondary school age children in the locality were taught together in one school. Impressed by the American spirit of equality of

5.9 Shena with her grandson Alan and her daughter-in-law Joan (1943). Source: SSP M14/4/3.

opportunity in education, she praised the American system for extending free secondary education to a far higher proportion of children than in Britain. She noted how as a result class distinctions were far less marked than in Britain. Shena, however, still believed that a tripartite system of specialised schools would get more from each child's aptitudes than the American comprehensive model.[89]

Having campaigned successfully for an equalised tripartite system during her tenure on the Consultative Committee, Shena mostly welcomed Butler's 1944 Education Act and was pleased to see Mancunian Ellen Wilkinson take over the Ministry of Education following Labour's 1945 electoral victory.[90] In line with the act's professed aim of ensuring parity of esteem for schools of different types, Shena was anxious that schools in Manchester were brought up to equal standard – with proper basic amenities such as hot water, playing fields and a separate dining room – as rapidly as possible.[91] For Shena, the act most of all symbolised a real step towards equality of educational opportunity:

> Instead of the present competition, and the narrow gate through which all children now have to struggle, there will be no gate, but a broad highway with three turnings, and children will be put along the turning which everybody thinks will be best for them.[92]

By 1948, however, Shena had come to see the three-way division of secondary education as flawed. Making her case in her book *Three Schools or One?* (1948), she called for its replacement with comprehensive schooling. Shena argued that grammar schools still benefited the well-off. While fees had been abolished, working-class children who were eligible to attend a grammar school could often not do so because their families had limited means; and therefore they would likely be sent to a Secondary Modern instead, where they would leave school at fifteen to work due to the necessity of having to earn. On the other hand, middle-class children faced no such difficulties, with their more affluent parents able to keep them in education up to eighteen.[93] Secondly, and crucially, Shena had come to realise that children could not be simply categorised into three types 'corresponding with three types of schools'. Individual children had varying aptitudes and interests, many of which they developed after they had been selected at eleven to go into a specific school. In making her argument, Shena considered her own educational development. Shining at history from a young age, she also developed a keen interest in economics, but at the same time she was not one for mathematics, English literature or French. The answer to creating an educational system which allowed children to be taught according to their aptitudes, therefore, was to teach all children together in one school and to place them in different sets for each subject, so that they could be taught alongside others who had similar capabilities. The additional benefit of teaching children together would be to redress 'the bitter

5.10 The cover of Three Schools or One? (1948). From Lady Simon of Wythenshawe, *Three Schools or One? Secondary Education in England, Scotland, and the U.S.A.* (London: Fredrick Muller Ltd, 1948).

class division' post-primary education had augmented in Britain. It would help instead to build a society, like the one she had witnessed in America, which was more democratic and in line with the spirit of postwar reform. Comprehensives would help to build the new Jerusalem.[94]

Final decades

In 1947, Ernest was ennobled as a Labour peer; and so he and Shena became Lord and Lady Simon of Wythenshawe, a title which celebrated the garden city they had both helped to create. In the same year, Ernest was also appointed chairman of the BBC, and he and Shena therefore spent much of their time during the early postwar years in London. At their flat at Marsham Court, they hosted social gatherings to learn more about the corporation and foster ties with its senior administrators. As the director-general of the BBC during Ernest's tenure, William Haley, recalled:

> The small parties in the Marsham Court flat became famous inside the Corporation; two of them sometimes going on simultaneously on different sides of the curtain, with Lord Simon of Wythenshawe eagerly canvassing some point with men producers in one room and Lady Simon of Wythenshawe getting the women producers to be equally frank and forthright in the other.[95]

Shena herself was unremittingly forthright as ever in her public work and was still an active campaigner as her eighth decade approached in the 1950s. Shena continued to press for equal educational opportunity. Berating the 'two nations in school', she criticised how richer parents could send their children who did not win a place in a grammar school to private schools, which did not suffer from overcrowding and unsanitary buildings. To overcome this division in society, she called for local authorities to do more to improve educational provision and for private schools to be taxed out of existence. Comprehensive schooling, however, was the crucial keystone to creating 'a real democratic system giving equal opportunity for all our children'.[96]

Shena's deep passion for comprehensive schooling was captured in a heated debate in 1951 with Dr Eric James, high master of Manchester Grammar School, at the Manchester Literary and Philosophical Society. The debate was based on James' book *Education and Leadership* (1951) and concerned how Britain's future politicians were to be educated. James believed that grammar school children should form the intelligent elite who would govern over society, an idea, as Shena made clear in the debate, she considered anathema:

> He thinks that education can produce leaders … select them on high intelligence basis and send them to grammar schools – and there you will have your future leaders … He has great contempt for the masses of people and thinks they can't really have much in the way of taste or morals

Shena, in contrast, argued that every child had to have 'an equal chance in education', adding that while 'Dr James despises the masses' it was ultimately 'the masses who settle who our leaders are going to be!' In his rebuttal, James argued that Shena's 'common culture' approach was wrong and, in contrast, asserted that some people were inherently intelligent and others were not: 'some people like to read Proust, others the Sunday Pictorial'. For James, leadership in the future would be grounded on 'high intelligence', so children who possessed the 'pre-requisite of intelligence' could 'break into the charmed circle of old Etonians and political power'. Future working-class politicians in the mould of the late Ernest Bevin and Shena's WEA colleague George Tomlinson, who had managed to rise to office through merit, having received little education, would now 'go to the grammar school', an assertion which was met by Shena exclaiming 'No!'[97] Shena's campaigning for comprehensive education finally started to bear fruit when, in 1956, the Manchester Education Committee, after much wrangling with the Ministry of Education, oversaw the opening of Manchester's first comprehensive, Yew Tree School, in Wythenshawe.[98] A decade later, Shena was actively involved in preparing for the transition to introduce comprehensive education in the city from 1965 to 1967.[99]

Shena's position as a leading progressive educationist saw her invited to the USSR in 1955 to once again investigate education there. Reporting on her visit, she was struck by the expansion of education and the regard citizens felt for education, albeit 'the result of continuous propaganda'. Her findings led her to believe that the Soviet Union would soon 'have the most highly educated population in the world'.[100] In light of this, Shena believed education was just as important as defence in the context of the Cold War, as developing nations would soon start to see 'knowledge' as 'indistinguishable from Communism'. The trip confirmed to her once again 'that equal educational opportunity' was 'more nearly achieved in the Soviet Union than elsewhere' and she was pleased to see that many girls studied science and engineering. Shena was also intrigued by the state's provision of leisure activities and extracurricular education through the Young Pioneers. While far from condoning the state's overbearing control over children's lives, it led her to ponder if more could done to afford children in Britain 'much more stimulating and worthwhile occupations for their leisure time'.[101]

In 1960, Ernest died following a stroke. With Ernest gone, Shena deliberated whether to return to London to be nearer to friends and family or to stay in Manchester and continue pressing for better educational provision there. Opting for the latter, she departed Broomcroft, making room for Simon fellows, academics sponsored by Ernest's endowment, and moved into a slightly smaller house a few yards opposite with the same name.[102]

The 1960s saw a flood of honours for Shena in recognition of her and her late husband's work. In 1961, she laid the foundation stone for

5.11 Shena at the laying of the foundation stone at Wythenshawe civic centre (1969). Source: private family papers.

the new Simon Engineering Laboratories at the University of Manchester (now the Simon Building).[103] In the same year, she also opened Simon Court, a municipal multistorey block of flats in Wythenshawe for older people.[104] Still taking much interest in Wythenshawe's inhabitants, she became the honorary chairman of the court's residents' association and, in 1969, she was pleased to witness the laying of the foundation stone for Wythenshawe's long-awaited civic centre.[105] In 1965, she was awarded an honorary fellowship by the LSE, an institution which had proved formative in forging her career as a social reformer, and in 1966, following her retirement from the Council of the University of Manchester, she received an honorary degree from the university. These awards were complemented by the conferring of the Freedom of the City of Manchester upon Shena in 1964. Only the third woman to enjoy the honour, she took the opportunity in her acceptance speech to advocate her feminist ideas by highlighting the 'wastage … in not developing the resources of women power'. She criticised how, in Britain, there remained a stubborn belief that women should still not go out to work and that there were inadequate provisions to enable them to do so. Furthermore, she called on women, especially teachers, who had received a grant while in higher education, not to give up working when they had a family, for in her eyes they owed the community for their training. She also used her speech to praise the hard work of teachers in Manchester. Shena spoke of how, when she was frustrated on the council, she would visit schools in the city, and her witnessing of how well-run and cheerful the classrooms were would spur her to continue her work.[106]

In 1970, Shena retired from public work. Ending her decades of service on the Manchester Education Committee, she was interviewed by a journalist from *The Times Educational Supplement*. Surprised by her eagerness not to reminisce but to look to the future, he noted Shena's combination of 'Edwardian style with a most modern and enquiring mind'. Retirement allowed her to indulge in her favourite pastimes. Owning a full collection of Agatha Christie's works, she delved into reading detective novels. She frequented the cinema and also watched Coronation Street as it provided her, with her privileged position, an insight into the lives of ordinary people in Manchester.[107] Two years after retirement, she died in July 1972 at the age of eighty-eight.[108]

Conclusion

Shena Simon was resolute and meticulous in her work in social reform. Her reluctance to compromise on what she thought was right often placed her in a minority position, and her focus on the tiniest details could, as in the case of Wythenshawe, hurt her career. Simultaneously, her integrity, proficiency in handling great amounts of information and political shrewdness enabled her to forward reforms which improved the lives and opportunities of people in Manchester and Britain.

Shena's main contribution to society was in equalising and expanding educational provision. Her devotion to reforming education originated out of her great interest in Manchester's children, something that grew following the loss of her daughter.[109] Inspired by schooling in America and the USSR, the driving force behind her work in reforming education was to equalise opportunity so that each child could benefit from an education suited to their aptitudes in order to realise their potential. Her efforts to tackle historic educational disparities, however, still resonate with contemporary challenges to inequalities in educational opportunity. Alongside education, feminism was an intrinsic component of Shena's life. Given the Simons' reliance on domestic servants, Shena was never in a position to fully comprehend the challenges most women face in pursuing a career and raising children, but her ideas about the family and women's position in society are still pertinent today. From adolescence to old age, Shena challenged customary thinking that women should largely lead lives of domesticity, and instead believed that their interests and that

5.12 Shena (c. 1960s). Source: SSP M14/4/15.

of the community could only be properly realised if women had an equal sway over public affairs. Shena's influence and radical ideas, alongside her intellectual exchange with Virginia Woolf, demonstrate her intellect and significance as a feminist, and she is more deserving than the scant attention given to her in past histories of women in social reform and politics in twentieth-century Britain.[110]

While much of Shena's career involved bureaucratic work and took place behind the doors of committee rooms, her efforts were underscored by a real concern for ordinary people, especially those in Manchester. She cared deeply for the welfare of the city's mothers and infants and wanted its women to take their place as equal citizens. She took pride in the residents of Wythenshawe, and was inspired by the city's teachers and pupils. She was a Simon of Manchester.

Notes

1 We would like to thank Charlotte Wildman for her helpful comments when we composed this chapter.

2 SSP M14/4/21, Shena Simon to Virginia Woolf, 12 June 1938. The letters referenced in this chapter between Shena and Virginia and Leonard Woolf are copies of the originals which are held at the University of Sussex in the Monks House Papers.
3 'Lady Simon Unfailing Friendship', *The Times* (5 August 1972), p. 14.
4 Jane Martin, 'Shena Simon (1883–1972) and the "Religion of Humanity"', in Jane Martin and Joyce Goodman, *Women and Education, 1800–1980* (Basingstoke: Palgrave, 2004), pp. 118–40.
5 Hsiao-Yuh Ku, *Education for Democracy in England in World War II* (Abingdon: Routledge, 2020), pp. 113–33.
6 Marian A. Horrocks, The Contribution to Education and Society of Lady Simon of Wythenshawe (1912–1972) (Unpublished MPhil dissertation, University of Manchester, 1990); Joan Simon, *Shena Simon Feminist and Educationist* (privately printed: 1986) [copy held by the University of Manchester Main Library]; Joan Simon, 'The Shaping of the Spens Report on Secondary Education 1933–1938: An Inside View: Part I', *British Journal of Educational Studies*, 25:1 (1977); Joan Simon, 'The Shaping of the Spens Report on Secondary Education 1933–1938: An Inside View: Part II', *British Journal of Educational Studies*, 25:2 (1977), 170–85.
7 'Lady Simon a Leading Educationist', *The Times* (18 July 1972), p. 14.
8 Simon, *Shena Simon*, Chapter (henceforth Ch.) I, p. 2; 'Deaths', *The Times* (5 July 1946), p. 1.; 'Obituary. Mr. John Wilson Potter', *The Times* (24 August 1933), p. 12; 'Mr. J. Wilson Potter', *The Times* (25 August 1933), p. 12; 'Death of Geo. Thompson of Pitmedden', *Aberdeen Journal* (12 April 1895), p. 5; Peter H. King, *The Aberdeen Line: George Thompson Jnr's Incomparable Shipping Enterprise* (Stroud: The History Press, 2017), pp. 11, 87–93, 223.
9 Simon, *Shena Simon*, Ch. I, pp. 2–3, Ch. II, pp. 6, 11–12; Lady Simon of Wythenshawe, *Three Schools or One? Secondary Education in England, Scotland, and the U.S.A.* (London: Fredrick Muller Ltd, 1948), p. 87; Horrocks, *The Contribution to Education and Society of Lady Simon of Wythenshawe*, p. 25.
10 Lady Simon of Wythenshawe, *Three Schools or One?*, p. 87; Simon, *Shena Simon*, Ch. I, pp. 5, 8.
11 Janet Beveridge, *An Epic of Clare Market: Birth and Early Days of the London School of Economics* (London: G. Bell & Sons, 1960), p. 75.
12 Diana Hopkinson, *Family Inheritance: A Life of Eva Hubback* (London: Staples Press, 1954), pp. 42–5.
13 Simon, *Shena Simon*, Ch. I, pp. 13–15.
14 Beveridge, *An Epic of Clare Market*, pp. 75–6.
15 SSP M14/4/21, Shena Simon to Leonard Woolf, 8 June 1964; Simon, *Shena Simon*, Ch. II, p. 2.
16 Simon to Leonard Woolf, 8 June 1964.
17 Beveridge, *An Epic of Clare Market*, p. 75.
18 Simon, *Shena Simon*, Ch. I, pp. 19–21; 'Women Workers and the Insurance Act', *Manchester Guardian* (3 October 1912), p. 5; 'Advantages of Joining a Society', *The Times* (27 June 1912), p. 10.
19 'The Interests of Women', *The Times* (12 October 1911), p. 6.
20 Simon, *Shena Simon*, Ch. I, pp. 30, 34.
21 Shena D. Simon, 'Virginia Woolf', *The Women Citizen* (June 1941), pp. 2–3.
22 Simon to Virginia Woolf, 12 June 1938; Simon, *Shena Simon*, Ch. II, pp. 24–5.
23 Hopkinson, *Family Inheritance*, p. 70; ESD, 20 July 1912.
24 Simon, *Shena Simon*, Ch. I p. 2, Ch. II p. 1a; SSP M14/4/2, Letter from Shena Simon to Eva Hubback, 1911.
25 Simon, *Shena Simon*, Ch. I pp. 32, 35; ESD, 20 July 1912.
26 ESD, 26 December 1912.
27 Simon, *Shena Simon*, Ch. II, pp. 18–19.

28 ESD, 13 October 1915, 11 December, 1915, 26 March 1915, 21 August 1917.
29 Beveridge, *An Epic of Clare Market*, p. 75; Shena Simon, 'Women Citizens Associations – II'. *Common Cause* (14 July 1916); ESD, 5 June 1916.
30 'Scholarships for Women', *Manchester Guardian* (8 February 1919), p. 6.
31 Simon, *Shena Simon*, Ch. II, pp. 29a-30, 45–6. Gary McCulloch, Antonio F. Canales and Hsiao-Yuh Ku, *Brian Simon and the Struggle for Education* (London: UCL Press, 2023), p. 9; private family information.
32 SSP M14/6/5, 'Women and Hospital Management', *Manchester Guardian* (26 November 1921); 'Women and Hospital Management', *Manchester Guardian* (15 March 1922), p. 9.
33 SSP M14/6/7, 'Slaves of the Home', *News Chronicle* (30 July 1922); SSP M14/6/5, newspaper clipping: 'Give Dolls to the Boys' (8 December 1921).
34 Mary Stocks, *Ernest Simon of Manchester* (Manchester: Manchester University Press, 1963), pp. 66–7.
35 SSP M14/7/13, Mabel Tylecote, *The Work of Lady Simon of Wythenshawe for Education in Manchester*, 28 November 1974, p. 3.
36 SSP M14/6/9, Shena D. Simon 'To the Electors of Chorlton-cum-Hardy', 1 November 1923; SSP M14/6/9, Mrs E. D. Simon, 'Call to Married Women', *Daily Dispatch* (26 October 1923).
37 'Municipal Election Results', *Manchester Guardian* (2 November 1923), p. 14; SSP M14/6/9, Shena D. Simon, 'To the Electors of Chorlton-cum-Hardy', 10 October 1924; 'Municipal Election Results', *Manchester Guardian* (3 November 1924), p. 10.
38 SSP M14/2/1/2, 'Brian Jackson Writes'.
39 'The Manchester Education Estimates', *Manchester Guardian* (25 May 1925), p. 14.
40 'The Dismissal of Women Teachers', *Manchester Guardian* (9 February 1928), p. 20; 'Manchester City Council Scenes', *Manchester Guardian* (8 March 1928), p. 13.
41 A. B. Robertson, 'Hey, Spurley', in *Oxford Dictionary of National Biography*.
42 SSP M14/4/2, Spurley Hey to Shena Simon, 9 February 1927; SSP M14/4/2, Spurley Hey to Shena Simon, 9 August 1928.
43 Stocks, *Ernest Simon of Manchester*, pp. 81–2; ESD, 23 October 1928.
44 Simon, *Shena Simon*, Introduction, p. 11.
45 UOMVCA/7/234 folder 4, Mitzi Cunliffe, 'To Shena Simon with Love: A Personal Souvenir', 31 August 1972.
46 Simon, *Shena Simon*, Introduction, p. 12.
47 Stocks, *Ernest Simon of Manchester*, pp. 100–1; Sir Ernest and Lady Simon, 'Wythenshawe', in E. D. Simon and J. Inman, *The Rebuilding of Manchester* (London: Longmans Green & Co, 1935), pp. 36–8, 42.
48 SSP M14/1/2a, Shena Simon to Barry Parker, 8 March 1934; SSP M14/1/2a, Barry Parker to Shena Simon, 9 March 1934.
49 ESD, 2 April 1932; Horrocks, 'The Contribution to Education and Society of Lady Simon of Wythenshawe', pp. 380–2.
50 SSP M14/1/7, 'Wythenshawe Residents Association', *Wythenshawe Gazette and Weekly News* (15 September 1933); 'City Flower Shows', *Manchester Guardian* 20 August 1934, p. 6.
51 Horrocks, 'The Contribution to Education and Society of Lady Simon of Wythenshawe', pp. 382–4.
52 ESD, 2 April 1932; SSP M14/6/10, election leaflet by Shena Simon, 'Lady Simon the Independent Candidate'.
53 'Anti-Waste Wins', *Daily Mail* (4 November 1933), p. 10.
54 Simon, *Shena Simon*, Introduction, p. 7, 'The Drink Report', *New Statesman and Nation* (9 January 1932), p. 32.
55 For a more detailed discussion of this aspect of Shena's work, see Chapter 7 in this volume by Charlotte Wildman.

56 SSP M14/3/2/1, *Rates and the Householder: A Criticism of the Government's Rating Proposals* (revised edition), November 1928, p. 5.
57 Report to the Minister of Health by the Departmental Committee on Valuation for Rates 1939 (London: HMSO, 1944), pp. 1, 4, 36–8.
58 Lady (Shena) Simon, 'Paying the Piper: The Case for a Municipal Income-Tax', *Local Government Service* 21:12 (1941), pp. 272–3.
59 'Lady Simon's Campaign in Wythenshawe', *Manchester Guardian* (16 October 1934), p. 15; 'The Elections', *Manchester Guardian* (2 November 1934), p. 8.
60 'Lady (Ernest) Simon', *Manchester Guardian* (7 April 1936), p. 15.
61 Tylecote, *The Work of Lady Simon of Wythenshawe For Education in Manchester*, pp. 3–4.
62 Simon, 'The Shaping of the Spens Report on Secondary Education 1933–1938: An Inside View: Part I', 64–5; SSP M14/2/3/7, Speech by Shena Simon, 'Tawney's half-century', 1 February 1962, pp. 1–2.
63 Simon, 'The Shaping of the Spens Report on Secondary Education 1933–1938: An Inside View: Part I', 66–7; Simon, *Three Schools or One?*, p. 15.
64 SSP, M14/2/3/4, Shena D. Simon, *The School Leaving Age and Day Continuation Schools* (London: Workers Educational Association: 1940), pp. 4–5.
65 Simon, 'The Shaping of the Spens Report on Secondary Education 1933–1938: An Inside View: Part I', 64.
66 *Report of the Consultative Committee of Secondary Education* (London: HMSO, 1939), p. iv.
67 Martin and Goodman, *Women and Education*, pp. 131, 133.
68 Simon, 'The Shaping of the Spens Report on Secondary Education 1933–1938': An Inside View: Part I', 71–4, 77–8; *Report of the Consultative Committee of Secondary Education*, pp. 311–315.
69 Simon, 'The Shaping of the Spens Report on Secondary Education 1933–1938: An Inside View: Part II', 171–3.
70 *Report of the Consultative Committee of Secondary Education*, pp. 306, 308–10.
71 Simon to Virginia Woolf, 12 June 1938.
72 Simon, 'The Shaping of the Spens Report on Secondary Education 1933–1938: An Inside View: Part II, 179.
73 Shena D. Simon, *A Century of City Government, Manchester 1838–1938* (London: George Allen & Unwin Ltd, 1938).
74 SSP M14/2/3/2, 'If Lady Simon became Educational Dictator', *Teachers' World* (31 October 1934), p. 163.
75 Lady Simon, 'Education', in Sir E. D. Simon, Lady Simon, W. A. Robson and J. Jewkes, *Moscow in the Making* (London: Longmans Green and Co., 1937), pp. 95, 124–9, 139, 141.
76 SSP M14/4/21, Shena Simon to Virginia Woolf, 8 January 1940.
77 SSP M14/4/21, Virginia Woolf to Shena Simon, 25 March 1933; SSP M14/4/21, Shena Simon to Virginia Woolf, 29 March 1933.
78 SSP M14/4/21, Shena Simon to Virginia Woolf, 5 July 1938; SSP M14/4/21, Shena Simon to Leonard Woolf, 5 April 1941.
79 SSP M14/4/21, Leonard Woolf to Shena Simon, 22 April 1941; SSP M14/4/21, Virginia Woolf to Shena Simon, 16 December 1939; SSP M14/4/21, Virginia Woolf to Shena Simon, 22 January 1940.
80 SSP M14/4/21, Simon to Leonard Woolf, 5 April 1941; Simon to Virginia Woolf, 12 June 1938.
81 King, *The Aberdeen Line*, pp. 13, 223.
82 Simon to Leonard Woolf, 5 April 1941.
83 Simon, 'Virginia Woolf', pp. 2–3.
84 Shena D. Simon, 'The Evacuation Problem', *Manchester Guardian* (1 November 1939), p. 6.

85 SSP M14/2/3/3, Shena D. Simon, *The Children in War-Time: How to Rebuild the Educational System* (London: Workers Educational Association, 1939).
86 SSP M14/4/2, Ernest Green to Shena Simon (23 February 1940); 'Early Return to Compulsory Education', *Manchester Guardian* (8 February 1940), p. 3.
87 SSP M14/4/21, note by Joan Simon, p. 7.
88 Stocks, *Ernest Simon of Manchester*, p. 118.
89 SSP M14/2/3/4, Shena D. Simon, *Impressions of American High School Education* (1943), pp. 2–7, 11–12, 17–21, 24–5, 30.
90 Lady Simon, 'The Way Ahead in Education', *The Highway* (October 1945), pp. 7–8.
91 SSP M14/2/3/5, Lady (Shena) Simon and Edgar Gates, 'Clean Slate for Our Schools', *Manchester Evening News* (30 July 1946).
92 'Lady Simon on the Act', *Education* (6 October 1944), 392.
93 Simon, *Three Schools or One?*, p. 53.
94 Simon, *Three Schools or One?*, pp. 85–95.
95 Sir William Haley, 'Chairman of the B.B.C. 1947–1952', in *80th Birthday Book for Ernest Darwin Simon, Lord Simon of Wythenshawe, b. 9th October 1879* (Cheadle Heath: The Cloister Press, 1959), p. 53.
96 Shena D. Simon, 'Two Nations in School', *New Statesman and Nation* (19 March 1955), pp. 377–8.
97 'How Can Britain Breed Leaders?', *News Chronicle* (20 December 1951), p. 3.
98 'School's Future Undecided' *Manchester Guardian* (22 November 1955), p. 14; 'School to Become Comprehensive', *Manchester Guardian* (10 April 1956), p. 1.
99 Horrocks, 'The Contribution to Education and Society of Lady Simon of Wythenshawe', pp. 182–94.
100 Shena D. Simon, 'Education in the Soviet Union 1936 & 1955', *Anglo-Soviet Journal*, 21:3 (1955), 2; Lady Simon of Wythenshawe, 'Education in the Soviet Union', *Fabian International Review* (May 1956), 11, 13.
101 Lady Simon of Wythenshawe, 'The Soviet Scene', *Education* (8 July 1955), 81; Lady Simon of Wythenshawe, 'Education in the Soviet Union', 12.
102 Simon, *Shena Simon*, 'Introduction', pp. 22–3. For information about the Simon Fellowship, see: Chapter 9 in this volume by H. S. Jones and Chris Godden.
103 SSP M14/7/11, 'Laying of Commemorative Stone naming the Simon Engineering Laboratories'.
104 'Simon Court "Launched"', *Guardian* (5 May 1961), p. 26.
105 SSP M14/4/10, Shena Simon to G. E. Stearns, 3 August 1961; Tylecote, 'The Work of Lady Simon of Wythenshawe For Education in Manchester', p. 11.
106 SSP M14/4/15, Speech by Lady Simon of Wythenshawe on the Occasion of the Freedom of the City of Manchester 14th April 1964, pp. 2–3, 11–13.
107 SSP M14/2/3/7, Paul Medlicott, 'An 87-year old radical', *The Times Educational Supplement* (10 July 1970). SSP M14/2/3/7, 'Lady Simon, 80, Looks to the Future', *Daily Telegraph* (15 April 1970). Private family information.
108 'Lady Simon of Wythenshawe', *Guardian* (18 July 1972), p. 5.
109 Simon, *Shena Simon*, Introduction, p. 12.
110 There is no mention of Shena in: Martin Pugh, *Women and the Women's Movement in Britain, 1914–1959* (Basingstoke: Palgrave Macmillan, 2000); Barbara Caine, *English Feminism 1780–1980* (Oxford: Oxford University Press, 1997) or Johanna Alberti, *Beyond Suffrage, Feminists in War and Peace, 1914–28* (Basingstoke: Macmillan, 1989). Shena is only very briefly mentioned as a friend of Eva Hubback in Brian Harrison, *Prudent Revolutionaries: Portraits of British Feminists between the Wars* (Oxford: Clarendon Press, 1987), pp. 284–5, and in Pat Thane, 'Women, Liberalism and Citizenship', in Eugenio Biagini (ed.), *Citizenship and Community. Liberals, Radicals and Collective Identities in the British Isles, 1865–1931* (Cambridge: Cambridge University Press, 1996), p. 72. In contrast, see Chapter 7 in this volume by Charlotte Wildman on Shena's work in municipal politics and reform.

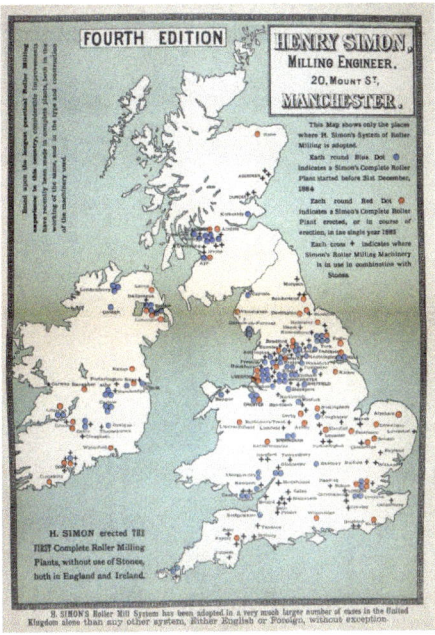

Plate 1 Henry Simon Ltd marketing map (1886). Source: Source: JRL SEGA/1. Copyright the University of Manchester (CC BY-NC-SA 4.0).

Plate 2 Henry Simon Ltd marketing map (1892). Source: Martin Dodge.

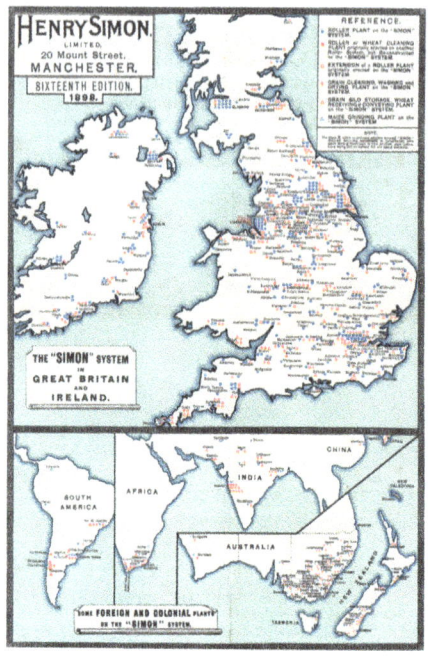

Plate 3 Henry Simon Ltd marketing map (1896). Source: Martin Dodge.

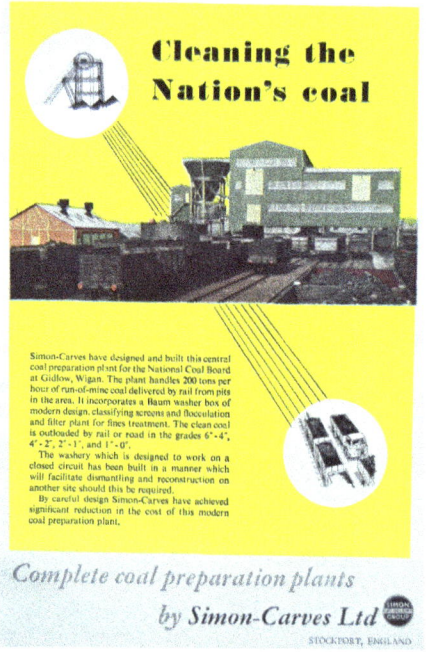

Plate 4 Simon Carves advert promoting their work designing and building new colliery plants for the NCB (1950s). Source: Martin Dodge.

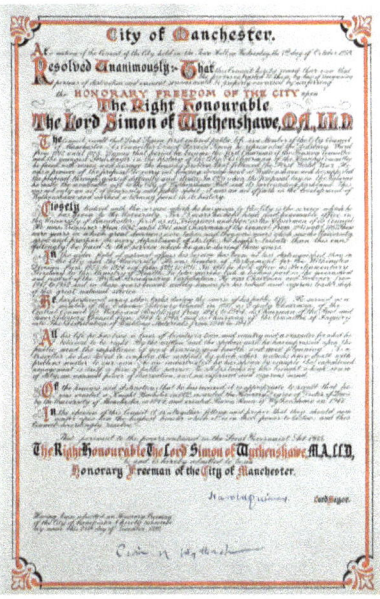

Plate 5 Certificate bestowing Ernest Simon the Freedom of the City of Manchester (1959). Source: MCL M797/2/1.

Plate 6 Map of Manchester in 1935 from *The Rebuilding of Manchester* (1935). Source: Ernest Simon and J. Inman, *The Rebuilding of Manchester* (London: Longmans, Green and Co., 1935).

Plate 7 Portrait of Henry Simon by Clara Von Rappard. Courtesy of Margaret Simon.

Plate 8 Portrait of Ernest Simon by Thomas Cantrell Dugdale (1944/45). Courtesy of Margaret Simon.

Plate 9 Emily Simon. Source: SSP M14/4/24.

Plate 10 Shena Simon (*c.* 1920). Courtesy of Margaret Simon.

Plate 11 Ernest, Joan, Shena, and Alan and Martin Simon at Broomcroft (1958). Source: SSP M14/4/3.

Plate 12 The stained-glass window at Lawnhurst with the word 'Maitri'. Photo by Janet Wolff.

Plate 13 The plaque at Wythenshawe Hall commemorating Ernest and Shena's purchase and gifting of the Hall and park to Manchester. Photo by John Ayshford.

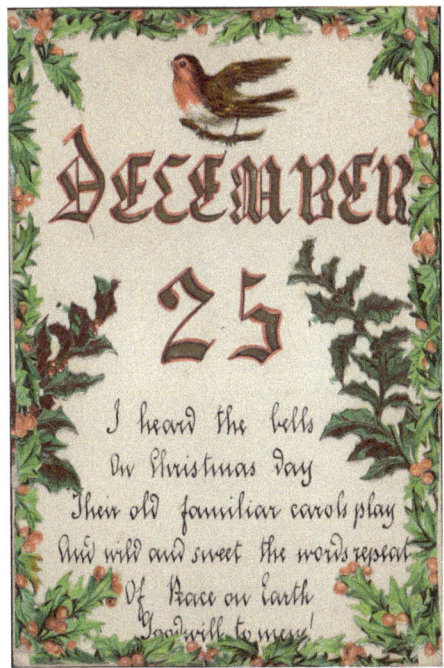

Plate 14 Card from the Simon Calendar (c. 1890). Source JRL HSC Temp/1. Copyright the University of Manchester (CC BY-NC-SA 4.0).

Plate 15 Lawnhurst (2023). Photo by John Ayshford.

PART II
The Simons' contribution to society

6

Busy making good money: the development of the Simon engineering businesses

Martin Dodge

My father, Henry Simon, introduced into Britain two new industrial processes of considerable importance. Starting without capital or influence he built the first complete roller flour milling plant in Britain in 1878 and the first by-product coke oven installation in 1881. He died in 1899. By that time flour milling had been revolutionised; practically all the millstones had disappeared, and the great bulk of British flour mills were working on the Simon system, which my father had also introduced widely into a dozen other countries. The revolution in coke ovens had not gone so far, but progress had been made and Simon-Carves Ltd had become the leading British firm in by-product coke oven contracting.[1]

Introduction

The building of his two engineering businesses from scratch was at the heart of Henry Simon's life in Manchester; and the successful expansion and diversification of the family firms over five decades by Ernest Simon was a central underpinning of his considerable public work. The businesses proudly carried the 'Simon' name into the wider world, while the day-to-day work of running the companies would have been an ever-present part of family life. The growing personal income the businesses generated from the later 1880s onwards supported an increasingly comfortable upper middle-class life for the Simon family, including large homes, domestic servants and extensive overseas travel.

Yet, the development of the family engineering businesses has often been overlooked and taken as a given in more recent consideration of the Simons, with the focus being on their philanthropic and political endeavours.[2] But without the entrepreneurial success in multiple specialised engineering fields, much of the public work and charitable generosity would not have been possible.

There is no detailed scholarly business history of the Simon engineering firms, nor any critical examination of the changing business practices of the firms or the management approach taken by Henry and then Ernest.[3] This chapter provides a largely chronological documentation of the businesses from the late 1870s to the early 1960s and the death of Ernest using readily available information, mostly published secondary sources.[4] The businesses developed through to the 1990s, but do not exist today after multiple takeovers, mergers and reorganisations, although the Simon name and heritage is employed by some descendant companies for branding purposes.[5]

Henry Simon starting out in business in Manchester

Following Henry's relocation to the city in 1860, aged twenty-four, he worked for others in Manchester, including as resident engineer for Jametal company and as a consulting engineer undertaking projects in Italy and France in 1863. He also acted as a broker in specialised industrial machinery from continental suppliers. As he established himself as a consultant and merchant, he took his own office at 28 Deansgate. During these early years he was perhaps a bit of 'wheeler-dealer' in business, a smart man on the make, cultivating useful contacts and creating opportunities, willing to work for others, particularly on railway related projects, but also seeking to forge his own more lucrative engineering contracts. He travelled extensively in Europe on business (also visiting family and relatives) and seems to have built a stable of contacts with specialised machinery manufacturers in Germany, Austria and Switzerland. In 1867, he devoted a great deal of time to the English participation at the International Exhibition in Paris, where he also won a prize. An entry in a directory for Manchester in 1868 shows his business address as 7 St Peter's Square, in the city centre, and describes him as a '[c]ivil and consulting engineer, contractor, exporter of machinery and agent for foreign patents'.[6]

Through the 1870s, Henry seems to have enjoyed increasing success in business and growing personal wealth, derived from fees and commission. For example, in 1872 he earned a substantial commission of £1,424 from Manchester railway engine manufacturing firm Beyer Peacock.[7] Around this time, he started to seriously try to bring the best roller milling machinery from Switzerland into wide application in flour mills in England. Although he lacked much in the way of capital or a track-record in the milling field, he had a depth of engineering knowledge, innate energy, focus and wider intellectual ability.

MODERN
FLOUR MILL MACHINERY

WITH MAP OF THE WORLD, SHOWING THE DEVELOPMENT OF THE
SIMON ROLLER SYSTEM; WITH PLATES OF TYPICAL MILLS; WITH ILLUSTRATIONS
AND FULL DESCRIPTIONS OF THE MACHINERY USED THEREIN

MESSRS T ROWSE & SONS, PROBUS, CORNWALL.

HENRY SIMON, Limited
MANCHESTER

OFFICES: 20 MOUNT STREET   WORKS: EAST STREET

LONDON BRANCH OFFICE: 82 MARK LANE, E.C.

AUSTRALIAN BRANCH OFFICE AND WORKS: MEADOWBANK, SYDNEY, N.S.W.

REPRESENTATIVES ABROAD:

WESTERN INDIA AND MADRAS	MESSRS. GREAVES, COTTON & CO., BOMBAY
EASTERN INDIA AND BURMAH	MESSRS. MARSHALL, SONS & CO., LTD., CALCUTTA
CHINA	MESSRS. WALTER SCHAERFF & CO., SHANGHAI
ARGENTINA	MESSRS. AGAR, CROSS & CO., BUENOS AYRES
CHILI	MESSRS. WILLIAMSON, BALFOUR & CO., VALPARAISO
PERU	MESSRS. MILNE & CO., LIMA

1898

6.1 Title page from Henry Simon Ltd promotional catalogue (1898). Source: Martin Dodge.

Roller milling of flour and rise of the Simon System

> A valued and ancient servant as the millstone is now being rapidly replaced by the roller-mill, a machine entirely different in principle.[8]

Cereal milling to produce flour for bread in the nineteenth century was a vital industry in feeding the nation, but it was largely overlooked by the British public. Henry Simon saw his contribution to milling as wider than technical success in a niche area of mechanical engineering. It would have wider economic significance to Britain by considerably improving the efficiency of flour mills through investment in an expertly designed new system of production. As he noted, '[i]t is certainly a subject of national importance that such a vast amount of valuable material [wheat flour for bread] should be treated in the best manner possible, and that all waste in its treatment should be avoided'.[9] Henry seems to have had something of a secular mission to improve the health and wealth of the nation. Importantly, he was not the inventor of a new way of roller milling wheat into flour, as is sometimes presented, but, by his energy and creativity, he became the best at exploiting new innovations in milling in Britain (and later abroad) to transform the whole industry through the 1880s and 1890s.

The long-established processes of milling home-grown wheat in Britain using millstones was fairly effective but not without its disadvantages. The resulting flour was browner in colour as it contained more of the branny outside of the wheat seed, and also germ which tended to make it musty and gave it a short self-life. The traditional English flour made from this approach also lacked 'strength', that is the ability to form dough that would rise into light bread. Consequently, the replacement of traditional grinding stones with the roller milling system offered many possibilities, and decades-long development and improvement, particularly in Hungary, had perfected a system of 'high grinding' with grains gradually reduced to flour over multiple stages to produce purer white flour. There were various attempts to implement this gradual reduction approach using roller milling into Britain in the 1870s, but none seemed to have been successful and it was not widely adopted.[10]

Henry had observed firsthand in Austria and Switzerland the 'gradual reduction' method using linked series of roller machines, and sought to bring such a milling system to Britain. He advocated this way of milling because it could produce a larger percentage of superior flour from the same amount of grain. Moreover, new roller mill machinery was often more compact and lighter than stones and could easily fit inside existing mill buildings. New purpose-built mills using only roller milling could be built to be smaller and cheaper than previously required. They would also be safer. Historically, flour milling was hazardous because of the amount of highly flammable fine dust created; contacts of rapidly spinning grinding stones could occasionally cause sparks that ignited the dust. Roller milling could reduce the amount of dust and thus the risks of explosions. Operation of the new roller machinery also required less horsepower and was cheaper to maintain because traditional grinding stones had to be frequently resurfaced, a costly procedure as it required skilled craft people.[11]

Henry's first commercial roller milling installation was for the McDougall Brothers millers in Manchester in 1877. It is unclear whether Henry already knew the company director Arthur McDougall through his previous business activities in Manchester and gained his confidence, or simply approached the firm speculatively because they were a well-known local company.[12] The installation, initially at experimental scale, was deemed a success and by 1878 the whole of McDougall's mill in Ancoats was using Simon's roller milling machines to produce flour without any grinding stones.[13] The reconstruction of McDougall's mill in 1878 marked the real beginning of Henry's business success, although much

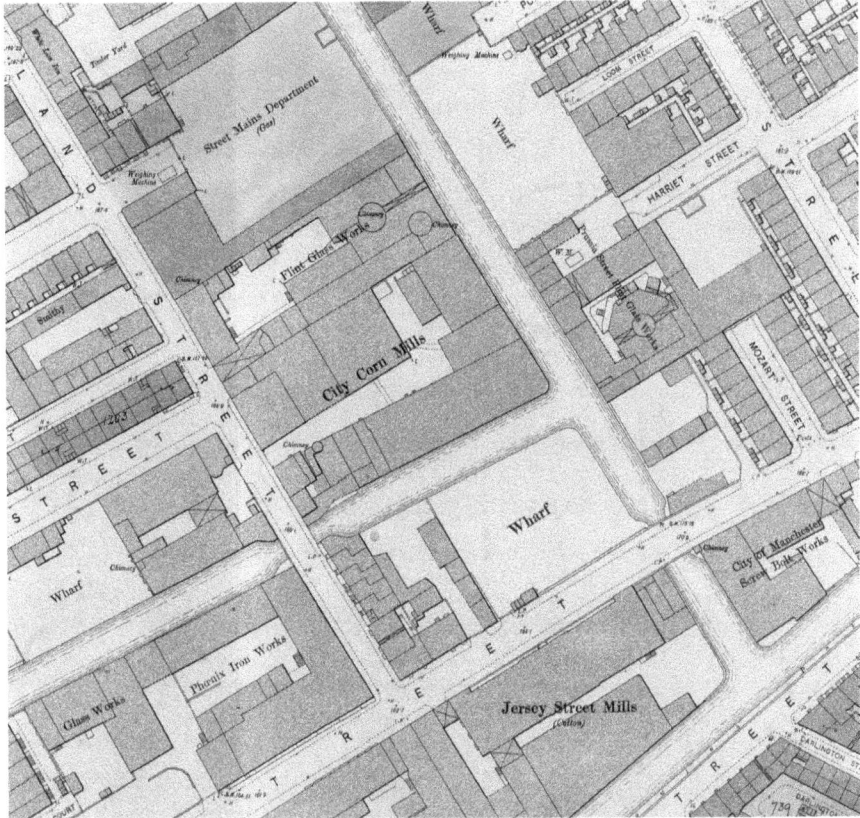

6.2 The City Corn Mill in Ancoats, operated by Arthur McDougall, where Henry installed his first complete roller milling system in 1878. Source: Excerpt from Ordnance Survey 10-foot plan sheet Lancashire CIV.7.12. University of Manchester Library, ref. JRL1300117.

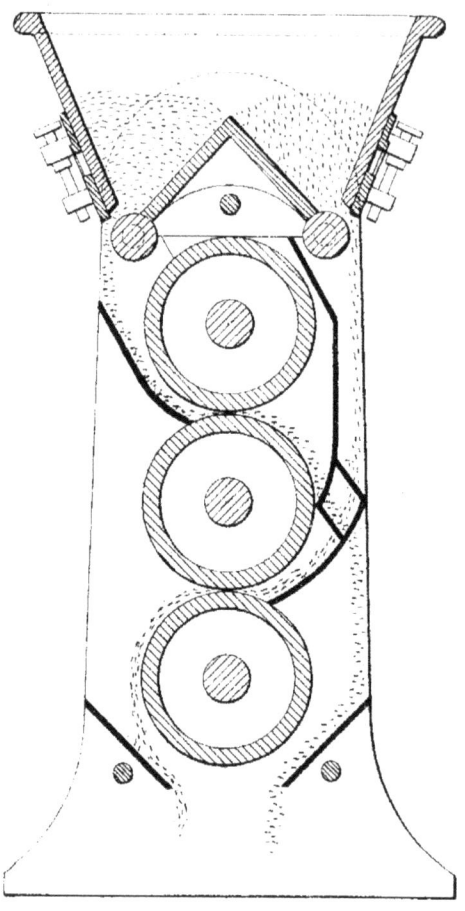

SECTIONAL ELEVATION OF ROLLER-MILL.

6.3 The internal layout of the Daverio designed roller milling machine used by Henry Simon in his first installations. Source: Henry Simon, 'Modern Flour-Milling in England', *Proceedings of the Institution of Civil Engineers*, 70 (1882).

effort would be required over subsequent decades, not least because he was not, at this point, designing or building milling machinery himself.

For his first few years of mill installations in Britain, Simon's chosen roller machinery was the Daverio design, manufactured by the Swiss firm Daverio, Siessardt and Geisler. The Daverio design used chilled-iron rollers arranged in an innovative vertical configuration which was efficient as two separate grinding surfaces were created by using three rollers rather than four; this meant a saving on materials and bearings and reduced the power needed to drive the machinery.[14]

After the breakthrough work for McDougall's, Simon quickly undertook further installations with other important millers. This included the first complete roller milling installation in Ireland in 1879 for millers Shackleton and Sons of Carlow. Henry was also invited in 1879 to give a paper to the first meeting of the National Association of British and Irish Millers, 'On roller-milling', which prophesied (and promoted) the rapid demise of grinding with mill stones.[15] Henry faced opposition and competition, he was not the only one selling new milling machinery and there were several competing firms in Britain in the late 1870s and into the 1880s, including a long-established Rochdale firm, Thomas Robinson & Son. But empirical evidence indicates Simon was the most successful.[16] He was good at winning new orders, realised the importance of providing ongoing advice and good customer service and was also effective at self-promotion, including with marketing maps. He frequently penned convincing technical articles advocating for the new system in the trade press. His company was still very small at this point; there were only fourteen employees by 1883.[17] Henry had a large responsibility although he was also reliant on a younger lieutenant, Joseph Ingleby, who had a depth of practical experience in milling and an extrovert personality that would have been a useful contrast to Henry's rather more reclusive character in terms of salesmanship and negotiations with sceptical millers.[18]

The company strove for continuous improvement in machinery and the integration of various stages in the milling process and more practical experience was gained in designing new mills for a number of companies in different places. A notable achievement in this regard in these early years was the design of a new mill in Chester for large local firm F. A. Frost and Sons that was described as being the first automatic flour mill in the world. It used a sequence of mechanical handling devices to move the grain and middlings between the separate machines without manual labour; '[t]his was a major step in transforming a slow, laborious, and costly "batch" process into an automatic continuous process'.[19] In 1882, Henry read a substantial forty-one-page paper, packed full of empirical evidence as to the potential of roller milling, to the Institution of Civil Engineers, the leading professional body for engineers in Britain; the paper's publication in their August proceedings would have been a key marker of credibility for the Simon company. The paper called for a systematic approach to milling through careful planning, close integration of machinery for gradual reduction milling and automation to raise the quality of output and improve productivity (partly by a reduction in skilled labour). This became known as the 'Simon System', and would feature throughout the company's marketing for years to come. In the 1882 paper, Henry claimed there was '£7 15s. extra in profit in every 5 tons of wheat ground, or 5s. on every sack of flour produced by the Simon systems' compared to conventional low grinding mills using stones.[20] The paper also recorded the successes of the Simon firm, with twenty-five different milling companies in Britain and Ireland having fully or partially adopted his roller technology. As he asserted '[t]he principal advantage of roller-milling is that the bran or husk, and the germ of the grain, are flattened out by the action of rolling, and can consequently easily be sifted out by proper application of dressing machinery' and the resultant reconfiguration of the milling industry on a national scale meant that '[t]he number of second-hand millstones and appurtenances for sale in England is consequently considerable and daily increasing'.[21]

The success of Simon's campaign for rolling milling to replace traditional stones can be seen in the marketing maps he published periodically. The first such map from 1883 shows fifty-two complete installations across many key markets in Britain and Ireland, in mills ranging from Exeter to Kirkcaldy. The major concentration for the Simon company at this point was unsurprisingly in Lancashire and Yorkshire, with weaker penetration in the London area. Some mills were only partial installations with older stones kept to carry out part of the process alongside new machinery from Simon (shown by the '+' symbol on the map, Figure 6.4). The key London market dominated by Seth Taylor, who had been strong advocates of milling by stones, converted completely to the Simon roller system in 1884.[22] An increasingly rapid growth in the number of mill contracts won by the Simon company was evident, and in 1886 the company distributed

6.4 The first marketing map Henry published (1883). Source: Mills Archive ref. GJON-IMG-02A.

a substantial marketing catalogue with an extensive introductory essay by Henry and detailed exposition of flour mill layouts for different scales of production, along with a forty-page listing of the full range of machinery sold by the company. The catalogue also included the fourth edition of the marketing map (Plate 1), demonstrating the extent of sustained growth. With 113 total dots in Britain and 37 in Ireland, in 1885 there were 53 new installations of 'Simon's complete roller plant'. Interestingly there were still considerable number of mills that were combining new roller milling machinery with existing stones, demonstrating a degree of inertia in the industry to the change.

There were other macro forces during the 1880s encouraging British millers to adapt new machinery and techniques, including a copious supply of hard wheat from US farmers that was better processed using gradual reduction on rollers; the need to compete against cheaper, better quality flour from large American mills and, importantly, a growing consumer demand for white bread.[23] As Henry noted in 1882, 'an increasing demand for superior well-cleaned and white flour has thus gradually been established, which it is as yet difficult for most English millers to respond to'.[24] Through the 1880s, there also was change in the milling industry with a concentration of production into a smaller number of larger firms, with new, much larger, mills being built adjacent to key ports. These changes tended to favour capital intensive investment in new machinery and more efficient production processes; Henry Simon's company clearly benefited.[25]

In 1887, Henry was successfully nominated to be a member of the Institution of Civil Engineers, a marker of his prestige in the field. He was by that time already an active member of the Institution of Mechanical Engineers and the Institute of Iron and Steel in Britain, as well as belonging to the Society of Civil Engineers of France and the Society of Engineers and Architects of Austria.[26]

Henry Simon seeks to transform coke making

As well as the struggle to get flour millers to adopt his Simon System, in the early 1880s Henry was also devoting considerable time and energy to get another technical innovation accepted in a quite different industrial field. In 1881, he worked to install his first by-product coke ovens, using a design he had seen successfully in use in France during a field trip with fellow engineers in 1878 organised by the Iron and Steel Institute.[27]

Conventionally coke, the vital fuel for iron making, was obtained by burning raw coal in open kilns, nicknamed 'beehives' because of their shape. This was effective but the burning process gave off tarry gases and ammonia that were simply left to pollute the surrounding area. The improved process, which Henry wanted to promote, turned raw coal into

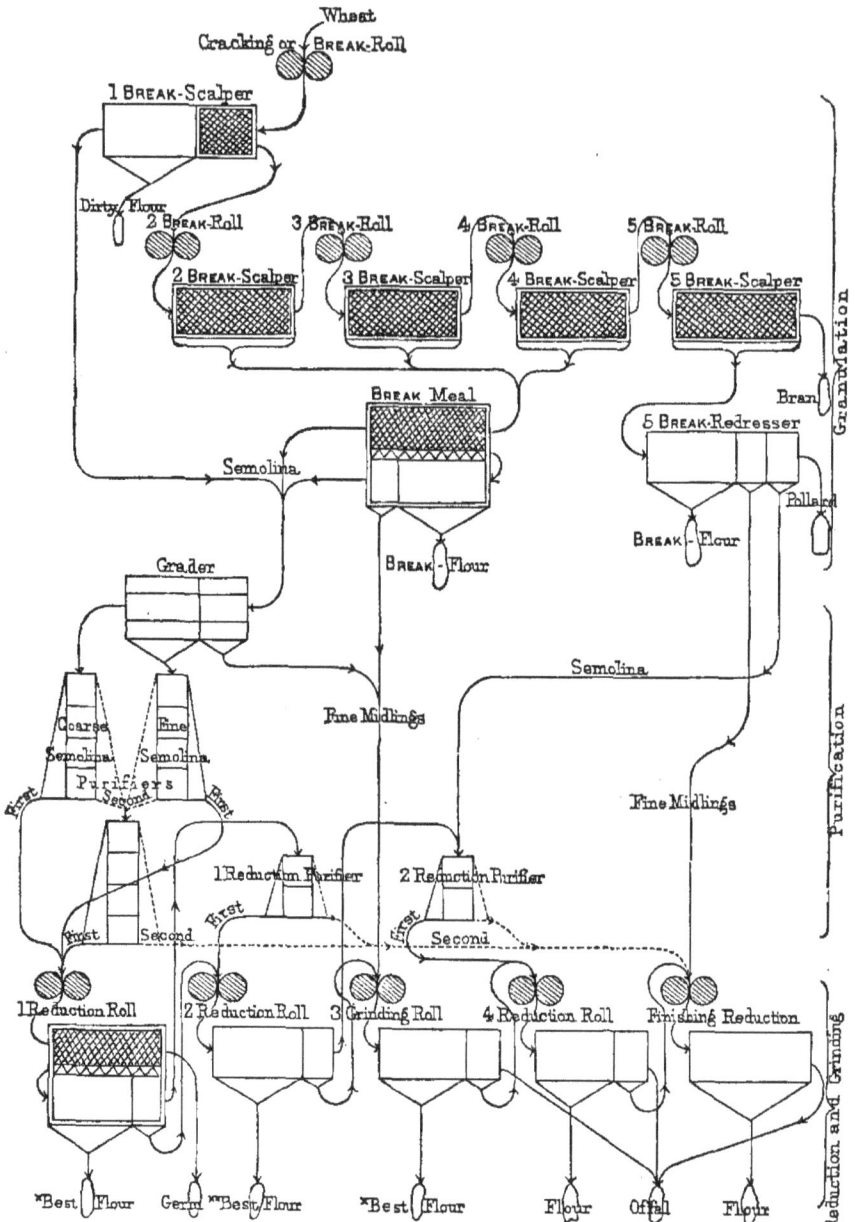

6.5 Diagram of a Simon System gradual reduction roller milling installation from the early 1880s showing the sequence of grinding and sifting out of impurities to obtain the maximum amount of top-quality white flour. Source: Henry Simon, 'Modern Flour-milling in England', *Proceedings of the Institution of Civil Engineers*, 70 (1882).

coke by controlled heating in airless retorts with the gas and tar gradually siphoned off and stored. These by-products had value as input for other chemical processes and could be sold, thereby improving the overall profitability of coke production. The use of similar airless retorts to carbonise coal was becoming common in Britain to generate methane gas ('town gas') for lighting and other uses. But many colliers and iron masters were much more sceptical about airless ovens to make coke suitable for their needs.[28]

As was Henry's preferred business strategy, he strove to introduce the by-product coke oven to collieries and steel plants in Britain by going into partnership with François Carves, a well-established French engineer specialising in coke oven design. A joint company, Simon-Carves was set up in 1880. Henry's entry into the coke oven business was signalled to people in the industry by his May 1880 paper read before the Iron and Steel Institute, with a strongly argued economic case for the profitability of its by-products. But the paper also advocated on the grounds of efficiency and environmental protection.

> It would ... seem desirable, from every standpoint, that such an extraordinary waste should not be allowed to go on [because] the utilisation of the bye-products, besides being very profitable, reduces the evil consequences which the manufacture of coke creates in its vicinity.[29]

The first installation of the Simon-Carves by-product system, replacing traditional beehive coke ovens, was at the Pease & Partners colliery at Crook, Co. Durham in 1881. A bank of twenty-five coke ovens was precisely built, using fireclay bricks, each 23 ft long and 6 ft 6 inches high, surrounded by flues to carry hot gas to bake the coal within. Each oven was charged with 4.5 tons of coal at a time. Each cycle took six hours and then the oven doors were opened, and mechanical rams pushed the red-hot coke out and fresh coal was loaded. In a reciprocal manner, some of the coal gas given off was burnt to provide the heating of the ovens and waste heat from the flues was fed to steam boilers to provide the energy needed to drive the fans and pumps to handle the by-products. It was an energy efficient and continuous production process. The overall efficacy and cost effectiveness of the new by-product coke ovens at the Pease & Partner's colliery was reported in the press in the summer of 1883, prompting Henry to write a letter to the *Manchester Guardian* pointing out that they were 'the first constructed in England under my license and according to plans furnished from my office'. Careful comparison of the earlier beehive oven process and the new Simon-Carves system at Bankfoot showed a 15 per cent increase in yield of coke.[30] Some critics claimed the quality was not as good and a number of established and vocal iron masters in this period asserted that beehive produced coke was best for their operations.[31]

With the entry into the coke oven field and the formation of Simon-Carves company, Henry's expanding business operations needed more office space. In 1884, the company took space in an imposing five-storey office building, 20 Mount Street next to Central Station and a stone's throw from Manchester Town Hall. It is not clear how much of the building the company occupied initially, but in later years large signs promoting both Henry Simon and Simon-Carves companies were displayed on the outside.

Simon-Carves undertook further installations in the early 1880s but progress in convincing established interests in the coking sector to adopt a new process was tough-going, particularly in comparison to the Henry Simon company's rate of success in flour roller milling. A paper read by Henry to the Iron and Steel Institute in 1885 documented the progress, including large projects for fifty by-product coke ovens for Bear-Park Coal and Coke Co. in Durham.[32] To encourage more collieries and steel makers to switch to the Simon-Carves by-product coke ovens, Henry offered capital financing of construction in return for a share of revenue from selling the chemical by-products.[33] This shifted the risk from the owners onto Henry's shoulders, but strongly demonstrated his confidence in the superiority of this new process over the conventional 'beehive' oven. He was proved right in the value of chemical by-products, and the experience Simon-Carves gained in processing different chemicals would subsequently help the company expand into the design of complex chemical facilities, including ones manufacturing sulphuric acid and ammonia. This specialised field proved a profitable one, particularly during the First World War and subsequently.

6.6 The original 'beehive' coke ovens at Pease's West colliery are shown on the left of this painting, W. Wheldon, 'North Eastern coalfield: colliery pit-head and coking ovens in England'. (c. 1845). Source: Science Museum Group Collection, ref. co521755.

COKE OVENS.

To the Editor of the Manchester Guardian.

Sir,—My attention has been drawn to an article which appeared in your issue of July 24, referring to the new coke ovens at work at the Messrs. Pease's West Collieries, near Darlington. Allow me to say that these coke ovens, patented to me, are the first constructed in England under my licence and according to plans furnished from my office. The figures given by you are in the main correct, but there is one important inaccuracy. You state that the new ovens cost £185, as against £65, the cost of the old and wasteful "Bee Hive" ovens. Now very much the reverse is the case. The capital required for constructing a plant of coke ovens such as is being used at the Messrs. Pease's is for a given quantity of coke positively less than for any other system if the cost of the apparatus necessary for collecting the by-products be excluded. This part of the plant is much the same as in gasworks, and should of course not be included in the cost of the coke ovens proper. It may interest your readers to hear that Messrs. Pease are extending the application of this system, and that other similar coke ovens are in course of erection in Yorkshire and elsewhere.—Yours, &c.,   HENRY SIMON.
 7, St. Peter's Square, Manchester, July 25, 1883.

6.7 Letter from Henry Simon to the editor of the *Manchester Guardian* about the installation of the Simon-Carves Ovens at Pease's West Collieries. Source: *Manchester Guardian* (27 July 1883), p. 7.

6.8 The Mount Street offices. Source: title page of *Flour Mill Machinery*, Henry Simon Ltd, 1923.

The coke oven business continued to be more challenging than flour milling for Henry's companies. Production statistics, for example, show that even in 1905 the sector was still dominated by the traditional beehive oven process. Only 15 per cent of coke produced in Britain came from the by-product system, and of this, Simon Carves had a 13 per cent share, some 726 ovens, which was a fraction of the market leader, which had 2,233 operating ovens.[34]

Henry's successful management of a growing engineering enterprise

As the 1880s was drawing to a close, Henry had succeeded in building up two large engineering companies, promulgating the Simon name proudly into the wider world. He had put a tremendous amount of time and energy into cultivating these specialised businesses, winning new customers and gaining repeat orders, developing and refining the technical processes, beginning to design his own machinery and taking out patents. His philosophy for business success, codified in 1888 formed part of a small book, *Rathschlaege für meine Kinder* [*Advice for my Children*], written for his children and repeated down the years by his son Ernest, focused firstly on the intrinsic value in taking a synoptic view of scientific and technological developments, and looking to synthesise and practically apply innovations. As Henry noted 'for my boys' in the booklet, '[y]ou must keep your eyes open for a speciality. A new system or patent to achieve better results in some large industry.'[35]

Henry cultivated wide scientific knowledge in his participation in learned societies locally, such as the Manchester Geographical Society, along with his membership of important national institutions like the Royal Geographical Society, the Society of Arts (now the RSA) and professional engineering bodies in Britain and Europe. Again, in his book of advice, he tutored his sons, 'read good periodicals in different languages and remain posted in all that is going on in science'. Henry himself was fluent in French as well as German and English, travelled frequently in Europe and maintained wide contacts with leading engineering firms on the continent. As noted above, his 'discovery' of the Carves design of coke ovens had happened on a study tour of France in 1878.

A second element in Henry's approach to business was a sense of due caution and seeking sustainable growth through partnerships to spread the risk. The goal was to use capital generated by profits for reinvestment into growing the company, rather than rapid expansion using debt finance. As Henry wrote in the *Rathschlaege für meine Kinder*, '[d]o not risk your capital until you are as certain as possible of success. Rather begin by working with or for others, to divide the risk until you can afford to risk alone.' Ernest also later reflected in the 1940s, '[a]mong the few notes my father left for his sons was one urging us, if in business, always to be in a position to send for our bankers rather than letting the bankers send for us'.[36] As the companies became larger, this approach remained possible as major shareholders were family members who were supportive and willing to forgo dividends to support endogenous growth.

A drive for quality and cultivating customers for the long term was the third strain of Henry's business acumen. In an age of exaggerated promises and companies that failed to deliver, Henry Simon Ltd was reliable and evidently built a strong reputation for honest dealing, delivery of machinery and plant designs that worked as advertised, along with evident depth of technical expertise in what they were selling. This necessitated forging a small and dedicated cadre of engineers at his companies that over the years built up real experience in what they were doing. Decades later this was described as Henry's 'consistent refusal merely to compete on price and his determination to offer nothing but the best milling system, the best machinery and the best technical service'.[37] In this the two companies succeeded in being recognised as leading centres of practical knowledge and experience in specific fields of mechanical and chemical engineering. This translated into decades of healthy profits.

In 1889, Henry read a major paper to the Institution of Mechanical Engineers with the aim to draw 'attention to the very extraordinary revolution … in progress in the manufacture of flour by the substitution of the roller system for the ancient method of grinding by stones'.[38] The paper demonstrated the positive impact of the re-organisation and wholesale automation of processes from raw wheat to finished flour that had raised productivity and reduced costs. Henry asserted in the paper that his company had completed over 200 mill installations since 1878, some costing up to £40,000. Interestingly, the case study chosen to illustrate the paper was not an example close to home, but a major new mill and granary installation in Rio De Janeiro, demonstrating very directly how the company was gaining international success and prestige. The winning of overseas contracts would be increasingly important to business growth and was a major source of pride and used in marketing. The tenth edition of the marketing map (1892) (Plate 2) featured an inset to show 'some of foreign & colonial plants on the H. Simon's system', including multiple installations in Southern Africa, India, Australia and New Zealand.[39] The company had a permanent branch office in Sydney by this point and, given growing success in the country, established a separate Australian subsidiary in 1893. The Henry Simon company introduced their roller milling system to the Japanese market in 1892 when they built a plant in Nagasaki, their first in Asia. The most remote milling contract undertaken in this period was in New Caledonia, in the South Pacific, built under special commission for the French Government as it was still a penal colony. It is noteworthy that Henry was not pursuing milling contracts in Europe at this point, presumably because some of his patent licenses with key machinery companies in German precluded his entry into this market. It remains unclear why the company did not pursue contracts in North America at this time.

The Henry Simon milling machinery catalogue from 1892 gives more statistics on the expansion of the Simon System, noting that by June that year the company had installed 394 roller-mill plants. The Simon company dominated major clusters of large flour mills in key British port cities: 'in Liverpool 13 mills with an aggregate output of about 1.5 million sacks ... have been erected on the Simon System'.[40] Other evidence of the prominence of the company in the field cited in the catalogue were the thirty-seven complete roller mills using competitors' machinery that had been 'remodelled and reconstructed on the Simon System'.[41]

Henry was reliant on a small but first-rate staff of engineers, draughtsmen and sales agents, but was evidently a 'hands-on' manager and fully engaged with the technical detail as well as charting the strategic course for the two companies' growth. In today's parlance, he might be described as a 'workaholic'. Throughout his early career he seems to have been effective at juggling competing projects and consulting jobs, as well as taking an active interest in different innovations. For example, in 1877 he read a detailed paper to the Iron and Steel Institute which demonstrated his technical knowledge and active interest in exploiting a novel construction technique based on the ideas of Belgian mining engineer Joseph Chaudron; and then the following year Henry was taking out a patent (with Charles Fairbairn) for a 'machine for impressing screw threads on bolts, etc.'.[42] Besides activities in technical engineering disciplines and demanding everyday business tasks, into the 1890s Henry was becoming ever more engaged in civic work in Manchester. Such high levels of intense work and accompanying stress had an impact on his long-term health and likely contributed to his worsening heart condition.

In October 1892, Henry started the 'Circular to his clients and others' in the milling business, a publicity bulletin designed to flag new developments, celebrate major contracts won and build the 'Simon' brand.[43] Some of the content was evidently personal, written in the first person, especially in the early years. Part of his successful salesmanship was based on his own character and trustworthiness. Included with the December 1892 Circular was a 'motto calendar' for the coming year; the issuing of such calendars, created by family members, became a longstanding tradition of the company.[44] In due course the Circulars would also be produced in French, Spanish and German to better communicate with international clients, and thousands of copies were despatched across the world. Also, in 1892 a branch milling machinery production outfit was established in Germany – Simon, Buhler and Baumann company. Growing business success was reflected in his personal circumstances, with his family having moved into Lawnhurst, a large mansion on the edge of Didsbury, by 1893.

A key part of Henry's business success was based on the use of patents. He was keen-eyed in finding useful patents by other machine makers and innovators to exploit. He also spent considerable time and money taking out new patents on his own ideas. Significantly, by the mid-1890s he was also involved in litigating against infringement of patents. Some of these legal battles were costly and a major drain on his time that could have been more productively applied. But evidently Henry thought it important to win in terms of business operations and perhaps more so for his professional reputation. In early 1893, Henry (and others), who held the patent rights for the UK and European market for the 'Cyclone' dust collector (it was invented in the USA by the Knickerbocker Company, of Jackson, Michigan), went to court claiming infringement of by the manufacturer Pieter Van-Gelder and his machine called 'The Tornado'. Henry won the case and substantial compensation. In the next year, Henry was the defendant in an infringement lawsuit brought by Messrs Tom and George Marsden Parkinson, flour millers from Doncaster, concerning his patented purifier machine. The plaintiff's legal action was backed by Robinson & Sons Ltd of Rochdale, who were the major rival to Henry Simon in the milling machinery sector. The *Parkinson v. Simon* case was decided in the High Court in Henry's favour in March 1894, but the plaintiffs appealed, and the case eventually was heard in the House of Lords. The verdict in July 1895 affirmed the judgement of the Court of Appeal and the case was dismissed without Henry's barristers being called to present evidence. The costs were high in financial terms – estimated at £10,000 including fees to expensive legal representation – but also a 'waste of time and brainwork'. Henry attended court and was called as a witness, and the stress seemingly contributed to his worsening health at this time.[45]

It was evident that by the mid-1890s the Simon System in flour milling was dominant across key cities in Britain and, crucially, by this point this included London. The large mills which the company had equipped were producing two-thirds of the total flour manufactured in London by mid-1895.[46] The business was also moving beyond milling machinery to become a recognised design consultancy for large grain silos for storage and distribution. This kind of high value-added design services work would generate an increasing share of profits in the future. In 1897, Henry changed the business structure into a limited liability company with shareholders (many of whom were in the family) to provide Henry Simon Ltd with a more stable financial footing going forward.

The scale of success of Henry Simon Ltd was noted in the Occasional Letters in the later 1890s, with a roll call of major mill and granary projects delivered and record order books. This was clearly not an unbiased source of information, but one can gain a sense of the extensive geography of the milling business by comparing the company's marketing maps from 1892 and 1898 and what was achieved in those busy six years (Plates 2, 3). There were burgeoning numbers of installations across the UK, particularly in the key port cities, but also multiple contracts won in Australia, southern Africa and across India. Some of the export success was facilitated by strong colonial connections and the primacy of the English language in commerce favouring British companies in places like India and South Africa. More unexpected was the strength of business ties Henry Simon Ltd developed with South American countries, with many large mill and granary contracts won in Argentina in particular. Within the UK, a signature project for Henry Simon Ltd during this period was the design and equipping of a completely new double-mill on the docks at Birkenhead for W. Vernon and Son's, the most important millers in Liverpool and one of the leading firms nationally. The mills represented a major capital investment of over £200,000 and could produce 12,000 sacks of flour per week. The mills were celebrated as the pinnacle of efficiency, due in large part to the design expertise of Henry Simon Ltd, which the company had refined over the previous twenty years:

> throughout the mill one is impressed by the thorough uniformity which has prevailed in its erection and equipment; architect, engineer, and miller alike having happily combined to produce ... a system of machinery as would constitute one harmonious whole – one gigantic automatic piece of mechanism complete in all its parts.[47]

Sadly, Henry would not live to see the full operation of Vernon and Son's state-of-the-art Simon System mill, as he died in 1899.

The 1900s and the second-generation family firms

Henry was cremated in July 1899, in a facility he had been instrumental in founding and using furnaces he had designed. His professional contribution to engineering was recorded in lengthy obituaries published by the journals of the Institutions of Civil Engineers and Mechanical Engineers and the Iron and Steel Institute.[48] His death marked a period of transition for the businesses but did not disrupt their growth and prosperity unduly. While Henry had been the driving force and source of ideas, he had been, particularly from the later 1890s, supported by loyal and talented lieutenants in both Henry Simon Ltd and Simon-Carves Ltd. His death was also not unexpected, as he had suffered several years of ill health and substantial periods away from day-to-day business to recuperate. At an Extraordinary General Meeting in November 1899, Joseph Ingleby, who had worked with Henry since 1871 and been the key business partner through the years of struggle in the 1880s and contributed to the success enjoyed in the 1890s, was appointed chairman. Two other long-serving senior staff, William Mehlhaus and George Huxley, were made directors.[49] The companies enjoyed enviable reputations in their fields for quality and innovation and were operating debt free.

Despite the changes in senior management, Henry Simon Ltd continued to do brisk business. As documented in the March 1901 Occasional Letter, during 1900 Henry Simon Ltd had managed the construction of forty new flour mills as well as reconstruction and extensions of existing mills. The company installed grain preparation plants for eighteen clients and supervised the building of seven large new storage granaries. Moreover, 'complete new roller plants have been erected at many places abroad [including] Cawnpore, India; Lima and Buenos Ayres, South America; Port Elizabeth, South Africa; Tamwork, Laggan, Pittsworth, Australia; Ulverston, Launcheston, Tasmania'.[50]

Ernest Simon was still a student at Cambridge University, undertaking an engineering degree, when his father Henry died. Ernest did not much enjoy student days by all accounts, but successfully completed a first-class degree, despite the shock of the loss of his father. Upon graduation in 1901, he began to work in both family businesses, and from a young age of twenty-two, he gained experience quickly and enjoyed the confidence of senior staff appointed by Henry.

Ernest was clearly intelligent, diligent and with a real aptitude for the engineering business, but he had much to learn. He missed the guidance of his father and felt the heavy burden of responsibility being the senior Simon son involved in running the companies successfully and supporting the wider family financially. Mary Stocks' biography of Ernest reports that he found the period 1901–11 the worse decade in his life. Yet he acknowledged in 1953 that the continued growth and development of the family firms had not 'been as difficult as the work accomplished by my father in laying the foundations of the business'.[51]

With the support of shareholders, composed largely of his family, in less than ten years he was beginning to run the businesses himself; as he reflected later in life: 'my father's trustees appointed me as Governing Director at the age of twenty-nine [1908] partly because they thought me competent, mainly because I was my father's son. It would have been very difficult to remove me if things had gone wrong.'[52] Ingleby retired as chairman of Henry Simon Ltd in 1908 but remained chairman of Simon-Carves Ltd for several more years. By 1910, Ernest had assumed the role of governing director of both Henry Simon Ltd and Simon-Carves Ltd. The companies had 350 employees by then, up from just fourteen in 1883.[53]

By the early 1910s, Ernest was also becoming active in politics as a local councillor. The businesses were expanding and undertaking extensive contracts abroad. In 1912, Henry Simon Ltd also signed a large contract for the Manchester Ship Canal Company to design and equip a massive new granary in the middle of Salford docks. In 1912, Manchester docks imported 528,000 tons of grain and the existing grain elevator on Trafford Wharf could not handle further growth. Granary no. 2 was a huge 160-ft tall steel-reinforced

6.9 Cover of a promotional booklet for a new grain elevator designed by Henry Simon Ltd for the Manchester Ship Canal Company (c. 1915). Source: Martin Dodge.

concrete edifice comprising 260 storage bins capable of holding 40,000 tons of grain when full, along with the means to select and weigh it, and discharge it into barges, rail wagons or trucks for onward distribution.

Simon businesses at war, 1914–18

> It is of course essential that the flour mills of the Empire should be kept in work and in an efficient state, and we have no doubt that we shall continue to be able to … obtain permission to carry out such orders.[54]

The First World War was a testing time for the Simon engineering companies and deeply tragic personally for the Simon family. The companies had to take on much specialised war work at short notice and with initially a diminished roster as staff volunteered to serve in the military. Ernest lost three of his brothers during the conflict and took up the additional burden of supporting their surviving families.

Henry Simon Ltd engineering works in Bredbury and Stalybridge were placed under the direction of the Ministry of Munitions and were enlarged to handle more urgent war work. Over the course of the war, they turned out hundreds of thousands of casings for explosive shells for the army artillery and the Admiralty. The conscription of many existing workshop staff meant the company had to employ about 1,000 more unskilled workers, about half of which were female. The demand meant that for many months a three-shift system was necessary at the Stalybridge works.[55]

With the reduction of available manual labour at docks and warehouses, Henry Simon Ltd was called upon to produce new pneumatic handling systems and portable conveyor systems to help keep goods flowing into the country. The assemblage of large floating grain elevators was an important aspect of their war work, some of which were supplied for use in French ports. The Simon-Carves company, given its relevant expertise, was commissioned by the government to design and supervise the construction of sulphuric acid chemical plants that were deemed vital to the war effort. By 1918, the range and intensity of war work meant its staff trebled in size.[56]

Ernest also grappled with a dilemma on how best to serve his country at the start of the war and rued the fact that the government did not provide ready guidance. In the end, Ernest believed he could contribute more by staying in charge of the businesses rather than signing up for military service, like his three younger brothers. 'He felt that his continued presence was absolutely necessary to both companies, though it is clear that this conclusion did not leave him with a quiet mind.'[57]

Making their own machinery and the Cheadle Heath factory

For the early decades of the milling business, when Henry was in charge, the company had not manufactured its own flour milling and processing machinery. Instead, it had licensed and resold other companies' machinery – typically putting a 'Henry Simon' badge on the cover – or it had its own patented designs for milling machinery built under contract by other firms (usually in Germany). Henry also contracted with Seck Bros Company in Dresden and used their 'Reform' brand name in Britain. He was involved as a financial partner in Buhler, Baumann and Co. in Frankfurt, from 1892, that built milling machinery for him. The Henry Simon company had a small workshop in Manchester on East Street, but this seems to have been for the testing and maintenance of machinery.

Henry Simon Ltd began producing its own machinery in its first UK factory in 1902, when it acquired a direct interest in the Eagle Ironworks in Stalybridge operated by Messrs Bailey & Garnett. In 1906, it acquired the factory outright and over subsequent years it was enlarged. The manufacturing capacity was further enhanced in 1915 when Henry Simon acquired the milling engineering business and existing factory of Briddon and Fowler in Bredbury. Simon-Carves always remained a specialist in design and supervision of installations; it never manufactured the components of the coke ovens, coal washers or steam boilers itself.

Following the return to civilian work after the war, the Simon companies enjoyed full order books, in part because competitors in Europe, particularly skilled engineering firms in Germany, had been so disrupted. But the company was aware of the threat of competition from continental firms in the milling business, particularly well-organised German machine makers, which would reappear in due course.

There was a strategic decision taken in the early 1920s to bring together all the milling machinery manufacturing into a large, purpose-built new factory and associated administrative offices. Initially, the site for a model factory was sought in Fallowfield, Manchester but the planning application faced strong opposition from local residents and the company shifted focus and acquired a greenfield site south of the city at Cheadle Heath on which to build.[58] The facility was carefully designed for efficiency of manufacturing and to be a good place to work. It was also conveniently located for Ernest, being a short drive south from his home in Didsbury. He was also proud that the works had been financed internally from accumulated profits over ten years rather than through borrowing.[59]

6.10 The new factory for Henry Simon Ltd on Bird Hall Lane, Cheadle Heath. (*c.* 1927). Source: SSP M14/6/4.

The factory, covering about four acres, was a conventional single-storey building, comprising a specialised wood-working shop, sheet-metal shop, machine and fitting shop, erecting bays, and painting and packing shops. There were also offices, a laboratory, a large staff dining-room and an experimental bakery, and finally ample outside space for sports of various kinds. The factory was formally opened in 1926 and production ceased in Stalybridge and Bredbury. Within a year, around 400 workers were in the factory and in later years the facilities would be expanded, including large drawing offices and space for research and development for both the Henry Simon milling business and Simon-Carves, and subsidiaries. Office staff were moved out of the Mount Street building, which was fully vacated by 1930. The works were gradually surrounded by residential development and other light industry due to the interwar suburban sprawl of Manchester and Stockport.

By the mid-1920s, the early postwar boom had faded, and the British economy was struggling with large-scale unemployment and much industrial unrest, culminating in the General Strike. In these conditions the Simon business struggled to secure new orders domestically, but profits were buoyed by international success. In 1926, Henry Simon Ltd had orders for over £900,000 from different parts of the world, the best in the company's history.[60] The milling and silo department were winning many orders in South America. For example, in 1927 the company won a contract in Argentina from the Buenos Aires Great Southern Railway Co. valued at £800,000 to construct a huge new granary at the port of Bahia Blanca capable of storing 80,000 tons of grain.[61] The business opportunities proved to be so strong in Argentina that the company decided to create a branch office in the country rather than rely on a separate agent. Business in Australia was also booming, and the company decided to expand its subsidiary with more manufacturing capacity to keep its prices competitive in the face of high import tariffs from the government.

Ernest Simon's style of management and the nature of the family firms

How did Ernest drive the Simon businesses forward and achieve sustained growth and diversification, and also – in parallel – build a successful career in public campaigning and political office? After the first decade of the 1900s of full-time work in business, Ernest consciously stood back from the daily running of the Simon engineering companies and sought a more 'hands-off' approach, to spend time only on high-level strategy and on the appointment and promotion of key management personnel. 'In 1912 I joined the Manchester City Council, and from that time on I never gave more than half my time to the business; at certain times, as for instance when I was in Parliament ... much less.'[62] Certainly he seems to have been able to stick to this strategy and to carve out vital time for public work, which became more pressing in the 1920s when he was made Lord Mayor of Manchester in 1921–22 and was also seriously ill for several months with tuberculosis (and yet still also found time to publish his first book, *The Smokeless City*!) and during his first spell as an MP in Westminster in 1924.

Following his father's lead, Ernest believed success for large organisations and commercial firms depended on the brains and drive of a few men at the top of the management. As chairman and governing director he was prepared to delegate a lot of power to managing directors and the key people running separate departments in the Simon companies, granting them a lot of operational independence and responsibility for contracts and thus also carrying the risks. This approach seems to have generated the reward of a motivated senior staff and scope for innovation. As Ernest reflected in 1947: 'It is far better to err on the side of giving too much responsibility than on the side of too much interference.'[63] This was clearly in marked contrast with Henry's much more 'hands-on' approach to business management.

Moreover, Ernest believed himself to be a good judge of a person's capacity and character and was demonstrably willing to promote younger people he believed capable in the businesses and give them authority and responsibility at a time when many organisations were rigidly hierarchical and seniority was earnt by years of service rather than latent abilities. As Stocks writes about Ernest in the 1910s, he clearly recognised 'his power to deal with men'. In 1910, he wrote in his diary: 'I feel sure that the extensive reorganization of the business I have already carried through has come just in time. We are in for a real hard fight, but I feel that I am a much better man than any of my English competitors anyway.'[64] Along with the willingness to delegate power and leaving daily decision-making to trusted lieutenants was a ruthless pragmaticism to remove people who failed to deliver. In this respect he characterised himself as having an autocratic style of management, despite his philosophical commitment to democracy.[65]

Another vital element in Ernest's successful management was that he was evidently extremely hardworking. His work approach was also highly productive – he had mental focus, an ability to compartmentalise and decisiveness in action – common traits in successful people. 'Nature and heredity have endowed [Ernest] with unusual gifts, which he has sedulously cultivated. His mind moves with exceptional speed and incisiveness and his powers of concentration is formidable; no one wastes less time; no one more swiftly grasps essentials or more ruthlessly casts aside irrelevance and triviality.'[66] His early affluence meant he also had ample help from diligent assistants, secretaries and researchers. His son Brian commented that 'I fully recognised the efficiency of his office arrangements only when dealing with his papers after his death. There were two highly skilled and devoted secretaries of long service, one for business affairs, one for personal activities.'[67] He had a private chauffeured car at his beck and call and travelled in first-class comfort, so was able to work on frequent train journeys to London and longer overseas trips on steam ships.

Ernest's work ethic was allied to a genuine interest in engineering – his membership of the Institutions of Civil and Mechanical Engineers was not for show – demonstrated by his ability and willingness to keep up with technical developments in milling, and giving learned papers on these, whilst also pursuing politics and public work so intensely. This was evidenced in 1930 when he published a technical book *The Physical Science of Flour Milling*,[68] while he was MP for Withington and pushing for housing reform off the back of his book *How to Abolish the Slums* (1929).

In early 1934, he consciously stepped back further from the businesses when he formally resigned as chairman of Henry Simon Ltd (although he remained on the board as governing director; and also a major shareholder), noting 'owing to the very difficult times through which the country is passing, I have decided that it is desirable to give more of my time to public work in order to render any help that lies in my power'.[69] While he sought more vital time for political engagement, one gets the sense that his imprint on the direction and ethos of the companies was by then firmly set.

A key part of the ethos, where Ernest followed Henry's 'guiding policy' of keeping up with scientific developments and new methods, was a willingness to invest significantly in applied research and later more formalised R&D strategies at the companies. Allied to this was the value in investing in employee training, particularly as it was difficult to recruit new staff with specialised skills: 'the necessary experts are simply not available; it can only be built up over a period of years by a process of skilled and continuous selection, training and promotion'.[70] From the 1920s onwards, the companies also saw the value in recruiting more university science graduates, but a lack of a degree was no barrier to the promotion of the most capable people to senior positions. Ernest was also proud of the working conditions provided to both office staff and shop floor workers and sought to offer good salaries, security of employment and to develop good labour relations. The Simon businesses were benevolent employers, and they expected the best from the staff and were rewarded for it.

The Simon name was proudly embedded in the company names, but how much were they 'family' firms after Henry's death and during Ernest's tenure? In terms of ownership, they were strongly controlled by the family; for example, by 1953, around twenty of Henry Simon's immediate children and grandchildren were the majority shareholders.[71] In terms of senior staff, this topic was one upon which Ernest felt it necessary to elucidate in his introductory essay in the 1947 promotional book *The Simon Engineering Group*, perhaps fearing accusations of nepotism and favouritism. As he asserted:

We have welcomed any competent member of the large Simon family who wished to join us, and have tried to treat him exactly in the same way as every other recruit ... It would be a disaster if any member of the family were given a job beyond his capacity just because his name was Simon; I would never dream of agreeing to it under any circumstances.

Of Henry's five sons, interest in the engineering businesses was shown only by Ernest and Harry. Harry Simon (1880–1917) studied engineering at Cambridge, like Ernest, and joined Henry Simon Ltd and made significant contributions in developing the grain silo engineering department into a successful counterpart of the existing milling machinery business. He became a director in Henry Simon Ltd by the 1910s. One can only speculate about what he might have contributed to the businesses had he not been killed in the war. His influence on the business did live on, however, through his sons Anthony and Christopher who went on to hold senior roles in the firms.

Several senior staff and company directors were also from the immediate family through marriage rather than birth. This included Ernest's brother-in-law Tufton Beamish who had married Margaret Simon in 1914. He had a distinguished career in the British Navy reaching the rank of rear admiral. In 1919, he was appointed to the board of Henry Simon Ltd.

Rupert Potter (1899–1970), Shena's younger brother, joined the Simon-Carves firm straight from completing an engineering degree at Cambridge University in 1921. He learnt the business initially in the boiler department and his ability meant he rose in the company, being appointed a director of Simon-Carves in 1931 and then chairman in 1939. He eventually became chairman of the newly merged Simon Engineering Group (SEG) in 1960.

The Second World War and the Simon businesses

The engineering expertise across the Simon businesses was pressed into war service from 1939, with much of its activities controlled by the Ministry of Supply. The large machinery workshop at Cheadle Heath, for example, was directed by the government to make armaments of all kinds. The Occasional Letter of June 1946 explained that 'owing to the difficulty of adapting a works like ours to mass production ... most of our output consisted of highly skilled jobs in limited quantities'. This included parts for tanks and components for anti-aircraft guns. The workforce increased by about 75 per cent and employed a large number of new women workers.[72]

There was little work for the milling department of Henry Simon Ltd beyond necessary repairs to bomb-damaged mills, but the conveying department was called upon to produce all manner of mechanical handling solutions for the ports to keep the food flowing and to speed up production at critical industrial plants. The pressure to grow more food domestically meant an increase in grain harvests, and the Ministry of Food needed more storage and drying capacity and commissioned Henry Simon Ltd to build and equip eight new silos.

The experience of chemical process engineering in Simon-Carves Ltd departments meant the company was commissioned by the government to build seventeen new plants to produce ammonia and eighteen plants to manufacture toluene, in addition to over twenty sulphuric acid plants, including at seven explosives factories.

During the Second World War, Ernest's depth of experience in management and engineering was put to use to help better organise workforces and the allocation of material and speed up aircraft production. From 1940, he was the area officer for the Ministry of Aircraft Production in the north-western region and was made regional advisor to the ministry a year later. He was also served on the board of Bristol-based firm Parnell Aircraft to reduce their overheads.[73]

In October 1944, Ernest turned sixty-five, and to mark the occasion staff at all the Simon companies subscribed to buy a birthday gift of a large oil portrait by the one of the leading artists of the time, Thomas Cantrell

6.11 Presentation of the birthday portrait to Ernest by J. Mallard, Shop Stewards' Convenor, Henry Simon Ltd (1945). On the wall behind Ernest is the portrait of Henry Simon by Clara von Rappard. Source: SSP M14/4/24.

Dugdale (Figure 6.11; Plate 8). This was formally presented to Ernest in March 1945 after the Annual General Meetings of Henry Simon Ltd and Simon-Carves Ltd.[74] In a speech at the ceremony, leading shop steward Mr Mallard expressed the 'wonder and admiration felt by all who knew Sir Ernest at his astonishing capacity to combine the energetic control of two large firms and several subsidiaries with an amount of public work that most men would regard as a full time occupation in itself'.[75]

Postwar growth and the emergence of the diversified Simon Engineering Group

The Simon firms won a great deal of new work in the immediate postwar boom as their engineering skills were in demand for reconstruction and re-equipping factories, mills, collieries, power stations and chemical plants in Britain and abroad, as well as the broader economic realignment to civilian production after six years of war. The Simon companies had just under 4,000 employees and in 1946 and they booked £10.5m in new orders.[76] There were few competitors in some of their specialised fields of engineering and consulting, given the shattered economies of major European countries.

The seventy years of the Simon businesses, spanning the era of Henry's pioneering leadership and then Ernest's direction and diversification, had given rise to a substantial cluster of separate but allied companies involved in a range of fields of mechanical and chemical process engineering. The original key companies of Henry Simon Ltd and Simon-Carves Ltd had separate senior management and boards of directors but were pooling resources (such as HR and accounting) and sharing facilities on the expanded Cheadle Heath site. They were both still owned and controlled by the same small cadres of family shareholders. After the war, this collection of companies, and distinct contracting and consulting departments, began to be referred to in official documents and publicity as the Simon Engineering Group (SEG). The growth and diversification of the businesses was captured in a substantial self-published 170-page promotional book in 1947 that gave some historical details and was full of photographs of mills and plants the group's companies had recently built or equipped. In the late 1940s, there was a centrally directed campaign of brand advertising in relevant trade magazines and to an industrial business readership to imprint the notion of the Simon Engineering Group – although it was not a set of companies with a profile in the wider public imagination as they produced no consumer goods or services. The marketing tagline in the adverts that the group 'serves the fundamental needs of civilisation' was seemingly a rather grandiose claim but clearly resonated with Henry's ethos (Figure 6.13).

The details in the 1947 Simon Engineering Group book make it clear how far the original two companies focused on flour milling and coke-oven

THE SCOPE OF THE SIMON ENGINEERING GROUP

HENRY SIMON LTD.
  Milling Department — *Flour mills.*
  Provender Milling Department — *Provender mills.*
  Flour Treatment Department — *Chemical and physical flour treatment.*
    Mill fumigation.
    Entoleter infestation control.
    Mill laboratory service.
    Mill laboratory equipment.
  Silks and Wires Department — *Silk and wire covers.*
  Spare Parts Department — *Spare parts and mill accessories.*
  Conveying Department — *Mill silos.*
    Granaries.
    Warehouses.
    Mechanical handling.
    Pneumatic handling.
    Ship loading and discharging plants.
    Automatic weighing, blending and separating.
    Structural engineering.
  Soap Department — *Soap machinery.*
  Power Department — *Contractors for steam, gas, oil and electric power plants.*
  General Goods Department — *Paper-makers' supplies.*
    Merchandise goods.

TURBINE GEARS LTD. — *Gears and gear units.*
  Gear-cutting.

HENRY SIMON (ENG. WORKS) LTD. — *Engineering manufacture.*

TYRESOLES LTD. — *Tyre retreading.*
  Tyre repairing.
  Retreading and repair equipment.

TYRE PRODUCTS LTD. — *Rubber engineering components.*
  Rubber mats.
  General rubber products.

SIMON-CARVES LTD.
  Coke Oven and Washer Department — *By-product coke ovens.*
    By-product recovery plant.
    Gas producers.
    Coal and coke handling.
    Coal washers.
    Coal screening, blending and weighing.
    Coal storage.
    Colliery surface plant.
  Chemical Plant Department — *Sulphuric acid plants.*
    Sulphuric acid recovery and concentration plants.
    Chemical plant.
    Gasworks by-product plants.
    Electrostatic precipitators.
  Boiler Department — *Complete central and industrial power schemes.*
    Steam-raising plant.
    Boiler firing plant.
    Coal and ash handling plants.
    Associated civil engineering works.
  Building Department — *Industrial buildings.*
    Civil engineering.

DUDLEY FOUNDRY CO. LTD. — *Ironfounders.*
THOMAS ADSHEAD & SON LTD. — *Non-ferrous castings.*
  Light engineering manufacture.
  Bedsteads and household goods.

SANDHOLME IRON CO. LTD. — *Iron, steel and special alloy castings.*
  General engineers.

6.12 The span of the SEG companies and departments by the start of the postwar period. Source: Anthony Simon, *The Simon Engineering Group* (1947).

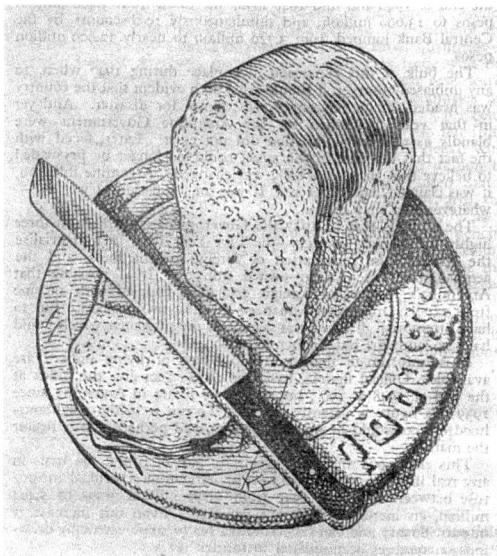

6.13 Example of brand marketing for the SEG in the postwar period. Source: *The Economist* (9 April 1949).

design founded by Henry had expanded and diversified into relevant specialties. The Henry Simon milling business had diversified into mechanical and pneumatic handling in the 1910s and this proved to be a major success for them, which was particularly evident in the two world wars. In 1911, it formed a separate conveying department based on years of experience building grain silos for flour mills and kitting them out. They further developed pneumatic systems of handling for other bulk materials like coal, ash and oxides and had installed many pneumatic plants of various types for use at ports, mills, power stations, gas works and breweries.

Simon-Carves' core was initially based around chemicals derived from coal, so it was logical – and proved profitable – to diversify into heavy machinery for collieries and specialised design of chemical plants, and later into coal-fired steam boilers for power stations. From 1900, a separate department exploited the Baum coal washer patent from Germany for use in British collieries. The First World War saw the birth of the chemical plant department, the product of wartime contracts for the building of sulphuric acid plants. The department grew significantly during the Second World War, constructing most of the sulphuric acid factories erected in Britain during the conflict.[77]

The growth in the SEG was not solely endogenous from the original two companies, as there were several significant external acquisitions and moves into new lines of business. In 1931, Turbine Gears Ltd was purchased, in part to keep work flowing in the economic troughs of the early 1930s when Henry Simon Ltd and Simon-Carves Ltd struggled to gain new contracts and suffered from bad debts and greater competition from efficient German firms. Acquisitions for supply chain security were made with controlling stakes taken in Thomas Adshead & Son Ltd and the Dudley Foundry, who made metal castings and components for the machinery assembled at the Cheadle Heath works. The Dudley company would become Simon Engineering (Midlands) Ltd in the 1950s and enjoyed considerable success designing vehicle-mounted hydraulic lifting platforms, including the celebrated Simon Snorkel firefighting appliance.[78] In the early 1930s, the Simon firms also acquired the patent rights from America for Tyresoles, a novel technique to retread old vehicle tyres for resale. This was a distinct new line of business but a justifiable direction, as the SEG book noted: 'It seemed to be precisely the kind of speciality that Henry Simon had once advised his sons to search for – "a new system or patent to achieve better results in some large industry".'[79] After an initial struggle to convince customers and build a market, the Tyresoles Ltd company was making a sizable profit by the 1940s. A decision was taken in 1953 to sell the UK business to Dunlop and use the capital gained to strengthen Tyresoles operations in international markets.[80]

Ernest's role in the SEG gradually changed after the war as he became solely the 'governing director' of the companies, stepping further back from management decision-making. He was approaching his later sixties and past formal retirement age. He seemed confident in a strong cadre of managing directors and executive boards that he had hand-picked and promoted in previous decades. It is clear, though, that Ernest remained connected with what still felt like the Simon family businesses – particularly when he was present in Manchester and able to visit Cheadle Heath or meet senior staff at Broomcroft. And undoubtedly, given his dominant personality and decades of commitment to the companies (plus his substantial shareholdings), he was a powerful figure in their overarching philosophy. The companies proudly acknowledged him as Lord Simon after his peerage in 1947. He also provided sage council to senior directors even though he devoted himself full time to the chairmanship of the BBC from 1947 to 1952. His position as something of an 'elder statesman' was, for example, visually resonant in a group photograph of Henry Simon Ltd managers published in the company newsletter in 1951 (Figure 6.14). The wider family still had a strong influence in terms of management positions, directorships and share ownership, with the rise to power of Ernest's nephews Anthony Simon and Christopher Simon, along with Shena's much younger brother Rupert Potter, which represented the passing of the reins of management in the running of Simon Engineering Group to a third generation of Simons.

An example of Ernest setting some of the strategic directions in this period was his alertness to the significance of the nationalisation of the coal industry and what that might mean for the family businesses, with it particularly changing the customer base for Simon-Carves Ltd and its subsidiaries. At the time, coal was the dominant source of energy in Britain and security of supply vital to the national economy. During the interwar period, the coal industry was widely viewed as inefficient due to its fragmented structure, with numerous small private mining companies unable to invest sufficiently to raise productivity. Labour relations were poor, and the sector suffered numerous strikes. But the hundreds of separate collieries had proved to be a good market for Simon-Carves Ltd. In these interwar decades, Ernest had a liberal view of economic matters and had long been wary of what he considered to be a dogmatic commitment of the Labour Party to the public ownership of key industries, including the collieries. In conjunction to running the risk of alienating customers for the Simon engineering businesses, this was a main rationale for him not to follow Shena in joining the Labour Party in the interwar years, despite it being largely otherwise aligned to his social and political objectives.[81]

By the early 1940s, and with his experience in wartime state-planning of production in the national interest, he came to see the benefits of the nationalisation of the coal mines for more economical operation for wider public benefit rather than private profit. Ernest joined the Labour Party in 1946, and in his maiden speech in the House of Lords in March 1947 spoke

Taken whilst some of our overseas representatives were assembled for a conference at Cheadle Heath earlier this year, this photograph shows on the front row (l. to r.) Messrs. G. H. Sugden, H. Bowes, P. Henry, J. F. Lockwood, Lord Simon of Wythenshawe, Sir Patrick Hamilton, Messrs. C. H. Marsh, C. H. Wooll, E. Olson, C. G. H. Simon, C. Pierson D'Autrey, and on the back row (l. to r.) Messrs. N. O. Simmons, B. C. Stamford, E. Swales, B. Smit, P. Dujoux, A. Ingvaldsen, W. T. Farmer, E. A. Stanger, C. A. Ashcroft, M. H. Rodway.

6.14 Ernest was still symbolically at the heart of the Henry Simon Ltd company, as illustrated in this publicity photograph from 1951. Seated next to him is his brother-in-law, Patrick Hamilton. Also pictured is Christopher Simon, Ernest's nephew. Source: JRL SEGA, 22, Occasional Letter, 214, October 1951. Copyright the University of Manchester (CC BY-NC-SA 4.0).

strongly in favour of nationalisation as the best way to raise the productivity of the miners. The debate was taking place just after the 'fuel crisis' in the harsh winter of 1946/47 when shortages of coal were acute. As Ernest said in the debate:

> I am that rather strange animal, a capitalist who is also a Socialist. I am actually responsible for a group of engineering firms, which I hope are rendering good service to the state at the present time. I am far from suggesting that capitalist industry is always inefficient ... But I do say, with confidence, that the capitalist system in conjunction with the governments that existed in the interwar years did make a very conspicuous failure of the coal industry.[82]

In the end, Simon-Carves found plenty of profitable business opportunities with the newly constituted National Coal Board as a single, large customer when the board embarked on an ambitious investment programme to raise the productivity of existing coal mines and develop new high-output 'super' pits. Simon-Carves cultivated this sector to bring technical know-how in mechanical handling to improve coal washing and grading plants at collieries (Plate 4). Simon-Carves was also winning large orders with other domestic nationalised industry, including steam boilers for the power station plant for the British Electricity Authority and coke ovens for new steel works for the Iron and Steel Corporation of Great Britain.

The Simon companies seem to have enjoyed a robust and growing order book into the 1950s and expanding profits. For example, annual profits before tax in Simon-Carves Ltd grew from just £154,000 in 1946 to over £1m in 1954.[83] The longstanding Simon ethos of investing back into the business for continued improvement and sustainable growth was reflected in the expansion of the Cheadle Heath site into what might be regarded in contemporary terminology as a corporate campus. In July 1951, a new R&D centre was opened for use across the SEG. This included a prominent tower containing a working model flour mill on which new machinery could be tested; it also served as a technical showroom for prospective customers. Keeping the companies ahead of the competition through investment in applied research and development of techniques was an approach that would have been familiar to, and approved by, Henry Simon. The size of the company in terms of staff numbers had also more than doubled in less than a decade, growing from 3,605 at the start of 1946 to over 7,800 by the beginning 1953; of these around 9 per cent were engineers and senior managers, 11 per cent were draughtsmen; the bulk were classed as skilled manual workers (59 per cent).[84]

The extent of investment in Cheadle Heath also signified the depth of connection to the greater Manchester region, despite the growing pressure on successful firms to join the drift of high-value engineering away from traditional northern strongholds to what were seen by many as more productive and modern sites in the south-east of England. Ernest was not tempted:

We have always firmly resisted the considerable temptations and advantages of London; we are convinced that for a business like ours the outskirts of Manchester provide pleasanter and better facilities for the staff and are on the whole more conducive to efficient and economical work. Moreover, London is already far too big; anybody who can refrain from adding to its size, in the national interest, should do so.[85]

The company did open a larger London office – Simon House on Dover Street in 1956 – but it was at that time still a branch office and not a headquarters. Likewise, Ernest and Shena were spending a lot of time in London in the 1950s, but they always saw their private apartment at Marsham Court as a working base and home remained at Broomcroft, Didsbury. The majority of staff were based at the Cheadle Heath site, but the SEG was truly international by the 1950s, winning contracts in wide range of countries, and also had a permanent presence in Australia, Argentina and South Africa.

Atomic power, stock market profits and mergers

From the mid-1950s, one innovative area pursued by Simon-Carves was that of atomic power engineering. This was in partnership with General Electric Company (GEC) Ltd and was a logical development for the company given their work on steam boilers for power stations, along with their strength in complex contracting, and practical experience in designing chemical plants that had to efficiently and safely process hazardous substances. Britain was at the forefront of civil nuclear energy with the

6.15 The expanded SEG site at Cheadle Heath (c. 1954). Source: *Steam Power Plant*, Simon-Carves Ltd (1955).

6.16 The tower containing a working model flour mill at Cheadle Heath topped off by a prominent 'SIMON' sign. Source: JRL SEGA, 23, Occasional Letter, 225, June 1953, p. 3. Copyright the University of Manchester (CC BY-NC-SA 4.0).

opening of the Calder Hall power station in 1956. The company was willing to devote significant resources of skilled engineering staff and capital (£100,000 was invested in 1956) to get into this new field.[86] It was in line with the ethos originated by Henry Simon to exploit new technical processes, but was not without its controversy, particularly given how closely civil atomic electrical power generation was bound to the secret world of nuclear weapons production. The new field also had invisible and unquantified dangers of radiation, which was exposed by the fire at the Windscale nuclear reactor in Cumbria in 1957. Nonetheless, the Simon-Carves Nuclear Power Division were successful in winning a major part of the construction of the Hunterston magnox power station in Scotland in 1957; and keeping up the export-oriented work, they were in the consortium awarded a contract to build the first atomic power station in Japan in 1959.[87] Quite how Ernest viewed this commercial pursuit of atomic energy work by the Simon-Carves' subsidiary is unclear, but what we do know is that he did become concerned about the wider scale threat of nuclear weapons and began to actively support CND in 1958. He chaired a high-profile CND rally at the Free Trade Hall in Manchester, acted as the president of the Manchester branch and one of his last speeches in the House of Lords in 1959 was on disarmament.[88] However, by this point his formal involvement with the companies was as honorific president, having stepped down from the chairmanship of Simon-Carves Ltd in 1954 in favour of Rupert Potter.

In the previous year, the holding company for Henry Simon Ltd subsidiaries seems to have become more avaricious with a significant public share offering on the stock market. This followed a similar share offering by Simon-Carves Ltd in autumn of 1955.[89] Some 20 per cent of the Henry Simon (Holdings) Ltd company were offered for sale, for the first time to the wider public, at 16s 9d per ordinary share.[90] The sale proved successful and increased the shareholder base from around 300 to over 1,200 – including some 280 SEG employees.[91] The power of longstanding family shareholders was diluted, but at the same they enjoyed a significant boost in financial value from the public share offerings and the increased stock market transactions. The unearned nature of this wealth troubled Ernest's conscience, 'but pride in the enterprise founded by his father and cherished by himself outweighed the thought that such enterprise was enabling a number of people, much as he loved them, to live in affluence on the labour of others'.[92]

In what turned out to be Ernest's final year, the Simon Engineering companies were significantly reorganised financially with the formal merging of the two major parts – Henry Simon and Simon-Carves. The announcement of the merger in March 1960 seemed to initiate a strange attempt to thwart the process, with a surprise takeover bid launched by EMI (Electric and Musical Industries company) to purchase Henry Simon Ltd outright. At the time the chairman of EMI was Joseph Lockwood, who had worked for Henry Simon Ltd since the 1930s, was chairman in the 1950s and was still a board member. (He is pictured sitting directly alongside Ernest in the 1951 photograph, Figure 6.14.) The company's board recommended shareholders reject the takeover, and it was subsequently withdrawn.[93] Ernest was on holiday with Shena in Cornwall while these

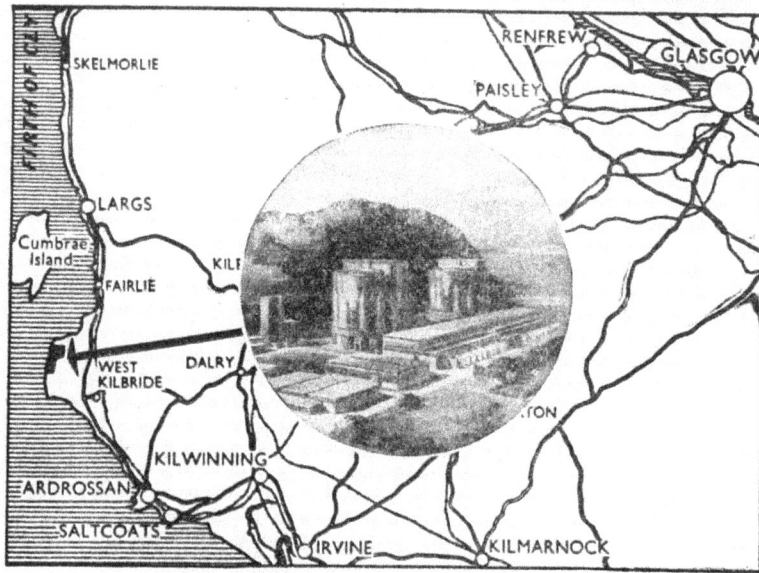

6.17 Simon-Carves Ltd advert celebrating their awarding of the Hunterston atomic power station contract. Source: *Financial Times* (13 November 1958).

events unfolded, and it seems he was not consulted, perhaps because he would not have been in favour of the financial 'wheeler-dealing'.[94] Rupert Potter, chairman of Simon-Carves Ltd, recommended the merger deal in his May 1960 annual report, 'I am convinced that the shareholders ... will benefit in the future from this landmark in our company history.'[95] The merger took effect in July 1960, unlocking the capital of the combined group – valued at £30m (which would be about £574m today) – and, again, there were unearned profits flowing to shareholders, which Ernest recorded as a 'most deplorable aspect of capitalism'.[96] Ernest died in October 1960. In their first year, the new Simon Engineering Group Ltd booked revenues of over £41m and a post-tax profits £2.8m.[97] It was controlled by Rupert Potter and the only Simon family member on the board was Christopher Simon, who also served as company secretary.

Conclusion

In the eight decades from late 1870s to 1960, the two Simon generations, father and son, had built a large, successful and well-regarded set of engineering companies. Henry's real success came from being a systems integrator, and also evidently from being a good salesman and self-promoter. In the initial two fields of flour milling and coke production, his ingenuity and drive meant he convinced companies to reorganise through all stages for efficiency of output using the Simon System.

The importance of Ernest's role through the first half of the twentieth century in steering the businesses forward should not be underestimated either. Despite taking a consciously 'hands-off' approach and devoting a great deal of time and energy to public work and politics, particularly after the First World War, his undoubted intellectual capacity and genuine interest in the technicalities of process engineering meant he had a significant positive impact on the steady growth of the family businesses. According to his biographer Stocks, 'there can be little doubt that his continued policy direction was a major factor in the spectacular expansion of both companies and their final evolution into the Simon Engineering Group with commitments for the installation of engineering plant[s] in four continents'.[98]

They were specialised firms and were little, if at all, known to the general public as they produced no consumer goods or services. However, they seemed to have enjoyed a strong reputation within their respective industrial engineering fields for quality, and as prudent and well-managed businesses within financial markets. Locally, in the Manchester area, the Simon firms were well known as excellent companies to work for.[99]

Importantly, they largely remained family businesses through to the 1960s which embodied the ethos of Henry, inherited and promulgated by Ernest, in doing 'good business' and deserving of the rewards of success because they were also creating wider benefits to society by improving the efficiency of key industrial processes. Furthermore, a good deal of the profits were purposefully reinvested into the business (often to the benefit of clients and staff ahead of the directors and shareholders). Moreover, much of the personal wealth flowing to Henry and Ernest from the business was directed into philanthropic projects and supporting their public work.

They were doing good business in several senses of economic value and social values:

> [Henry's] view, which still prevails, was that the family firms should have higher aims than the mere earning of dividends for the shareholders; they should provide the best possible conditions of long and secure employment, and they should discharge their full share in applying scientific invention and progress to the improvement of standards of living throughout the nation and the world. They should be, in short, a credit to British industry.[100]

The Simon family engineering businesses were evidently that.

Notes

1 Quote from Ernest Simon's reflection on the development of the family companies, after his being in charge for nearly forty years. Ernest Simon in: Anthony Simon, *The Simon Engineering Group* (Cheadle Heath: privately printed, 1947), p. ix.

2 Ernest consciously downplayed his business work as he became engaged in national political life, yet he remained central to the success of the companies. The biography of Ernest by Mary Stocks (Mary Stocks, *Ernest Simon of Manchester* (Manchester: Manchester University Press, 1963)) has relatively little coverage of his involvement in the engineering companies. The lengthy obituary to Ernest in the *Guardian* (4 October 1960), p. 4, barely mentions his substantial work directing the family businesses.

3 There are promotional books titled *The Simon Engineering Group*, privately published by the firms in two editions, 1947 and 1953, by Anthony Simon. (Henceforth, referenced as *SEG* (1947) and *SEG* (1953).) These provide considerable historical details but an unsurprisingly positive reading of business developments. Early editions of the marketing catalogues produced for customers by the Simon milling company contain lengthy introductory essays by Henry that chart the development of the business. The 1886 catalogue *On Roller Milling* is held in the John Rylands Library; the 1892 catalogue *The Present Position of Roller Flour Milling* is available on Google Books; a copy of the 1898 catalogue *Modern Flour Mill Machinery* is held by the author. Henry Simon also wrote substantial articles about milling published in *Proceedings of the Institution of Civil Engineers* in 1882 and in *Proceedings of the Institution of Mechanical Engineers* in 1889 which provide useful sources of information, although clearly have a self-interested perspective. He also wrote two articles on the coke-oven business in *The Journal of the Iron and Steel Institute* in 1880 and 1885. There is academic examination of the historical development of roller flour milling that does provide some details of Henry Simon's contribution: Jennifer Tann and R. Glyn Jones, 'Technology and Transformation: The Diffusion of the Roller Mill in British Flour Milling Industry, 1870–1907', *Technology and Culture*, 37:1 (1996), 36–69; Glyn Jones, *The Millers: A Story of Technological Endeavour and Industrial Success, 1870–2001* (Lancaster: Carnegie Publishing Ltd, 2001). The coke oven sector, developed as Simon-Carves company is much less well examined, although see D. G. Edwards, 'Financing the Construction of Early By-product Coking Plants', *Business Archives: Sources and History*, 74 (November 1997), 45–52.

4 There are some valuable historic materials on the companies in public archives. Manchester Libraries, Information and Archives hold business records for Simon-Carves Ltd from 1898–1967, ref. GB124.B.CAR. The University of Manchester

Library special collections holds materials relating to Henry Simon Ltd in the Simon Engineering Group archive.
5   For example, www.simoncorrugating.com/history; www.henrysimonmilling.com/aboutus/company-heritage; www.ottosimon.co.uk/history (all accessed 10 October 2023). Also see the Conclusion to this volume.
6   Brian Simon, *In Search of a Grandfather: Henry Simon, 1835–1899* (Leicester: Pendene Press, 1997), p. 40. There are scant details on Henry's early years working in Manchester and largely identical information is given in the obituaries of him in the *Manchester Guardian* (24 July 1899, p. 9) and in *Proceedings of The Institution of Civil Engineers and Mechanical Engineers*.
7   Simon, *In Search of a Grandfather*, p. 40.
8   Henry Simon, 'Modern Flour-milling in England', *Proceedings of the Institution of Civil Engineers*, 70 (1882), 198.
9   Simon, 'Modern Flour-milling in England', 194.
10 Tann and Jones, 'Technology and Transformation', 43–6.
11 Simon, 'Modern Flour-milling in England', pp. 191–233; Richard Perren, 'Structural Change and Market Growth in the Food Industry: Flour Milling in Britain, Europe, and America, 1850–1914', *Economic History Review*, 43:3 (1990), 423–4.
12 Alexander McDougall (1809–99), originally from Coldstream in Scotland, had relocated to Manchester by the 1850s and worked as a manufacturing chemist. He created self-raising flour by the addition of a yeast substitute chemical to make the dough rise. To profit from his innovation he started, with his sons, their eponymous flour business in Manchester in 1864. They went into the milling business by end of 1860s including opening City Mill in Ancoats. From the 1880s, the business was run by Arthur McDougall (1847–1912).
13 Henry Simon, 'On the Latest Development of Roller Flour Milling', *Proceedings of the Institution of Mechanical Engineers* 40 (1889), 148–92.
14 Simon, 'Modern Flour-milling in England'.
15 Simon, 'On the Latest Development of Roller Flour Milling'.
16 Tann and Jones, 'Technology and Transformation', 49.
17 *SEG* (1953), p. xlii
18 Simon, *In Search of a Grandfather*, pp. 54–5
19 *SEG* (1953), p. 12.
20 Simon, 'Modern Flour-milling in England'.
21 Simon, 'Modern Flour-milling in England', 209, 216.
22 Jennifer Tann, 'Simon, Henry (1835–1899), Industrialist and Inventor', in *Oxford Dictionary of National Biography*; Tann and Jones, 'Technology and Transformation', 51.
23 Perren, 'Structural Change and Market Growth in the Food Industry', 420–37.
24 Simon, 'Modern Flour-milling in England', 192.
25 See: Perren, 'Structural Change and Market Growth in the Food Industry'.
26 *On Roller Milling* catalogue (1886).
27 Simon, *In Search of a Grandfather*, p. 53.
28 Edwards, 'Financing the Construction of Early By-product Coking Plants'.
29 Henry Simon, 'An Improved System for the Utilisation of Bye-products in the Manufacture of Coke', *Journal of the Iron and Steel Institute*, 1 (1880), 137–62.
30 R. Dixon, 'On the Cost and the Results of the Simon-Carves Coke Ovens', *Journal of the Iron and Steel Institute*, 2 (1883), 494–503.
31 Editors, 'On the Manufacture of Coke: Discussion', *Journal of the Iron and Steel Institute*, 2 (1883), 515–51.
32 Henry Simon, 'Recent Results and Further Development of the Simon-Carves Coking Process (Utilisation of Bye-products)', *Journal of the Iron and Steel Institute*, 5 (1885), 108–19.
33 Edwards, 'Financing the Construction of Early By-product Coking Plants'.

34 *The Coal Trade Bulletin*, 18:4 (15 January 1908), p. 51.
35 Private family papers, Henry Simon *Rathschaelage für Meine Kinder* (Manchester: c. 1899), p. 55.
36 *SEG* (1947), p. xvi.
37 *SEG* (1953), p. 13.
38 Simon, 'On the Latest Development of Roller Flour Milling', 148–63.
39 1892 Henry Simon Milling catalogue.
40 1892 Henry Simon Milling catalogue, p. 4.
41 1892 Henry Simon Milling catalogue, p. 9.
42 Henry Simon, 'Chaudron's Method of Shaft Sinking through Water-bearing Strata without Pumping and the Results Obtained By It', *Journal of the Iron and Steel Institute* 1 (1877), 187–202; Henry Simon and Charles Fairbairn 'Improvement in machines for impressing screw-threads on bolts, etc.', Letters Patent No. 200, 522 (19 February 1878).
43 They were published frequently, up to at least 1957. In later years they were titled 'Occasional Letters'. Whilst not unbiased, they provide fascinating details on the Henry Simon milling company. A complete bound set is held by JRL in SEGA.
44 See Chapter 3 in this volume by Diana Leitch.
45 Simon, *In Search of a Grandfather*, pp. 106, 108.
46 JRL SEGA, 16, Henry Simon, Circular to Clients, no. XXV, June 1895, p. 1.
47 Richard Bennett and John Elton, *History of Corn Milling*, 4 vols (London: Simpkin, Marshall and Company Ltd, 1900–04), III, p. 314.
48 *Minutes of the Proceedings of the Institution of Civil Engineers*, 138 (1899), 494–7; *Memoirs of Proceedings of the Institution of Mechanical Engineers*, 56 (1899), 270–2.
49 JRL SEGA, 17, *Circular to Clients*, LIII, December 1899, p. 1.
50 JRL SEGA, 18, Occasional Letter, LVIII, March 1901, p. 1.
51 *SEG* (1953), p. viii.
52 *SEG* (1953), p. xxiv.
53 *SEG* (1953), p. xlii.
54 JRL SEGA, 19, Occasional Letter, 102, January 1916, p. 2.
55 JRL SEGA, 20, Occasional Letter, 107, December 1918.
56 Stocks, *Ernest Simon of Manchester*, p. 51.
57 Stocks, *Ernest Simon of Manchester*, p. 47.
58 'From Fallowfield to Cheadle Heath: Model Factory Plans Changed', *Manchester Guardian* (16 May 1923), p. 11.
59 *SEG* (1947), p. xvi.
60 SSP M14/6/4, 'Henry Simon Ltd., Manchester. A Review of the Past Year's Activities by the Chairman' (24 January 1927).
61 'A Modern Granary', *Nature*, 131 (25 March 1933), 431–2.
62 *SEG* (1953), p. xiii.
63 *SEG* (1947), p. xiv.
64 Stocks, *Ernest Simon of Manchester*, p. 13.
65 ESD, 7 February 1920.
66 JRL SEGA, 21, Occasional Letter, 173, July 1945, p. 4.
67 Brian Simon, *Henry Simon's Children* (Leicester: The Pendene Press, 1999), p. 49.
68 The book was over 220 pages long and grew out of technical papers Ernest had presented to the National Association of British and Irish Millers in 1913, 1923 and 1928. For the authorship he was able to lean upon expert help from the engineering and scientific staff at the company, of course.
69 JRL SEGA, 21, Occasional Letter, 153, January 1934, p. 1.
70 *SEG* (1947), p. xx.
71 *SEG* (1953), pp. xlv–xlvi.
72 JRL SEGA, 21, Occasional Letter, 176, June 1946, p. 1.

73 Stocks, *Ernest Simon of Manchester*, pp. 114–17; 'Parnell Aircraft Board', the *Financial Times* (18 February 1943), p. 1.
74 'Sir Ernest Simon: Employees' Tribute', *Manchester Guardian* (27 March 1945), p. 6.
75 JRL SEGA, 21, Occasional Letter, 173, July 1945, p. 1.
76 *SEG* (1947), p. xii.
77 *SEG* (1953), pp. x–xi, 80–1.
78 'Snorkel to the Rescue: Versatile Aid for Firemen', *Guardian* (15 September 1961), p. 3.
79 *SEG* (1947), p. 85.
80 *SEG* (1953), p. xii.
81 Stocks, *Ernest Simon of Manchester*, p. 76.
82 Hansard (Lords), 19 March 1947, vol. 146, cols 531–32.
83 Simon-Carves Ltd advertisement, *Manchester Guardian* (26 September 1955), p. 9.
84 *SEG* (1953), p. xlii.
85 *SEG* (1953), p. xlii.
86 '£100,000 of Profit Set Aside: Nuclear Power Research', *Manchester Guardian* (19 June 1956), p. 14.
87 '30M. A-plant for Japan', *Manchester Guardian* (30 March 1959), p. 1. Much closer to home, Simon-Carves were successful in winning a contract with Manchester City Council to build the new municipal swimming baths in Wythenshawe in 1958!
88 Stocks, *Ernest Simon of Manchester*, pp. 146–51.
89 'Simon-Carves Offer: New Issue Queue Still Growing', *Manchester Guardian*, (20 September 1955), p. 10.
90 'A Family Business Comes to Market', *The Economist* (9 November 1957), p. 526.
91 'Henry Simon (Holdings) Limited: Record Profit under Increasingly Competitive Conditions', *Manchester Guardian* (23 June 1958), p. 8.
92 Stocks, *Ernest Simon of Manchester*, p. 136.
93 'Simon Firms Merge: E.M.I Drops Bid', *Guardian* (10 March 1960), p. 20.
94 Stocks, *Ernest Simon of Manchester*, p. 161.
95 'Simon-Carves Limited', *Financial Times* (26 May 1960), p. 6.
96 'Simon Group Merger', *Financial Times* (25 May 1960), p. 1. Approximate 2023 valuation taken from Bank of England inflation calculator.
97 'Simon Engineering Limited: First Consolidated Results Since Merger', *Guardian* (26 May 1961), p. 17.
98 Stocks, *Ernest Simon of Manchester*, pp. 39–40.
99 Anecdotal comments from older local people in Manchester and former employees to the editors of this volume.
100 JRL SEGA, 21, Occasional Letter, 173, July 1945, p. 2.

7

Shena Simon: feminism, civic patriotism and the strength of local government

Charlotte Wildman

Shena Simon became a Manchester citizen in 1912 aged twenty-eight after meeting and marrying Ernest Simon that same year. Shena's friend and colleague, the Labour politician and local councillor Mabel Tylecote, noted that when she arrived in the city Shena 'was beautiful and highly intelligent, already deeply committed to economic studies and social work and had a wide acquaintance among the social and political thinkers of her day'.[1] This commitment to public service ensured Shena became one of the most high-profile members of the Simon family and one of the most influential women to contribute to local government in the early and mid-twentieth century. Shena has largely been remembered for her valuable contributions to education, particularly as the first woman to chair the Manchester Education Committee in 1932, as well as her involvement in developing the Wythenshawe housing estate. Yet, Shena's commitment to reforming local taxation, and especially through her opposition to the rates system, placed her at the forefront of debates around the design, function and financing of municipal government. Although Shena was unsuccessful in her own lifetime in achieving the repeal of the rates, its replacement by the Poll tax and, subsequently, by Council tax, and ongoing discussions around fiscal devolution, illustrates Shena's innovative approach and expert understanding of local government.

Born in Croydon to an affluent family, Shena was educated at home before studying economics at Newnham College, Cambridge, from 1904 to 1907. After striking up correspondence with Beatrice Webb, Shena began research on the Labour party at the London School of Economics in 1907. This project remained unfinished, however, as she became drawn into work investigating the sweated industries, visited Australia and New Zealand to study their use of wage boards, and campaigned with the social reformer Margaret MacDonald. She first visited Manchester to stay with her friend, the feminist and family planning campaigner Eva Hubback, in 1912. Eva was friends with Ernest's cousin, Edith Eckhard, who introduced Shena to Ernest. Shena and Ernest married in November 1912, having only met each other seven times before their engagement. Making their home in Didsbury, Manchester, their first child, Roger, was born in October 1913 and their second son, Brian, was born in 1915. Their daughter Antonia was born in 1917 but sadly died aged twelve. Beatrice Webb captured something of their devastation about the tragic loss of Antonia when she recounted a visit from the Simons to her home: 'E.D. Simon and his wife here for weekend. Broken hearted about the death of a dearly loved child after three or four years slowly developing cancer of the face and hand – eating away the eye and then affecting the brain. But about this they did not speak.'[2] In light of this unimaginable personal tragedy, Shena's achievements are only more impressive. She was the Liberal councillor for the Chorlton-cum-Hardy ward from 1924 until 1933 and in 1932 became

7.1 Shena in 1912. Source: SSP M14/4/3.

the first woman chairman of the Manchester Education Committee. She also became chairman of the Rating and Valuation Association in 1955, received the Freedom of Manchester in 1964, and finally retired from the Manchester Education Committee in 1970, just two years before her death.

Shena's success and influence helps to challenge two important gaps in historical scholarship. Firstly, although women were involved in local politics from the late nineteenth century and could stand for elections to borough and county councils from 1907, we know little about their role as municipal politicians. In contrast, there is a broad body of research on the campaign for women's enfranchisement and on national women's movements.[3] However, scholarship addressing women's political involvement following their national enfranchisement has centred on women MPs or on forms of activism outside of formal power structures.[4] The important work of Patricia Hollis remains the only comprehensive account of women's involvement in local politics and focuses on the pre-1914 period to situate women's contribution to local government within the wider path to universal suffrage. Hollis argues that women were drawn to local government 'not only as a place of political power in its own right but as a stepping-stone to national power'.[5] Shena was known to support women's suffrage and championed women's rights more generally; however, her priority was to improve living standards by delivering comprehensive public services that were financially secure. Hollis also suggests that local government provided a more straightforward space for women than national politics as it offered 'more women's content' and 'they occupied, and clearly felt comfortable in, a semi-detached space of their own'.[6] Shena's career and contributions to local politics in Manchester complicates this narrative. Although her work in education and housing could be considered a reflection of women's domestic role and responsibilities, it was underpinned by her understanding of municipal financial infrastructure. Shena's largely overlooked contributions in shaping new ideas about local taxation show that women's contributions in finance and policy need greater acknowledgement.

Secondly, Shena's career and accomplishments challenge the notion of decline in the strength and role of local government in Britain during the early and mid-twentieth century. Along with the work of her husband, Ernest, Shena's achievements undermine the assumptions that the contributions of local elites to large municipal projects decreased. Urban historians, such as Simon Gunn and Robert Morris, have emphasised the retreat of the upper middle classes from urban spaces from the early twentieth century and as the working classes increasingly occupied centre stage.[7] Shena's focus on housing and education supports more recent research which not only illuminates the strength of civic patriotism and the continued investment of urban elites, but also shows how municipal projects emphasised the importance of local citizenship after 1918. For example,

Tom Hulme argues local government's interwar investment in education was used to foster greater civic duty and suggests the emphasis on teaching 'civics' reinforced 'the relationship between local state, the city, liberty and active citizenship'.[8] In her own 1938 publication, *A Century of City Government*, Shena suggested that a 'serious handicap to good government is the lack of local interest in municipal affairs'. For Shena, citizenship needed to be reciprocal, and she lamented that 'too many citizens feel they have done all that is required of them when they have paid their rates'.[9] Hulme's approach helps to understand Shena's investment in education as part of a broader civic project to strengthen municipal culture and engender civic patriotism within inhabitants. Similarly, my own research has situated the Wythenshawe housing estate, a project Shena was closely connected to, within a broader period of flourishing civic pride and emphasised its portrayal as a break with the city's Victorian past and its associations with stark inequalities.[10] Taken together, we can see that Shena's commitment to local government, public services and tax reform was reflective of her commitment to the strength and autonomy of municipal government and civic citizenship. Although her achievements and the scale of her work were exceptional, Shena was part of a broader movement of civic patriots who contributed to the vitality of municipal culture in the face of increasing centralisation and intervention from central government in mid-twentieth century Britain.[11]

This chapter therefore examines the career and contributions made by Shena in local government. It draws on the archival collection of Shena's papers, press coverage (which was almost entirely favourable in the *Manchester Guardian*, owing to her links with the Scott family) and from biographical studies, such as that written by her daughter-in-law Joan Simon in 1986.[12] It analyses her key achievements and beliefs in relation to housing, education, women's rights and maternity care and taxation. This assessment of her career, her ideas and the strategies she deployed within these areas, shows historians need to understand more about the contributions of women in local government and illustrates the ongoing commitment to cultures of civic pride by the local elite. However, it also reveals that Shena deserves greater recognition for shaping approaches to public services and their funding. Perhaps by illuminating her achievements we can more comprehensively recognise the role women played to ensure the vitality of local government throughout the twentieth century.

Politics and women's rights

Shena's interest in women's rights was well established by the time she arrived in Manchester. Shena supported female suffrage but did not participate in any militancy herself, owing to her parents' opposition.[13] During her postgraduate studies, Shena had been honorary secretary of the Legislation Committee of the National Union of Women Workers when Margaret MacDonald was chairman. Shena also assisted Margaret on a Committee for Safeguarding Women's Interests in relation to the 1911 National Insurance Act, which Shena criticised for not doing enough for women or for female, casualised, low-paid workers. Yet, when Shena first engaged in Manchester's public life, 'she appeared ready to take up an active role in the women's movement, but adopted a more cautious approach to women's rights'.[14] In 1913, Shena acknowledged the need to engage with women municipal voters in Didsbury and Withington along nonparty lines as a way to bring about reform on social issues, particularly those impacting women and children. Subsequently, in 1914, she helped to establish the Manchester and Salford Women Citizens Association (WCA). Its purpose focused on '"interesting women in the good government of the city" for its sake and theirs'. By 1916, there were twelve branches averaging seventy members, five of which were composed of almost entirely working women, and the association was starting to spread to other cities.[15] It aimed to remain apolitical and their work hoped to ensure that 'women voters shall realise how much they can do for women and children by pressing for better housing, more efficient cleansing, and more open spaces' and to encourage women to stand as candidates for the Board of Guardians and the Council.[16] The association was successful and engaged significant numbers of women and, in 1930, 2,000 women attended a gathering for the association at the Town Hall hosted by the Lord Mayor and Lady Mayoress of Manchester. The Lord Mayor praised the association for 'doing splendid work in developing the interest of women in civic life and work'.[17]

Despite her initial caution, Shena was thrown further into civic and political life in Manchester once Ernest became Lord Mayor in 1921. Shena later recalled that she had found the position of Lady Mayoress surprisingly empowering because it had enabled her 'to stimulate and encourage those activities' that she believed 'to be in the best interest of the city'.[18] She caused significant outcry in December 1921 when she refused to give out the Christmas presents to children at St Mary's hospital in the city because of its lack of women on the management and staff. The women's group of the Fabian Society subsequently passed a motion in support of Shena, asserting that it was 'only through publicity of this nature that women will be able to be helped in their struggle for professional justice'.[19] Shena used her platform as Lady Mayoress to encourage women to contribute to municipal government more fully and to promote the work of the WCA. She argued women's involvement was key because the rates 'come out of the family budget, and everyone knew it was the woman who arranged that budget'.[20] Shena campaigned successfully with the WCA to improve maternity care and convinced Manchester Corporation to introduce municipal maternity centres. Shena worked with Ernest, who was on the Sanitary Committee, and its chairman, Alderman William Turner Jackson, to establish these centres in 1914–15, with financial support via a grant from central government. Ernest acknowledged the 'urgent need' to improve child and maternal health, noting that in 1913 around 2,500 children in Manchester had died before reaching their first birthday.[21] Shena explained that the centres were 'the only way to ensure a comprehensive, efficient and permanent scheme' and 'because work of such importance to the nation should be paid for out of public funds and administered by councillors responsible to the ratepayers'.[22] This approach was part of a broader, gradual shift towards greater state involvement in welfare, facilitated by the Liberal government social reforms.[23] As Manchester Corporation acknowledged, intervention had become more pressing in the context of the death and destruction caused by the First World War.[24] The scheme also reflected Shena's foresight in understanding the need for the local state to invest in local infrastructure to alleviate hardship. It set up a comprehensive system of support starting during pregnancy and ensured 'the interest of the child will be safeguarded before it is born and right through its infancy and school days'.[25] These centres were very successful and, in 1926, Ernest wrote that 'the scheme has worked excellently', as infant deaths under the age of one year old had fallen from 173 per thousand between 1901–05, to 96 per thousand for the period, 1920–24.[26] Shena also ensured the WCA became a kind of informal pressure group for the treatment of women in hospitals. In 1934, it was represented at the inquiry of a woman who had died shortly after her baby had been born at St Mary's hospital. The association sent a woman counsel who explained that its members – at that time numbering between 3,000 and 4,000 – 'had found that public confidence had been disturbed' by the case and wanted the hospital to provide an explanation 'so that the confidence of the women of the city should be restored. Confidence was an essential condition to the reduction of maternal mortality.'[27] As an example, it provides some sense of Shena's conception of civic citizenship that was both gendered and also linked to broader kinds of activism and the contribution made by women's voluntary organisations to the women's movement more generally after the First World War.[28]

Shena also conceived of civic citizenship as a way for married women to make positive contributions to society. At a Manchester high school speech day, she said that marriage alone was not enough to be a worthy and productive citizen: 'any woman who is not doing a full day's work is a parasite to the community'.[29] When Shena was made Freeman of Manchester in 1964, she used her speech to complain about the 'wastage in not developing the country's resources of women power'. She stressed that girls who received a grant for training 'were not entitled morally to throw up their vocation for marriage', particularly those who were qualified teachers.[30] Shena understood the barriers that married women faced

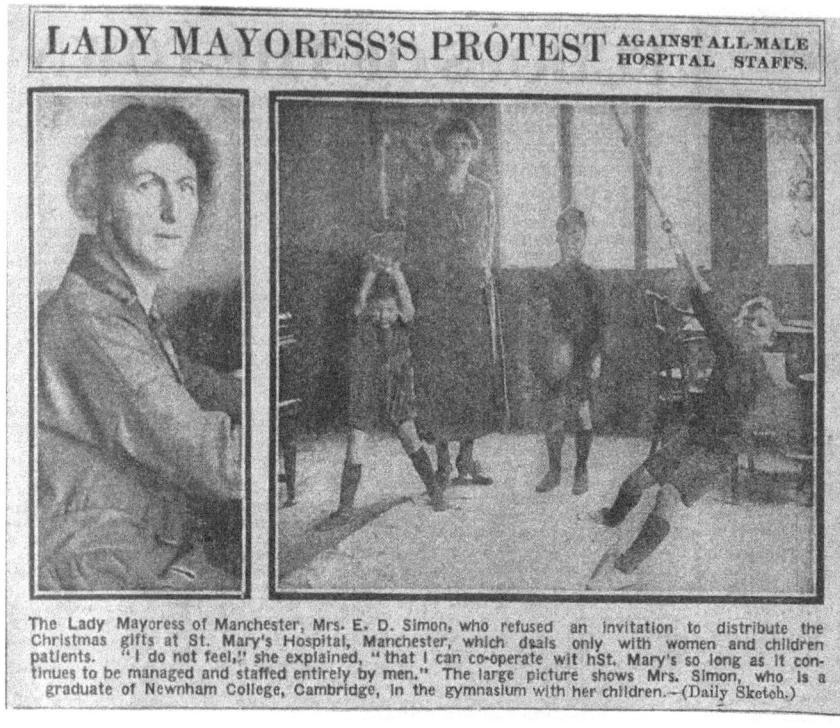

7.2 A news clipping about Shena's protest at the lack of women managers at St Mary's hospital. From *Daily Sketch* (26 November 1921). Source: M14/6/7.

in trying to contribute to the public sphere, particularly when they were mothers. Consequently, when asked what her greatest achievement was later in life, she stated that it was her 1928 victory in getting women teachers in Manchester permission to continue working after having children.[31] The decision was widely celebrated within feminist circles, such as in the periodical the *Woman's Leader and the Common Cause*, published by the National Union of Societies for Equal Citizenship. It praised the work of Shena and her colleague and ally Wright Robinson, for having 'fought a most excellent fight for the liberties, status, and opportunities of women'.[32] Her awareness of women's roles outside the home also motivated and shaped Shena's interest in the provision of nursery schools. In 1921, Shena and Ernest provided the use of the house and grounds known as Kirklees in Didsbury for the Education Department to use as a day nursery and she became increasingly committed to the provision of educational spaces for the under-fives.[33]

Shena certainly sought to live by her own beliefs. She first stood for local election in Chorlton in 1923. It was a challenging ward to contest, both because of the popularity of the incumbent Conservative candidate and because it was the largest ward in the city with 17,500 voters.

7.3 Shena and Ernest visiting a babies' hospital (1922). Source: M14/6/7.

Shena 'fought a hard campaign … and held more meetings than any other candidate in the city'.[34] The *Manchester Guardian* reported Shena's campaign positively and suggested that 'bred in a high tradition of social service, a student of local government, a ready, incisive speaker, she would speedily become a distinguished figure in the City Council'.[35] Shena lost by just over two hundred votes, a remarkable achievement both in light of the significant challenges of contesting the Chorlton ward and because of the lack of support women candidates generally received, including from the political parties they sought to represent, as 'women found it hard to be selected for council seats and even harder to win them'.[36] The following year, Shena 'won Chorlton-cum-Hardy brilliantly, with an impressive majority of 579'.[37] By 1930, Shena's majority was over 5,000 and reflected her popularity as a councillor and her visible public presence in municipal politics.[38] The main focus of her work within the council was for the Sanitary Committee and the Education Committee and she also became interested in housing. Her biographer and daughter-in-law, Joan Simon, speculated that Shena's involvement in these three large areas of council business reduced the time she could spend with her constituents, which contributed to her losing her seat in 1933.[39]

7.4 Shena's campaign pamphlet for the 1924 local elections. Source: SSP M14/6/9.

Despite this long commitment to public service, Shena's upper-class lifestyle drew criticisms and she and Ernest were often seen as out of touch. Tylecote suggested that the comfort of their surroundings shielded them from the harsh realities of life in interwar Manchester:

> Their devotion to causes seemed almost of necessity to lead to an unawareness of the feelings of other people, differently motivated, many of whom they gathered around them in their home at Broomcroft to launch some social programme ... but they were isolated by their wealth from much common experience, despite the strength of their human sympathies. As one senior member of what may be described as a Manchester University family once summed the matter up, 'The trouble with the Simons is that they have never ridden in a tram.'[40]

Consequently, the privileges afforded by her upper-class life and the sheer scale of her achievements meant Shena was not universally popular and had a reputation for being intimidating and exacting. Tylecote also recalled that 'there is no doubt that she inspired fear in the hearts of many people, that her criticism could be sharp and her questioning relentless. Inefficiency and indecision annoyed her greatly and she could be persistently argumentative in committee and authoritative in manner.'[41] Yet such anecdotes only help to understand how Shena was able to achieve so much in difficult circumstances. Beatrice Webb described Shena and Ernest as 'handsome, intellectual and public spirited ... This admirable couple have indeed only one defect – they are a little too "superior"; and regard most of their fellows with kindly contempt – especially the wife in her attitude towards her fellow town councillors in general and towards the labour men in particular.'[42] However, this insight provides some sense of how Shena may have coped with and responded to the inevitable hostility she experienced as one of the few women in local government, particularly one that challenged the views and ideas of so many of the men councillors that she encountered. As Hollis has shown, women found it particularly difficult to win seats on the councils of large city councils such as Manchester, and notes that 'many people were unpersuaded that council work was suitable work for women'.[43] It is difficult to comprehend the kinds of hostility women in the sphere of local politics endured and this makes the scale of Shena's successes even more notable.

Housing and education

Despite her electoral disappointments, Shena made significant progress in addressing the housing problem. Improving housing was a key aim of the work of the WCA and the Salford branch authored a report into housing in the St Matthias Ward in 1931. Shena moved the adoption on the report at their annual meeting and 'said that she hoped the Association would continue to agitate about housing until the slum problem of both cities was solved'.[44] Its annual meeting of 1933 continued this campaign work and Shena's speech encouraged members to push councillors on the need to build more family houses in Manchester: 'You will not get people rehoused unless you make a great deal more fuss about it than you do at present.'[45] Perhaps one of the greatest symbols of interwar civic pride was Ernest and Shena's purchase of land at Wythenshawe that they donated to Manchester Corporation to help address the shortage of working-class housing. Shena was a member of Wythenshawe Estate Special Committee from its creation in 1926 and its chairman 1931–33. For Shena, the investment in housing was crucial in her approach towards public services; explaining that Wythenshawe was central in 'my endeavour ... [which] has always been to provide the municipal service necessary to ensure eventually the goal of equal opportunity for every child in the city'.[46] Shena has been accused of disliking the houses built on the Wythenshawe estate, but Andrzej Olechnowicz argues this is unfair because the aesthetics of the homes were crucial for the success of the development. 'A concern with the appearance of houses was sensible when Manchester Conservatives and others were looking for any excuse to attack the development', suggests Olechnowicz, and he notes that Shena wanted appealing houses that would draw in middle-class residents, as well as the working classes.[47] Shena also understood the problems relating to community for new residents of the estate and she remained connected to Wythenshawe, receiving many invitations to participate in events by residents and letters for assistance.[48]

Shena's achievements in education were arguably more impressive and her name became synonymous with new measures to tackle the impact of social inequalities on education. The resolution providing Shena with the Freedom of Manchester explained that:

> In all her work, she has been inspired by a profound faith in the value of ever-expanding educational opportunity and its power to influence the wider destiny of man ... For her eminent services as well as for her intellectual distinction, her humanitarian sympathies and her high sense of public duty she is everywhere recognised as one of the leading citizens of Manchester and one of the foremost educationalists of our time.[49]

Her reforms focused on the development of a single Code of Regulations for schools, the removal of fees for secondary schools and championing the comprehensive education system. Jane Martin, in her and Joyce Goodman's history of women and education, argues that for Shena Simon, 'the injunction to promote the common good was not just an intellectual matter, but also a moral priority'. Martin stresses that Shena's approach to education was part of a broader endeavour by middle-class social reformers who emphasised the value of service. She explains that Shena saw schools as having the potential to be 'agencies of social change to reduce social inequalities'.[50] This ideology about the role of education manifested itself explicitly in her opposition to the eleven plus and she was known to be very pleased about Manchester's adoption of the comprehensive system of schooling in 1967.[51] Despite losing her council seat in 1933, Shena served as a co-opted member of the Manchester Education Committee between 1936 and 1970. This service was described in her obituary in the *Guardian*, which noted that Shena spent forty-three years on the education committee supporting motions 'consistently in favour of working-class education'.[52] Shena was 'committed to a belief in the educability of *all* children and the principle of everyone of secondary school age going to schools designed for all abilities. She was optimistic that the common school could create social cohesion and provide the arena in which a really democratic community could be attained.'[53] Like housing, therefore, Shena understood education as a crucial provision within a suite of public services that would nurture and sustain a democratic society in which all would prosper.

In developing her ethos towards educational reform, Shena was notably influenced by the work of Richard H. Tawney, the economic historian and campaigner for adult education.[54] Shena was also very close to Spurley Hey, director of education in Manchester from 1914 until his sudden death in 1930. In 1928, he wrote to Shena to 'pay tribute to the work you have accomplished on behalf of education. I have never known a better member of an education committee.'[55] Hsiao-Yuh Ku highlights the importance of Shena's trip to visit the Soviet Union in 1936, during which she examined their methods of education provision. Ku concludes that Shena's 'ideal of "equality of educational opportunity", acted constantly as a solid foundation for all her reform proposals'.[56] Shena's commitment to education was the catalyst for joining the Labour Party in 1935, in response to 'the government's treatment of education, which I feel to be the most fundamental of all social questions'.[57] Shena did not limit her contribution to education to schools, however, and both she and Ernest served on the council of Manchester University, where research fellowships still bear their name. The university named a teaching building after them in the 1960s, and included a café originally named Potters in honour of Shena's maiden name. The Shena Simon campus, originally a sixth form college formed in 1982 and now part of the Manchester College in Manchester city centre, reflects the ongoing legacy of Shena's work and the city's acknowledgement of her contributions to supporting and improving educational provision for the city's youth.

Shena's previous electoral success and her significant contribution to municipal politics made her loss in 1933 to the Conservative Party particularly striking. The election was the first occasion when Shena faced candidates from both the Conservative and Labour parties, which made it especially difficult for her to defend her seat.[58] Shena had suffered from rumours that she was financially profiting from the Wythenshawe estate, with various untrue accusations circulating claiming that she and Ernest had sold land to the council; that Shena received £10,000 from ground rents at Wythenshawe; and that she received £5 from every house built on the new estate. Her allies were confident that 'these rumours did Lady Simon considerable harm in the election'.[59] Allegedly having received 700 personal requests to stand in Wythenshawe the following year, she did so as an independent. The *Manchester Guardian* wrote on her candidature, that she:

> desires to place the good and economic government of the city above party considerations. Her Liberalism is unquestioned, but it is as a municipal administrator whose record on the Council is a guarantee of her ability and desire to serve the city that she will come before electors.[60]

Shena lost to the returning Conservative candidate by just 150 votes, having suffered from ill health throughout the campaign. Shena tried again, for the last time, and stood as a Labour candidate for Moston in

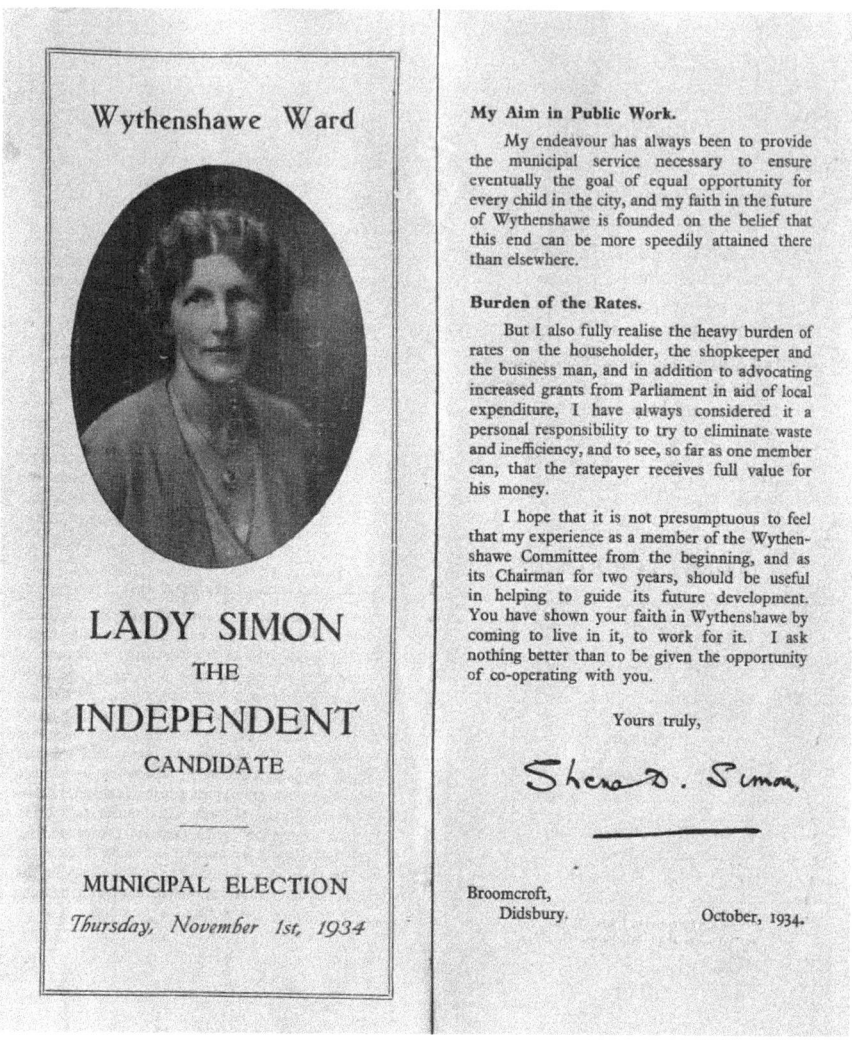

7.5 Shena's campaign leaflet to voters in Wythenshawe (1934). Source: SSP M14/6/10.

1936, but was unsuccessful. Despite this disappointment, however, Shena was able to maintain significant influence in municipal government, especially through her lobbying and campaign work on municipal taxation.

Taxation

Perhaps Shena's least well-known, but no less impressive and influential, work was on the issue of local taxation. She joined local government amid a period of crisis in municipal funding due to rising costs, particularly for welfare. 'As a result,' argues Martin Daunton, 'local government did not have access to any buoyant or responsive tax, and increasingly came to rely on subventions from the central government.' However, central government was keen to limit local authority spending because of their own financial pressures and responded by moving to a block, or fixed, grant system, and tried to remove power from those local governments that were seen as too extravagant.[61] Shena recognised these attempts by national government to shift greater costs onto local government, particularly on local ratepayers. Part of Shena's contribution to local government, therefore, should be seen as challenging this policy and by maintaining the autonomy and independence of Manchester Corporation, complaining in 1928 that 'Parliament is continually putting fresh burdens upon the municipalities'.[62] This conflict persisted throughout the twentieth century and beyond, reflected in ongoing discussions around the responsibilities and powers of local government, including around fiscal devolution.[63] Shena started what became a lifelong challenge against the rates following an increase in Manchester in 1926 and amid the recommendations of the Rating and Valuation Act 1925 which made valuation the responsibility of the council. Writing to the *Manchester Guardian*, Shena described the increase as 'a serious matter and one that is rightly rousing considerable interest among the ratepayers of the city'. Shena also complained that criticism was levied towards the local councillors, rather than central government, and argued that it was 'the duty of every citizen, whilst keeping a vigilant watch on the expenditure of the City Council and Board of Guardians, to protest to his member of Parliament against the false economy and unfair discrimination of taking burdens from the taxpayer and thrusting them upon the shoulder of the ratepayer'.[64]

The problem of the rates system of taxation was acute after the First World War ended. Structural issues, including the housing shortage and price increases, caused a significant rise in rents, whilst the rateable value of dwellings was acknowledged to be variable and inaccurate.[65] Shena identified the burden this placed on poorer families, reflecting the sustained influence of Shena's education at the LSE and especially from Tawney's research undertaken before the First World War that highlighted the disproportionate impact of indirect taxes on the poor. As Daunton explains, 'the main beneficiaries of the Liberal fiscal reforms were middle-class men with families; taxes on the poor were not reduced, and on the rich were increased by the super-tax and differentiation'.[66] The rise in rates, as Shena understood, would exacerbate this situation for the poorest householders. In 'Rates and the Householder' read at the Liberal Summer School in 1928, she used the example of families living in Manchester's Hulme, 'one of our most congested slum areas', where she examined twenty-one families with an income of under £3.5.0 a week. She claimed that the percentage of rates as a proportion of weekly income varied between 4 and 9 per cent, but, if they lived in better housing, it would be 7 and 17 percent and an average of nearly 11 per cent.[67] In 1943, she used figures from municipal housing estates situated within London County Council and Manchester Corporation that had identified that rent and rates accounted for 21–23 per cent of chief earners' income where the average wage was below three pounds. Shena noted that since '73.5% of *all* families are those in which the chief wage-earner earns £4 and under, the meaning of these heavy percentages, for a prime necessity of life, can be appreciated.'[68]

For Shena, this issue presented an additional problem beyond that of immediate hardship that she would return to often – that of the lack of incentive for families to try and move out of slum housing. She wrote:

> a man who makes considerable personal sacrifices to move his family out of a slum and house them on a Corporation estate, and who is rightly asked to pay higher rent because he is getting a better house, is actually penalised by our present system of rating and made to pay 5 per cent extra every week, although his family will cost the city no more and may be expected to cost it less because they will be living in healthier surroundings.[69]

This argument underpinned belief that sustainable and affordable models of funding were crucial to ensure the success of investment programmes, beyond that of standalone prestige projects. In 1943, Shena discussed the significant inconsistencies in the rates costs of houses following the interwar crisis in valuation. She cited 'Williams', a workman living in a two-up, two-down urban house with his family who had been offered a Corporation home and who was willing to pay more rent 'because the house is much better than the one I am living in, and although my wages will not go up I can manage it if I cut down my beer and smokes, But why should I pay more in rates when I shall be in the same city?' For Shena, this problem threatened the broader programmes of investment in working-class living standards that she and Ernest had been so committed to, as Williams asked, 'I thought I should be doing the right thing in moving the family to this new estate, where they can get more fresh air and more room in the house than they can in our present place. If I am doing the right thing, why should the City Council make me pay more rates? Lots of chaps I know are sticking in the slums and keeping their children there ... Why are they allowed to pay lower rates than I shall have to pay?'[70] In sum, Shena's work on rating reform highlighted the need for comprehensive restructuring and emphasised that affordability was a crucial step in achieving successful housing reform. But it also reveals Shena's knowledge and understanding in the role and function of local government more generally and the importance of local finance in maintaining municipal autonomy and effectiveness.

The rates were not the only problematic aspect of municipal finances and Shena worked to challenge central government's use of block grants

7.6 The cover of Shena's pamphlet, *Local Rates and Post-War Housing*. Source: SSP M14/3/2/1, Shena D. Simon, *Local Rates and Post-War Housing* (Letchworth: J.M Dent and Sons, LTD., 1943).

over percentage grants. The Treasury's position was 'to maintain a high level of taxation and to increase the sum available for debt redemption through cuts in expenditure'.[71] Shena argued against the policy of block grants because she claimed it gave local government little financial security and reduced the amount of funding they actually received. Shena took issue with the claims of those who opposed percentage grants, who 'talk of encouraging local extravagance'. Using the example of the 1915 Maternity and Child Welfare Scheme, which received a 50 per cent grant from central government, Shena suggested this funding was 'a direct encouragement to local authorities' to invest in these kinds of crucial reforms.[72] Shena was concerned that block grants would not reflect the needs of each locale and risked stripping away the important role and influence of local voluntary societies who delivered extensive public services without payment.[73] Instead, Shena argued that the use of percentage grants 'affords the best stimulus without undue interference with local freedom and initiative'.[74] Shena's financial model emphasised sustainability for municipal governments, in terms both of monetary income and of independence and power, and Shena understood that successful funding models were crucial to maintain the agency and authority of local governments in the face of increased intervention from central government.

Shena valued the enduring vitality and independence of local government because she knew that pressures on the provision of local services would not decrease: 'I cannot honestly say that I think there will be any substantial reduction in the expenditure of the city in the future' and identified the 'only hope for easing the burden upon the ratepayer ... lies in either discovering new sources of income', such as a local income tax or extending government percentage grants to other municipal services.[75] Shena dealt with particularly difficult circumstances as a councillor as finances were increasingly squeezed by the impact of economic depression. In 1930, Shena campaigned against Manchester Corporation's decision to raise the rates by ninepence, arguing that current ratepayers should not shoulder the entire financial burden. Shena recommended Manchester borrow more money and spread the repayments across the rates in future years, as it was 'not the time to be generous to future ratepayers at the expense of the present ones'.[76] Yet Shena was defeated in her attempts to reverse the introduction of a new policy of levying threepence on the rates to meet items of capital expenditure.[77] Later that same year, as she sought re-election, Shena emphasised the attempts of the Liberal Party to save money by opposing the Labour Party's threepence rise and stated that 'she did not think there had ever been a time when trade had been worse in Manchester than at present, and the Liberals in the City Council felt that this was the time to make every effort to keep rates as low as possible consistent with giving the ratepayers efficient services'. Shena again emphasised that it 'was certainly not a time for putting extra burdens on the ratepayers of today in order to save the ratepayers of tomorrow.'[78] Shena won with a majority of more than 5,000, but achieving a cut in the rates proved to be an impossible task. Pressures on public spending caused the corporation to limit their expenditure but, still, the cost of the rates rose again in 1932 to fifteen shillings and sixpence.[79] Meeting with her Chorlton constituents in 1932, she outlined the difficulties the city faced when, for the first time, the rateable value of Manchester was falling, and the 'serious position had therefore been reached that, on the one hand, the city's expenditure was rising and, on the other, the source from which it got the money for the expenditure was declining'.[80]

Knowing the hardship that the rates caused to poor families and understanding the limited funding that large corporations like Manchester faced, Shena sought to develop an alternative model of municipal finance. 'No one who has any first-hand knowledge of our rating system can think it is good,' she declared in 1941, 'it is not only complicated to administer, but impossible to explain satisfactorily to the ratepayer.' Shena objected to the way that the rates bore no relation to the ability to pay and suggested that using houses as the basis for taxation was 'fundamentally unsound'.[81] Shena was invited to contribute to the departmental committee on valuation for rates in 1939, but refused to endorse the recommendations of the committee's 1944 report to the Minister of Health. Instead, Shena's minority report argued that the focus on housing for tax was unfair in light of interwar housing reform, which, she claimed, 'has caused all except those tenants who are still living in pre-war controlled houses, to pay a larger proportion of their income in rent or house purchase payments and rates, than they did before'. Shena suggested that in many family homes, a third of the income had to be spent in rent and rates.[82] This problem would get even worse after the war, Shena argued, when the return to municipal activities would 'raise the question of the burden of rates in a much more acute form'.[83] Similarly, in 1945, she told the Manchester Fabian Society that the local rates system was the 'greatest stumbling-block to social reform' and were 'so unfair and put such a burden on the poor'. Shena also emphasised that the re-evaluation of houses was a disaster in waiting and warned 'we were all going to be faced with a serious problem'.[84] The recommendations of the 1938 report were eventually shelved and re-evaluation finally took place in the 1960s. As Joan Simon argued, it included 'substantial modifications in favour of domestic ratepayers', which represented 'ample justification of Shena Simon's stand in the 1930s'.[85] This success reflected Shena's persistence against the disproportionate burden the rates placed on the poor and particularly her recognition that housing reform could exacerbate the already challenging circumstances of poorer householders. Shena also criticised the rates system because the more affluent area outside of Manchester in Cheshire and Derbyshire had become 'a dormitory of Manchester'. She complained that richer commuters could still use the city's services, paid for by its poorer inhabitants: 'if they want to have the best of both worlds, then they should be prepared to pay for both worlds'.[86] It is not far-fetched to presume that Shena would have approved of the Manchester City Visitor Charge, introduced in 2023 to improve the city's tourism industry.[87] This form of targeted tax that operated on a municipal level was precisely the kind of fiscal innovation that Shena had envisioned for Manchester.

Keen to explore new methods of public funding, Shena travelled around Sweden and Denmark in 1938 to examine their model of a local income tax.[88] She noted that nowhere had copied the English tax system because 'it was fundamentally bad and unfair, as it was not based on ability to pay'. Rather, she recommended the local income tax system in Stockholm, where the average rate was 6.3 per cent overall, but varied between 2 and 40 per cent.[89] This model became Shena's preferred idea for municipal funding and formed the basis of her campaigns throughout the 1940s. In 1945, she explained it would mean that 'local taxation would be equitably distributed according to people's ability to pay and we should avoid a severe tax on the first necessity of life, the people's houses'.[90] She returned to this model of finance in the postwar years when Manchester's finances were looking more positive. In 1959, she responded to the Manchester Finance Committee's report on rates that calculated the increase required to maintain public services:

> We cannot pretend that, as a whole, the citizens of Manchester are poor. Yet the cost of making it a city of which we could all be proud is considered to be too high. Surely this is because rates are an unfair tax since they are levied on a necessity of life and not related, as are income and profits and taxes, to ability to pay.[91]

In 1964, Shena wrote to *The Times* in response to the re-evaluation of the rateable value of housing and complained that 'it highlighted that unlike income tax, rates are assessed irrespective of the individual's ability to pay'. Shena reiterated her calls for a local income tax as 'not a complete substitute for rates, but a supplement to them', adding that 'it would also have the advantage of bringing into the picture the men or women who now are completely exempt because, living with families or as a lodger, they neither own nor rent a house'.[92] Although unsuccessful in achieving the reform that she wanted, her ideas for taxation and for the funding of public services need to be analysed more thoroughly in the context of the abolition of the rating system, which became the focus of clashes between local and national government in the late 1970s and 1980s. Shena had foreseen the problem of the rates and since the wholesale reform she recommended was not adopted, local government and its financial structures experienced disastrous problems and continued upheaval.

Conclusion

When Shena was made Freeman of the City of Manchester in 1964 (the third woman to receive the honour), she recalled that Ernest often claimed that on their marriage, she fell in love with Manchester and the children of the city. 'It is easy enough to understand the children,' she conceded,

> but I have often in the years that have passed, wondered what it was that made me fall in love with Manchester. It was not her beauty ... Fifty years ago she was less attractive than she is today. There were no housing estates with gardens and spaciousness to break up the continuous stretch of red brick.

There was much more grime ... It was Manchester's heart of gold that first attracted me, and has held me ever since.⁹³

Ernest had died in 1960, and she explained she had decided against returning to London after his death: 'I will not join the drift from the North to the South. Although I may not live to see the drift back to the North, I feel sure that it will take place, once we have cleaned up the scars of the first industrial revolution.'⁹⁴ Understandably, the city mourned her death in 1972, with Brian Jackson, a fellow educationist, writing in the *Guardian* that 'her death ends a special age in Manchester's history'. He noted that thousands of children and their parents 'will recall the frail, stick-leaning lady' visiting classrooms.⁹⁵ The article alludes to the area that Shena has been mostly remembered for – that of education – but, as we have seen here, her work and contributions were much more varied and reflect both the strength of local government and the opportunities for women to contribute to civic culture and the strength of municipal cultures in mid-twentieth century Britain.

7.7   Shena receiving the Freedom of the City of Manchester. Source: SSP M14/4/3.

The extent of Shena's work both in Manchester and in municipal government more generally has perhaps been overshadowed in light of the sweeping reforms of the post-Second World War welfare state and increased centralisation of government. Yet, by using her contributions and achievements as a prism through which to explore local government more generally, we can see that Shena's life epitomised a flourishing and committed elite for whom the challenges of post-1918 Britain only cemented their dedication to improving the lives and opportunities of the urban communities they served. Nevertheless, this interpretation should not undermine or downplay Shena's individual achievements: the range of her activities and longstanding commitment to Manchester were remarkable. It suggests both that we need to understand more about women's contributions to local government and that, in doing so, we can revise assumptions about he perceived demise of civic pride and the role of local elites in municipal government. Finally, although Shena's contribution to education and housing have been well known, this chapter has particularly drawn attention to her work in tax reform and especially in relation to addressing the rates system. In doing so, it demonstrates that Shena's approach was comprehensive, as she saw all areas she focused her energy on – housing, education, child and maternity welfare, finance – as crucial parts of a universal system of public services. It was this philosophy, and the emphasis on public services as a way to achieve a successful democratic community, that was perhaps Shena's most important and valuable contribution to twentieth-century society and it remains relevant amid ongoing discussions about the role of the state in addressing social inequalities. Shena's understanding of the role of local government, therefore, still has much to contribute and highlighting her contributions to the concept of public service itself can only add to how local politicians may respond to the ongoing challenges they face.

Notes

1 SSP M14/7/13, Mabel Tylecote, *The Work of Lady Simon of Wythenshawe for Education in Manchester*, 28 November 1974, p. 1.
2 LSE Digital Library PASSFIELD/1/2, Beatrice Webb's Diary, 29 March 1930.
3 See, among many examples, Martin Pugh, *Women and the Women's Movement in Britain 1914–1959* (London: Macmillan, 1992); June Purvis, *Emmeline Pankhurst: A Biography* (London: Routledge, 2003); Lyndsey Jenkins, *Sisters and Sisterhood: The Kenney Sisters, Class and Suffrage c.1890–1965* (Oxford: Oxford University Press, 2021); Krista Cowman, *Women in British Politics, c.1689–1979* (Basingstoke: Palgrave MacMillan, 2010); Barbara Caine, *English Feminism 1780–1980* (Oxford: Oxford University Press, 1997).
4 Laura Beers, *Red Ellen: The Life of Ellen Wilkinson, Socialist, Feminist, Internationalist* (London: Harvard University Press, 2016); Susan Pederson, *Eleanor Rathbone and the Politics of Conscience* (London: Yale University Press, 2004); Maggie Andrews, *The Acceptable Face of Feminism: The Women's Institute as a Social Movement* (London: Lawrence & Wishart, 1997); Caitriona Beaumont, *Housewives and*

Citizens: Domesticity and the Women's Movement in England, 1918–64 (Manchester: Manchester University Press, 2013).
5 Patricia Hollis, *Ladies Elect: Women in English Local Government, 1865–1914* (Oxford: Clarendon, 1987), p. 462.
6 Hollis, *Ladies Elect*, p. 471.
7 Simon Gunn, 'Class, Identity and the Urban: The Middle Class in England, c.1790–1950,' *Urban History*, 31:1 (2004), 29–47; R. J. Morris, 'Structure, Culture and Society in British Towns', in Martin Daunton (ed.), *The Cambridge Urban History of Britain, Volume III. 1840–1950* (Cambridge: Cambridge University Press, 2000), 395–426.
8 Tom Hulme, 'Putting the City Back into Citizenship: Civics Education and Local Government in Britain, 1918–45', *20th Century British History*, 26:1 (2015), 36.
9 Shena Simon, *A Century of City Government, Manchester 1838–1938* (London: George Allen & Unwin Ltd, 1938), pp. 420–1.
10 Charlotte Wildman, *Urban Redevelopment and Modernity in Liverpool and Manchester, 1918–1939* (London: Bloomsbury, 2016), p. 31.
11 See: Wildman, *Urban Redevelopment and Modernity*, pp. 23–8; James Greenhalgh, *Reconstructing Modernity: Space, Power and Governance in Mid-Twentieth Century British Cities* (Manchester: Manchester University Press, 2018), pp. 29–35; Peter Shapely, 'Civic Pride and Redevelopment in the Post-war British City', *Urban History*, 39:2 (2012), 310–28.
12 Joan Simon, *Shena Simon, Feminist and Educationist* (privately printed, 1986).
13 Brendon Jones, 'Simon [née Potter], Shena Dorothy, Lady Simon of Wythenshawe', in *Oxford Dictionary of National Biography*.
14 Marian A. Horrocks, The Contribution to Education and Society of Lady Simon of Wythenshawe (1912–1972) (Unpublished MPhil dissertation, University of Manchester, 1990), p. 203.
15 Simon, *Shena Simon*, Chapter (henceforth Ch.) II, p. 23c.
16 'Women Citizens' Work', *Manchester Guardian* (19 March 1914), p. 12.
17 'Women Citizens' Association: Manchester Town Hall Reception', *Manchester Guardian* (25 January 1930), p. 12.
18 Simon, *Shena Simon*, Ch. II., p. 35.
19 'Women and the Hospitals', *Manchester Guardian* (19 December 1921), p. 9.
20 'Woman as Citizen', *Manchester Guardian* (11 October 1922), p. 9.
21 'Correspondence', *Manchester Guardian* (29 March 1915), p. 5.
22 'Municipal Maternity Centres', *Manchester Guardian* (8 March 1915), p. 4.
23 Martin Daunton, *Wealth and Welfare: An Economic and Social History of Britain 1851–1951* (Oxford: Oxford University Press, 2007), p. 539; John Cooper, *The British Welfare Revolution, 1906–14* (London: Bloomsbury, 2019), pp. 39–77.
24 'Child Welfare', *Manchester Guardian* (8 April 1915), p. 3.
25 'The New Child Welfare Scheme', *Manchester Guardian* (8 April 1915), p. 6.
26 Ernest Simon, *A City Council from Within* (London: Longmans Green and Co., 1926), p. 28.
27 'Young Mother's Death', *Manchester Guardian* (22 September 1934), p. 15.
28 Beaumont, *Housewives and Citizens*, pp. 8–39.
29 Horrocks, The Contribution to Education and Society of Lady Simon of Wythenshawe, p. 207.
30 'City's tribute to a leading Lady', *Guardian* (15 April 1964), p. 20.
31 Horrocks, The Contribution to Education and Society of Lady Simon of Wythenshawe, p. 402.
32 *The Woman's Leader and the Common Cause*, 10 August 1928, p. 1.
33 'The First Seven Years', *Manchester Guardian*, 6 January 1933, p. 4.
34 Horrocks, The Contribution to Education and Society of Lady Simon of Wythenshawe, p. 45.

35 'The City Elections', *Manchester Guardian* (26 October 1923), p. 11.
36 'Municipal Election Results', *Manchester Guardian* (2 November 1923), p. 14; Hollis, *Ladies Elect*, p. 422.
37 'Municipal Election Results', *Manchester Guardian* (3 November 1924), p. 10.
38 'The Municipal Elections', *Manchester Guardian* (3 November 1930), p. 12.
39 Simon, *Shena Simon*, Chp III, p. 1.
40 Tylecote, *The Work of Lady Simon of Wythenshawe*, p. 13.
41 Tylecote, *The Work of Lady Simon of Wythenshawe*, p. 12.
42 LSE Digital Library PASSFIELD/1/2, Beatrice Webb's diary, 11 October 1927.
43 Hollis, *Ladies Elect*, pp. 398, 418.
44 'Women Citizens and Housing', *Manchester Guardian* (12 February 1931), p. 10.
45 'Women Citizens and Slum Clearance', *Manchester Guardian* (7 April 1933), p. 3.
46 'Manchester Municipal Elections', *Manchester Guardian* (15 October 1934), p. 16.
47 Andrzej Olechnowicz, 'Civic Leadership and Education for Democracy: The Simons and the Wythenshawe Estate', *Contemporary British History*, 14:1 (2000), 5.
48 Olechnowicz, 'Civic Leadership and Education for Democracy', 7.
49 'City's Tribute to a Leading Lady', *Guardian* (15 April 1964), p. 20.
50 Jane Martin, 'Shena Simon (1883–1972) and the "Religion of Humanity"', in Jane Martin and Joyce Goodman, *Women and Education, 1800–1980* (Basingstoke: Palgrave, 2004), pp. 118–19.
51 'City's Tribute to a Leading Lady'.
52 'Shena Simon,' *Guardian* (8 August 1972), p. 15.
53 Martin, 'Shena Simon', p. 139.
54 Lawrence Goldman, 'Tawney, Richard Henry (1880–1962), historian and political thinker,' *Oxford Dictionary of National Biography*, 2004.
55 As quoted in Simon, *Shena Simon*, Ch. III, p. 10.
56 Hsiao-Yuh Ku, 'In Pursuit of Social Democracy: Shena Simon and the Reform of Secondary Education in England, 1938–1948', *History of Education*, 47:1 (2018), 71.
57 As quoted in Tylecote, *The Work of Lady Simon of Wythenshawe*, p. 3.
58 'Municipal Election Results', *Manchester Guardian* (2 November 1933), p. 12.
59 'Sir Ernest and Lady Simon: A Baseless Slander', *Manchester Guardian* (21 December 1933), p. 11.
60 'Lady Simon', *Manchester Guardian* (28 June 1934), p. 13.
61 Daunton, *Wealth and Welfare*, p. 469.
62 SSP M14/3/2/1, 'Rates and the Householder' read at the Liberal Summer School, Oxford 1928.
63 Jessica Studdert, 'Fiscal Devolution: Why We Need It and How to Make it Work', *New Local* (April 2023), www.newlocal.org.uk/articles/fiscal-devolution/ (accessed 24 July 2023).
64 SSP M14/3/2/1, Letter from Shena Simon to the *Manchester Guardian*, 12 July 1926.
65 SSP M14/3/2/1, Rating and Valuation Act, 1925, First series of representations received by the Minister of Health from the Central Valuation Committee, pp. 7–8.
66 Martin Daunton, *Just Taxes: The Politics of Taxation in Britain, 1914–1979* (Cambridge: Cambridge University Press, 2002), p. 118.
67 Simon, 'Rates and the Householder'.
68 SSP M14/3/2/1, Shena D. Simon, *Local Rates and Post-war Housing* (Letchworth: J.M Dent and Sons, LTD., 1943), p. 17.
69 Simon, 'Rates and the Householder'.
70 Simon, *Local Rates and Post-war Housing*, p. 6.
71 Daunton, *Just Taxes*, p. 127.
72 Simon, 'Rates and the Householder'.
73 SSP M14/3/2/1, Shena Simon, 'The Government's rating reform and maternity and child welfare,' p. 3.

74 SSP M14/3/2/1, 'Percentage and Block Grants' Mrs E. D. Simon, the *Nation and Athenaeum* 44 (1928), pp. 283–4.
75 Simon, 'Rates and the Householder'.
76 'Manchester Rates', *Manchester Guardian* (24 February 1930), p. 11.
77 'Cutting the Rates', *Manchester Guardian* (5 February 1931), p. 5.
78 'Rates and Housing', *Manchester Guardian* (24 October 1930), p. 11.
79 SSP M14/3/2/1, Shena Simon, 'Municipal Finance', The Manchester School, III: 1, 1932, p. 19.
80 'City's Economy Plans', *Manchester Guardian* (19 January 1932), p. 13.
81 SSP M14/3/2/3, Shena Simon, 'Paying the Piper: The Case for a Municipal Income Tax', *Local Government Service*, 21:12 (1941).
82 SSP M14/3/2/3, Report to the Minister of Health by the Departmental Committee on Valuation for Rates 1939 (London, 1944), p. 39.
83 'Rates and Post-War Housing', *Manchester Guardian* (6 August 1943), p. 4.
84 'Rating Problems', *Manchester Guardian* (10 February 1945), p. 6.
85 Simon, *Shena Simon*, Introduction, p. 9.
86 Simon, *A Century of City Government*, p. 422.
87 'Manchester's £1-a-night tourist tax comes into force', *Guardian* (31 March 2023) www.theguardian.com/travel/2023/mar/31/manchester-1-a-night-tax-on-tourists-comes-into-force (accessed 24 July 2023).
88 Horrocks, The Contribution to Education and Society of Lady Simon of Wythenshawe, p. 395.
89 'Lady Ernest and a Local Income Tax', *Manchester Guardian* (19 October 1938), p. 11.
90 'Local Income Tax', *Manchester Guardian* (7 February 1945), p. 7.
91 'Municipal Finance', *Guardian* (3 December 1959), p. 13.
92 'Raising the Rates', *The Times* (3 June 1964), p. 13.
93 SSP M14/4/15, Speech by Lady Simon of Wythenshawe on the Occasion of the Freedom of the City of Manchester 14th April 1964, p. 3.
94 Speech by Lady Simon of Wythenshawe on the Occasion of the Freedom of the City of Manchester, p. 3.
95 Brian Jackson, 'Shena Simon', *Guardian* (8 August 1972), p. 15.

8

Building Jerusalem: the Simons' role in housing reform and town planning

Stephen V. Ward and Martin Dodge

Manchester is a huge overgrown village, built according to no definite plan. ... The interests and convenience of individual manufacturers and owners of property has determined the growth of the town and the manner of that growth, while the comfort, health and happiness of the inhabitants have not been considered ... Every advantage has been sacrificed to the getting of money.[1]

Great concern for the comfort, health and happiness of Manchester's people was shown by Emily, Henry, Shena and Ernest Simon. The energetic and innovative public work to improve physical conditions in the city through housing reform and town planning by these two generations of the Simon family is considered in this chapter. As the 'shock city' of the industrial age, Manchester posed many challenges and all four Simons actively sought practical solutions to reduce pollution, overcrowding, lack of open space, widespread ill-health and insanitary homes.[2] Whilst Ernest's work was most prominent, we consider the largely unexamined earlier work of Henry and Emily, before examining Shena's concern around housing in regard to the development of Wythenshawe. While the main focus is on Manchester, their work reflects wider reform trends, from the late Victorian beginnings of social housing with small-scale worker tenement schemes, to the Edwardian garden suburb movement and then the interwar push for large municipal housing estates.

Ernest's public work, firstly locally and then nationally, in housing policy and planning from the 1920s was most extensive. He became an acknowledged expert in these fields; he was awarded his knighthood in 1932 and peerage in 1947 partly for this reason. However, space does not allow a detailed examination of Ernest's Manchester work.[3] Instead, we shine a light on a lesser-known aspect of his career to show how he developed his wider thinking about planning over the later 1930s and

8.1 Dense Victorian terraced housing around St Mary's Church in Hulme, an inner neighbourhood of Manchester (1920s). Source: MCL ref. m67728.

early 1940s. We examine his research trips to the Soviet Union, the Nordic countries, Switzerland and the USA, and demonstrate how, during the Second World War, he drew on this international learning to propose how to rebuild Britain according to a definite plan.[4]

Henry Simon and the Manchester Labourers' Dwellings Company

In late Victorian Britain, the extent, visibility and dire health consequences of unplanned insanitary housing led to many small-scale 'model' tenement schemes being built for the poor. Medical Officers of Health, newly appointed by city authorities at this time, began documenting the problems but were unable to take large-scale remedial action beyond closing and demolishing the most squalid back-to-back courts and cellar dwellings.[5] Despite new sanitary legislation, many politicians did not want councils building new accommodation themselves, seeing housing as the private market's domain. Instead, numerous charitable initiatives by philanthropists and industrialists in this period provided decent affordable housing for 'workers', including in Manchester and Salford.[6]

Henry Simon was deeply involved in one such housing initiative, leading the formation in 1891 of the Manchester Labourers' Dwellings

Company and serving for five years as its chairman. The company's primary motive clearly reflected Henry's personal outlook as it sought to support the 'less favoured portion of the community, and not the return of large remuneration upon the outlay, as it is intended to afford the very poorest the opportunity of living under healthy conditions without loss of self-respect and independence'.[7] The company issued 4,000 shares at £5 each, aiming through rental income to be a self-sustaining enterprise and, ultimately, make a modest return of 4 per cent on capital to shareholders.

The company's first scheme, announced in March 1891, involved acquiring and converting a large disused cotton mill into a basic but sanitary tenement, subsequently named Jersey Street Dwellings. The mill adjoined the Rochdale Canal in Ancoats, a dense industrial area in central Manchester.[8] Henry would have known the conditions in the area as the first flour mill where he successfully installed his roller milling machinery in 1878 was nearby.

The six-storey mill building was altered to create 149 separate small, mostly two-room, dwellings. New towers were added at both ends of the building, providing open staircases and shared toilets for each floor. Access to individual dwellings was from newly added external metal balconies; these were divided in the middle because, it was claimed, 'in the case of an [disease] outbreak of any kind it would be possible to isolate one part of the building from another'.[9] Existing adjacent storage sheds were converted to house bathrooms, a laundry and space for a small co-op shop and two club rooms. The outdoor quadrangle, covered in cinders, was made into a children's playground (Figure 8.2). Rents ranged from 2/0d to 4/9d a week, including rates, gas-lighting and running hot and cold water.

The tenement was opened in a public ceremony by the Lady Mayoress of Manchester in May 1892. It was reported that the scheme provided airy, well-lit and sanitary dwellings, a distinct improvement on most cheap accommodation for workers in Ancoats. It was judged a success by the company's directors, with 105 dwellings already let, housing 360 occupants. The tenants' views were unrecorded but many likely appreciated the significantly better facilities than in nearby existing accommodation. Henry Simon made a speech commending the scheme, including a humorous allusion,

> [t]he situation of the building at the junction of two canals ensured large open spaces, and on a fine day, with a bit of convenient imagination, [the tenants] might from their balconies fancy themselves in Venice … (laughter), and from personal experience he [Henry] backed the Manchester canals for sweeter average smells than similar-sized canals during a great part of the year in Venice (laughter).

Yet Henry Simon and the other directors were not simply benevolent landlords. Like many philanthropic providers of housing for the 'working

The Simons' role in housing reform and town planning

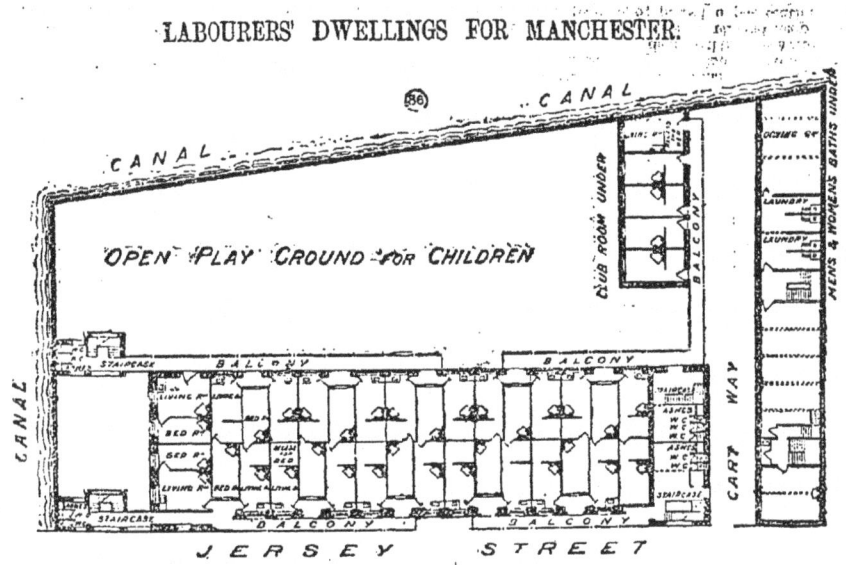

8.2 Sketch plan of the Jersey Street Dwellings. Source: *Manchester Guardian* (17 March 1891), p. 9.

classes' at this time, they had a strongly paternalistic urge to improve the behaviour and moral character of the poor while also providing a secure roof over their heads. As Henry concluded his speech, the company 'sincerely hoped that their tenants might soon come to feel that they form, as it were, one large family, and that every one of them would do his or her best by respectable behaviour to raise the character of the small community, so that to belong to it might gradually become a matter of pride as well as an advantage (applause)'.[10] Such words perhaps reflected something of Henry's approach to his own family. By 1892, Henry and Emily had seven children and Henry sought to inculcate morals in his children in writing, for example, a small book *Rathschlaege für meine Kinder* [*Advice For My Children*] in c. 1899.[11] The family's increasing affluence from Henry's business success allowed their life in their large Didsbury home to be supported, according to the 1891 census return, by four domestic servants and a governess for the children.

At the 1898 annual meeting, Thomas Coglan Horsfall, another director (and prominent housing reformer), noted that the:

> experience of the Company had made it clear that it was not enough to put poor, ignorant people into wholesome dwellings, and leave them to work out their own salvation from a social and sanitary point of view. They must be assisted in various ways, and the Company, as well as the tenants, were greatly indebted to Miss Hankinson and her friends for their useful work.[12]

Annie Hankinson served for many years at Jersey Street as a kind of social worker and educator. Such 'useful work' was not just supportive and educative but helped inculcate codes of 'good' behaviour and 'proper' levels of cleanliness in the poor.[13]

Initially, the Labourers' Dwellings Company struggled to reach financial viability at Jersey Street.[14] Nor did it build any more housing after this first scheme. (The nearby Victoria Square tenements were opened by the City Corporation in 1894.)[15] Yet, in late 1898, the Jersey Street tenement was practically fully occupied, housing 125 men, 118 women and 374 children. From the company's paternalistic perspective, there had been management challenges, with 'twelve families removed in the night, taking their belongings with them, and ten had to be ejected for disorderly conduct and for using bad language'.[16] By then, however, Henry had stepped back from managing the company, likely due to significant health problems; his good friend Charles Behrens now became chairman.[17]

The Company continued into the early twentieth century, and the largely unchanged Jersey Street tenement remained occupied into the 1930s. By then, social reformers saw the tenement as a horribly overcrowded Victorian 'barracks'; a 'model' improvement scheme of the 1890s was by then seen as unfit for use. A 1932 newspaper article on the Manchester University Settlement's work saw it as the city's worst tenement block, a 'gaunt, six-storey structure of unparalleled hideousness'. For all Henry Simon's original philanthropic ambitions, these 1930s housing reformers thought it 'incredible that this insanitary rabbit warren should be the home of 141 families at the present day'.[18] It is unclear when the tenement was closed and the company wound up, but evidence from detailed Ordnance Survey plans shows the block gone by the late 1940s.

Emily Simon and Edwardian garden suburbs

By the Edwardian period, Manchester's worst industrial slums and mean rows of Victorian terraces were slowly giving way to better by-law housing, but the sheer scale of existing problems remained a daunting challenge. However, radically better ways to lay out towns and design good housing were emerging, informed largely by the garden city movement (influenced by Ebenezer Howard's 1902 book *Garden Cities of To-morrow*). The approach sought to combine the beneficial aspects of countryside – natural light, fresh air and green space – with urban living, enabled by collective land ownership and prevention of speculative development. Its planning principles included careful zoning of activities, separation of homes from factories and well-laid-out low-density residential areas with well-built cottages. The first garden city was at Letchworth, Hertfordshire, developed from 1903. Howard's ideas pervaded early developments in town planning and appealed to campaigners, not least the Simons, seeking ways to rehouse thousands of working people living in crowded industrial cities in better conditions.

Such efforts to improve Manchester's working-class housing during this period were most palpable in the work of Thomas Horsfall[19] and Thomas Marr. In 1902, they formed the Citizens Association for the Improvement of the Unwholesome Dwellings and Surroundings of the People and published a major report, *Housing Conditions in Manchester and Salford* in 1904. Based on detailed street-level investigations and social surveys, the report called for comprehensive policy towards planning and housing that:

> would provide not only for the demolition of unwholesome dwellings and the statutory obligation to re-house the occupants but would also definitely provide for the growth of the towns, planning roads, streets and open spaces for the new districts long before they are actually required for building.[20]

Ernest Simon strongly advocated this approach decades later in his *Rebuilding Britain–A Twenty Year plan* (1945) book (see below) and it was actually realised after the Second World War.

Edwardian housing reformers, like Horsfall and Marr, contributed to a growing national political debate about the state's role in providing good-quality homes. Government legislation, including the 1909 Housing and Town Planning Act, enabled local authorities to intervene more significantly in residential planning and in building homes for rent. Manchester Corporation took small steps to building suburban council housing for the poor in the Edwardian period, starting with a small estate of 150 workers' cottages at Blackley completed in 1904.[21] However, little happened nationally to encourage large-scale municipal housebuilding until after the First World War.

Modest attempts to provide decent homes also came from socially minded architect developers who applied some of the Garden City ideals when building small suburban estates for rent, often operated on cooperative or copartnership (a near variant) principles. Several such 'garden suburbs' were created around Manchester before 1914.[22] Three notable ones were located close to each other in south Manchester, and near the Simons' homes. These schemes in Burnage, Chorlton and Didsbury were all small estates of cottages constructed by cooperative societies, supported by local philanthropic investors. Their specific financial basis and design quality varied, but all provided new family homes with 'vegetation, light, and air'.[23]

The first was Didsbury Garden Suburb Provident Cooperative Society Limited, begun in 1907. Directed by prominent local housebuilder Amos Mason, the Society gained the strong support of Emily Simon early on. It sought to 'to erect sanitary dwellings amid healthy surroundings, at reasonable rents, and on terms that would enable the tenants, who were shareholders, to become absolute owners of the houses they lived in'.[24]

Tenants had first to pay £10 to become shareholders in the society but, unlike most otherwise similar schemes, it was conceived as a 'rent-to-own' model. The society purchased two and a quarter acres of farmland near the new Levenshulme to Wilmslow railway line in Didsbury. The first phase of thirty semi-detached houses adopted a conventional linear street layout but with generous individual gardens, and land permanently retained for a playground. At fifteen dwellings per acre, its density was slightly higher than other garden suburb schemes but was much less dense than by-law terraced housing being built elsewhere in Manchester before 1914. The society financed construction using loans, a mortgage and funds from tenant shareholders. It was anticipated that tenants would own their house after twenty years of renting. Each house cost about £200, then considered a moderate sum, and initial rents were 7s 6d a week. The first four houses were formally opened in October 1907 with ceremonial tree planting by Emily and other prominent women social reformers in the Simons' friendship circle (Mrs Hans Renold, Mrs Gustav Eckhard, Mrs J. Watt, Miss Margaret Ashton).[25]

Emily remained on the committee running the society, giving the keynote speech at the formal ceremony when all thirty planned houses were completed in October 1909.[26] She stressed that 'tenants must be shareholders, and it is to their interest to see that the property is kept in good repair, for they are part owners'.[27] Local Liberal MP Harry Nuttall also praised garden suburbs, but posed a key question: 'Where do the poorest class of people come in in these schemes?' After the speeches came sports organised for the children and a firework display at dusk.[28]

The garden suburb schemes in Didsbury, Burnage and Chorlton were successfully realised but limited in scope. As was the case with similar housing schemes elsewhere in Britain, their funding model was unable to provide the thousands of new homes Manchester actually needed. Moreover, the size and locations of the houses, and the requirement that tenants invest as shareholders, meant such schemes were unaffordable for most poorer families in inner Manchester. They were occupied by more affluent skilled workers and lower middle-class professionals. Despite their founders' idealism, these estates barely touched the main housing problem. Far more ambitious national government policies and municipal solutions were needed.

Into the 1920s and the Simons' role in the struggle for Wythenshawe

The First World War was a major shock to social norms, indirectly giving new impetus for interventionist urban planning. Its ending also brought major housing policy changes. In 1918, the government's Tudor Walters report was published, much influenced by leading garden city architect

MRS SIMON ANNOUNCES COMPLETION OF THE SCHEME.

Mrs Simon, who had a hearty reception, was then called upon to announce the completion of the scheme. She said: Those of us who knew the village of Didsbury almost half a century ago have seen many changes and a great deal of building, and we could wish that there had been more forethought exercised, and that the idea of garden cities and garden suburbs had arisen before any extension of the village had been planned. The first garden city at Letchworth is such a success that the example is being followed in many parts of the country, and in Manchester we are not lagging behind. The Burnage estate is nearing completion, and this small effort on similar lines in our own village is now practically completed. It arose through the action of a few working-men, who approached Mr Amos Mason, and with his assistance formed the Didsbury Garden Suburb and Provident Co-operative Society, Ltd. The great advantage this society affords is co-operation. The tenants must be shareholders, and it is to their interest to see that the property is kept in good repair, for they are part owners as well as tenants, and any profits that accrue will go to increase the shares of the tenants until in time they may own their own houses entirely. The rents are very low, no equally good houses with gardens are to be had elsewhere in Didsbury, and this has been made possible through the economy in building. A garden suburb is laid out as a whole on a pre-conceived plan, instead of each lot being disposed of to a different builder, and the result is a pleasing group of houses. This movement was started three years ago, and in October of 1907 the first four houses were completed, and formally opened by Mrs Hans Renold. I have a photograph of a group of friends taken on that occasion, and one was with us then who has so recently been called away that I am sure there is not one here to-day who is not missing Dr Rhodes, for he was a friend alike to rich and poor, and ever ready with sympathy and encouragement in every good work that was started. His work was of national importance, but we are mourning for him as a neighbour and a friend. The first houses were occupied as soon as they were finished, and by the end of December, 1908, 21 houses were occupied, and had it not been for lack of funds the whole scheme would have been completed last year. Now it has been brought to a successful issue, and a happy community is established in this garden suburb. It would not have been complete without some special provision for the children, and they have not been forgotten. The plot of ground on which they have held their sports is dedicated to the use of the children, and can never be built upon or taken from them. The gardens are a most attractive feature of this suburb, and I think every inch of ground is utilised, for they are gay with flowers in front, and full of vegetables and fruits at the back. There seems to be much friendly rivalry as to who shall have the finest display of flowers—it is not only flowers, but babies also that flourish here, for was it not one of the tenants babies that gained a prize at the South Manchester show. (Applause). One of the greatest evils of modern days is the constant flitting from house to house. But when you own your house and are proud of it, you want to take root and make it a real home. I hope that the tenants will take up more shares, and in declaring the scheme completed, I wish long life and happiness to the dwellers in the Didsbury garden suburb. (Applause).

Mr Nuttall, M.P., on being called upon,

8.3 Report of Emily's speech at the ceremony marking the completion of the Didsbury Garden Suburb. Source: *Alderley & Wilmslow Advertiser*, (8 October 1909), p. 8.

Raymond Unwin. It called for new working-class houses to be well-spaced, well-lit by sunlight, with good ventilation, a garden and a bathroom. It also recommended planned street layouts, favouring cul-de-sacs, stating that new houses should be '[t]wo-storied cottages, built in groups of four or six, with medium or low-pitched roofs and little exterior decoration, set amongst gardens and trees'.[29] After winning the general election in December 1918, Prime Minister David Lloyd George pledged to build 'Homes Fit for Heroes'. His government passed the Addison Act in 1919 which gave local authorities like Manchester City Council generous financial subsidies to build houses for rent on a large scale suitable for working people.

Ernest and Shena Simon had become involved in Manchester municipal politics before 1914, seeking to advance various progressive causes. But it was only after the war that Ernest gained detailed practical experience of town planning on Manchester City Council. In November 1919, he became chairman of the new Housing Committee and began looking beyond mere civic paternalism towards a comprehensive concept of planning that was both effective and democratic.[30] In November 1921, the Simons became Lord Mayor and Lady Mayoress of Manchester, and Ernest used this high-profile platform to press for greater and more effective

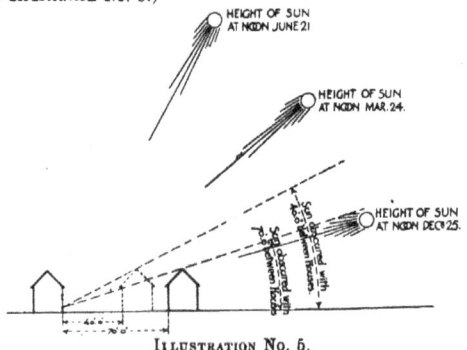

8.4 The practical case for low-density housing to allow daylight made in the influential Tudor Walters report. Source: John Tudor Walters, *Report of the Committee Appointed by the President of the Local Government Board and the Secretary for Scotland to Consider Questions of Building Construction in Connection with the Provision of Dwellings for the Working Classes in England and Wales, and Scotland* (London: HMSO, 1918).

municipal intervention. In his acceptance speech, he urged extending the city's boundaries 'to develop either self-contained garden cities or dormitory cities ... and to transfer to those cities large portions of the population now forced to live in slums'.[31]

To move beyond tentative Edwardian efforts and effectively rehouse tens of thousands, in accordance with the ideals of the first garden city at Letchworth and Tudor Walters standards, required Manchester Corporation to have enough space for low-density residential development. Flat, open farmland just across the Mersey River in Cheshire seemed the ideal choice, provided it could be acquired and developed. Most of it belonged to the aristocratic Tatton estate, centred on the impressive Wythenshawe Hall. The idea of a satellite garden city on this land was strongly advocated by Labour Alderman William Turner Jackson in November 1919, who 'thought Manchester had a good case for the compulsory acquisition of an estate like this'.[32]

The Housing Committee, chaired by Ernest, tasked the city surveyor and leading town planner Patrick Abercrombie with assessing the feasibility of the council developing the Wythenshawe area as a large satellite city. Their reports, produced in December 1919 and March 1920, were strongly supportive, giving powerful political ammunition to Jackson and Ernest in the battle to realise their hopes. The Housing Committee as a result recommended that the council purchase the Wythenshawe estate, yet the birth of Manchester's garden city proved protracted and politically difficult.[33]

It took over twelve years from the initial idea in 1919 before the Wythenshawe area officially became part of Manchester and large-scale house building could proceed. The immediate obstacle was landowner Thomas Egerton Tatton's refusal to sell his Wythenshawe estate to the council. After he died in 1924, however, his heir proved more amenable. The real possibility of acquiring Wythenshawe then triggered serious wrangling within Manchester City Council about the wisdom of purchasing so much land. With no real progress made, Ernest and Shena made a move which would prove critical for the Wythenshawe's future and the shape of Manchester as whole. In early April 1926, the Simons told the Lord Mayor and the council they were privately purchasing Wythenshawe Hall and its surrounding parklands and would donate their acquisition directly to the council as open space for Manchester's people.[34] This was a politically shrewd but personally expensive move.[35] It reduced the financial burden facing the council and galvanised it into action, with the council buying the rest of the Wythenshawe estate the following month. A single paragraph at the bottom of the *Manchester Guardian* frontpage on the 6 May 1926 tersely summarised this momentous decision (Figure 8.6). The council purchased 2,568 acres, mostly farmland, across the northeast Cheshire parishes of Baguley, Northenden and Northen Etchells.[36]

CORRESPONDENCE.

TOWN-PLANNING FOR MANCHESTER.

To the Editor of the Manchester Guardian.

Sir,—The Lord Mayor, on May 18, said of Manchester that "it just happened," and that is true. And things that "just happen" are never done right, and therefore require a lot of putting straight. To this end the proposals for dealing, on the best town-planning lines, with a considerable area around Manchester put forward so ably by Professor Abercrombie on the same occasion are admirable. But I would suggest that to be truly effective such efforts must be supplemented by efforts of quite another kind. Satellite towns on new areas at a distance of 25 miles or so from the city could be designed and built so as to be most effective and economic, industrially, commercially, and from the point of view of health and efficiency, and would greatly relieve the difficulties of Manchester.

Therefore, when the satellite town at Welwyn, within 20 miles of London, is well under way the Garden Cities and Town-planning Association, which is largely responsible for its foundation, will certainly turn its attention to the problem of Manchester, which is perhaps more than equally urgent.—Yours, &c.,

EBENEZER HOWARD.
The Garden Cities and Town-planning
Association, 3, Gray's Inn Place,
Gray's Inn, London, W.C., May 25.

8.5 Ebenezer Howard commenting on Patrick Abercrombie's report on Wythenshawe. Source: *Manchester Guardian* (27 May 1920), p. 5.

Further purchases of adjacent land parcels by the council occurred over subsequent years.

Yet the city's ownership of the necessary land did not immediately see Manchester's satellite garden city being built. Although owning the land, Manchester City Council lacked administrative authority over the area. The small local district authorities and Cheshire County Council were reluctant themselves to fund the substantial infrastructure, such as drainage and sewers, needed to build so many homes for Manchester people. To resolve

> **MANCHESTER TO BUY WYTHENSHAWE.**
>
> After a long discussion the Manchester City Council yesterday adopted by 62 votes to 49 the recommendation for the purchase of the Wythenshawe estate. A proposal to defer the application for borrowing powers to make the purchase was heavily defeated. The Council also accepted the "princely gift" of Wythenshawe Hall from Mr. and Mrs. E. D. Simon.

8.6 The announcement of the council's decision to purchase the Wythenshawe estate. Source: *Manchester Guardian* (6 May 1926), p. 1.

this, Manchester sought Parliamentary approval for a boundary extension to give it full control. After stiff resistance, approval came in April 1931, and Wythenshawe was legally incorporated into Manchester. With this additional 5,567 acres of land, the city's area grew by about a quarter, forever changing the regional map.[37]

Shena Simon's active involvement in planning the Wythenshawe estate

From the mid-1920s, Ernest's involvement in housing and planning matters became more nationally focused. It was Shena who took over to help shape Wythenshawe's early development as a municipal garden city. In 1924, she was elected a Liberal councillor for the Chorlton-cum-Hardy ward and joined the Council's Education Committee, beginning her more than four decades of service on this committee. She also joined the Wythenshawe Estate Special Committee in 1926, supervising housing development. Led by Alderman Jackson, the Committee commissioned the leading garden city architect-planner Barry Parker, co-designer of Letchworth, to prepare a masterplan for this new satellite garden city.[38]

Shena became immersed in the practical planning of housing development, at times working closely with Parker.[39] She was especially concerned that community facilities often arrived long after dwellings were built. Shena also showed her wider concerns about urban design, stating in a speech in Manchester Art Gallery in 1930 that town planning and architecture were:

> at a rather low ebb. Not only in Manchester but all over the country we seem to have lost that sense of beauty which presumably we once possessed, as can be seen in our old villages and country towns, that sense of beauty in architecture and lay-out. I suppose it was part of the price – a very large price – that we had

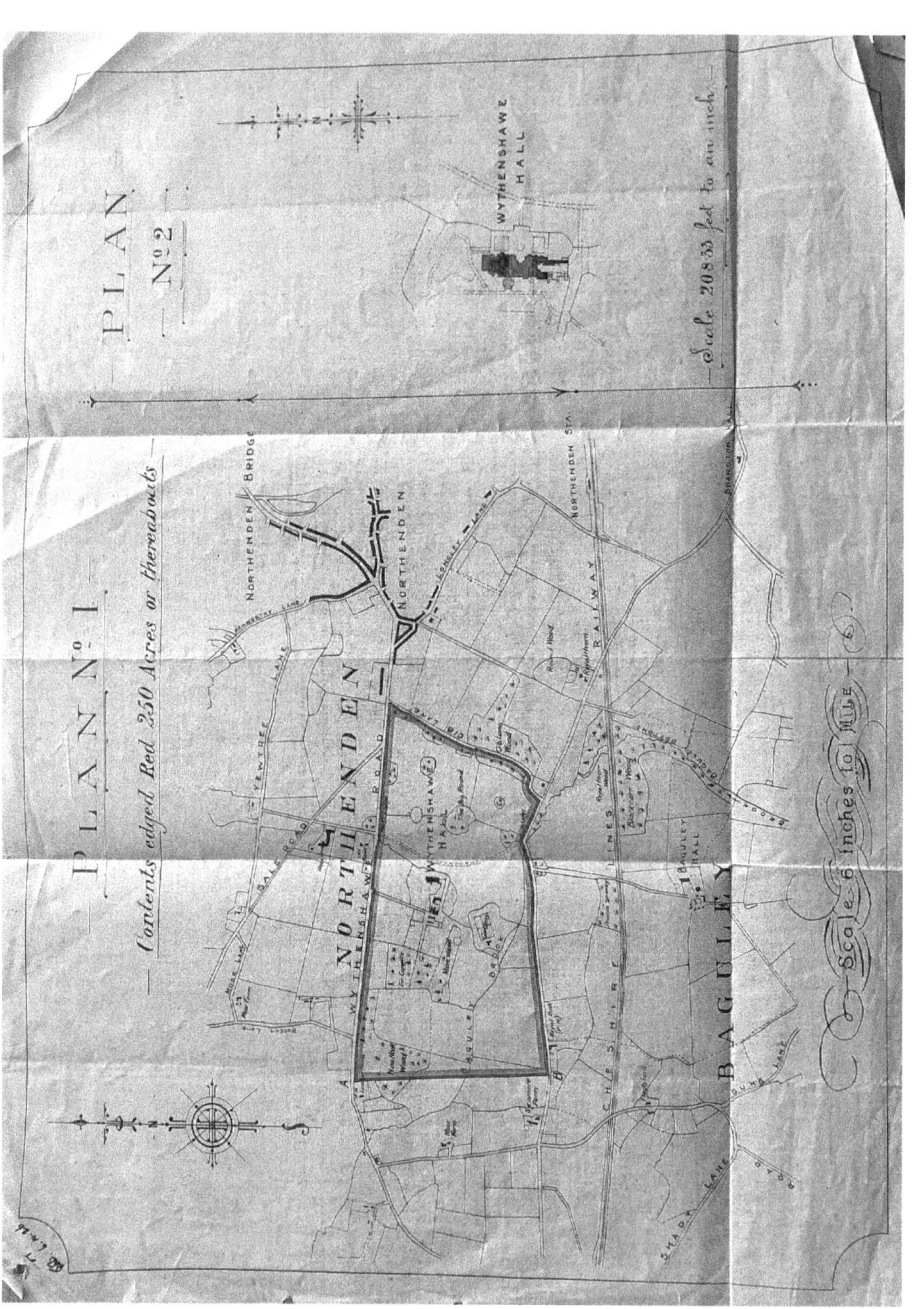

8.7 The deed plan for the purchase of Wythenshawe Hall and grounds by the Simons (1926). Courtesy of Legal Records Centre, Manchester City Council.

to pay for the great extension of industry commonly known as the industrial revolution. What is depressing is that we still go on paying that price.[40]

The objective for Wythenshawe was to create a self-contained satellite town for Manchester, housing around 100,000 people and surrounded by an agricultural green belt. It would be built in phases over decades, comprising several distinct neighbourhoods of more than 10,000 people, with each neighbourhood having its own local shopping facilities and schools. Housing density would be no more than twelve dwellings to an acre, contrasting with forty to fifty homes per acre in inner Manchester. To achieve these goals Parker's masterplan for Wythenshawe zoned separate areas for specific purposes (Figure 8.8).

Residential neighbourhoods would comprise clusters of houses around small greens and in geometrical patterns of cul-de-sacs. Parker favoured hexagonal layouts to maximise land use. In reality, however, few were actually built in Wythenshawe. The planning also preserved existing local place names and country lanes. Many ponds and spinneys were also retained. The design of early houses reflected the ideals of the Arts and Crafts movement, with each family home designed with open space at the front and a substantial back garden.

Another important Parker contribution was to knit the satellite town together, using major roads similar to American parkways, with wide, planted verges containing separate pedestrian footpaths. The goal was to visually soften the transport corridors and reduce traffic noise for nearby dwellings.[41]

Shena strongly supported Parker's vision for Wythenshawe. In a BBC Radio broadcast in 1930, she described her vision of a utopian city, believing, like Ebenezer Howard, that the Wythenshawe garden city could harmoniously combine the urban and the rural,

> Slums and overcrowding will be regarded by the citizen of the future as something which they can barely imagine. Above all, the houses will be beautiful outside as well as convenient inside. I am afraid that some of our housing estates have not added to the beauty of the country in which they have been placed, but this will not happen in Utopia. I think each house will have a separate garden.[42]

In November 1931, Shena took over from Jackson as Wythenshawe Estate Special Committee chair, just as growth was quickening. In February 1932, Princess Road was extended, with a new bridge over the River Mersey into Wythenshawe providing a fast road connection to the city. Despite the economic depression, housing construction proceeded quickly in several different neighbourhoods. Over 4,600 new council houses had been completed by 1934, seeing Wythenshawe's population swell from 7,000 in 1931 to 25,000 by the mid-1930s.[43] It was intended that the estate would have owner-occupied properties as well as rented homes to provide

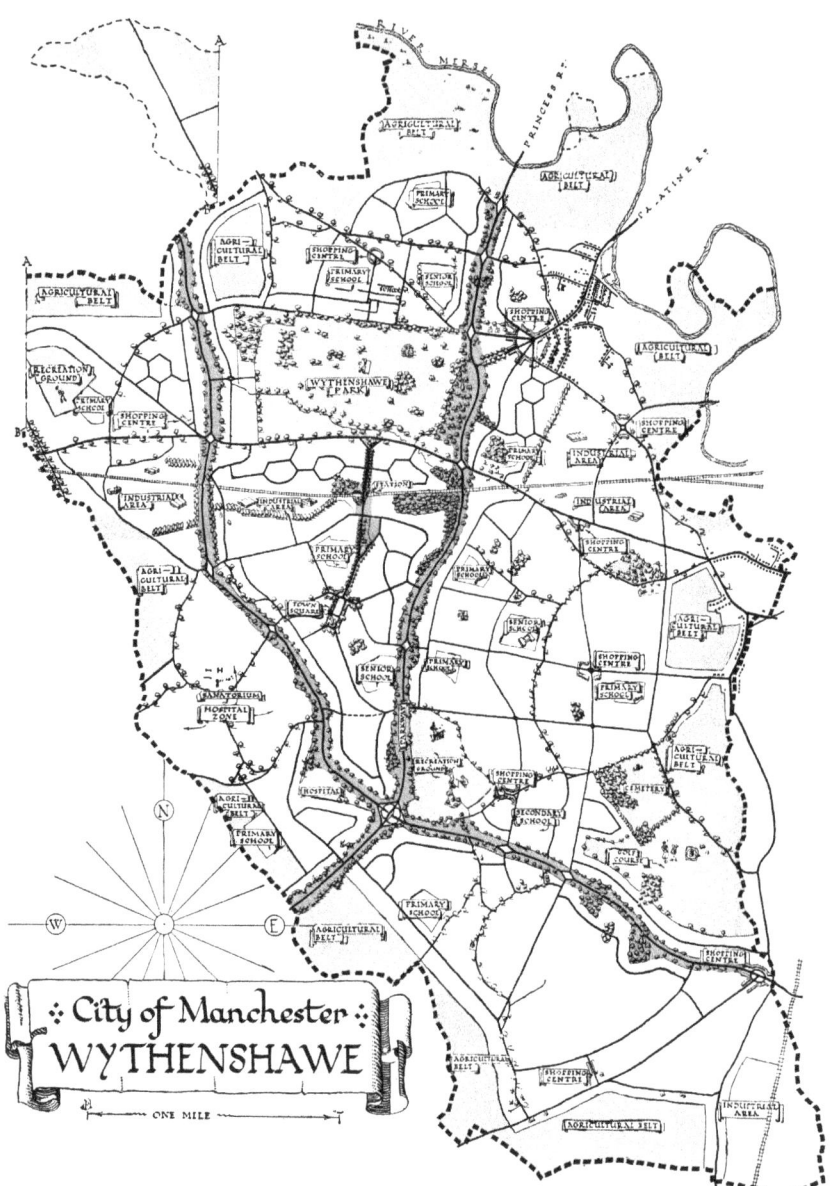

8.8 Parker's sketch plan of the estate (1931). Source: Dugald MacFayden, *Sir Ebenezer Howard and the Town Planning Movement* (Manchester: Manchester University Press, 1933).

a social mix that was part of the garden city ethos, but relatively few were built. Even with new housing going up in Wythenshawe, there were still acres of slums across inner Manchester in the mid-1930s, as starkly mapped in Ernest's book *The Rebuilding of Manchester* (1935) (Plate 6).

SPADE WORK.—The building of houses by private enterprise on the Manchester Corporation estate at Wythenshawe was inaugurated to-day by Lady (Ernest) Simon, here seen cutting the first sod on land taken over by Lord's Estates, Ltd.

8.9 Shena Simon captured in a press photo of the ceremonial digging of the first sod on the site of the first privately constructed homes in Wythenshawe. From the *Evening Chronicle* (16 February 1933), p. 10. Source: SSP M14/6/10.

Ernest Simon's international planning 'quests', 1936–43

An important progressive reformist concern in Britain in the 1930s, and one of particular interest to Ernest Simon, was finding an effective and democratic approach to planning. It grew from the widely perceived inability of liberal democracy to tackle the major challenges of the interwar years, contrasting with the seeming decisiveness of totalitarian regimes. Some with these concerns themselves shifted to the extreme left or right. But more democratically disposed reformers sought a middle way, between unfettered capitalism and the centrally planned approach of the dictatorial regimes.[44] There were differing versions of this progressive 'middle opinion' in the 1930s, but each wanted their notion of planning by the state to play a larger role in shaping wider economic and social development.

The Second World War heightened the significance of these ideas, especially those variants wanting more state intervention.

A specific aspect of this wider concern, one that especially engaged Ernest's interest, also involved a bolder and more comprehensive town and regional planning, closely integrated with social and economic development. His own experience was based in Britain, particularly Manchester, but he also investigated several international cases. This wider knowledge was gained on research fieldtrips made in a voluntary capacity to the USSR (1936), the Nordic countries and Switzerland (1938) and, in an official capacity, to the US (1942–43). Although especially concerned with housing and town planning, his foreign fact-finding often had a wider scope, as in the case of the Nordic countries and Switzerland where he investigated their democratic government.

The first trip to Moscow in 1936 was similar to other Western visits to the Soviet Union during these years.[45] Lasting four weeks, it was arranged by the Society for Cultural Relations between the British Commonwealth and the USSR, an Anglo–Soviet friendship society sympathetic to the Soviet Union. Ivan Maisky, Soviet Ambassador in London, also gave additional support. VOKS (All-Union Society for Cultural Relations with Foreign Countries) and the Soviet travel agency Intourist assisted at the Moscow end, identifying many interviewees and sites to visit and providing interpreters. Ernest was joined by Shena, William A. Robson, a constitutional law and local government expert from the London School of Economics, and John Jewkes, an industrial and regional economist from the University of Manchester. Ernest knew Robson as a fellow Fabian Society member and Jewkes (not a Fabian adherent) from university life in Manchester. The group examined the work of the Mossoviet, the Moscow City Government, under the great 1935 general plan to reconstruct the Russian capital. It was an approach dominated by Fabian thinking, especially that of Sidney and Beatrice Webb, who also gave encouragement and made many detailed suggestions.[46]

The party arrived at Leningrad on 28 August 1936 and thence to Moscow. After some sightseeing, several weeks of intensive interviews and visits began on 31 August.[47] Ernest's loose leaf Moscow diary records meetings with approximately thirty-eight people. Additional information came from inspecting and observing activities at schools or housing blocks. Opinions of anonymous Russians (mainly supervisors) at these sites were often sought. The visitors also saw a little of Soviet life for themselves. Its rigid inflexibilities were obvious even at the opulent Metropole hotel where they stayed – and far more so beyond it. Thus, their public note-taking during street walks often drew challenges from security personnel. Inflexibility also took more draconian forms, directly restricting what the visitors saw. Thus, when they saw construction sites on the Moscow–Volga canal using prisoner labour, under armed guard, requests to stop were denied.[48]

Other distortions were more subtle. For instance, although Ernest reckoned to have inspected fifty flats of various types, they excluded the most seriously overcrowded families.[49] He estimated that about 50 per cent of Moscow's families lived at below 3 square metres per head in so-called grade IV accommodation. However, 'I did not see any of these grade IV houses; they are not normally shown to visitors'.[50] Nevertheless he observed the worst overcrowding in other ways, including on evening walks in poorer districts. Through lighted windows, he saw barrack-style worker accommodation where many shared one large dormitory room.

Effective but undemocratic planning in Moscow

Despite its poor housing record, many things excited Ernest about Moscow and the bold way its development was planned and managed. He noted his overall impressions in his unpublished diary in breathlessly unpunctuated sentences. The visit was, he thought, the '[m]ost thrilling 4 weeks of life at intervals quite carried away – wonderful opportunity build fine city'.[51] He was also impressed by the 'enthusiasm devotion unity of aim' and that the Soviet Union offered a 'good life for mass of people'. He saw that implementing the 1935 plan represented an 'immense construction job' because machines, houses and experienced workers were all lacking. Yet he envied the absence of opposing vested interests or conservatism and greatly admired those leading Moscow's reconstruction efforts.

More specifically, he saw how public ownership of land removed a prime obstacle to effective planning.[52] He also admired the commitment to keep Moscow's population (then about 3.67 million) below 5 million.[53] Admired too were schemes to control the Moskva river, raise its level and improve the banks; the Moscow–Volga Canal; the new Metro subway and the effort and resources focused on social services.[54] Above all, however, it was the foresight, energy, resolve and leadership behind the whole venture that most inspired Ernest. Concluding, he felt Moscow was far better able to address metropolitan planning than London or any other major city in the world. In ten years, he believed Moscow would be well on the way to being 'the best planned great city the world has ever known'.[55]

Unlike many other 1930s Western visitors, however, he had few illusions about the USSR's dark side. Despite Soviet minders, the group learned something about the repressive system. Shena saw, for instance, how mass indoctrination occurred within education.[56] The group had arrived immediately after the executions of Zinoviev and Kamenev, once Bolshevik revolutionary heroes yet now, after a show trial, reviled as traitors.[57] Ernest was downhearted that even intelligent Soviet citizens apparently believed all accusations of treason unquestioningly.

Moscow in the Making, a substantial volume of findings and reflections on the visit, appeared in 1937. In the penultimate chapter, Ernest

8.10 The cover of *Moscow in the Making* (1937). From Sir E. D. Simon, Lady Simon, W. A. Robson and J Jewkes, *Moscow in the Making* (London: Longmans Green and Co., 1937).

considered whether the benefits achieved under the Soviet system outweighed its negative features. He concluded that, in the Russian context, it might do, provided this one-party dictatorship soon became more democratic and less brutal. But he was clear that Soviet methods would be utterly unthinkable in Britain.[58]

To Stockholm and Zurich

The dangerous expansionism of totalitarian states during the late 1930s only heightened the urgency of Ernest's quest for forms of governance that could effectively tackle the serious problems of those years without sacrificing their democratic character. In this respect, he admired those smaller European democracies, the four Nordic countries and Switzerland, which seemed to be successfully striking this balance. Originally, Ernest intended Switzerland as his primary focus, following James Bryce's firm endorsement of its robust democracy and his own prior awareness of it.[59] However, Victor Gollancz, the publisher of *The Smaller Democracies* – Ernest's book on these investigations – had suggested expanding the Swedish section to examine unemployment policies.[60] In fact, Ernest was already thinking along similar lines. Both he and Gollancz were influenced, like many others, by the American author Marquis Childs's notable 1936 book, *Sweden: The Middle Way*. This did much to cement Sweden's growing image as a near utopia that avoided both the evils generated by American capitalism and the brutal authoritarianism of the Soviet Union's repressive state-led dictatorship. Ernest realised that Childs's picture was too good to be true, but it spurred his interest so that, in the end, the biggest section of the book examined Sweden.[61]

From the outset, Ernest had wanted to examine Stockholm's housing and town planning.[62] Here was a case study within his own field of the perceived success of Swedish democracy. He also gave some attention to urban planning in Zurich and, to a lesser extent, Bern. But Switzerland eventually accounted for a much smaller part of the book, mainly focusing on rural local democracy. The other countries were examined in less detail which, in the end, did not include urban planning. Nevertheless, Ernest's diaries show a typically rigorous round of interviews with key figures in each country to garner information. The book's eventual Swedish focus was reflected in the approximately thirty-five people he interviewed there, mainly during August 1938.[63]

For both Zurich and Stockholm, Ernest noted how their attractive qualities reflected their natural settings and that city planners were careful to protect these.[64] He also observed that factories and railways had far less damaging impacts than in larger British settlements, largely reflecting greater electricity use. The greater British reliance on coal generated serious problems of urban smoke. As in Moscow, Ernest admired the willingness and ability of both cities to take land into public ownership. In Stockholm's suburban fringe 80 per cent of land was municipally owned and values were kept low as a result, but he thought the council too timid in pursuing this policy in the inner city (only 28 per cent municipal ownership); a further 41 per cent was also state owned but, despite that high public ownership, inner-city land values remained very high.[65]

The clearest single lesson he drew was how much money both Zurich and Stockholm devoted to city planning.[66] Although both were smaller than Manchester, each spent more on their planning departments. He also admired Zurich city council's willingness to spend on cultural projects and Stockholm's to buy nearby tracts of attractive coast for recreational use.[67] Yet his praise was not universal, and he felt that British cities performed better on the quality and quantity of new social housing. Admittedly, housing needs in British cities exceeded those of Zurich and Stockholm. But he judged the Stockholm new suburb of Bromma inferior to Manchester's new garden city satellite at Wythenshawe.[68]

The origins of the American visit

By September 1939, Ernest Simon had established from his trips to Stockholm and Zurich that some democracies could plan their cities effectively. They might not be perfect, but then neither was Moscow. The key difference was that, in robust democracies like Sweden and Switzerland, governments could be challenged and changed in a consensual way. What was still unclear, however, was if bigger democracies, especially the largest of all, could govern and plan their cities effectively. At best their record, like that of Manchester, was patchy.

Meanwhile, Ernest's experience and talents were being put to good use by the wartime government.[69] At the Ministry of Works, he was soon thinking about postwar reconstruction. The experience of his prewar visits, to Moscow especially, took on a new relevance, even though his knowledge was now a little dated.

The appointment in January 1941 of the Uthwatt Expert Committee on Compensation and Betterment by Lord Reith, the Minister of Works, was another spur. Uthwatt sought to prevent private land ownership, especially fragmented ownership, frustrating public efforts to comprehensively plan urban reconstruction. Again, Ernest's Moscow and, less completely, Stockholm and Zurich findings underlined the value of public, or at least unified, land ownership, rather than the multiple piecemeal holdings typical of British cities. By March 1941, he was pressing the Deputy Prime Minister, Labour Party leader Clement Attlee, to act, arguing that nationalisation was the only practical step.[70] Ernest understood the political difficulties but felt that war had created a fluid situation. But Attlee, a key member of the Conservative-dominated wartime Coalition government, thought it politically impracticable.[71]

Meanwhile, apart from Ernest's work at the Ministry of Works and Planning (as it became in early 1942), he was actively raising public awareness about postwar reconstruction.[72] The Simons' public activities prompted the Ministry of Information to recruit them to go to the United States. Ernest would tell American audiences about Britain's postwar rebuilding plans, while Shena would speak about its local government in wartime.[73] The visit would also allow Ernest to learn more about how American democracy was governing and planning its own cities.

Finding some effective planning in democratic America

On 19 September 1942, the Simons flew from Ireland, via Newfoundland, to New York.[74] Coming straight from wartime Britain into a land of plenty, both were, from the first, entranced by the United States.[75] And, this infatuation was warmly reciprocated by everyone they encountered. This made it relatively easy to gather information compared to the greater formality of the other international visits.

The Simons were positive about many things they encountered in the United States. Top of this list was the Tennessee Valley Authority (TVA), the New Deal regional development project begun by President Roosevelt in 1933. It had been reported in Britain shortly after by the biologist, Julian Huxley, and in a PEP report.[76] Ernest saw it in late November 1942, describing it as '[t]he most exhilarating thing in the USA. First rate democratic planning ….'[77] As in Moscow, the quality, vision and drive of its leaders hugely impressed him, particularly the chairman, David Lilienthal, who he judged the 'finest type of businessman & citizen'. In April 1943, Ernest published a short booklet about the TVA, amongst the first of several important wartime British publications about it.[78] By then, Ernest rated the TVA as 'probably the world's most successful experiment in large scale and long-range democratic planning'.[79]

For city planning, New York stood out particularly because of its express highways and parks.[80] Ernest was apparently (according to Robert Moses, the 'very powerful personality' largely responsible) the first Englishman to inquire seriously about the city's highways programme. In an unpublished December 1942 report to brief his own and other ministries, Ernest wrote that New York had 'led the way' in the United States.[81] Its highways and parkways were 'so good that it would seem almost essential that England should study them, especially from the point of view of the replanning of London and our other great conurbations'. Overall, Ernest saw New York's efforts as 'probably the outstanding example of large-scale democratic city planning in the world'. Moses, he thought, was 'doing an incomparable job', even though he '[d]oes not listen' and 'knows comparatively little

Sir Ernest goes 'slumming'
Expert on housing in Britain where Nazi bombs have done effective slum clearing, Sir Ernest Simon tours Chicago "blighted areas", to get first-hand information on slum situation here.

8.11 Newspaper clipping from the *Daily Times* (Chicago) (30 October 1942). Courtesy of Helen David.

outside NY'.[82] He was also shocked by some aspects of the United States, including the prevalence of blight, especially in some cities, quite different to the huge slum problems of British cities. In Detroit, for example, he noted examples near downtown. Deteriorating areas, abandoned by affluent aspirant and mobile suburbanites, were now occupied by poor white and African American migrants from the South.[83]

> THE WHITE HOUSE
> WASHINGTON
>
> December 22, 1942
>
> Dear Sir Ernest:
>
> I am so glad that you had the opportunity of personally investigating the workings of TVA and to know that you feel it is such an outstanding example of successful long-range planning.
>
> Did you have the opportunity of talking with Senator George Norris, with whom, as you probably know, these developments are almost an obsession?
>
> I hope you will advise me later on about what success you have in applying the idea within the British Commonwealth.
>
> Very sincerely yours,
>
> Franklin D. Roosevelt
>
> Sir Ernest Simon,
> Hotel New Weston,
> Madison Avenue at 50th Street,
> New York, N. Y.

8.12 Letter from the President Franklin D. Roosevelt to Ernest, 22 December 1942. Courtesy of Helen David.

Ernest Simon – when British democracy rebuilds

The lessons Ernest drew from America were, though mixed, mainly positive ones. Towards the end of a 100-day American journey during which he had lectured fifty times about rebuilding postwar Britain and discussed planning with many people, he planned another book. He noted that his thinking on rebuilding had become clearer 'as one contemplated Britain from a distance ... comparing it with the USA; my opinion of British Democracy grew steadily more favourable! While immensely liking America. A happy experience.'[84] Zigzagging slowly back to Liverpool in January 1943 in an Atlantic convoy pursued by a U-boat, Ernest began to set out his thoughts in greater detail.[85]

In lectures after he returned to Britain, he referred extensively to his foreign experiences, for example to the Architectural Association in October and the Institute of Landscape Architects in November 1943.[86] Earlier, in July, he had written an article on rebuilding Britain for publication in Moscow.[87] He had also proposed the book, though this only proceeded seriously the following year. After further delays, *Rebuilding Britain – A Twenty Year Plan* finally appeared in January 1945.

In *Rebuilding Britain*, Ernest distilled the mature lessons of his international visits.[88] Some thirty-two pages of 219 were exclusively devoted to foreign examples. Twenty-three pages were on the United States, nine on the TVA alone. However, this numerical balance understates the role of the foreign examples in the book's arguments. Thus Moscow, 'The Planner's Paradise', was invoked in support of his arguments for land nationalisation and the United States for more forward-looking approaches to highways planning.[89] Moscow and Zurich were cited in discussion about ideal city sizes. These lessons were also applied specifically to Manchester. He wanted it to emulate several American and European cities as a fully fledged regional capital with fewer and better main rail terminals, more grand buildings (including a major skyscraper) and a richer cultural life.[90]

Rebuilding Britain was well received, prompting Minister of Works, Duncan Sandys, to appoint Ernest his housing advisor.[91] The book's most distinctive feature was its emphasis, not just on planning, but on detailed implementation.[92] This involved assessing the supply of labour, materials and land, linking physical and economic planning.[93] The approach certainly owed something to his Moscow experience, but this was to be democratic planning. Concluding, he contrasted the abundantly funded command structures that were successfully prosecuting the war, even in democratic countries, with how, under the Soviet system, a similar structure also operated in peacetime.[94] National prosperity and low interest rates would also be needed to fulfil his proposed rebuilding programme, but he thought the critical factor would be public opinion. He ended *Rebuilding Britain* with words expressing these hopes: 'Let us plan and build healthy and pleasant cities, the finest the world has known, and a monument to the ideals and efficiency of British democracy.'[95]

Discussion

Few planners today use such language. Even then, Sir Ernest Simon was unusual in so often explicitly linking urban planning to wider political values and governmental regimes. A few professional town planners spoke or wrote this way in the 1930s and 1940s, but most preferred a more technical discourse where political values remained implicit. Yet Ernest, though widely respected across the built environment professions, was not a professional planner. His grounding as an engineer certainly meant that he understood the technical values of the expert. But he had also absorbed the principles of welfare liberalism and a deep commitment to Fabian values. Added to these was an active involvement in public life and a strong concern for urban reform and to empirical research into local governance. These attitudes, competencies and experiences meant he could connect the technical aspects of planning with the political values that underpinned them. He could also articulate that connection in a cogent and engaging manner that transcended specific party interest. His more explicit language on these themes expressed a dominant strand in wartime thinking and had provided the ideological compass for his international journeying.

In visiting these places, however, Ernest did not simply confirm prior expectations. He could extol Mossoviet's effectiveness (while recognising its failure to provide enough decent housing), but be deeply unhappy about Soviet repression. Even Stockholm, superb though its planning was, left him less impressed with its housing policies compared to Manchester. As regards the United States, however, he returned far more admiring than anticipated, seeing it, at its best, as a powerhouse of democracy, actively planning for its future. He obviously grasped that in many places it fell short, where individual city governments (albeit less corrupt than formerly) remained too willing to appease private real estate or other interests. Beyond this, there were other aspects to which he seemed oblivious. The great racial inequality of American democracy passed without comment, a symptom of urban blight but apparently accepted as a fact of nature.

Amidst the very intense circulation of policy knowledge during the later 1930s and 1940s, the specific impact of Ernest Simon's international learning on British policy discourse and action is difficult to isolate. His position within, but not centrally part of, the government machine in the war years allowed easy access to many decision makers. There is ample evidence that he was heard and taken seriously within government, the professions and more widely. In part, of course, this reflected his purely British experience. Yet, by being able also to speak with such authority about key international experiences, he was bringing something unique to the policy debate. Here were cities being more effectively planned than in Britain because greater resources were devoted to planning, land was more effectively controlled for public purposes and there was more decisiveness regarding the key determinants of the efficiency and wider quality of urban life. A part of the postwar drive for a stronger British planning system certainly fed on such knowledge.

Creating that stronger system was to be the work of others, however. Ernest Simon's own active role within planning policy largely ended after 1945. His remarkable talents and commitment to public service were now largely deployed in the University of Manchester and the BBC. Yet, in these and his other campaigning interests such as promoting population control in the 1950s, he never lost his habit of seeking and drawing lessons from relevant foreign experiences.[96]

The Simons' continuing connections to Wythenshawe after 1945

Wythenshawe's development continued after the Second World War, although now more as a large municipal housing estate rather than a satellite garden city; ensuring its success was a key element in the influential 1945 City of Manchester Plan.[97] The Simons' connections to Wythenshawe also continued, signalled most powerfully when Ernest adopted it as the title for his barony in 1947.

By the early 1950s, more than 12,000 council homes had been constructed in Wythenshawe, by then accommodating well over 60,000 people. Already it had greatly surpassed the earlier garden cities at Letchworth and Welwyn – and was continuing to grow.[98] Parker's careful zoning of residential neighbourhoods, separated by large access roads, had largely been enacted (Figure 8.13). The civic and larger retailing centres, whilst designated, would only be finished by the early 1970s. Low housing density was maintained generally, despite pressure for more dwellings (subsequently some maisonettes and low-rise flats were built). The 5,500-acre Wythenshawe estate comprised around 3,000 acres for housing and about 1,000 acres for open space, including a large golf course and the 250-acre public park that the Simons had gifted to the city in 1926. There were concerted attempts to bring light manufacturing and logistics jobs to Wythenshawe. Despite advantages of space for new factories, access to the trunk road network and the nearby expanding airport at Ringway, the area struggled to attract businesses.[99]

When Ernest, now Lord Simon of Wythenshawe, received the Freedom of the City of Manchester in November 1959, he reflected on the development and significance of the estate:

> Wythenshawe is far from perfect; a major trouble is that we still have no civic centre. But thousands of families are living under housing conditions so good that if we could provide similar conditions for all our families, the housing problem would be satisfactorily and finally solved. In spite of serious difficulties, Wythenshawe is undoubtedly a very great achievement. It was certainly the best instance of a satellite garden town in the inter-war years. It set an example which had an important influence on the building of new towns; undoubtedly the best feature of the post-war planning development.[100]

Ernest died in October 1960, just shy of eighty-one. Shena kept in touch with developments at Wythenshawe and remained politically engaged, leaving the Education Committee only in 1970. In 1961, she opened Simon Court in Wythenshawe, a nine-storey block of flats for older residents. It was the first system-built multistorey block that Manchester constructed after the war. Although named to honour the Simons, the use of high-rise

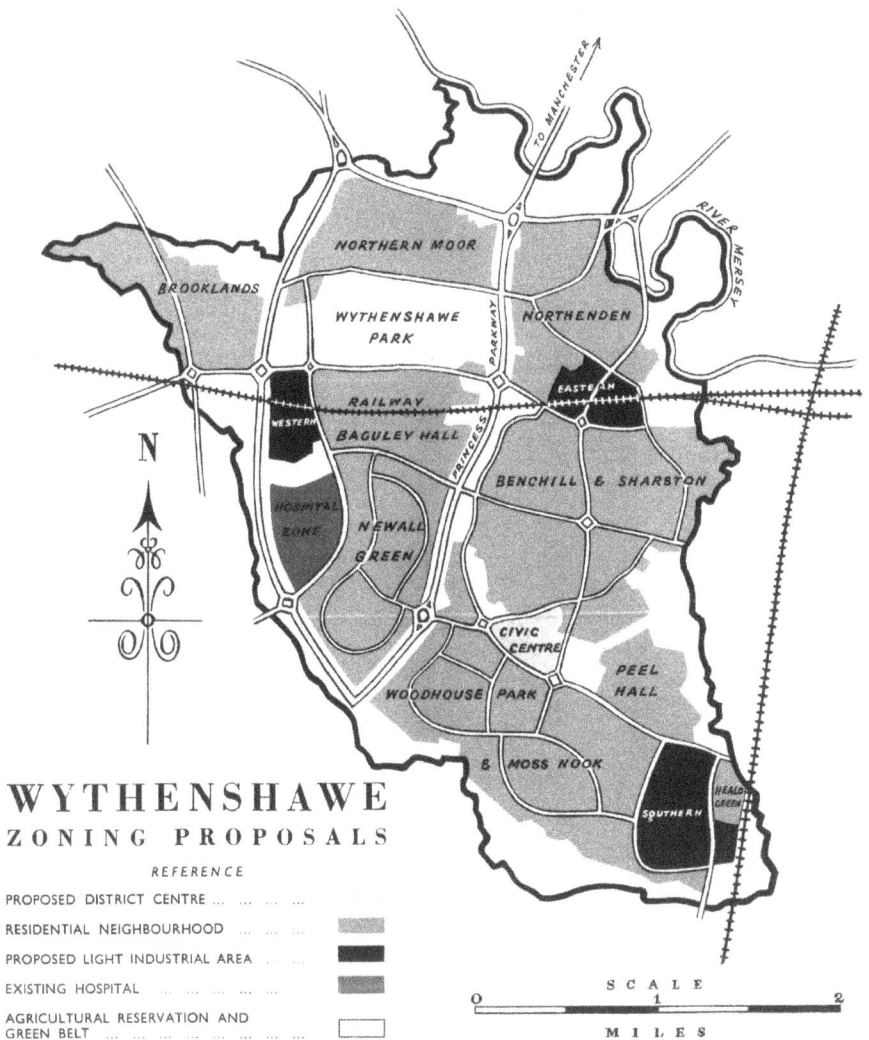

8.13 Zoning plan from *Wythenshawe Plan and Reality*. (Manchester Municipal Information Bureau, c. 1953). Source: Martin Dodge.

flats rather than cottages with gardens would have been an anathema to an earlier Ernest Simon.[101] The Freedom of the City of Manchester was granted to Shena in recognition of her public work in 1964. One of her last public appearances, aged eighty-six, was at the ceremonial laying of the foundation stone for Wythenshawe's long overdue civic centre in 1969.[102] Shena died in 1972.

By 1970, around 102,000 residents lived in some 23,000 council homes and 4,400 privately owned houses in Wythenshawe.[103] Subsequently, the area suffered social problems and significant pockets of deprivation such that, by the 1980s, it had a tarnished reputation as a municipally mismanaged 'sink estate'. Yet, as the planning historian Peter Hall reflected, 'for all its latter-day shabbiness, it fully deserves the appellation of the third garden city'.[104]

Since the work of these two remarkable Simon generations, town planning and social housing have markedly changed, yet many pre-existing housing problems remain, and new challenges have appeared. The impact of council house sales following the 1980s Thatcher reforms on places like Wythenshawe is marked in terms of social divisions. Former industrial cities like Manchester have also been reimagined, with old mills being gentrified and a marked growth in city-centre living after years of population deconcentration. But there are systemic housing problems in terms of availability and affordability for ordinary families, so while the many new high-rise apartment blocks are creating a 'MancHattan' skyline, homeless numbers on the streets are growing.[105] There is also renewed suburban sprawl and a battle over Manchester's green belt reminiscent of the 1920s. More widely, governments again struggle to effectively deliver the important projects and programmes that society and the economy needs while maintaining democratic principles. Sadly perhaps, this account of the public service of two remarkable generations of Simons continues to have a profound relevance for the housing and planning issues facing us today.

Notes

1. Dr John Roberton, a Manchester surgeon, in evidence to the Parliamentary Committee on the Health of Towns, 1840, pp. 221–2. Available from the Wellcome Collection, https://wellcomecollection.org/works/zfykg69p (accessed 1 September 2023).
2. Asa Briggs, *Victorian Cities* (Harmondsworth: Penguin Books, 1968); Mark Crinson, *Shock City: Image and Architecture in Industrial Manchester* (London: Yale University Press, 2022).
3. This has been well documented elsewhere – including in his own extensive writing. See: E. D. Simon, *A City Council from Within* (London: Longmans Green & Co., 1926); E. D. Simon and J. Inman, *The Rebuilding of Manchester* (London: Longmans Green & Co, 1935). Also, see Mary Stocks, *Ernest Simon of Manchester* (Manchester: Manchester University Press, 1963) and Chapter 4 of this volume by John Ayshford and Brendon Jones.
4. This section draws upon material originally published in Stephen V. Ward, 'Searching for Effective and Democratic Town Planning: The International Travels of Sir Ernest Simon, 1936–1943', *Planning Perspectives*, 32:3 (2017), 353–71.
5. The first Medical Officer of Health appointed by Manchester Corporation in 1868 was John Leigh and his first annual report was published in 1869.
6. John J. Parkinson-Bailey, *Manchester: An Architectural History* (Manchester: Manchester University Press, 2000).
7. 'Model dwellings in Manchester', *Manchester Guardian* (31 May 1892), p. 9.
8. Ancoats was the first dedicated industrial area laid out for cotton factories in the 1800s with the coming of the Ashton and Rochdale Canals into central Manchester. By the 1890s, the Ancoats ward had one of the highest death rates in the city. Michael E. Rose, Keith Falconer and Julian Holder, *Ancoats: Cradle of Industrialisation* (Swindon: English Heritage, 2011).

9 'Some Model Artisans' Dwellings at Manchester', *British Architect* (20 May 1892), p. 381.
10 'Model dwellings in Manchester'.
11 See Chapter 2 in this volume by Janet Wolff.
12 'Joint-Stock Companies: Manchester Labourers' Dwellings Company, Limited', *Manchester Guardian* (20 December 1898), p. 9.
13 Hankinson became a well-regarded social worker and sanitary reformer in Manchester and went on to found the Manchester Housing Company, which followed Octavia Hill's model of social housing; 'Obituary: The Late Miss Hankinson', *Manchester Guardian* (10 April 1929), p. 12.
14 'The Jersey-Street Dwellings', *Manchester Guardian* (12 December 1895), p. 4.
15 This was its first council housing comprising a large five-storey tenement block of 522 dwellings and located on Oldham Road. The building still stands and was Grade II listed in 1988.
16 'Joint-Stock Companies: Manchester Labourers' Dwellings Company, Limited', *Manchester Guardian* (20 December 1898), p. 9.
17 For details on Henry's network of close friends and associates in his public work, see Janet Wolff's Chapter 2 in this volume and Brian Simon, *In Search of a Grandfather: Henry Simon of Manchester 1835–1899* (Leicester: The Pendene Press, 1997).
18 'Tenement dwellings survey', *Manchester Guardian* (21 June 1932), p. 14.
19 His book *The Improvement of the Dwellings and Surroundings of the People: The Example of Germany* was published in 1904. Also, Horsfall's daughter Edith married into the Simon family, marrying Henry's third son Harry, and had four children. See: Brian Simon, *Henry Simon's Children* (Leicester: The Pendene Press, 1997), p. 85.
20 Thomas R. Marr, *Housing Conditions in Manchester & Salford* (Manchester: Sherratt and Hughes, Manchester University Press, 1904), p. 5.
21 *A Short History of Manchester Housing* (City of Manchester Housing Committee, 1947).
22 'Garden Suburbs: Five Schemes Around Manchester', *Manchester Guardian* (26 June 1912), p. 9.
23 'Housing Reform: A Didsbury Garden Suburb', *Manchester Guardian* (21 October 1907), p. 12.
24 'Didsbury Garden City Scheme: Celebration on Completion of Buildings', *Alderley & Wilmslow Advertiser* (8 October 1909), p. 8.
25 'Housing Reform: A Didsbury Garden Suburb'.
26 Reports of the society show that Ernest Simon also served on the management committee, perhaps one of the first examples of him taking on a role in social reform. At this point in his life, a great deal of his time was taken up in running the two family engineering businesses.
27 'Didsbury Garden City Scheme: Celebration on Completion of Buildings'.
28 'Co-operative Housing. A Garden City Scheme at Didsbury', *Manchester Guardian* (4 October 1909), p. 14.
29 John Tudor Walters, *Report of the Committee Appointed by the President of the Local Government Board and the Secretary for Scotland to Consider Questions of Building Construction in Connection with the Provision of Dwellings for the Working Classes in England and Wales, and Scotland* (London: HMSO, 1918).
30 ESD, 6 November 1919.
31 'A Greater Manchester: The New Lord Mayor on the Need for Wider Boundaries', *Manchester Guardian* (10 November 1921), p. 9.
32 'Wythenshawe Estate: Manchester & Compulsory Powers', *Manchester Guardian* (28 November 1919), p. 8.
33 Sir Ernest and Lady Simon, 'Wythenshawe', in E. D. Simon and J. Inman, *The Rebuilding of Manchester* (London: Longmans Green & Co, 1935), pp. 36–8.

34 SSP M14/1/16/5, Report of the Parks and Cemeteries Committee, 16 April 1926.
35 Costing them over £25,000, it was equivalent to over £1.2 million today according to the Bank of England inflation calculator. Joan Simon, *Shena Simon Feminist and Educationist* (Manchester: privately printed, 1986), Chapter III, p. 15.
36 *A Short History of Manchester Housing* (Manchester: City of Manchester Housing Committee, 1947).
37 Sir Ernest and Lady Simon, 'Wythenshawe', pp. 38–42.
38 Sir Ernest and Lady Simon, 'Wythenshawe', pp. 36, 42.
39 Marian A. Horrocks, *The Contribution to Education and Society of Lady Simon of Wythenshawe (1912–1972)* (Unpublished MPhil dissertation, University of Manchester, 1990), pp. 379–80.
40 'Ugliness in Daily Life: Public Art at Low Ebb', *Manchester Guardian* (26 September 1930), p. 13.
41 Audrey Kay, *Wythenshawe Circa 1932–1955: The Making of a Community?* (Unpublished PhD thesis, University of Manchester, 1993), pp. 124–36.
42 Mrs E. D. Simon, 'Towards Utopia – V. Cities of the Future', *The Listener* (9 April 1930), pp. 633–4.
43 *A Short History of Manchester Housing* (City of Manchester Housing Committee, 1947). Horrocks, *The* Contribution to Education and Society of Lady Simon of Wythenshawe, p. 380. Also see: *Manchester Guardian* (2 February 1932), p. 12.
44 Arthur Marwick, 'Middle Opinion in the Thirties: Planning, Progress and "Political Agreement"', *English Historical Review*, 79:311 (1964), 285–98; Daniel Ritschel, *The Politics of Planning: The Debate on Economic Planning in Britain in the 1930s* (Oxford: Clarendon, 1997).
45 Stephen Ward, 'Introduction', in Sir E. D. Simon, Lady Simon, W. A. Robson and J. Jewkes, *Moscow in the Making*, (Abingdon: Routledge, 2015 [1937]), pp. ix–xiii.
46 Sir E. D. Simon, 'Preface', in Sir E. D. Simon et al., *Moscow in the Making*, pp. v–vi.
47 ESP M11/15/11, 28 August 1936–30 August 1936.
48 Sir E. D. Simon, 'The Mossoviet: Is it Democratic?' in Sir E. D. Simon et al., *Moscow in the Making*, pp. 224–5
49 Sir E. D. Simon, 'Housing', in Sir E. D. Simon et al., *Moscow in the Making*, p. 147.
50 Simon, 'Housing', p. 153.
51 ESP M11/15/11, 'Notes on Freedom', p. 21
52 Sir E. D. Simon, 'The Mossoviet: Its Advantages for Town Planning', in Sir E. D. Simon et al., *Moscow in the Making*, pp. 212–13.
53 Sir E. D. Simon, 'The Ten Year Plan: Comments', in Sir E. D. Simon et al., *Moscow in the Making*, pp. 199–201; Nobuo Shimotomai, *Moscow under Stalinist Rule* (London: Macmillan, 1991), p. 7.
54 Simon, 'Comments', pp. 203–6; Sir E. D. Simon, 'The Mossoviet: Is it Efficient?' in Sir E. D. Simon et al., *Moscow in the Making*, 229–31.
55 Simon 'The Mossoviet: Is it Efficient?', p. 234.
56 Lady Simon, Education', in Sir E. D. Simon et al., *Moscow in the Making*, pp. 137–42.
57 ESP M11/15/11, 28 August 1936.
58 Simon, 'The Mossoviet: Is it Efficient?', pp. 226–7.
59 James Bryce, *Modern Democracies*, 2 vols (New York: Macmillan, 1921), I, pp. 327–454.
60 ESP M11/11/2, Victor Gollancz to Ernest Simon, 9 February 1939; ESP M11/11/2, Ernest Simon to Victor Gollancz, 11 February 1939.
61 Sir E. D. Simon, *The Smaller Democracies* (London: Victor Gollancz, 1939), p. 52.
62 Ernest Simon, 'Town Planning in Stockholm', *Journal of the Town Planning Institute*, 25:3 (1939), 81–5; Simon, *The Smaller Democracies*, pp. 89–90.
63 ESP M11/15/13, generally.
64 Simon, *The Smaller Democracies*, pp. 33–9, 89–114.
65 Simon, 'Town Planning in Stockholm', 82–4.

66 Simon, *The Smaller Democracies*, pp. 35, 91.
67 Simon, *The Smaller Democracies*, pp. 35–7, 95.
68 Simon, *The Smaller Democracies*, pp. 94, 97.
69 Stocks, *Ernest Simon of Manchester*, pp. 114–18.
70 ESP M11/11/2, Ernest Simon to Clement Attlee (19 March 1941).
71 Stocks, *Ernest Simon of Manchester*, p. 120.
72 ESP M11/16/15, Broadcast by Sir Ernest Simon 'Rebuilding our Cities', 22 February 1942; Ernest Simon, *The Rebuilding of Britain* (1942) [copy held by the University of Manchester Main Library].
73 Stocks, *Ernest Simon of Manchester*, p. 118.
74 ESP M11/15/15, p. 1.
75 ESP M11/15/15, pp. 1, 3.
76 Julian S. Huxley, 'The T.V.A., A great American Experiment, I – Large Scale Social Planning', *The Times* (21 May 1935), p. 17; Julian S. Huxley, 'The T.V.A., II – A Town in the Making', *The Times* (22 May 1935), p. 17; PEP [Political and Economic Planning], 'The Tennessee Valley Authority', *Planning*, 76:1 (1936), 1–16.
77 ESP M11/15/15, 29 November 1942 and 30 November 1942, pp. 9–10
78 Ernest Simon, *The Tennessee Valley Authority* (privately printed, 1943); Julian Huxley. *TVA: Adventure in Planning* (Cheam: Architectural Press, 1943); David E. Lilienthal, *TVA Tennessee Valley Authority: Democracy on the March* (Harmondsworth: Penguin, 1944).
79 Simon, *The Tennessee Valley Authority*, p. 1.
80 ESP M11/15/15, 10 December 1942, pp. 10, 76.
81 ESP M11/10/1, Express Highways in the United States, 19 December 1942.
82 ESP M11/15/15, 10 December 1942, p. 76.
83 ESP M11/15/15, 18 November 1942, p. 50.
84 ESP M11/15/15, p. 12.
85 Stocks, *Ernest Simon of Manchester*, p. 119.
86 ESP M11/11/2, Ernest Simon, Address to Landscape Architects, 8 November 1943.
87 ESP M11/11/2 H, Rebuilding Britain (text of Moscow broadcast), 20 July 1943.
88 E. D. Simon, *Rebuilding Britain – A Twenty Year Plan* (London: Victor Gollancz, 1945), pp. 127–62.
89 Simon, *Rebuilding Britain*, pp. 171–8.
90 Simon, *Rebuilding Britain*, pp. 194–211 (especially pp. 203–7).
91 ESP M11/11/2, Dorothy Horsman to Miss Green, 7 August 1945. [Miss Green was Ernest's private secretary, see Stocks, *Ernest Simon of Manchester*, p. 160]; ESP M11/11/2, Ernest Simon to Victor Gollancz, 5 April 1945.
92 Simon, *Rebuilding Britain*, pp. 15–66; ESP M11/11/2, Clough Williams-Ellis to Ernest Simon, 5 October 1944; ESP M11/11/2, 9 October 1944; Ernest Simon to Clough Williams-Ellis, 10 October 1944.
93 ESP M11/11/2, Ernest Simon to Victor Gollancz, 17 June 1944; Victor Gollancz to Simon, 21 June 1944; ESP M11/11/2, Ernest Simon to Victor Gollancz, 24 August 1944.
94 Simon, *Rebuilding Britain*, pp. 227–9.
95 Simon, *Rebuilding Britain*, p. 233.
96 ESP M11/11/15, Lord Simon of Wythenshawe, *Population and Resources of Barbados* (1954). Lord Simon of Wythenshawe, 'Broadcasting in other Countries', *Political Quarterly*, 24:3 (1953), 356–86.
97 Rowland Nicholas, *City of Manchester Plan* (Norwich: published for Manchester Corporation by Jarrold, 1945). A whole chapter in this extensive report is devoted to the Wythenshawe estate.
98 *Wythenshawe Plan and Reality* (Manchester: Manchester Municipal Information Bureau, 1953); Kay, Wythenshawe Circa 1932–1955, p. 451.

99 Derek Deakin, *Wythenshawe: The Story of a Garden City* (Bognor Regis: Phillimore, 1989).
100 Address by Lord Simon of Wythenshawe on the Occasion of the Presentation of the Freedom of the City of Manchester 25th November 1959 in the form of a farewell speech to the City Council', *Manchester Review*, 9 (1960), p. 7.
101 For example, in 1935, Ernest took part in a public debate on BBC Radio with Geoffrey Boumphrey and argued the case for cottages over flats. See: 'Can Flats Solve the Housing Problem?', *The Listener* (30 October 1935), pp. 741–4.
102 'Stone Laid 30 Years Late', *Guardian* (27 September 1969), p. 4.
103 Deakin, *Wythenshawe*.
104 Peter Hall, *Cities of Tomorrow: An Intellectual History of Urban Planning and Design Since 1880* (Oxford: Basil Blackwell, 1998), p. 111.
105 Richard Goulding, Adam Leaver and Jonathan Silver, 'From Homes to Assets: Transcalar Territorial Networks and the Financialization of Build to Rent in Greater Manchester', *Environment and Planning*, 55:4 (2023), 828–49.

9

Burghers and citizens: the Simons and the University of Manchester

H. S. Jones and Chris Godden

A family inheritance

'If I come to Manchester, I am inclined to make the university my chief job, and try to be chairman.' So wrote Ernest Simon in his diary in 1929, as he reached the age of fifty.[1] He had recently been elected for a second time as MP for Manchester Withington, and was deliberating about whether he should pursue his public career at Westminster or in Manchester: hence '*If* I come to Manchester'. The electors of Penryn and Falmouth made his decision for him in 1931, although his decision not to fight Withington and to contest a Cornish seat instead already indicated a flagging enthusiasm for a parliamentary career. Only then did he return to the choice between 'politics' and 'education' as rival vocations. He set out the choice in a number of letters addressed to his elder son Roger and, at greater length, to his old Liberal Summer School colleague Ramsay Muir in 1934. By that time he had been Treasurer of the University of Manchester for over a year, and was impressed with the opportunities it offered him. The Vice-Chancellor, Walter Moberly, was 'in every way a first-class V.C., an excellent man to work with; nobody could do the academic side better'; that said, 'He needs somebody to work with on the business side', and Ernest saw this as his role. He also expected, prematurely as it turned out, that he would soon succeed to the chairmanship.[2]

It was quite something for a lay (unpaid) governor of a university to contemplate committing to it as his 'chief job' in this way. Yet this was how Ernest's career developed, once he had put an end to his parliamentary ambitions.[3] He had been appointed to the University of Manchester's court of governors in 1915, and six months later to its council, the executive body, and would retain these two positions, more or less without interruption, until his death forty-five years later. He would go on to hold the two senior lay offices for exceptionally long periods, being treasurer from 1932 to 1941 and chairman of council from 1941 to 1957. His twenty-five-year service in senior office was unequalled in the University's history – and remains so.[4] He sustained his close involvement in the University's business even when he was chairman of the BBC (1947–52).[5] He also interpreted his role capaciously. Rarely did he confine himself to the established responsibilities of lay officers, and the boundary between their role and that of academics was one he overstepped with some relish. He had no hesitation in expressing strong views on chair appointments, which was very much an academic responsibility, and continued to do so even when reproached by the vice-chancellor.[6] He could be a difficult colleague, and had a strained relationship with Lord Woolton, who was the University's chancellor for almost the entirety of Ernest's service as chairman of council.[7] But he was deeply interested in the University as a force for social good and as an intellectual community, and saw himself as a part of that community. He was a munificent and interventionist donor, notably funding the innovative Simon fellowships in the social sciences. Moreover, his position in the University of Manchester also gave him the standing to make a remarkable contribution to the national conversation on the role of universities: he could even claim to have done more than anyone to initiate that conversation at the end of the Second World War.

Historians of British universities have shown curiously little interest in the contributions of lay governors, who, if they feature at all in university histories, appear cloaked in collective anonymity. Ernest Simon's relationship with the University of Manchester is illuminating, not because it was typical by any means, but because he was so distinctive. Of all such figures in the twentieth century, he was probably the most influential and certainly the one who thought and wrote most about what universities were for and how they could best serve the community.

In forming such a close relationship with the University, Ernest built on foundations laid by his father. Henry Simon's relationship with Owens College – the precursor of the Victoria University of Manchester – is opaque, however. When Henry arrived in Manchester in 1860, a graduate of Zurich Polytechnic, he would have found academic life in the city in a rudimentary state. Owens College, founded in Quay Street in the city centre in 1851, had struggled to overcome the scepticism of middle-class parents about the value of higher education, and the *Manchester Guardian* deemed it a 'mortifying failure' in 1858.[8] The Mechanics' Institution, which is now commemorated as if it were an embryonic UMIST, really dispensed an elementary education enriched by a smattering of high culture. But Henry arrived at an important moment in educational history. It was in the 1860s that demand for higher education started to take off, and Owens College began to flourish to such an extent that a movement was launched for its 'extension' – that is, institutional reform, expansion and relocation to the site on Oxford Road still occupied by the University of Manchester. Central to that movement, which came to fruition in 1870–73, was a new and symbiotic relationship between the college and Manchester's business and professional communities. Those communities, buoyed by civic pride, weighed in with generous benefactions; in return, a mode of governance was devised which established a subtle balance between academic self-government and accountability to civic notables. It was a structure that worked because it could draw on a strong tradition of civic service among the mercantile classes, or burghers, of Manchester. That structure, which came to be the norm for English civic universities, would provide the setting for much of Ernest's work.

Manchester's German community made an important contribution to the formation of the city's distinctive burgher spirit. This community had strong links with the reformed Owens College, supplying academics (Schorlemmer, Schuster), governors (the Behrens family in particular) and some of its greatest benefactors, including, most importantly, the railway engineer Charles Beyer. It was through the German community that the Simons first established their connection with the College. Henry Simon recalled as much in his speech on laying the foundation stone for the new Physics Building at Owens College in 1898. His connection with the College stretched all the way back to the early 1860s, when his friend Carl Schorlemmer introduced him to Henry Roscoe in the Quay Street building. Roscoe was professor of chemistry, a doctoral graduate of Heidelberg, and the intellectual visionary behind the college's extension. Schorlemmer, who like Roscoe had studied under Bunsen at Heidelberg and then moved on to work with Liebig at Giessen, was at this time working as Roscoe's assistant, but as the College expanded he was himself appointed professor of organic chemistry in 1874. Henry does not appear on the list of significant donors to Owens College at this time, no doubt because he was still establishing his business career and his local roots. His own contributions came much later, in the 1890s, when he endowed the Henry Simon Chair of German (1895) and then made the largest single donation towards the Physics Building, the building that would soon house Rutherford's laboratory.[9]

The origins of the chair of German are little known. Eda Sagarra wrote a short history of the chair to mark its centenary in 1996, but her focus was on the chair's occupants rather than its founder.[10] Correspondence between the professor of Latin, Augustus Samuel Wilkins, and the editor of the *Manchester Guardian*, C. P. Scott, suggests that Wilkins and other professorial colleagues made the case for the chair out of concern for the situation of the lecturer in German, Herman Hager, who happened to be Wilkins's brother-in-law. Hager was a distinguished scholar, and well known in academic circles as a member of council of the Victoria University. But he was underpaid for the work he did: £400 a year for

9.1 The foundation stone of the Physics (now Rutherford) Building laid by Henry Simon in 1899. Photo by Margaret Littler.

twenty hours' teaching a week. Wilkins suggested to Scott that the answer was to seek subscriptions from 'the wealthier Germans in Manchester', and he specifically identified Henry Simon as the man who 'could more easily than anyone carry it through', if he could be interested in the plan.[11] Since Hager taught German at Withington Girls' School as well as at Owens, his qualities were known to Simon, who was evidently taken by the plan. In the event Hager died, quite suddenly, early in 1895, after the gift had been offered but before the chair was filled, and the chair went instead to a lacklustre first incumbent.[12] But it subsequently attained considerable prestige as one of the leading German chairs in the country.

Still, Owens College was only one of the public causes that Henry Simon supported, and far from the most important: he never, for instance, served on the court of governors. He was more committed to the Royal Manchester College of Music, Withington Girls' School and the Hallé Orchestra. Ernest inherited from his father a sense of the public obligations that wealth entailed. But the fascination with universities, and the commitment to the University of Manchester in particular, was Ernest's.

The Burghers of Broomcroft

One factor that made Ernest opt against national politics in the 1930s in favour of Manchester and education was that he was looking for a vocation that he could share with his wife. He was profoundly attracted, as Shena was, by the Webbs' model of a partnership between husband and wife grounded in work they pursued in common.[13] While both were of the stature to pursue parliamentary ambitions, it would have been difficult to reconcile family life with two parliamentary careers. Instead, they devoted themselves to public service in Manchester, both with a focus on education, although Shena's main interest was secondary education, pursued though the education committee of the city council, whereas Ernest was chiefly drawn to higher education.[14]

The nature of Ernest's work for the University up to the Second World War has been fully described by Alex Robertson and Colin Lees.[15] They are especially good on his conduct of business in the University, and his contribution to material questions of University development, such as marketing, fundraising, expansion and the improvement of the campus, areas in which he was closely involved as treasurer from 1932. They recognise that he was much more than an archetypal businessman in his relations with the University, but nevertheless the side of him that comes out most strongly in their account is the man of action who was frustrated by some of the formalities of university life and wanted to cut a swathe through some of its inefficiencies. He favoured specialisation, arguing that the University should concentrate on doing some things outstandingly well rather than trying to do everything competently: it was better to fund Rutherford generously, he argued in 1918, than to have chairs in Russian, Italian and Spanish.[16]

During his long tenure of the senior lay offices in the University, Ernest always interpreted his role expansively. Deeply involved as he was in questions of university policy, in Manchester and nationally, he was never simply a policy-maker. He and Shena were immersed in the social and intellectual life of the University, and he used his position to make contact with a wide range of members of the University community and to facilitate intellectual exchange. Always a man of method, he kept files of notes on all the important conversations he had, typically over lunch or dinner, whether at the University or at Broomcroft, their Didsbury home. These notes are an unusually rich source for reconstructing a picture of the University as an intellectual community, something all too easily lost from institutional histories.[17]

A sense of what Ernest contributed to and derived from university life as a life of ideas can be explored through his relationship with Michael Polanyi. Polanyi was a figure of towering importance in the intellectual history of the twentieth century, yet one who is curiously lost from the institutional memory of the university in which he served for a quarter of a century. Born into a family of secular Jews in Ukrainian Hungary, he held a chair of chemistry in Berlin at the time of the Nazis' accession to power in 1933, whereupon he moved to be professor of physical chemistry at Manchester. Eminent as he was as a chemist, he was also profoundly interested in the philosophy of knowledge and in wider questions of social and political philosophy, and in 1948 moved to a specially created chair of social studies, almost a research professorship, which he held until his retirement from Manchester in 1958. Intellectually he had affinities with Cold War liberalism, but combined with a deep religious sensibility too: he was a Catholic convert, and also had a profound love of the Anglican Book of Common Prayer. Polanyi was a passionate opponent of planning, both of the economy and of science, and a central pillar of his thought was a belief in the importance of the 'tacit dimension' of knowledge: we know much more than we can articulate, and much of our knowledge is embedded in and transmitted through traditions and practices. This aspect of his thinking has had a profound influence on the history of science as a discipline.[18]

Polanyi and Simon were not natural allies. Ernest was profoundly convinced that what the universities needed was planning through a national system; Polanyi thought what they needed was freedom.[19] Still, they became close friends who retained a deep admiration for each other. When Ernest finally relinquished the chairmanship of the council in 1957, Polanyi wrote effusively: 'Time has robbed me of most of my earlier compagnons at the University, but none of these departures has changed the physiognomy of the university so much as yours will.' He added that he must have been to Broomcroft a hundred times in the twenty-four years he had spent in Manchester: 'You and Lady Simon have made us feel at home in Manchester from the first day. Your superhuman patience with my wretched tennis has left a specially soft spot in my heart.'[20] Ernest was almost equally warm when Polanyi retired in 1958 and left Manchester for Oxford: 'I have very much enjoyed and, I think, in spite of the difference of our outlook, got a good deal of stimulus from our occasional talks.'[21] The ability to seek stimulus in spite of, or perhaps from, difference of outlook was very much part of his personality.

Polanyi's correspondence makes it clear how important Broomcroft, and hence Shena too, were to Ernest's relationship with the University. Shena's significance to the University tends to be overlooked, since her own focus was on primary and secondary schooling, as a member for many years of Manchester City Council's education committee and as a nationally known advocate for the cause of comprehensive schooling.[22] But she is important in this story for three reasons in particular.

Shena certainly reinforced Ernest's passionate interest in the social sciences. He was an engineer by educational background and by profession, though one who soon turned in a sociological direction; whereas she read for the economics tripos at Newnham before starting a research degree at LSE under Graham Wallas and L. T. Hobhouse.[23] He jestingly called her 'My Sociological Wife'.[24] Ernest was persuaded by the case for social science with a practical orientation to actual social problems; Shena shared that conviction, and in particular made the case for a kind of economics more geared to the problems of industrial society than was the discipline she had encountered at Cambridge.[25] She had, however, a stronger commitment to fundamental social research too. This was the recollection of Max Gluckman, professor of social anthropology, whose department benefited hugely from Ernest's largesse towards the social sciences: 'Lady Simon quickly saw the point of studying everything human. I think Lord Simon was a little more taken aback at the amount of work on small societies in Africa that the Fund was assisting; but for him too, *nihil humani illi alienum erat*, and he quickly became fascinated by the account of what was common, and what were the variations, in those societies and our own.'[26]

Second, Shena was herself a member of the University's council for an extraordinarily long period, from 1920 to 1966: longer even than Ernest.[27] Before she joined council, she was vice-chair of a committee chaired by C. P. Scott to raise funds (the '1918 Fund') for scholarships for women, and Ernest recorded in his diary that she presided over her first meeting 'with business-like firmness (even putting Tout in his place) and irresistible charm'.[28] Subsequently she sat on the governing body of Ashburne Hall, the oldest of the women's halls.[29] She was also a governor of the College of Technology and then UMIST; and also of several of the colleges that eventually came to join Manchester Polytechnic, including both Didsbury College of Education and the Domestic and Trades College (Hollings College).[30] She belonged to the University community almost as much as Ernest did. As an ordinary member of council, and not an officer, she is mostly invisible in the archival record, but it is clear that some causes were ones in which she took a passionate interest over many years. These included the position of academic staff on temporary contracts, the tutorial relationship between academic staff and students and the nurturing of the student community, especially through the halls of residence.[31] She was tenacious in pursuing the causes she thought worth fighting: Sir Bernard Lovell recalled that it was she who insisted that the University should buy sufficient land at Jodrell Bank for the development of the radio astronomy facility.[32] She was especially important in acting as a bridge between the university and the city council, and in identifying ways in which the University could contribute more to the life of the city. Jodrell Bank was one of example of this: she was among the first to see the possibilities it opened up for a new kind of public engagement with the university's research, and the opportunity for the university 'to do something rather dramatic which would impinge on the citizens of Manchester and make them proud of having the University at their doorstep'.[33]

Third, after Ernest's death in 1960, she was the guardian of his legacy, not least in taking a close interest in the Simon fellows: in their work, in their welfare and in their life after Manchester. Broomcroft Hall (as it was now to be known) was made over to a trust for the University's use, in the first place to accommodate the Simon fellows; and Shena had a house for herself (this took the name Broomcroft) built in the gardens. She was living alongside the fellows, and liked to entertain them in order to welcome them to the university and the city. Curiously, it is ingrained in the university's mythology that Ernest, by a quixotic final act, made it impossible for it to sell Broomcroft by stipulating that if it did so the proceeds would go to Cambridge. But in fact he left the property absolutely and unconditionally to Shena. It was she who offered the house to the university for its use (though it was certainly his hope too); and she who stipulated that were it to be sold the beneficiaries should be her own residuary legatees, two of the three women's colleges at Cambridge.[34]

9.2 Shena receiving her honorary degree from the University of Manchester (1966). Source: SSP M14/4/3.

Citizenship and the social sciences

That Ernest and Shena devoted so much time and attention to the university was a manifestation not simply of a sense of public duty, but also of a passionate commitment to the idea of the university. But what kind of intellectual vision inspired them? They absolutely did not want to turn the university into a business, but were passionately interested in the university as an intellectual community; and they were interested in that intellectual community above all for its ability to foster leadership in a democracy.

'Education for citizenship' had been a significant preoccupation for British public intellectuals since the university extension movement of the late-Victorian period, but it reached the peak of its influence in the interwar period.[35] The WEA, the linear descendant of the extension movement, was an important incubator of the idea that democracy required an educated citizenry: Ernest started supporting it in 1910, when he called it 'a splendid organisation for giving university training to working class leaders'; the following year, he hosted his fellow Rugbeian, the future archbishop William Temple, at Lawnhurst when Temple addressed a WEA meeting.[36] In July 1912, he and Shena went to the WEA Summer School in Oxford, where they got engaged, appropriately enough, while attending lectures on 'The Biological Study of the Home' by the Unitarian minister and eugenicist Dr J. Lionel Tayler: Ernest thought Tayler an 'idiot', but found his ideas interesting.[37] Undeterred, Shena subsequently became even more closely involved in the WEA.[38] From a different perspective, James Bryce's magisterial *Modern Democracies* (1921) – a work that was a recurrent point of reference for Ernest – helped entrench the idea that democracy flourished in those societies, like Switzerland, that both through schooling and through practical experience provided an effective education in citizenship.[39] These were the intellectual traditions on which the Simons drew in launching their Association for Education in Citizenship in 1934.

We should add another tradition to this eclectic mix: a religious one. Conventional religious practice, whether Christian or Jewish, did not attract Ernest, but he was strongly drawn to the 'religion of humanity'.[40] His idea of a religion grounded in service to others seems to have been drawn eclectically from John Stuart Mill, the Webbs and H. G. Wells, as well as from Auguste Comte, the progenitor of the religion of humanity.[41] The idea of a quasi-religious duty of service to humanity preoccupied Ernest, especially in the years just before his marriage to Shena. 'My religion is getting stronger', he recorded in his diary in April 1912, three months before his engagement:

> I deliberately want to work in whatever direction I am likely to be effective for the common good, & am steadily taking more pleasure in such work, & less

in pure amusement. Though I enjoy polo as much as ever. But the thing that really matters to me in life now is to feel that I am preparing myself, I am on the whole living the right kind of life.⁴²

Then, a week or so before his engagement, he reiterated that 'one's whole duty is to work for the common good', and that while the development of one's own personality mattered, it nevertheless 'must be subordinated to the good of the community as a whole', and the point of any religion must be to ensure that subordination. Prayer, by which Ernest meant reflection on one's aims in life, was 'most essential' to one's development of 'a real religion, an active faith'.⁴³

But to understand how Ernest got from the religion of humanity to education for citizenship, we have to attend to his engagement with the world of classical antiquity. A civic spirit was the way in which the ethic of service to others was brought down to the realm of practicality. It was not practically possible to be a good cosmopolitan or humanitarian without being a good citizen.

In his educational thinking, Ernest started off with a strong animus against the classics. When, back in 1909, he first envisaged getting involved with the university, he was attracted by 'opportunities of encouraging scientific & social education as against classical'.⁴⁴ But his position softened over the next few years as he came to appreciate how much support the cause of citizenship education received from classicists. Two books in particular helped arouse his interest in the classical world. One was *The Greek Commonwealth* (1911), by the young Oxford classicist Alfred Eckhard Zimmern. It no doubt helped that Zimmern was a nephew of Henry Simon's executor (and Emily's brother-in-law) Gustav Eckhard, as well as the cousin of Ernest's Manchester friend Willie Zimmern.⁴⁵ Ernest said that the book gave him for the first time 'real interest in & admiration for the Greeks', because it 'shews that humanity can, given the right conditions, rise above their baser selves, & live for something higher than cash & comfort'. He looked in vain for comparable 'civic spirit' in modern England, except perhaps in Joseph Chamberlain's Birmingham. Manchester was in a 'deplorable' state, since the business and professional classes aimed to make money and flee to Cheshire, taking little interest in the city other than 'subscribing to a hospital or two'.⁴⁶

The other book that made him more sympathetic to the case for the classics was by another Oxford classicist. Richard Livingstone's *Defence of Classical Education* (1916) was inspired by the need to respond to new-found wartime militancy on the part of advocates of scientific education, such as Ray Lankester and H. G. Wells. Ernest regarded Wells as one his intellectual heroes, but now he found himself agreeing with Livingstone that the central focus of education should be the human mind, and that natural science did not provide a suitable foundation.⁴⁷ Significantly,

Livingstone later served as president of Ernest's Association for Education in Citizenship.[48]

Ernest remained convinced of the superiority of a modern over a classical education, but his position was now more nuanced. We can gauge the extent of the 'classical turn' in his thinking by the fact that by 1920, Pericles's Funeral Oration (as recorded by Thucydides) had become his and Shena's favourite text. Ernest recommended it to their children, an extract was hung on the wall of the children's room at Broomcroft, and it was included on the Simons' Christmas cards to the schools of Manchester during Ernest's mayoralty. Ernest's fascination with Pericles almost certainly came from Zimmern, for whom Thucydides was the fundamental source. For Zimmern, the Oration was 'that highest expression of the art of life in the City State'.[49]

The Simons' longstanding commitment to education for citizenship is well known, but what is less well understood is just how important the universities were to their vision of democratic citizenship. Although Ernest wrote in the 1930s chiefly on citizenship education in schools, his association had universities very much in its sights from the outset. 'It should hardly be necessary to stress the importance of the universities as a training ground for citizenship', wrote his collaborator, Eva Hubback, in 1934. 'Here we find those who are to constitute the future leaders of thought, both in practical affairs and in research.'[50] Ernest's interview notes with academics show him starting to focus on this problem from around 1933, which was obviously a significant date for anyone concerned about the fate of democratic citizenship.[51] At the founding of the Manchester branch of the association at Broomcroft in 1935, he recalled that his interest in citizenship had come from his parents, and from the influence of works by H. G. Wells and Sidney Webb; his education at Rugby and Cambridge had left him 'completely ignorant of the modern world'.[52]

A particular interest of Ernest's was in questioning the concept of 'transfer': the idea that citizenship could be sufficiently fostered indirectly through the teaching of other subjects, including the classics. In his notes on an interview with the distinguished philosopher Samuel Alexander in 1933 he recorded that Alexander 'does not seem to have considered the problem of transfer seriously'.[53] The good scholar did not necessarily make a good citizen.[54]

This was the subject on which he wrote in the association's 1936 volume, *Education for Citizenship in Secondary Schools*. He commissioned papers from a number of psychologists to help him think through this problem: Dr R. H. Thouless of Glasgow and later Cambridge, Professor Godfrey Thomson of Edinburgh, and the now notorious Professor Cyril Burt of University College, London.[55] They confirmed him in his belief that 'Transfer of training from one subject to another takes place on a much smaller scale than used to be believed.' Hence, the best way of training

THE LORD MAYOR (Coun. E. D. Simon).

I will make this Manchester of mine into a modern and a larger Athens.

To serve that old city was the object of all worthy Athenians.

Do you know who the worthy people of Athens were? They were the people of Athens who were worthy.

Let us serve our city of Manchester! Let us die for her. Nay, more, let us live for her.

By contrast with Birmingham, who has 45,000 acres, this city of ours, with her 23,000 acres, has but a few units of space.

This is too meagre, it is niggardly; it is neither august nor expansive.

Let us absorb new and even larger slices of the beautiful country on our southern boundary—and on any other boundary where the slices are beautiful and the people are rich. And thus, some day if we persist long enough, Manchester may call herself England, and England Manchester.

9.3 A satirical sketch of Ernest as an Athenian statesman. From *Manchester Evening News* (30 December 1921). Source: SSP M14/6/7.

young people for citizenship was through subjects directly relevant to the life of the citizen.[56]

One of the lessons Ernest drew was that civic education required a greater focus on modern (not medieval) history, on modern rather than classical languages, on 'area studies' and above all on the social sciences. He had long been working for the expansion of the social sciences at the university: with Ramsay Muir (professor of modern history at Manchester, 1914–21) he pressed for the establishment of a chair of political science, and hoped that Henry Simon Ltd would contribute towards the endowment. Muir and Simon envisaged at Manchester something comparable to the honour school in philosophy, politics and economics ('Modern Greats') that Oxford was just setting up, but financial retrenchment at the end of the First World War proved an insuperable obstacle.[57] Instead, Ernest personally and anonymously funded Henry Clay's salary as professor of social economics, to enable him to engage in practical economic research focused on the problems of the regional economy.[58] For Ernest, applied social research was a natural complement to civic education focused on understanding the contemporary world.

The engagement between academic research and the outside world was important to Ernest's vision. So, in parallel, was a broad rather than narrowly specialist university education. In the summer of 1936, he addressed the Council of the Association of University Teachers, giving the title of his talk 'A Citizen Challenges the Universities'. He urged the universities to do more to help build 'a better social order', notably by providing leadership for public opinion. That meant producing graduates with skills in critical and disinterested thinking, but also with 'a knowledge of public affairs'. He approved of what the LSE was doing, and he also thought that Modern Greats at Oxford was an 'outstanding' attempt to create 'a course in citizenship'. Ernest returned again to the problem of transfer: he insisted that citizenship must be 'learnt by the direct study of the thought and life and actions of men in society'. What did that mean in practice? History had long been regarded in Britain as offering the ideal school for citizens and statesmen. Ernest agreed, but asked: what sort of history? He distinguished between 'pure history, based on an interest in the study of the past for its own sake', and 'history for life', a somewhat Nietzschean expression, by which he meant 'the study of history in order to enable the student to understand the world of to-day'. The former – embodied, he thought, in the mediaevalism of the Manchester history school – was an indulgence; the latter was wholly vital for the future of humanity.[59]

It was the commitment to education for citizenship, as well as to applied social research, that inspired the Simons' most important single contribution to the university, the establishment in 1944 of the Simon Fund to support fellowships and visiting professorships in the social sciences.[60] The arrangements for this gift were set out in a letter to the vice-chancellor in December 1943, whereby Ernest donated to the university shares in both of his engineering businesses: 15,000 ordinary shares in Henry Simon Ltd, and 5,000 pre-preference shares in Simon-Carves Ltd. These produced an original dividend income for the scheme of something more than £3,000 per annum (in 2024 values, more than £100,000).[61] The terms of the gift did not restrict how the university spent the income, but Ernest made his wishes very clear. His intention was that the dividend income be used for the provision of fellowships for 'men and women of mature years' to pursue research and teaching in the social sciences, defined as consisting of sociology, social psychology, economics, political science, philosophy, public administration, jurisprudence and education. Specifically, he was keen to promote 'work which is likely to prove of practical importance'.[62]

Ernest was also unusually explicit about the intellectual purposes that motivated his gift. Government and public opinion were interested in universities only for the scientific research they produced, and Ernest fully agreed on its importance; but the most urgent problem for the postwar world was 'our failure to control the democratic state', and that failure was due above all to inadequate education in citizenship. He saw it as a core postwar mission of universities to educate leaders of public opinion, and hence to support democracy through wider knowledge and understanding of political, social, economic and industrial affairs.[63] 'My object in creating the Simon Fund,' he recalled at the end of 1957, 'was to encourage education for citizenship in the University.'[64]

In seeing the social sciences as key disciplines for postwar Britain, Ernest was hardly unique. The Clapham Committee on Provision for Social and Economic Research, appointed by the wartime coalition government, reported in July 1946; and while it stopped well short of recommending a research council, it urged a major expansion of provision for the social sciences in the universities.[65] Its members included three close associates of Ernest: Tawney, Clay and Moberly. Clay was by now warden of Nuffield College, Oxford, endowed in 1937 as a graduate and research college specialising in the social sciences, and with a particular remit to pursue research in conjunction with practitioners, especially in the field of public policy. A. D. Lindsay, the Oxford vice-chancellor who was chiefly responsible for persuading Lord Nuffield to give the money for this purpose, stressed the need to remedy the 'divorce between theory and practice in the study of contemporary society' by nurturing collaboration between scholars and 'practical men'.[66] This vision was close to Simon's.

Ernest expected to be consulted about the purpose to which the university applied the Simon Fund, and to be involved in the administration of the Simon fellowships.[67] Such a role was possible as he held the unusual position of being both donor and chair of the body (the council) which had control over how the money was spent. Ernest's interventionist approach was evident from the outset. When academic departments tried to stretch the definition of the scheme they were swiftly rebuffed, as when the geography department sought funding to support young postgraduate researchers, and when the dental hospital asked whether dentistry could also fall within the scope of the scheme.[68] Ernest also expressed some impatience with the slow development and administration of the fellowship scheme. He told the vice-chancellor in December 1946 that only two of the fellowships awarded had fully met the criteria for the scheme as set out in 1943. He suggested that a 'very small committee' be established (consisting of just the vice-chancellor and himself) to undertake a preliminary review of all fellowship applications before deciding which were to be submitted to the main Simon Fund committee.[69] Eight years later, Ernest was still dissatisfied with the applicants the Simon Fund was attracting: 'I think the applications [this year] are a very disappointing lot; there is only one person who seems to be first-rate.'[70] Nor was he averse to more direct criticism of the committee's decisions, especially when he was displeased with the kind of research topics that the Simon Fund was supporting. The proposal to award a fellowship to Dr Bernice Hamilton for research on Spanish political thought of the sixteenth and early seventeenth centuries antagonised him. Hamilton's research, he argued, could not meet the criterion of practical importance as set out in the terms of his 1943 gift. A robust defence of the committee's decision was provided by the philosopher Dorothy Emmet, the university's sole woman professor. Emmet argued skilfully that Hamilton's proposed research was not remote in time, but actually had clear contemporary relevance, by calling attention to the liberal democratic tradition of political theory in Catholic thought.[71] Hamilton was duly appointed to the fellowship; but Ernest continued to express disappointment that fellowships were being awarded for work 'of historical and academic' rather than practical importance in addressing contemporary social problems.[72]

For the first half-century of its existence, the Simon Fund was used primarily to finance fellowships and visiting professorships intended for 'mature' scholars, who were usually established academics working on a major project, or in some cases people with professional experience in other fields (public administration, business, the professions) who wanted the opportunity to bring their experience into dialogue with academic researchers.[73] While Ernest may have had his own questions about the operation (and even success) of the scheme, it was nonetheless clear that its recipients held it in very high regard. One Simon fellow, Professor Max Marwick of the University of Witwatersrand, assured Shena that 'the Simon Fellowships are a live, lasting and socially useful reminder of your late husband's foresight and generosity'.[74]

The Simon Fund had a profound and positive impact on the university, and on the wider academic world; but not always in the way that Ernest had intended. Two disciplines in which Manchester was a leader exemplify the impact of the Simon Fund. Under Max Gluckman, social anthropology at Manchester established a global reputation; in fact, not social anthropology alone, but social anthropology *and* sociology, for his department embraced both. He was quite open about the key role the Simon fellowships had played in enabling him to build up the 'Manchester School'.[75] The list of names is a roll-call of the stars of the discipline: John Barnes, Elizabeth Colson, Clyde Mitchell, Hilda Kuper, Victor Turner and Max Marwick.[76] Often they progressed from Simon fellowships to permanent positions at Manchester, as did Colson, Mitchell and Turner, who finished their careers at Berkeley, Oxford and Chicago respectively.

Gluckman was exceptionally entrepreneurial in seeing and exploiting the opportunities presented by the fund, but there were other instances in which the fund was used to help get round bureaucratic obstacles to desirable outcomes. It was Simon funding that made it possible for Polanyi to transfer to a chair in social studies, for example. Even more striking was the importance of the Simon Fund in the creation of new academic fields such as American studies. Manchester was the first university in the United Kingdom to set up a department of American studies after the Second World War: very much in line with Ernest's sense of the importance of area studies to the development of world citizenship. But the story of how this happened is intriguing. The first professor of American studies was Isaac Kandel, who held the chair from 1948 to 1950.[77] But he had essentially no background in the field. His field was educational studies, which he had studied at Manchester under Michael Sadler, the future vice-chancellor of the University of Leeds and a longstanding proponent of civic education. Sadler encouraged Kandel to go to Columbia University for his PhD, and he went on to make his career in the United States. In the 1930s, he became interested in education for world citizenship, and it was probably this work that brought him to Ernest's attention, possibly through Richard Oliver. In any case, Kandel contributed to *The Citizen*, the organ of the Association for Education and Citizenship, before the war.[78] At its inception in 1946, Ernest's *Universities Quarterly* listed Kandel as a future contributor; the following year he came to Manchester as a Simon fellow, apparently with Simon's active involvement in making the financial arrangements for this appointment.[79] During his fellowship, Kandel advised on the creation of an American studies programme, and was appointed to the chair. The premature death of his wife in his first summer vacation led him to resign earlier than hoped, though he was sixty-nine at the time. In recording its appreciation, the university council (chaired, of course, by Ernest) wrote that 'to a University which for years has been searching in vain for a Professor of American Studies, Professor Kandel provided the ideal answer'. Simon told him that 'you have set a very high standard for future Simon visiting Professors'.[80]

The cases of Polanyi and Kandel tell us much about the way in which Ernest envisaged the operation of the Simon Fund. He wanted the university's academic leaders to have some discretionary income that would enable them to seize opportunities to attract and retain exceptional academic talent. That was what Gluckman appreciated, and even if Ernest was surprised to find himself funding so much research on 'small societies in Africa', Gluckman operated in exactly the kind of enterprising manner that Ernest applauded.

The future of British universities

In stressing the key role that universities had to play in sustaining democratic politics and defending modern civilisation, Ernest was of one mind with an important strain in intellectual opinion at the end of the war.[81] His former Manchester colleague Sir Walter Moberly made the case from a Christian point of view in his *Crisis in the University* (1949), while Ernest's own son Brian, already a member of the Communist Party and a recent president of the National Union of Students, wrote along curiously similar lines in *A Student's View of the Universities* (1943).[82] It was in this context that Ernest Simon launched the *Universities Quarterly* in 1946. In 1949, this carried a symposium on Moberly's book, including an article by Ernest himself entitled 'University Crisis? A Consumer's View'. This argued that British universities had been successful in doing what the government wanted and was prepared to pay for, and had expanded the number of graduates in the areas the government had prioritised. They had been less successful in addressing either the productivity crisis in industry or the moral crisis facing Western democracies; the latter being Moberly's concern.[83]

Ernest wrote that 'The *Universities Quarterly* was originally founded by the Association for Education in Citizenship in the hope that it might do something to help in the directions which Moberly desires.'[84] The association was, indeed, the formal proprietor: its ownership of the journal functioned to allow Ernest to maintain control without seeming too egotistical. It had a national editorial board to give it weight and credibility, but its members included several with connections to Manchester or the Simons, and in practice the journal was run by a Manchester editorial board. This was chaired by Ernest and included a galaxy of notables: Stopford, the young Bernard Lovell, and the Langworthy Professor of Physics, Patrick Blackett. Ernest's key collaborator, however, was R. A. C. Oliver, professor of education at Manchester from 1938 to 1970, an educational psychologist who had made his name devising intelligence tests for use on Africans; significantly, his Edinburgh mentor and supervisor Godfrey Thomson was on the national board.[85] Oliver later reminisced about the role of the editorial board of *Universities Quarterly*: 'to some of us members our chief and delectable duty must surely have been to be his guests at dinner, discussing future issues'.[86] He suspected that Ernest 'had his own unorthodox methods of balancing the budget of a non-profit-making publishing venture': that is, he met the deficit from his own pocket. Oliver seems to have formed an inner group with Ernest and Eva Hubback.[87] Richard Oliver wrote prolifically on the kind of subjects that interested Ernest, such as 'general education' in universities and indeed in sixth forms, and 'Liberal education in a technical age'.[88] Significantly, he was drawn towards American experiments in a common curriculum: 'Western Civ.', as it became.[89] He and his wife, Anna, a junior lecturer in English, were notably close to the Simons: Richard Oliver addressed him 'Dear Ernest', which was well nigh unknown among the university community.[90]

Ernest's aim in establishing the *Universities Quarterly* was primarily to help shape opinion about higher education policy. He was a leading proponent of the view that universities should be considered as a system – and managed as a system. He welcomed the rapid growth of student numbers in the postwar period, but saw that it was entirely changing the character of existing universities and the kind of education they could offer: in particular, it threatened to erode their character as communities. Towards the end of his life, he became the foremost advocate of a systematic investigation of the future of higher education; and as the instigator of a major House of Lords debate on the subject, he could be regarded as the main architect of what became the Robbins Committee.[91]

Conclusion

It is in the nature of the role that lay officers rarely steer university strategy. That is the role of vice-chancellors, whereas chairs of council and the like have the job of oversight to ensure effective governance. The Simons were different. They (both Ernest and Shena) formed part of the university community as few counterparts have done; they had an intellectually serious vision for the university; and Ernest had the resources to make strategic donations to influence policy. Ernest and Shena both relished the life of ideas, but their particular aptitude was for the translation of intellectual visions into realisable plans for action. In that sense it is appropriate that their most important contribution to the University of Manchester was the endowment of a fund to support social research with the potential for practical application.

The Simons' vision for universities encompassed both education for citizenship and social research geared to addressing real-world problems. These two conceptions of universities have very different intellectual lineages: the first is usually thought to be rooted in Hellenism, and transmitted via Oxford Greats; the second depends on a more instrumental conception of universities as serving the needs of modern industrial societies.

9.4 Ernest having received his honorary degree from the University of Manchester (1944). Source: SSP M14/4/24.

The early history of the Simon fellowship scheme exhibits the tension between the two: the fellowships were demonstrably successful in nurturing social research, including much with a practical focus; but whether they ever did much for civic education is much more questionable.

Notes

1. ESD (1929–35), October 1929. This is mis-cited by Alex Robertson and Colin Lees, 'Ernest Simon and University Policy and Development', *Bulletin of the John Rylands Library*, 84:1–2 (2002), 223: they date it to November 1920 in the diary for 1920–28.
2. Private family papers, Sir Ernest Simon to Ramsay Muir, 2 February 1934; private family papers, Simon to Roger Simon, 16 February 1934. Christopher Needham was appointed chairman in 1934, and was succeeded by Sir Ernest Simon in 1941.
3. He made one final attempt to return to Parliament as an independent candidate in the by-election for the Combined English Universities constituency in 1946.
4. In 2004, the governance structure was significantly overhauled and these two offices no longer exist in the same form.
5. Lord Stopford of Fallowfield, 'The University', in *80th Birthday Book for Ernest Darwin Simon, Lord Simon of Wythenshawe, b. 9th October 1879* (Cheadle Heath: Cloister Press, 1959), p. 27.

6 Robertson and Lees, 'Ernest Simon and University Policy and Development', 236–7.
7 Marguerite Dupree (ed.), *Lancashire and Whitehall: The Diary of Sir Raymond Streat*, 2 vols (Manchester: Manchester University Press, 1987) II, pp. 783–4; Brian Pullan with Michele Abendstern, *A History of the University of Manchester 1951–73* (Manchester: Manchester University Press, 2000), pp. 80–1; Bodleian Library MS Woolton 43 ff. 27–8, 148, 177–8, 204–5, 210–15: Ernest Simon to Woolton 13 April, 16 November, 8 December 1955; Woolton to Ernest Simon 14 April, 21 November, 2 December, 9 December 1955.
8 *Manchester Guardian* (9 July 1858), p. 2; William Whyte, *Redbrick: A Social and Architectural History of Britain's Civic Universities* (Oxford: Oxford University Press, 2015), p. 72.
9 Brian Simon, *In Search of a Grandfather: Henry Simon of Manchester 1835–1899* (Leicester: Pendene Press, 1997), p. 127.
10 Eda Sagarra, 'The Centenary of the Henry Simon Chair of German at the University of Manchester (1996): Commemorative Address', *German Life and Letters*, 51 (1998), 509–24.
11 JRL Guardian Archive, GDN 120/5, A. S. Wilkins to C. P. Scott, 9 January 1894. Edinburgh University did indeed appoint its first lecturer in German in 1894: Dr Otto Schlapp.
12 Sagarra, 'The Centenary of the Henry Simon Chair', 512; 'The Late Dr Hager', *Manchester Guardian* (23 February 1895), p. 8.
13 Ernest explicitly invoked this model in ESD (1920–28), 9 November 1922 to 1 September 1923: 'We believe we can lead useful & interesting lives in Manchester, continuing to work on our present lines. We should both be in the inner councils of the MLF [Manchester Liberal Federation], the Liberal group in the City Council, & the University Council. It would be a delightful life of cooperation, as close as the classic case of the Sidney Webbs.'
14 Simon to Ramsay Muir, 2 February 1934.
15 Robertson and Lees, 'Ernest Simon and University Policy and Development', 221–76.
16 ESD, 2 July 1918.
17 ESP M11/3, 'Universities Manchester'.
18 Gerald Holton, 'Michael Polanyi and the History of Science', *Tradition and Discovery*, 19 (1992), 16–30.
19 On this question, see Geoffrey L. Price, 'The Expansion of British Universities and their Struggle to Maintain Autonomy: 1943–46', *Minerva*, 16 (1978), 357–81.
20 ESP M/11/13 Polanyi, Michael Polanyi to Lord Simon, 5 May 1957.
21 ESP M/11/13 Polanyi, Simon to Polanyi, 22 July 1958.
22 There are just two references – one very much in subordination to Ernest – in Pullan and Abendstern, *A History of the University of Manchester 1951–73*; and not much more in Robertson and Lees, 'Ernest Simon and University Policy and Development'.
23 UOMVCA/7/234 folder 4, Lady Simon to William Mansfield Cooper, 28 June 1961. Shena's certificates from Cambridge are in SSP M14/4/1.
24 ESD, 26 December 1912.
25 SSP M14/2/3/8, Shena Simon, 'The Study of Economics in a Modern University' (text of lecture she delivered in 1940).
26 Max Gluckman, 'Preface', *Directory of Simon Visiting Professors and Fellows 1944–1970* (Manchester: University of Manchester, 1972), p. viii. 'Nothing human was alien to him.'
27 Pullan and Abendstern, *History of the University of Manchester 1951–73*, p. 22. She was a governor from the end of 1918, when she was but thirty-five: the two Simons were for a time the youngest two governors: ESD, 12 November 1918.
28 ESD, 12 June 1918. This was Thomas Frederick Tout, the distinguished mediaeval historian. Ernest rather unfairly approved of putting him in his place.

29 SSP M14/2/3/6, 'Memo. on Residential Accommodation for Technical College Students' [2 August 1957], p. 1.
30 She chaired the governors of Hollings: see 'Miss E.M. Hollings' (Obituary), *Manchester Guardian* (5 July 1962), p. 18.
31 For example, UOMVCA/7/234 folder 4, Lady Simon to William Mansfield Cooper, 28 June 1961, 29 March 1962, 24 May 1963, 14 July 1969.
32 Sir Bernard Lovell, *The Story of Jodrell Bank* (London: Oxford University Press, 1968), pp. 99–100.
33 SSP M14/2/3/8, Lady Simon to Sir William Mansfield Cooper, 9 June 1964.
34 SSP M14/4/2, Lady Simon to William Mansfield Cooper, 14 November 1960. Shena was probably keen to be true to Virginia Woolf's *A Room of One's Own* (1929), which urged the need to increase the endowments for women's education. In this same letter she remarked that she and Ernest had considered offering Broomcroft to the university as a vice-chancellor's residence, 'but we realise that, at present, the University does not pay its Vice-Chancellor a large enough salary to enable him to maintain a house of this size in full occupation'.
35 On the intellectual background, H. S. Jones, 'The Civic Moment in British Social Thought: Civil Society and the Ethics of Citizenship, c. 1880–1914', in Lawrence Goldman (ed.), *Welfare and Social Policy in Britain since 1870: Essays in Honour of Jose Harris* (Oxford: Oxford University Press, 2019), pp. 29–43.
36 ESD, 19 February 1910, 16 April 1910, 20 October 1911.
37 ESD, 20 July 1912; 'Summer Classes, 1912', *The Highway*, 4:45 (June 1912): 141.
38 Mary Stocks, *Ernest Simon of Manchester* (Manchester: Manchester University Press, 1963), p. 53.
39 James Bryce, *Modern Democracies* (London: Macmillan, 1921), especially vol. 1, pp. 79–89. For Simon's debt to Bryce's book, Sir E. D. Simon, *The Smaller Democracies* (London: Gollancz, 1939), pp. 5, 14 ('Lord Bryce's great book'), 46, 50, 176–7; private family papers, Ernest Simon to Roger Simon, 5 April 1950.
40 Shena's debt to this tradition is noted by Jane Martin, 'Shena Simon (1883–1972) and the "Religion of Humanity"', in Jane Martin and Joyce Goodman, *Women and Education, 1800–1980* (Basingstoke: Palgrave, 2004), pp. 118–40. But it was Ernest who invoked it explicitly.
41 He read Mill's *Autobiography* and his essay on *The Utility of Religion* with enthusiasm in August 1911; Wells's *First and Last Things* he had encountered soon after its publication some three years before: ESD, 16 August 1911, 5 December 1911.
42 ESD, 19 April 1912.
43 ESD, 10 July 1912.
44 ESD, 30 March 1909 (printed heading 'Thursday, April 8').
45 Ernest later knew Zimmern well enough to invite himself to stay when in Oxford: Bodleian Library MS Zimmern 32 f. 195, Ernest Simon to Zimmern, 11 May 1933.
46 ESD, 14 July 1914.
47 ESD, 22 January 1917.
48 'Citizenship Training', *Manchester Guardian* (7 July 1943), p. 6.
49 Alfred E. Zimmern, *The Greek Commonwealth: Politics and Economics in Fifth-Century Athens* (Oxford: Clarendon, 1911), p. 54; ESD (1920–8), 3 February 1920, 'To my children': 'I hope you will read, & be as much impressed as we have been with Pericles Funeral Oration, & that you will select your career with regard not to money making, but to rendering services to your fellow men.' For the reference to Broomcroft, Joan Simon, *Shena Simon: Feminist and Educationist* (privately printed, 1986), Chapter II, p. 36.
50 ESP M11/11/15, Eva M. Hubback, 'What is and What Might Be?', in Eva M. Hubback and E. D. Simon, *Education for Citizenship* (Ashton-under-Lyme: J. Andrew & Co., 1934), p. 23.

51 ESP M11/15/3, interview with Samuel Alexander, 13 March 1933.
52 *Manchester Guardian* (9 July 1935), p. 15.
53 Interview with Samuel Alexander, 13 March 1933.
54 E. D. Simon, 'The Need for Training in Citizenship', in Simon and Hubback, *Education for Citizenship*, p. 10.
55 Brian Simon was an early critic of Burt, in *Intelligence Testing and the Comprehensive School* (London: Lawrence & Wishart, 1953).
56 Sir Ernest Simon, 'The Problem of Transfer', in *Education for Citizenship in Secondary Schools* (London: Oxford University Press, 1936), pp. 19–20.
57 Stocks, *Ernest Simon of Manchester*, pp. 52–3.
58 Robertson and Lees, 'Ernest Simon and University Policy and Development', 257. The records do not show conclusively that Simon was the anonymous donor, but it is very likely.
59 Sir E. D. Simon, 'A Citizen Challenges the Universities', *The Universities Review*, 9:1 (November 1936), 8–13.
60 This section draws heavily on archival research on the origins of the Simon and Hallsworth Funds undertaken some years ago for Chris Godden by Dr Patrick Doyle, now of the University of Limerick.
61 The strength of the two businesses meant that the dividend income had grown by 1956 to around £10,000 a year: a real terms increase of about 100 per cent in little more than a decade: UOMVCA/7/732, Ernest Simon to William Mansfield Cooper, 26 November 1956.
62 UOMVCA/7/8, Simon Research Fund 1943–52: 'Note for Members of the Simon Fund Committee from Sir Ernest Simon', 30 October 1944.
63 'Note for Members of the Simon Fund Committee', 30 October 1944.
64 UOMVCA/7/234, Lord Simon to William Mansfield Cooper, 31 December 1957.
65 Desmond King, 'Creating a Funding Regime for Social Research in Britain: The Heyworth Committee on Social Studies and the Founding of the Social Science Research Council', *Minerva*, 35 (1997), 2–4.
66 Nuffield College Archive 77/1/3, 'Speech made by the Vice-Chancellor in Congregation on 16 November 1937'.
67 UOMVCA/7/8, Simon Research Fund 1943–52: 'Note for Members of the Simon Fund Committee', 30 October 1944.
68 UOMVCA/7/8, Simon Research Fund 1943–52: Professor Fitzgerald to Vice-Chancellor, 26 April 1945; Letter to Professor E Matthews (n.d. 1946).
69 UOMVCA/7/8, Simon Research Fund 1943–56, 'Note for the Vice Chancellor', 2 December 1946.
70 UOMVCA/7/8, Simon Research Fund 1943–56, Simon to William Mansfield Cooper, 26 April 1954.
71 UOMVCA/7/8, Simon Research Fund 1943–56, Lord Simon to Sir John Stopford, 19 July 1952; Dorothy Emmet to Stopford, 30 July 1952.
72 UOMVCA/7/8 Simon Research Fund 1943–56, Lord Simon to William Mansfield Cooper, 26 April 1954.
73 In the mid-1950s, at Simon's suggestion, some of the substantial surplus the fund was generating was used to create sub-funds for entertainment by academic departments (intended to nurture community-building in the university) and for engineering. But here we focus on the main work of the fund in supporting research and teaching in the social sciences.
74 SSP M14/4/12, Professor Max Marwick to Lady Simon (n.d).
75 Simon once identified Gluckman's book on Barotse Jurisprudence in Northern Rhodesia (together with Arthur Lewis's book on economic growth) as typifying the kind of research that the Simon Fund should support. UOMVCA/7/8 Simon Research Fund 1943–56, 'Note by Lord Simon – Simon Fund: Lunch at the University', 6 December 1955.

76 On Gluckman's use of the Simon Fund to build up the Manchester department as a rival to Oxford, Katherine Ambler, 'The Manchester Department of Social Anthropology 1949–1975' (Unpublished PhD thesis, King's College London, 2022). We are grateful to Dr Ambler for allowing us to read and cite her thesis.
77 'Manchester Chair of American Studies', *Manchester Guardian* (20 March 1948), p. 3.
78 I. L. Kandel, 'Education for Citizenship in the United States', *The Citizen*, 8 (November 1938), 4–7.
79 UOMVCA/7/8 Simon Research Fund 1943–56, Professor IL Kandel to Sir John Stopford, 19 September 1946.
80 ESP M11/10/8 Kandel, USA, Lord Simon to I. L. Kandel, 1 November 1950. Kandel was in fact a Simon fellow, and not a visiting professor.
81 Matthew Grimley, 'Christianity, Culture and the Universities in Wartime England', in Michael Snape and Stuart Bell (eds), *British Christianity and the Second World War* (Woodbridge: Boydell, 2003), pp. 82–98.
82 Sir Walter Moberly, *The Crisis in the University* (London: SCM, 1949); Brian Simon, *A Student's View of the Universities* (London: Longmans, 1943).
83 Lord Simon of Wythenshawe, 'University Crisis? A Consumer's View', *Universities Quarterly*, 4:1 (November 1949), 73–81.
84 Simon, 'University Crisis?', 81.
85 On this episode, more intriguing than edifying, see Chloe Campbell, *Race and Empire: Eugenics in Colonial Kenya* (Manchester: Manchester University Press, 2007), Chapter 6. Also see: Richard A. C. Oliver, 'Mental Tests in the Study of the African', *Africa*, 7 (1934), 40–6; Richard A.C. Oliver, 'Mental Tests for Primitive Races', *Year Book of Education*, (1935), 560–70. One of the most influential post-war critics of intelligence testing was Brian Simon: Deborah Thom, 'Politics and the People: Brian Simon and the Campaign Against Intelligence Tests in British Schools', *History of Education*, 33:5 (2004), 515–29.
86 R. A. C. Oliver, 'Lord Simon and Universities Quarterly' (correspondence), *Higher Education Quarterly*, 14 (1960), 185.
87 ESP M11/5/3, Lord Simon to Elizabeth Layton, 6 September 1948.
88 Professor R. A. C. Oliver, 'A General Studies Paper. 1 – Sixth-Form Attitudes', *Manchester Guardian* (18 September 1957), p. 6; R. A. C. Oliver and D. G. Lewis, *The Content of Sixth Form General Studies* (Manchester: Manchester University Press, 1974); R. A. C. Oliver and D. G. Lewis, 'Elements in Sixth Form General Studies', *Journal of Curriculum Studies*, 2:2 (1970), 162–74; R. A. C. Oliver, Review of *Liberal Education in a Technical Age*, *British Journal of Educational Studies*, 4:1 (1955), 85–6.
89 R. A. C. Oliver, 'The undergraduate curriculum at Yale', *Higher Education Quarterly*, 1 (1947), 269–72; I. L. Kandel and R. A. C. Oliver, 'American Controversy on the Philosophy of Education', *Higher Education Quarterly*, 2 (1948), 131–5.
90 ESP M11/13/Oliver, R. A. C. Oliver to Lord Simon, 9 March 1960.
91 Stocks, *Ernest Simon of Manchester*, pp. 170–3.

Conclusion

The editors

It could hardly be claimed that the Simon name is an unknown one in Manchester in 2024. The main artery running through the Wythenshawe estate is called Simonsway, and many thousands use it each day. Walkers in south Manchester cross the Mersey on Simon's Bridge. In the city centre, many thousands of sixth-formers study at the Shena Simon Campus, the employer-facing branch of Manchester College in the heart of the city.[1] The University of Manchester marks the family name in the Simon Building, once the Simon Engineering Laboratories, and in the Henry Simon Chair of German (vacant since 2018), as well as in the Simon fellowships and visiting professorships, which still thrive. All that said, in popular consciousness it is just a name: the family commemorated in these ways has largely slipped from memory and their role in shaping the contemporary city is forgotten. The survival of a reputation is not helped by a tendency to confuse Ernest with Sir John Simon, and even, apparently, with the political scientist Herbert Simon or perhaps the politician Sir Herbert Samuel.[2]

This book has told a story of two generations spanning over a century of Manchester's history. That story is a diverse one, and the book has explored many themes: the making of an émigré mercantile community, industrial innovation, philanthropy, public service, town planning and housing reform and the building and management of civic, cultural and educational institutions. It is certainly not the story of a homogeneous Simonian worldview. Ernest was clear enough about the things that separated him from his father. While he too was an engineer, Henry, cultured though he was, had no interest in the social sciences, which were to be Ernest's abiding intellectual interest. Ernest acknowledged his mother's goodhearted selflessness, but evidently thought that he had little in common with her intellectually.[3] The contrast is starkest when we compare Emily and Shena: Emily the staunch anti-suffragist, eager to demonstrate that the suffragettes (or even the suffragists) had no claim to speak for most women; Shena, by contrast, a doughty fighter for women's political rights. We have seen that there were divisions within the wider family, as Emily's opposition to women's suffrage set her at odds with her own sister and, eventually, with one of her own daughters, as well as with Ernest and Shena. When we cast an eye at the wider family, the differences become still more apparent: Ernest eventually became a Labour peer, and his and Shena's two sons were Communists, but two of his sisters married future Conservative MPs. So the book has tried to depict these four Simons as individuals.

That said, we hope that the contributors to this volume have done enough to vindicate an approach based on the study of four members of one family over two generations. The salient rationale for this is that there was a powerful family ethos, built around a cult of the ancestor, Uncle Heinrich, and symbolised by the family's conservation of the official seal of the Frankfurt Parliament. Ernest's children and indeed grandchildren were brought up on a set of family stories about the hero of 1848, and Heinrich's early death certainly contributed to the myth-making. Twinned with memories of the ancestral past were values based on hard work, rationality

10.1 The Simon family at Pendyffryn Hall near Conwy (1896). From left to right are Henry, Ernest, Ingo, Harry, Emily, Eleanor Margaret, Victor, Eric and Dorothea. From: *Henry Simon's Occasional Letter to Miller's at Home & Abroad*, XXXVII, January 1897. Source: JRL SEGA, 17. Copyright the University of Manchester (CC BY-NC-SA 4.0).

10.2 Ernest, Shena and Brian and Roger (second from left top row, fourth from left middle row, and third and fourth from left bottom row) at the golden wedding anniversary of Shena's parents, John Wilson Potter and Jane Boyd Potter (1931). Source: SSP MI4/4/3.

and a commitment to leaving the world a better place than one found it. There was also a commitment to 'doing good business' which entailed a kind of business ethics in which the interests of the workforce and their families took a high place, as did the wider interests of society. These were passed on rather self-consciously from one generation to the next: Henry's *Rathschlaege für meine Kinder* [*Advice for my Children*], itself indebted to Heinrich, was the prototype, and Ernest gave his own sons a bound copy when they reached eighteen.[4] The Simon Calendar, initiated by Henry in 1892 and drawing on Emily's earlier initiative, was another vehicle for the transmission of the family's traditions and values, and on Henry's death Emily arranged for the private printing, under the title *Fragments of Thought*, of a selection of the edifying and instructive quotations he had used to supply the Calendar's daily mottos.[5] Ernest's diary includes similar sets of guidance for his own children. This was a family with an unusually strong sense of its identity.

The kind of values Henry and Ernest propounded were values of duty and public service, of reticence and self-sacrifice. These are the kinds of values conventionally labelled Victorian. That suggests two historiographical reflections. The first is that 'Victorian values' (a much

10.3 Heinrich Simon (1805–60). Courtesy of Eva-Maria Broomer.

contested term) were not confined to Britain, or to the English-speaking world. In the case of the Simons, the Victorian values they put to work in Manchester were demonstrably inherited from the German *Bürgertum*, and reinforced by the German mercantile and professional circles in which Henry and Emily moved. So the story of the Simons is an intriguing case study in the transferability of 'Burgher' virtues across national boundaries in the nineteenth century; a subject that deserves a more extensive study. That is a point about the spatial mobility of values. But, equally, the history of the Simon family reinforces what is now quite a well-established historiography that has demonstrated that values that we stereotype as Victorian were actually remarkably enduring in the first half of the twentieth century, and did much to shape the public institutions of twentieth-century Britain, from the BBC to the welfare state.[6] Ernest himself does not quite rank with Reith and Beveridge as one of the architects of twentieth-century Britain, but he is not out of place in that company; a comparison between him and Beveridge (an almost exact contemporary) would make a fascinating study. Much the same might be said of Shena and Eleanor Rathbone.

MRS. HENRY SIMON

We regret to announce the death, which took place at Didsbury on Sunday, of Mrs. Henry Simon. Mrs. Simon will be missed by many, and by none more than by the poor. Her goodness and her benevolence placed many in her debt; and all her deeds of charity were performed with a complete unostentation. She organised the lads' club at Didsbury; she bought houses and established in them a day nursery and a home for lonely old women. To these she gave a very personal care. She was one of the founders of the Withington Girls' School, and its treasurer after her husband's death. One of her last acts was to present to it a splendid addition to the playground. She turned her own house into a hospital for wounded soldiers, and worked in it indefatigably. She herself lost three sons in the war, and there can be no doubt that these labours and sorrows undermined her health. It seemed a matter of course for those who wanted advice and help to seek it from Mrs. Simon. These, and those more personal friends who knew the stability and fineness of a rare character, will find in her death an irreparable loss.

10.4 Emily Simon's obituary in the *Manchester Guardian* (9 November 1920), p. 8.

The focus on a *Simon* family ethos risks unconsciously or consciously privileging the male line. This book has attempted to give due weight to Emily and Shena as contributors to the Simon family, both in private life and in public service. In the case of Shena it is obvious that her relationship with Ernest was one of intellectual equals: if he brought great wealth to the partnership, she brought an inimitable strength of will, as well as a personability and charm that he knew he lacked. But we have also tried to rescue Emily from the shadows, uncovering both the significance of the Stoehr family connection and Emily's active role in the philanthropic work and civic service that shaped the family's identity.

The German roots were central to the family's sense of identity, especially up to the First World War. So (for our four Simons) was their allegiance to a progressive political tradition that, in their case, swept seamlessly forward from the liberalism of the Frankfurt Parliament through Edwardian New Liberalism to the Labour Party of the Attlee and Gaitskell years. But, in addition, an important and distinctive feature of the Simons' identity was the city of Manchester as the focus for the family's civic responsibilities. Good citizens could only be nurtured in a good city, they believed, which was why civic institution-building was such an important dimension of the lives of all four of our protagonists. Ernest was especially clear on this point, and it underpinned his conscious decision to turn away from a national political career and instead to devote himself to a career within the institutions of his native city. He deplored the tendency of Manchester businessmen to 'make money & clear out'.[7] Shena too argued that good municipal government was undermined by a lack of interest in civic affairs: if Manchester in the 1930s was 'a disgrace to civilisation', this was in large measure because 'far too many citizens feel that they have done all that is required of them when they have paid their rates'.[8] When Ernest's political career was at its zenith there were other national politicians who had made their reputations in local government: Neville Chamberlain and Herbert Morrison among them. But it was unusual enough to make Ernest's case intriguing. In making their lives and careers in Manchester, a city then regarded as in decline economically, culturally and politically, Ernest and Shena were self-consciously swimming against the tide. They were also, perhaps, guided by family traditions of civic service that Henry and Emily had laid down. A. J. P. Taylor wrote a famous essay on Manchester in 1957, the year that Ernest finally retired from his service to the university. 'The merchant princes have departed', wrote Taylor. 'They are playing at country life in Cheshire or trying to forget Manchester in Bournemouth or Torquay.'[9] Certainly, Ernest and Shena's careers as civic notables marked them out as distinctive in the middle of the twentieth century.

Precisely because the relationship between the family and the city is at the heart of this book, it does not make sense to take the story backwards or forwards. The German-Jewish roots are fascinating, and the story of

Henry Simon's other children and his grandchildren is absorbing in its way too, as we shall see shortly. But without Manchester at its heart it is essentially a different story. The story of Henry and Emily, of Ernest and Shena, has a unity conferred by commitment to the city of Manchester as well as by powerful family traditions transmitted with a degree of reverence. Because the focus is on Manchester, we have dwelt much more on the Simons' work in building civic institutions and wrestling with problems of urban planning and development. Ernest's equally fascinating enthusiasms for other causes, such as population control and nuclear disarmament, have had to be given short shrift.

The kind of world these four Simons inhabited now seems remote. Their Manchester was still one of the world's great cities. That was the theme of Taylor's essay: it was 'the last and greatest of the Hanseatic towns – a civilization created by traders without assistance from monarchs or territorial aristocracy'. But when he republished it in 1976, he thought that Manchester was no more than 'an agreeable provincial town'.[10] The *Manchester Guardian* had been central to the Simons' political, intellectual and cultural networks, but in 1959, the year before Ernest died, it dropped

10.5 Shena and Ernest on holiday (*c.* late 1920s – early 1930s). Source: private family papers.

'Manchester' from its title; soon afterwards, its editorial staff moved to London; and by the time of Shena's death in 1972, it had vacated its Manchester offices altogether.

But today there is increasing awareness that British (especially English) politics, government and public life are afflicted by an excess of centralisation, with its attendant dangers of apoplexy at the centre and paralysis at the extremities, in the words of a nineteenth-century critic of French over-centralisation.[11] Devolution of extensive powers to city-regions and their directly elected mayors is a notable response, and the fact that members of parliament have exchanged their seats at Westminster for mayoral office is an early indication that Westminster is no longer perceived as the only place to get things done. This looks like a reversal of the 'drift from north to south' of which Shena Simon in particular was so critical. But whether the mere transfer of powers to plebiscitary mayors will be enough to combat the civic indifference she also lamented is another matter. 'City deals' negotiated by elites are no substitute for an authentic sense of the city as a political community. It may be that the Simons' great cause of education for citizenship is due for a return: as, indeed, it enjoyed a brief moment in the sun a quarter of a century ago, when David Blunkett as education secretary invited his old mentor Professor Bernard Crick to devise a citizenship curriculum for schools.

Legacies
The end of the engineering empire

The twin engineering businesses of Henry Simon Ltd and Simon-Carves Ltd were an essential thread running through the Simon lives from the 1880s to the 1960s. The two companies formally merged into the Simon Engineering Group (SEG) Ltd just before the death of Ernest in 1960. The SEG seems to have enjoyed a good deal of success well into the 1980s and was a sizeable company; in 1981 it had a turnover of £339m and made a profit before tax of £20m. Five years later the turnover had increased to £503m but profits before tax had only grown modestly to £28m. Growth was coming primarily by acquisitions and the risks of over-diversification with a large burden of debt would cause subsequent problems when the company hit choppy waters. The last Simon family member involved in senior management, Michael Napier (descended from Susan Napier, Emily Simon's younger sister), retired in 1986. A consequential and symbolic structural change occurred a couple of years later when the SEG decided to sell its milling subsidiary to Thomas Robinson and Son. We can imagine how Henry would have been shocked and dismayed at this turn of events, as this was the firm that engaged in a bitter patent dispute with Henry, fought all the way to House of Lords, in 1894 that caused him such consternation. The combined business was called Robinson Milling

System Ltd. In 1991, the business was acquired by the Japanese firm Satake Corporation, to form Satake Robinson UK Ltd, later Satake UK Ltd. Satake made the decision to form a UK division which relocated to Bredbury, greater Manchester in 1998.

In the early 1990s, the SEG struggled and in 1993 almost went bankrupt under a £150m debt burden. A new strategic direction, under chief executive Maurice Dixson, saw many assets and long-established subsidiaries sold off to pay the debts. The business became more focused on docks and logistics and acquired substantial land on Humberside to develop new industrial port facilities. While the company dropped the 'Engineering' part of its name to become the Simon Group in 1997, the memory of Henry and Ernest was still present. As Brian Simon reported at the end of the 1990s, the company's London office still had Clara von Rappard's portrait of Henry Simon (Plate 7) hanging in the boardroom and in the foyer the 'striking [Jacob] Epstein black marble bust of Ernest greets the visitor on arrival'.[12] The second of the founders' engineering firms, Simon-Carves Ltd, would be sold for £12m in 2001 to SembCorp Industries of Singapore. They continued to operate under the Simon-Carves name from the Cheadle Heath site for several years before relocating to the Atlas

10.6 Bust of Henry Simon. Photo courtesy of Andrew Simon.

10.7 Bust of Ernest Simon. Photo courtesy of Andrew Simon.

Business Park in Wythenshawe. The company was subsequently brought by ECI Inc. in 2016.

In more recent years, some of the descendant companies have consciously employed the heritage and name of the Simon family as part of their branding.[13] These claims are more nominal than actual, given the numbers of takeovers and mergers they have been through. The milling machinery business in Bredbury, in particular, now uses 'Henry Simon' branding, and sports on its logo the strapline 'Manchester 1878' to signal a direct connection back to the origins of the firm.[14]

Places of legacy

Many of the houses that the various branches of the Simon family occupied at different times are long replaced or radically altered. The most significant, Lawnhurst, does survive and is largely intact. The exterior still features the 'HS 1891' signature plaque proudly in place over the front door and the stained-glass windows with various mottos remain too (Plate 12 and Figure 10.8). Ernest and Shena's house, Broomcroft, also still stands

10.8 The signature plaque above Lawnhurst. Photo by John Ayshford.

10.9 Lawnhurst and Broomcroft shown here on the Ordnance Survey 10-foot plan (1893). Source: Martin Dodge.

nearby. For some years, the official residence of the vice-chancellor of the University of Manchester, it remains on trust for the university's use.

In addition to Lawnhurst and Broomcroft, another physical reminder of the Simons is a substantial family memorial at the entrance of Manchester Crematorium. Henry is literally depicted as the head of the family with a carved portrait in the centre (finely delineated by the sculptor Conrad Dressler). It records in plain text the lives of Henry and Emily Simon, their three sons Harry, Victor and Eric killed in the First World War, along with Ernest, Shena and their daughter Antonia.

The best monument, we would argue, for Ernest and Shena is conspicuous yet overlooked. It is the Wythenshawe housing estate. Without the Simons' imagination, campaigning and work on the council in the 1920 and 1930s it might not have been realised. The purchase of the land and building of thousands of council homes transformed the map of Manchester forever and improved the living conditions of tens of thousands of Manchester's citizens. The Simons' great personal gift of Wythenshawe Hall and surrounding parks to the people of Manchester remains at the

10.10 The Simon memorial. Photo by John Ayshford.

centre of the place; it is a vital green lung for Wythenshawe residents. Tucked away on one wall of the hall is a blue plaque commemorating Ernest and Shena's gift (Plate 13).

The family legacy

The story of the Simons of *Manchester* may have ended in 1972 when Shena died, but the family story certainly did not finish then. A brief sketch can give a sense of how this creative and energetic family has continued to make its impact.

Henry's son, and Ernest's half-brother, Ingo Simon (1875–1964) and his third wife Erna (1894–1973) won acclaim as internationally renowned master archers. According to Mary Stocks, Ernest admired Ingo and even mimicked his tastes, but unlike Ernest, Ingo did not play a part in the family business and instead led a career as an international opera singer. Enjoying sailing, big game hunting, music and art, and studying the history of bows and firearms, he largely lived a life of leisure in contrast to Ernest's and Henry's work ethic. On Ingo's death, his vast collection of bows from across the world was donated to the Manchester Museum. He and Erna spent much of their married life in Devon, and Erna passed her remaining nine years there. She sponsored and organised charitable work to provide holidays for disabled and deprived people.[15]

Other notable Simon family members included Sir Patrick Hamilton (1908–2002) and his wife Winifred Mary, Lady Hamilton, known as Pix (1913–2000). Patrick was the son of Eleanor Simon, the second daughter of Emily and Henry who married the Conservative MP Sir George Hamilton. In 1941, Patrick married Pix Jenkins, who, having studied economics at Cambridge, served in the Ministry of Economic Warfare during the Second World War. The paralysis of Patrick's sister, Lindisfarne, in 1949 had a profound effect on the couple and they subsequently worked to improve the lives of thousands of disabled people, volunteering for, managing and financially supporting disability charities and organisations. Pix also collaborated with Wythenshawe MP Alf Morris on his landmark Chronically Sick and Disabled Persons Act (1970) and co-founded the Disabled Living Foundation with him. In a separate vein Patrick had a notable career as a businessman, serving as chairman of both Henry Simon Holdings Ltd and Henry Simon Engineering Ltd, as well as director of Lloyds Bank. He also invented the Simon snorkel which is a key component of modern fire engines, having been inspired by cherry-pickers in Canada.[16]

Patrick's obituary was authored by his cousin Christopher Simon (1914–2002), the son of Patrick's uncle Harry Simon. Having read economics at Cambridge under John Maynard Keynes, Christopher worked for the British Council until 1948, with a break for war service, and then for the next twenty-eight years for the Simon Group, for most of that time as a director and company secretary. He served on the Council of the University of Manchester and in a number of other public roles, in Greater Manchester and beyond, as a magistrate and school governor, and in the NHS. He was awarded an honorary degree by the University of Manchester.[17]

Two of Christopher's other cousins, Roger and Brian, the sons of Ernest and Shena Simon, became two leading left-wing intellectuals. Having been educated at Gresham's, the historic public school in Norfolk, Roger and Brian each spent a year at Salem School in Germany during the twilight and destruction of the Weimar Republic, before they both went to Cambridge University. At Cambridge, Roger and Brian were introduced to the works of Karl Marx and subsequently joined the Communist Party of Great Britain. Soon afterwards, during the Second World War, the siblings served in the Royal Signals. After the conflict, Roger, having qualified as a solicitor, continued his career as a civil servant in local government and in 1958 he joined the Labour Research Department (LRD) of which he became secretary in 1965. His work in the LRD proved influential, but his most marked contribution was his role in propagating the ideas of the Italian Marxist Antonio Gramsci in Britain. Roger and his brother Brian both died in 2002. Brian worked as school teacher in Manchester and Salford before becoming an academic at the University of Leicester. As a scholar, he established a reputation as a renowned Marxist historian of education and campaigned against intelligence testing and for comprehensive education. He rose to a senior position within the Communist Party, becoming chairman of its National Cultural Committee in 1962, and used his role to help steer the party towards accepting multi-party democracy and the adoption of humanist values in the 1960s. His life and work have been covered extensively in a 2023 biography.[18] In 1941, Brian married Joan Peel (1915–2005). A fellow Communist, Joan worked as a historian and education journalist. Part of the famous Communist Party historians' group, she won acclaim with her study of *Education and Society in Tudor England* (1966). In the 1950s, she and Brian developed a rapport with Soviet neuropsychologist Alexander Luria following a trip Brian took with his mother to the USSR in 1955. Influenced by his work, she translated his works into English to popularise his ideas and those of his mentor, Lev Vygotsky, to inform educational psychology and support the campaign against educational selection in Britain. Her work has been unduly neglected, but her life and contribution to the study of history were commemorated in a lecture by historian of education Jane Martin in 2013, eight years after her death.[19]

Notes

1. The brief web page on the history of the college mentions its progressive credentials but does not identify who Shena Simon was and her role in education. See: www.tmc.ac.uk/about/history/ (accessed 1 October 2023). It seems likely the name will disappear with the closure of the building in 2025.
2. Ernest appears as 'Sir Herbert Simon' in Ken Young, 'Re-reading the Municipal Progress: A Crisis Revisited', in Martin Loughlin, M. David Gelfand and Ken Young (eds), *Half a Century of Municipal Decline, 1935–1985* (London: Allen & Unwin, 1985), p. 20.
3. Private family papers, Ernest Simon, 'Mother', January 1920; ESD, 13 July 1912.
4. Private family papers, Henry Simon, *Rathshlaege für meine Kinder* (Manchester: privately printed, c. 1899); Brian Simon, *In Search of a Grandfather* (Leicester: The Pendene Press, 1997), p. 37.
5. Simon, *In Search of a Grandfather*, p. 77.
6. Susan Pedersen and Peter Mandler (eds), *After the Victorians: Private Conscience & Public Duty in Modern Britain* (London: Routledge, 1994).
7. ESD, 14 July 1914.
8. Shena D. Simon, *A Century of City Government, Manchester 1838–1938* (London: George Allen & Unwin Ltd, 1938), pp. 419–21.
9. A. J. P. Taylor, 'Manchester', *Encounter* (March 1957), 13.
10. A. J. P. Taylor, *Essays in English History* (Harmondsworth: Penguin, 1976), p. 307.
11. Félicité de Lamennais, quoted in Marx's *Civil War in France* and in many other places. Some versions have 'anemia' or other variants in place of 'paralysis'.
12. Brian Simon, *Henry Simon's Children* (Leicester: The Pendene Press, 1999), p. 116.
13. For example, Otto Simon Ltd, a specialised chemical process design consultancy based in Cheadle, Stockport: www.ottosimon.co.uk/history (accessed 20 October 2023).
14. See: www.henrysimonmilling.com/ (accessed 20 October 2023).
15. Mary Stocks, *Ernest Simon of Manchester* (Manchester: Manchester University Press, 1963), p. 5. Simon, *Henry Simon's Children*, pp. 11–33; www.museum.manchester.ac.uk/collections/archery/ (accessed 18/10/2023); 'Mrs Erna Simon', *The Times* (12 May 1973), p. 14; 'Latest Wills', *The Times* (19 July 1973), p. 20.
16. Simon, *Henry Simon's Children*, p. 112; 'Deaths', *The Times* (13 September 2000), p. 20; Christopher Simon, 'Obituary: Sir Patrick Hamilton Bt', *Guardian* (17 January 1992), p. 39; 'Celebrating DLF's 50th Anniversary', Disabled Living Foundation' (July 2020), p. 7 https://livingmadeeasy.blob.core.windows.net/dlf-live/lme/50-years-of-the-DLF-1969-to-2019.pdf (accessed 18 October 2023); Anthony Simon, *The Simon Engineering Group* (Cheadle Heath: privately printed, 1953), p. 10 (plate).
17. Information courtesy of Christopher's son, Andrew Simon. Private Correspondence (20 October 2023).
18. Pat Devine, 'Roger Simon', *Guardian* (25 October 2002), p. 24; Anne Corbett, 'Brian Simon', *Guardian* (22 January 2002), p. 18; Gary McCulloch, Antonio F. Canales and Hsiao-Yuh Ku, *Brian Simon and the Struggle for Education* (London: UCL Press, 2023). Roger played a major supporting role in the creation of Quintin Hoare's and Geoffrey Howell-Smith's (eds), *Selections from The Prison Note Books of Antonio Gramsci* (London: Lawrence and Wishart, 1971). It was the first significant edition of Gramsci's writings in English. He also wrote *Gramsci's Political Thought: An Introduction* (London: Lawrence and Wishart, 1982), the third edition of which was published in 2015.
19. Jane Martin, 'Neglected Women Historians: The Case of Joan Simon', *Forum* 56:3 (2014), 541–566.

Index

Illustrations and plates (*pl*) are denoted by the use of *italic* page numbers. The index is in letter-by-letter order.
Literary works can be found under authors' names.

Abercrombie, Patrick 227, *228*
Addison Act (1919) 98, 226
Aircraft Production, Ministry of 106–7, 136, 177
Albert Club 23–5
Albert, Prince 19, 24
Alderley Edge 65
Alexander, Samuel 261
Ashton, Letitia Mary (*née* Kessler) 73–4
Ashton, Margaret 74–6, 97, 224
Ashton, William Mark 74
Asquith, Herbert Henry 97
Athenaeum 11, 26
atomic power 185–9
Attlee, Clement 108–9, 238–9

Baldwin, Stanley 100
Balling, Michael 25
Beamish, Margaret Antonia (*née* Simon) 44, 67, *67*, 71, 76, *77*, 176
Beamish, Tufton 78
Beamish, Tufton Snr. 176
Bear-Park Coal and Coke Co., Durham 162
Bedales 73
Behrens, Abigail 14
Behrens, Charles 222
Behrens, Edward 14, 16, 62
Behrens, Gustav 16, 25, 38, 50–2
Behrens, Jacob 16, 63
Behrens, Leonard 16
Behrens, Louis 16, 24
Behrens, Nathan 16
Behrens, Soloman Levi (S. L.) 16, 24
Bevan, Aneurin 108, *109*
Beveridge, William 99, 278
Bevin, Ernest 140
Beyer, Charles Frederick 17, 253
Blackett, Patrick 267
Board of Education 119, 130, 132, 135
Borchardt, Louis 11, 24–5, 36, 63, 66
Bradford 9, 16, 61, 63–4, 67
Bright, Jacob 66
Bright, Ursula 66
Britain's Industrial Future (1928) 101
British Association for Advancement of Science *22*
Brodsky, Adolph 25, 51
Broomcroft, Didsbury *pl11*, 140, 182, 185, 202, 255–8, 261, 283, *284*, 285

Bryce, James 237, 259
Buddha statue 33–4, 54–6
Buenos Aires Great Southern Railway Co. 173
Bunsen, Robert 19–21
Burns, Mary 12–13
Burt, Prof Cyril 261
Butler, R. A. 133, 137

Cabutt, Louisa 26, 70
Cambridge, University of 69, 91, 94, 122,124, 169, 176, 194, 257–8, 261, 286
Cammell, J. T. 52
Campaign for Nuclear Disarmament (CND) 111, 187
Carves, François 38, 161
Cheadle Heath site 171–3, *172* 176, 178, 181, *183*, 184–5, *185–6*
Cheshire County Council 228
citizenship and the social sciences 259–67
City Corn Mill, Ancoats *155*
City of Manchester Plan (1945) 244
Clark, Theodora 121
Clay, Henry 263–4
Clean Air Act (1956) 94
Clifton College, Bristol 69
coal industry 159–64, 181, 182, 184, 237–8
Coates, Su 14, 15, 24
Colson, Elizabeth 266
comprehensive schools 136–40, 204, 256, 287
Comte, Auguste 259
Consultative Committee of the Board of Education 130–3
Continental Blockade (1806) 16, 23
Core, Thomas 70
Cowen, Frederic 50–2
Cross Street Unitarian Chapel 14–15, 64
Crowther, Joseph Stretch 65
Cunliffe, Antonia 128
Cunliffe, Marcus 128
Cunliffe, Mitzi 128
Curzon, Beatrice 79

Darwin House, Didsbury 40, *41*, 46, 66–7, 71, 89
Daunton, Martin 206–7
Daverio design 156, *156*
Didsbury Garden Suburb 223–4, *225*
Didsbury Institute and Lads' Club 82
Didsbury Library 74–5
Didsbury National School (now Didsbury Church of England Primary School) 73–4, *74*
Dixson, Maurice 282
Doctrine of the Trinity Act (1813) 14
Domestic Fuel Policy report (1946) 94
Dressler, Conrad 285
Dugdale, Thomas Cantrell *pl8*, 177–8, *177*

Eckhard, Edith 195
Eckhard, Gustav 38, 67, 260
Eckhard, Marie-Louise (*née* Stoehr) 63, 67, 70, 76, 224
Education Act (1944) 133, 137
Education in Citizenship, Association for 104–5, 259, 261, 266–7
Education, Ministry of 137, 140
Elm Grove houses, Didsbury 75, 82
EMI (Electric and Musical Industries Co.) 187
Emmet, Dorothy 265
E. M. Stoehr & Co 9, 63
Engels, Friedrich 12–13, 20, 21–2, 24–5, 53
Epstein, Jacob 282
Ermen & Engels 9, 12
Ermen, Godfrey 12, 24

Fabian 122, 236, 243
  Fabian Society 122, 198, 211, 234
Fairbairn, Charles 166
fascism 104–5
  Nazism, 104, 134, 256
  see also totalitarianism
Fellenberg, Philip Emmanuel von 26
Fettes College 52
Feuerbach, Ludwig 12
Firs, The (Rusholme) 61–3

First World War 69, 31n.85, *78*, *80*, 97, 125, 162, 170–1, 181, 189, 199, 263, 279
  Germanophobia 9, 27, 97
    Simons change pronunciation of name 78
  postwar reform 97–8, 103, 107, 199, 207, 223–4, 226
  Simon family loss 78–79, 97, 171, 285
Fitzgerald, Marion 94
Forsyth, James 25, 50–1
Frankland, Edward 19
Fraser, Bishop James 44–5
Frederick William IV 10
Free Trade Hall 24, 75, 93, 111, 187
Fröbel, Friedrich 26–7
  Fröbelian, 89
Fuchs, Carl 25

Gaddum, Henry Edwin 24
garden cities 129, 222–3, *225*, 226–7, *228*, 232, 244
  see also Wythenshawe
garden suburbs, Edwardian 222–4, *225*
Garfield, Simon 19
Gaskell, Elizabeth 14, 19
Gaskell William 14, 19, 64
General Elections 99–100, *99*, *100*, 101–2, 124, 226
General Electric Company (GEC) Ltd 185
German diaspora 1, 3, 9–27, 36, 38, 46 61–4, 69, 89–90, 97, 253–4, 278
  Bradford, 9, 63–4
  gymnastics 27
  'rational recreation' 26–7
  religion 13–16
  science 19–23, *22*
  see also Albert Club; Schiller Anstalt
German revolution (1848) xviii, 10–11, 29n.39, 34–6, 275
  exiles 16, 24, 27, 36, 63.
Gielgud, Val 109
Giessen University 19–21, *22*, 253
Gluckman, Max 257, 266, 267
Goldschmidt, Philip 24
Goodfellow, Thomas Ashton 81
Goodman, Joyce 204

grammar schools 131–2, 137, 139–140
Gramsci, Antonio 287
Grant, Margaret 83
Greenheys 14, *15*
Greenwood Housing Act (1930) 102
Greenwood, Joseph 17
Gumpert, Dr Eduard 24
Gunn, Simon 196

Hager, Herman 253–4
Haley, William *109*, 139
Hallé, Sir Charles 24–5, 50
Hallé Concerts Society 25, 50
Hall, Elsie Maude Stanley (*later* Stoehr) 70
Hallé Orchestra 3, 16, 25, 50, 254
Hall of Science 19
Hall, Peter 246
Hamilton, Bernice 265
Hamilton, Eleanor (Nell) Christadora (*née* Simon) 44, 48–9, 67, *67*, 71, 77, 82–3, *275*, 286
Hamilton, Sir George 77, 286
Hamilton, Lindisfarne 77, 81–2, 286
Hamilton, Sir Patrick 77, *183*, 286
Hamilton, Winifred Mary (Pix) (*née* Jenkins) 286
Hankinson, Annie 221–2
Hassan, Luly 79, *79*
Hegel, G. W. F. 12, 21, 55
Heidelberg University 19, 20–1, 23, 253
Henry Simon Ltd 6, 167–78
  becomes Ltd 36
  catalogue *153*, 159, 166
  diversification 181
  during wartime 162, 170–1, 176–7, 181, 189
  group photo 182, *183*
  marketing maps pls1–3, *158*, 159, 167
  public shares in 187
  Roller milling *5*, 36, 44, 151–2, 154–9, *155–6*, *160*, 162, 165–8
Henry Simon's Occasional Letter to Miller's at Home & Abroad 72, 167, 169, 176, 190, *275*
Herford, Caroline 70

Index

Herford, Marie Catherine (*née* Betge) 27
Herford, Siegfried Wedgwood 27, 31n.85
Herford, William Henry, 26–7, 70, 71, 89
Hess, Moses 12
Hey, Spurley 127–9, 205
Heywood, Benjamin 26
higher education expansion, postwar 111–12
Hiles, Henry 50–1
HMS Vanguard 78
Hobhouse, Leonard Trelawny 123, 257
Hofmann, August Wilhelm von 19
Hollis, Patricia 196, 203
Horrocks, Marian 121
Horsfall, Thomas Coglan 221, 223
Housing Conditions in Manchester and Salford (1904) 223
housing reform, Simons' involvement in 218–46, *219*
  see also Manchester City Council; Wythenshawe
Housing, Town Planning Act (1909) 223
Howard, Ebenezer, *228*, 231
  Garden Cities of To-morrow 222
Hubback, Eva (*née* Spielman) 94, 104–5, 121–2, 124, 195, 261, 268
Hulme, Tom 197
Hunt, Tristram 12
Huxley, George 168
Huxley, Julian 239

Industrial Revolution 11–12, 93, 213, 229, 231
Information, Ministry of 106, 136, 239
Ingleby, Joseph 157, 168, 169
Inman, John *pl6*, 103, *104*

Jackson, Annie 40
Jackson, Brian 213
Jackson, Sir Percy 132
Jackson, William Turner 199, 227, 229, 231
Jacob Behrens & Co. 16, 63
James, Eric, 139–40

Jersey Street Dwellings 220, *221*, 222
Jewish Board of Relief 15
Jewish Ladies' Visiting Society 14
Jewkes, John 106, 234, *236*
Jodrell Bank, Cheshire 257
Johnson, Rachel 25–6
Joseph and Fanny 48–9

Kandel, Prof Isaac 266
Keynes, John Maynard 99, 101, 286
Kidd, Alan 11
Kindergarten movement 26
King, Hilda 79
King, Peter H. 135
Kirchhoff, Gustav 19, 21, 23
Kirklees, Didsbury 75, 200
Ku, Hsiao-Yuh 120–1, 205
Kuper, Hilda 266
Kyllmann, Edward 69

Labour Research Department (LRD) 287
Lady Barn House School, (Withington) 26, 70, 73, 89–90
Lange, Hermann L. 17
Larches, The (Alderley Edge) 42, 65–6, *65*, 68
Lathbury, Stanley Chandos 33
Lawnhurst, Didsbury 46–8
  architects of 38, *48*
  Belgian refugees 69, 79,
  family at 67, 71, 166
  hospital, 79–81, *79–80*
  photos of *pl15*, *49*, *284*
  stained-glass windows *pl12*, 53–4, 283
  visitors to 75, 93, 259
Laybourn, Keith 103
Lee, Jennie *109*
Lees, Colin 255
Legacies of Simon family 281–7
Lejeune, Louisa 70, 71
Letchworth, Hertfordshire 222, 227, 229, 244
Levy, Winifred (*later* Simon) 73
liberalism 279
  British 11, 53, 89, 97–8, 101, 113n.1
  Cold War 256
  German 9–11, 13–14, 28n.6, 29n.39,

liberal democracy 105, 233, 265
Liberal Summer School movement 6,
    98–9, 101, 207, 251
  of Simon family members 10, 25,
    52–3, 182, 205, 243
Liberal Party 20, 65, 97–102, 114 n.2,
    199, 207, 224
  Didsbury Liberal Association 81
Liebig, Justus von 19–22, 30n.50, 253
Lilienthal, David 239
Lindsay, A. D. 264
Literary and Philosophical Society,
    (Manchester) 14, 19–20, 139
Livingstone, Richard 260–1
Lloyd George, David 97–9, 101–2,
    226
Lockwood, Joseph *183*, 187
London School of Economics (LSE) 94,
    122–3, 141, 194, 207, 257, 263
Lovell, Sir Bernard 257, 267
Luria, Alexander 287
Lusitania 9, 28n.3 97

MacDonald, Margaret 123, 194, 198
MacDonald, James Ramsay 102
McDougall Brothers 155, *155*
McDougall, Margaret 83
Maisky, Ivan 234
Maitri *pl12* 54, *54*, 78, *285*
Majer, Friedrich 55
Mallard, J. *177*, 178
Mallon, James J. 123
Manchester Cathedral 64
Manchester Central Library 80, 121
Manchester City Council, 3–4, 101,
    120, 125–128, 130, 142, 173,
    198, 201, 205, 210, 226–228,
    230, 285
  Education Committee 23, 126–8,
    130, 140, 142, 194 196, 201,
    204–5, 229, 244, 255–6
  Housing Committee 98, 102, 107,
    226–7
  Sanitary Committee 94, 125, 127,
    199, 201
Manchester College 205
Manchester Crematorium 1, 44–6, *47*,
    54, *54*, 73, 81, 285
Manchester Evening News 99, *262*

Manchester Governesses' Home 82
Manchester Guardian 26, 50–3, 63, 90,
    125, *221*, 252–3, 280–1
  coverage of Emily in 61, 80–1, *278*
  coverage of Shena in 197, 201,
    204–5, 213
  Emily's letters to 75
  Henry's letter to 161, *163*
  Ebenezer Howard's letter to *228*
  Shena's letters to 135, 207
  Wythenshawe estate purchase 227,
    229
Manchester Labourers' Dwellings
    Company 44, 219–22, *221*
Manchester Ship Canal Company
    169–70
Marr, Thomas 223
Marshall, Alfred 121
Marsham Court, London 139, 185
Martin, Jane 120, 204, 287
Marwick, Max 265–6
Marx, Karl 21–2, 24–5
maternal health, child and 96, 125,
    197–9, *201*, 209
Mechanics' Institution 19, 26–7, 252
Meek, Diana 77
Mehlhaus, William 168
Mendeleev, Dimitri *22*
mergers, company 187–9
'miasma theory' 20
Midland Hotel 9
Mill, John Stuart 65–6, 93, 121, 259,
    271n.41
Millencourt Cemetery, Somme 54
Milling journal 80
Mitchell, Clyde 266
Moberly, Walter 251, 264, 267
Moir, Cordelia 75
Mond, Ludwig 22
Montague, Charles Edward 63
Moore, Samuel 24
Morris, Alfred 286
Morris, Robert 196
Moscow 106–7, 134, 234–5, *236*,
    238–9, 242
Moses, Robert 239–40
Murg, Switzerland 36, 56n.12, 63
Muir, Ramsay 98, 251, 263
Munitions, Ministry of 171

Nansen, Fridtjof 44, 55
Napier, Lennox 82
Napier, Michael 281
Napier, Susannah (*née Stoehr*) 63, 69, 281
Napier, Walter John 69
National Insurance Act (1911) 94, 123, 198
National Union of Women's Suffrage Societies 76
National Union of Women Workers (NUWW) 123–4, 197–8
Natural History Society 19
New Statesman 93, 103
New York 239
Nicholson, Max 110
Nordic countries 105, 211–12, 219 234, 237–8, 243
nuclear war threat 111
Nuffield, William, 264
Nuttall, Harry 224

Oakfield, Rusholme 61–3, 65
'Oaks' Estate, Rusholme 61–3, *62*
Olechnowicz, Andrzej 203–4
Oliver, Anna 268
Oliver, Richard (R. A. C.) 266–8
Orrell, Mary Louisa 62
Osmaston, Dorothy (*later* Layton) 121–2
overpopulation 110
Owens College 17–23, 30n.62 34, 44, 55, 58n.57, 69–70, 252–4
  Beyer Building, Owens College 17, *18*
  Schorlemmer Organic Laboratory, 22

Pankhurst 74, 123
Parker, Barry 129, 229, 231, *232*, 244
Parkinson v. Simon (1894) 167
patents 4, 29n.41, 36, 44, 152, 164, 166–7, 171, 181, 281
Peacock, Richard 17
Pease & Partners colliery, Co. Durham 161, *162–3*
Peel, Robert 19
Pendyffryn Hall, Conwy 71, *275*
Pericles 261
Perkin, William 19

Pestalozzi, Johann Heinrich 26
Petschler, Helmut Carl Friedrich Martin 62
Petzold, Gertrud von 14
planning, town 218–46, *219*, *228*
Playfair, Lyon 20
Polanyi, Michael 255–6
pollution, air 93–4, 112–13
Potter, Jane Boyd (*née* Thompson), *xxii*, *120*, 121, *276*
Potter, John Wilson, *xxii*, 121, *276*
Potter, Millicent 121, *276*
Potter, Rupert 176, 182, 187–9, *276*
Prevention of Eviction Act (1924) 100
Prieger, Friederich Carl 63
Prieger, Stoehr & Co. 9, 63
Prussia 10–13, 16–17, 23, 27, 29n.26, 34, 58n.10

Rappard, Clara von *pl7*, *177*, 282
Rappard family 76
Rathbone, Eleanor 102, 108, 278
Red Cross Society, British 79–80, *79*
Reeves, Amber (*later* Blanco White) 122–3
Reform Club 23, 49
Reform movement (Judaism) 13–14
Reich Regency seal xx, 35, *35*, 275
Reith, John 238, 278
Relief of Really Deserving Distressed Foreigners, Society for the 15–16
Renold, Susan (née Herford) 70, 224
Richter, Hans 25, 50–2
Robbins Report (1963) 112, 268
Robertson, Alex 255
Robinson & Sons Ltd, Rochdale 157, 167, 281
Robinson, Wright 200
Robson, William A. 106, 234, *236*
Roosevelt, Franklin D. 107, 239, *241*
Roscoe, Henry Enfield 21–3, *22*, 253
Rowlinson, E. G. 132
Royal College of Chemistry 19
Royal Commission on Licensing (1929–31) 130
Royal Commission on Public Health (1843) 20

Royal Manchester College of Music (RMCM) 25, 254
Royal Manchester Institution 19–20, 25
Royal Manchester School of Music 25
Rugby School 34, 52, 68–9 73, 90–1, 93, 261
Russell, Bertrand 111
Rutherford, Ernest 1, 23, 111, 253, *254*, 255

Sadler, Michael 266
Sagarra, Eda 253
Salomons, Edward 24, 38, 46
Satake UK Ltd 282
Saxony 16–17
Schiller Anstalt 23–5, 30n.59, 35, 38, 44, 52–3, 57n.14, 58n.57
Schiller, Friedrich 24
Schlesinger, Hermann 64
Schopenhauer, Arthur 54–6
Schorlemmer, Carl 3, 21–4, *22*, 253
Schunck, Carl 20
Schunck, Henry Edward 16, 20, *22*
Schunck, Johann-Carl 16
Schunck, Martin 15–16, 20, 24
Schunck, Souchay & Co 9, 20
Schuster, Arthur 18, 21, 23
Schuster Brothers & Co. 23
Schuster family 16
Schuster, Felix Otto 23
Schwabe, Adolf 24
Schwabe, Julia 14
Schwabe, Salis 14, 16, 24
Scott family 90, 197
  Scott, C. P. 44, 51, 63, 70–1, 97, 125, 253–4, 257
  Scott, John 90
  Scott, Madeleine 71
  Scott, Rachel 70
secondary education 130–3, 136–40, 204, 255
Second World War 106–8, 134–6, 176–8, 234, 287
Selbie, Constance Mackay 79
SembCorp Industries 282
Shackleton and Sons, Carlow 157
Sharp, Roberts & Co. 17
Silesia 13, 16–17, 24, 29n.38, 34, 36
Simon, Alan *pl11*, *136*

Simon, Anthony 44, 52, 77, 80, 176, 182
Simon, Antonia (Tony), *xxii*, 97, 101–2, 124, *129*, 195
  illness and death 101–2, 128, 142, 195
Simon, Antonie Theodora (*née* Stöckel), *xxii*, 34
Simon, Brian, *xxii*, 57n.22–3, 267, 287
  childhood 97, 124–6, 195
  on Ernest Simon 174–5
  family portraits *129*, *276*
  on W. H. Herford 26–7
  on Henry Simon 33–6, 44, 282
Simon, Buhler and Baumann Co. 166
Simon Calendar *pl14*, 34, 52–3, 56n.5, 71, 83, 166, 277
Simon-Carves Ltd xvii, 38, 168–73, 176–8, 184–9
  colliery plant advert *pl4*, 184
  Hunterston contract *188*
  lack of growth 181
  public shares in 264
  Simon-Carves Ovens 159–64, *163*
  success of 151, 182, 282–3
Simon, Christopher 77, 176, 182, *183*, 189, 286–7
Simon Court, Wythenshawe 141, 244
Simon, Dorothea Antonia (later Murdoch) 44, 47, 67 71, 73, 77, *275*
Simon, Edith (*née* Horsfall) 78, 80
Simon, Emily Anne (*née* Stoehr) xvii, 1, 3–4, 6, 11, 40–4, 47, 61–83
  anti-suffragism 75–6
  and Edwardian garden suburbs 222–4, *225*
  awarded OBE 80
  illness and death 61, 80–3, *278*
  letters from Henry Simon *43*, 52
  letters to Harry Simon 49–50
  marriage 3, 38, 51, 66–70
  philanthropy xvii, 3, 46, 73–5, 83
    Didsbury National School 73–4, *74*
    wartime work 3, 69, 79–82,
    Withington Girls' School and Emily Simon Scholarship 70–71, 82–3
  portraits *2*, *pl9*, *60*, *67*, *77*, *82*, *275*

Simon Engineering Group (SEG) 176, 178–85, *179–80*, 189, 281–2
Simon, Eric Conrad
  childhood and education 44, 67, 73
  children 77
  death 54, 78–9, 97, 171
  portraits *67*, *77–8*, *275*
Simon, Erna 286
Simon, Ernest Emil Darwin xvii–xviii, *xxii*, 1, 3–6, 47, 82–3, 89–113
  Air pollution 93–4
  The Smokeless City 94, *95*
  America visits 107, *108*, 110, 238–42, *240*, 243
  BBC chairman 109–10, 252
  birthday portrait *pl8*, 177, *177*
  Britain's industrial future 101–2
  bust 282, *282*
  childhood and education 34, 40, 44, 52, 55, 67, 89–91, 169
  children and 78, *96*, 125–6
  citizenship
    education 104–5, 259, 261, 263
    the social sciences 264–67
    connections to Wythenshawe post-war 244–5
  death 112, 140
  depictions of *88*, *262*
  Economic Advisory Council 102
  engineering businesses 92, 112, 151–2, 172, 173–9, *177*, 181–2, *183*, 184–5, 187, 189–90
  family portraits *pl11*, *77*, *96*, *276*
  Freedom of the City of Manchester *pl5*, 112, 244
  holiday portraits *275*, *280*
  housing reform
    as Minister and MP, 100, 102
    Books 102–3, *103*, 107–8
    Housing Committee (Manchester) 98, 102, 107, 226–7
  How to Abolish the Slums 102, 175
  knighthood, 102
  Labour Party and 101, *109*
  letter from Roosevelt *241*
  Liberal politician
    councillor 96–8
    MP 100, 102
    see also liberalism
  on London 184–5
  as Lord Mayor 99, 198, *201*, 226–7
  Lords' maiden speech 182, 184
  loss of brothers 97, 170–1
  management style 112, 173–6, 182
  marriage and children 3, 78, 81, 94–7, 101–2, 124, 195, 279
  Moscow in the Making 106, 235, *236*, 237
  Nordic countries visits 105, 219 234, 237–8, 243
  peerage 108–9, 139, 244
  planning, 218–9
    international influences 106–8, 233–43, *236*
    relation to democracy 107–8, 241–2
  pneumonia 99, 126
  portraits *2*, *pl8*, *pl11*, *77*, *88*, *90–2*, *105*, *113*, *262*
  publicity photo *183*
  Rebuilding Britain – A Twenty Year Plan 107–8, 223, 242
  relationship with parents 90–1, 93, 274, 279
    advice from father 93, 164–5
  religion 92–4, 112, 259–60
  Second World War 106–8
  socialism and Labour Party, 98, 100–1, 106–9, 182, 184, 238–9
  Soviet Union visit 106–108, 234–7
  Switzerland visits 105–6, 110, 219 234, 237–8, 242
  The Anti-Slum Campaign 102
  The BBC from Within 110
  The Physical Science of Flour Milling 175
  The Rebuilding of Manchester pl6, 102, 103, *104*, 232
  The Smaller Democracies 105
  University of Manchester and 111, 251–69, *269*
Simon family ix, xvii, *xxii*, 1–6, *72*, *77*, *285*
  relation to engineering business, 175–6
  relation to Manchester, 1–2

Index 297

memorial (Southern Cemetery Manchester) 46, 54, *54*, 285, *285*
transmitted values and ethos xvii, 1, 3, 189–90, 275, 277–280
Simon, Friedrich Gustav, xxii, 34
Simon, Harry (Heinrich Helmuth) 47–8, 67, 77–80, 285
  childhood and education 44, 67, 176
  children, 77, 286
  death 78–9 97, 171
  letters from Henry 38, 46, 49–50, 52, 91
  portraits *78*, *275*
Simon, (Uncle) Heinrich, August xvii, xxii, 10, 16, 24, 34–8, *37*, 56n.12, 63–4, 66, 76, 93, 275, 277, *277*
Simon, Henry (Gustav Heinrich Victor Amandus) xvii, xxii, 1, 3–4, 6, 33–55, 277
  childhood and education, 10, 34, 252
  holiday portrait *275*
  ill health and death 44, 47–50, 73, 166, 168
  letter from uncle Heinrich Simon 36, *37*
  marriages and children 3, 26, 40–4, 54, 57n.17, 66–7
  memberships 159, 164
  philanthropy
    Henry Simon Chair of German 18, 44 253, 274
    Manchester Labourers' Dwellings Company 219–22
    Manchester Pure Milk Supply Company, 44
    Simon's Bridge 44, *45*
    physical laboratory 23, *254*
    see also Hallé Orchestra; Manchester Crematorium
  portraits *2*, *pl7*, *32*, *67*, *77*, 282
  Rathschlaege für meine Kinder 18, *22*, 38, *39*, 53, 55, 93, 164, 221, 277
  Schiller Anstalt, 25, 35, 38, 44, 52–3
  successful management of firms 151–2, 164–8
  transforming coke making 159–64
  Withington Girls' School, 44, 70–1
Simon, Herman 16
Simon, Hirsch 13
Simon House, London 185
Simon, Ingo Heinrich Julius William Gustav 40–1, 52, 55, 66, 67, 73, *275*, 286
Simon, Joan (*née* Peel) *pl11*, 121, 126, 132, *136*, 197, 201, 211, 287
Simon, John 77
Simon, Martin *pl11*
Simon, Mary Jane (*née* Lane) 38, 40, *40*, 42, 54
Simon, Michael 77
Simon, Monica 77
Simon, Oliver 77
Simon Population Trust 110–11
Simon, Roger xvii, xxii, *96*, 97, 124, *125*, *129*, 195, 251, *276*, 287
Simon, Shena Dorothy (*née* Potter) xvii–xviii, *xxii*, 1, 3–6, 119–43, 194–214
  A Century of City Government, 197
  America visit 107, 136–7, 139, 239
  Australia and New Zealand visit 123, 194
  awards and honours 141
  childhood and education, *120*, 121–4, 137
  children 78, 97, 101–2, 124–6 128, 142, *200*
  citizenship and the social sciences 259–67
  connections to Wythenshawe after 1945 244–6
  councillor 126–8, 194, 195, 200–1, *202*, 229
  councillor elections 205–6, *206*, 210
  death, 142, 245
  education, interest and work in 119, 126–128, 130, 137, 140, 142, 194, 196–7, 200–1, 203–5
    during the Second World War, 135–136
  education reform 130–3, 137, *138*, 139–40, 205
  'educational dictator' 133–4, *133*

Simon, Shena Dorothy (*cont.*)
   equality of educational opportunity 121, 133–4, 136–7, 139–40, 142, 205
   Wythenshawe 129, 203
   see also Consultative Committee of the Board of Education; comprehensive schools
   family portraits *pl11, 120, 125, 129, 136, 276, 280*
   feminism 119, 121, 126, 128, 134–5, 141–3, 199, 275
     married women teachers bar abolition 126, 200
     refusal to deliver presents at St Mary's Hospital 119, 126, 198–9, *200*
     Suffragette movement 123–4, 197
     Manchester and Salford Women Citizens' Association, (WCA) 96–7, 124–5, 198–9, 203
     National Insurance reform 94, 123, 198
     see also National Union of Women Workers; Woolf, Virginia
   final decades 139–42
   Freedom of the City of Manchester 199, 212–13, *213*, 245
   ill health 125
   Labour Party and 109, 130, 194, 205
   as Lady Mayoress 99, 126, *127*, 198, *201*
   marriage
     attitude towards 124, 199
     partnership with Ernest 3, 78, 94–6, 112, 124–6, 195, 212
   Moscow in the Making 236
   Nordic countries visit 211–12
   obituary 204, 213
   portraits *2, pl10, 118, 122, 131, 143, 195*
   religion of humanity 120, 126, 271n.40
   retirement 142
   Second World War 134–7
   Soviet Union visits 106, 134, 140, 205, 234–7, 287
   taxation, municipal 130, 194, 196, 206–12
   Local Rates and Post-War Housing 209
   Three Schools or One? 137–9, *138*
   University of Manchester and 125, 255–60, *258*, 265, 268
   Withington Girls' School and 71
   Wythenshawe estate planning 128–9, 203–4 229–32, *233*
Simon, Victor Herman 44, 48, 67, *67*, 77–8, 78–9, 97, *275*
S. L. Behrens & Co. 9, 14, 16
Smith, Henrietta Hayne 82
Smith, Robert Angus 20
Smoke Abatement League of Great Britain 94
Somervell, Arthur 75
Somervell, Edith 75
Souchay, Charles 24
Soviet Union 4, 106, 107, 111, 234, 243
   see also totalitarianism
Spens, William 132
SS Persia 78
Steinthal & Co. 9
Steinthal, Edwin Alfred 38, 46, 64
Steinthal family 63–4
Steinthal, Anna Marie (née Worms) 64
Steinthal, Francis Anton 64
Steinthal, Friedericke (née Emmanual) 64
Steinthal, Henry Michael 14, 36, 62, 63, 64, 69
Steinthal, Joseph 15
Steinthal, Ludwig 64
Steinthal, Moritz 64
Steinthal, Walter Oliver 64
Steinthal, Rev. Samuel Alfred 14, 15, 21, 38, 64–5
Steinthal, Wilhelmine Pauline 62, 64
Stephen family 135
Stiglitz, Regine Sara 75
Stockholm 212, 237–8, 243
Stocks, Mary Danvers (née Brinton) 46–7, 89, 108, 110, 114–5n.33, 169, 174, 189, 286
   Ernest Simon of Manchester 89, 190n.2

Stoehr, Charles Felix and Kathleen 68, 77–8
Stoehr, Charles William 61, 63, 64, 66, 68, 77–8
Stoehr, Clara Helene 63, 69
Stoehr, Emil Moritz 11, 33, 38 42, 61–4, 66, 68–9, 76
Stoehr family 61–6
Stoehr, Friederich (Fritz) Otto 63, 66, 68, 69, 70
Stoehr, Helene Margarethe (*née* Worms) 61, 63–4, 66, 68–70, 76, *77*
Stoehr, Matilde 61, 63, 64, 68, 76
Stoehr, Oscar Henry 33, 54–6, 63, 68
Stoehr, Oscar Humphrey 68, 78
Stoehr, Verena (Mary Georgina) (*née* Tonge) 68, 82
Stoehr Wilhelm, 63
Stopford, John 267
suffrage, women's 65, 75–6, 123–4, 196, 197
  Suffrage Petition (1866) 65
Sumner, James 19, 20, 23
Swanwick, Helena 75–6
Switzerland 105–6, 110, 234, 237–8, 242

Tawney, Richard Henry 93, 101, 130, 205, 207, 264
Tayler, Dr J. Lionel 259
Taylor, Alan John Percival 279
Taylor, John Edward 26
Taylor, Samuel and Mary 46
Temple, William 259
Tennessee Valley Authority (TVA) 107, 239, *241*, 242
Tetlow, Max 103
Thatched House Tavern, off Market Street 21
Theodores, Tobias 13, 18–19
Thomas Robinson & Son, Rochdale 157
Thompson, George 121
Thomson, Godfrey 261, 267
Thouless, R. H. 261
Times, The 212
Tomlinson, George 140
Tonge, Richard 68
Totalitarianism 104–6, 233–237

Town and Country Planning Act (1947) 108
Tudor Walters report (1918) 224, *226*, 227
Turner, Victor 266
Tylecote, Mabel 194, 202–3
Tyresoles Ltd 181

United States of America 4, 68, 107, 110, 136, 139, 142, 181, 234, 238–43
universities, future of British 267–8
Universities Quarterly 266, 267–8
University of Manchester 3, 5, *15*, 44, 111, 125, 134, 141, 202, 205, 234, 243 251–69, *254*, 274, 279, 285, 287
  Settlement Scheme 69
  Simon scholarships/fellowships 71, 83, 205, 252, 263–6
  see also Owens College
Unwin, Raymond 226

Verein (German clubs) 11, 23, 27
Victoria University 21, 23, 252–3
Vygotsky, Lev 287

Wallas, Graham 123, 257
Ward, Dr Adolphus 70
Ward, Mary 75
Waterhouse, Alfred 22, 62
Webb, Beatrice 93–4, 97, 101 106, 122–3, 194, 234, 255, 259
  on the Simons 195 203
Webb, Sidney 4, 93–4, 97, 101, 106, 123, 234, 255, 259, 261
Wells, H. G. 93, 123, 259, 261
Westaway, Jonathan 11, 23–4, 27
Westphalia 16
Whitelaw, Robert 91
Whitworth, Joseph 62
Wilkins, Augustus Samuel 253–4
Wilkinson, Ellen 94, 137
Withington Girls' School (WGS) 44, 70–1, 79, 82–3, *254*
Wolff, Wilhelm 24–5
Women's Leader and the Common Cause 76, 200
Wood, George William 26
Woolf, Leonard 135

Woolf, Virginia 119, 123–4, 132, 134–5, 143
Woolton, Frederick, 252
Workers' Educational Association (WEA) 93, 135, 140, 259
Works, Ministry of 107, 238, 239, 242
Worms, Alfred 64
Worms, Anna Maria (*later* Steinthal) 64
Worms, Charles and Emily 63–4
W. Vernon and Sons 168
Wyke, Terry 9, 11
Wythenshawe 1, 4, 142–3, 197, 203, 218, 245–6, 285
  civic centre 141, *141*, 245
  Simons' post 1945 connections with 244–5
  garden city 98, 101, 109, 128–30, 139, 227–9, 231–2, *232*, 238
  Shena as councillor candidate for 205, *206*
Wythenshawe Estate Special Committee, 129, 203, 229, 231
Wythenshawe Hall and Park *pl13*, 101, 128, 203, 227, *230*, 285–6
  residents 129, 143, 204, 245
  Wythenshawe Residents' Association 129
Wythenshawe, struggle for 224–9
  purchase by council, 101, 227–8 *229*

Yew Tree School, Wythenshawe 140
Young, Hilton 103, 111
Young, Wayland, 111

Zimmern, Alfred Eckhard 260, 261
Zimmern, William 260
Zurich 34, 36, 237–8, 242

Milton Keynes UK
Ingram Content Group UK Ltd.
UKHW020153091224
452196UK00011B/108